Collins

EASY
LONDON

G000122731

Contents

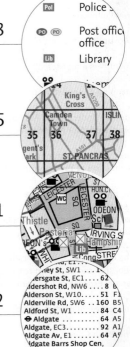

Pol   Police s

PO PO   Post offic
office

Lib   Library

King's
Cross

Camden
Town   ISLI

35 36 37 38

gent's
ark   ST. PANCRAS

LEICESTER

WC
SQ   ODEON
Sch

Thistle

Pastoria   SQ   IRVING S

EON's   Hampshir

Lib   STRE

ney St, SW1 ...1
ersgate St, EC1....62
Idershot Rd, NW6 8
Alderson St, W10.....51 F
Alderville Rd, SW6 ..160 B5
Aldford St, W1 ....84 C4
Aldgate 64 A5
Aldgate, EC3.........92 A1
Aldgate Av, E1 ......64 A
Idgate Barrs Shop Cen,
.................64
gate East .....

Published by Collins
An imprint of HarperCollins Publishers
77-85 Fulham Palace Road, Hammersmith, London W6 8JB

www.collins.co.uk

Copyright © HarperCollins Publishers Ltd 2006

Collins® is a registered trademark of HarperCollins Publishers Limited

Mapping generated from Collins Bartholomew digital databases

London Underground Map by permission of Transport Trading Limited
. Registered User No. 06/4302

The grid on this map is the National Grid taken from the Ordnance Survey map with the
permission of the Controller of Her Majesty's Stationery Office.

Printed in China

ISBN-13   978 0 00 720630 8
ISBN-10   0 00 720630 5   Imp 001   TM12159 / NDE

e-mail: roadcheck@harpercollins.co.uk

Key to map symbols

A4 (Dual)	Primary route
A40 (Dual)	'A' road
B504	'B' road
	Other road
→	One way street
	Street market
	Pedestrian street
·	Access restriction
------- -------	Track/Footpath
	Borough boundary
	Postal district boundary
	Congestion charging zone
	Congestion charging zone extension (from Feb 2007)
---⊕---	Pedestrian ferry with landing stage
⇌	Main national rail station
⊕	Other national rail station
⊖	Underground station
⊖	DLR station
●	Bus/Coach station
P	Car park
WC	Public toilet
i	Tourist information centre

Pol	Police station
PO PO	Post office/Postal delivery office
Lib	Library
🎥	Cinema
🎭	Theatre
⊠	Major hotel
⌐USA	Embassy
+	Church
☾	Mosque
✡	Synagogue
Mormon ■	Other place of worship
▢	Tower block
■ Amb Sta	Ambulance station
	Leisure/Tourism
	Shopping
	Administration/Law
	Health/Welfare
	Education
	Industry/Commerce
	Public open space
	Park/Garden/Sports ground
† † †	Cemetery

0   ¼   ½ mile

0   0.25   0.5   0.75 kilometre

Scale 1:7,500 8.5 inches (21.5cm) to 1 mile / 13.3 cm to 1 km

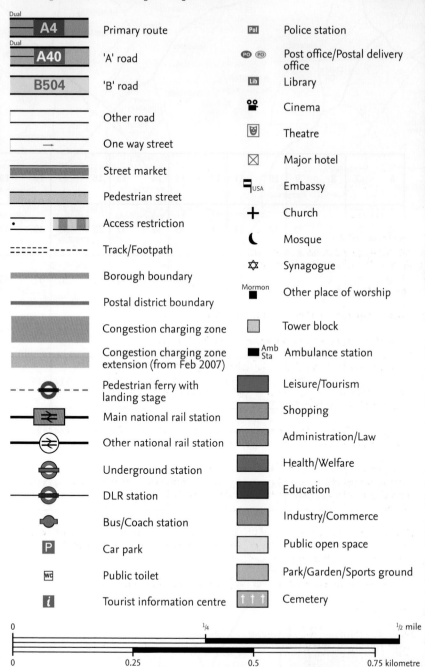

Key to map pages

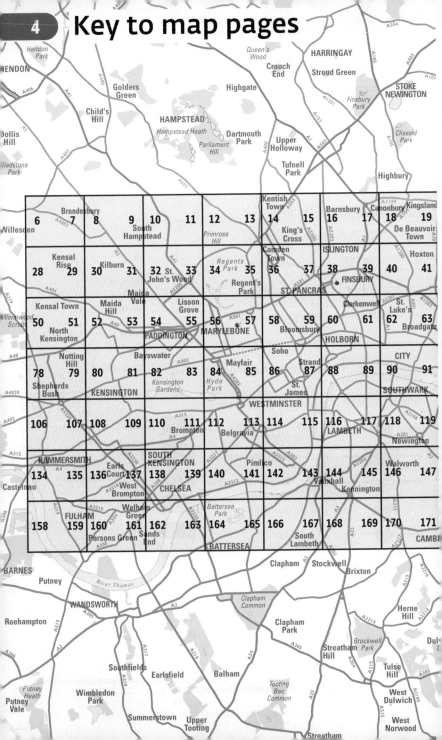

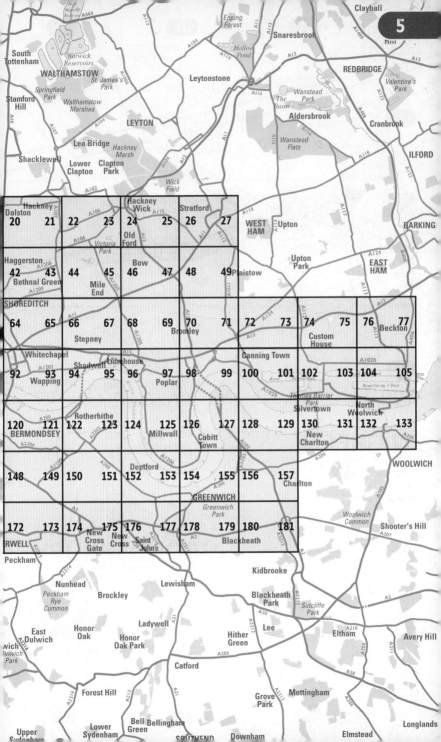

Clayhall
Hill
Epping Forest
Snaresbrook
Hollow Pond
South Tottenham
Warwick Reservoirs A503
WALTHAMSTOW
St. James's Park
Springfield Park
Stamford Hill
Walthamstow Marshes
LEYTON
Leytonstone
REDBRIDGE
Valentine's Park
Wanstead Park
The Basin
Aldersbrook
Cranbrook
ILFORD
Lea Bridge
Hackney Marsh
Shacklewell
Lower Clapton
Clapton Park
Wick Field
Wanstead Flats
BARKING

Hackney Dalston
20 **21** **22** **23**
Hackney Wick
24 **25**
Stratford
26 **27**
WEST HAM
Upton

Haggerston
42 **43** **44** **45**
Old Ford
Bow
46 **47** **48** **49** Plaistow
Bethnal Green
Mile End
Upton Park
EAST HAM

SHOREDITCH
64 **65** **66** **67** **68** **69** **70** **71** **72** **73** **74** **75** **76** **77**
Stepney Bromley Beckton
Custom House

Whitechapel
92 **93** **94** **95** **96** **97** **98** **99** **100** **101** **102** **103** **104** **105**
Wapping Shadwell Limehouse Poplar Canning Town
Royal Victoria Dock
Royal George V Dock
Thames Barrier Park
Silvertown
North Woolwich

120 **121** **122** **123** **124** **125** **126** **127** **128** **129** **130** **131** **132** **133**
BERMONDSEY Rotherhithe Millwall Cubitt Town New Charlton

148 **149** **150** **151** **152** **153** **154** **155** **156** **157**
Deptford GREENWICH Charlton
Greenwich Park
WOOLWICH
Woolwich Common
Shooter's Hill

172 **173** **174** **175** **176** **177** **178** **179** **180** **181**
ERWELL New Cross Gate New Cross Saint Johns Blackheath

Peckham
Nunhead Lewisham Kidbrooke
Brockley Blackheath Park Sutcliffe Park
Peckham Rye Common
East Dulwich Honor Oak Ladywell Lee Eltham Avery Hill
Honor Oak Park Hither Green
Catford
Forest Hill
Grove Park Mottingham Longlands
Upper Sydenham Lower Sydenham Bell Green Bellingham Downham Elmstead

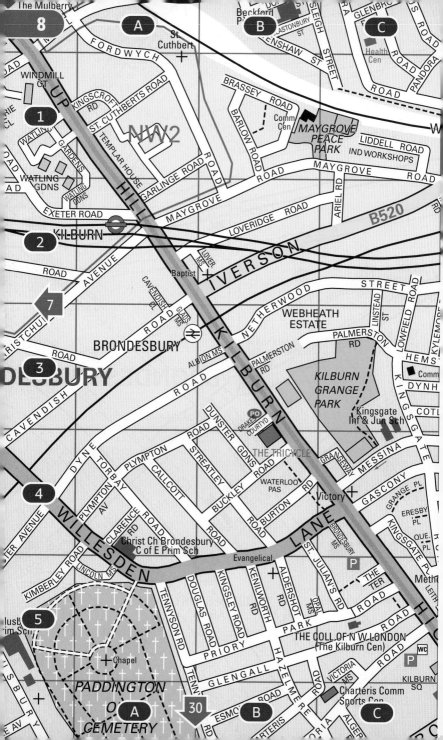

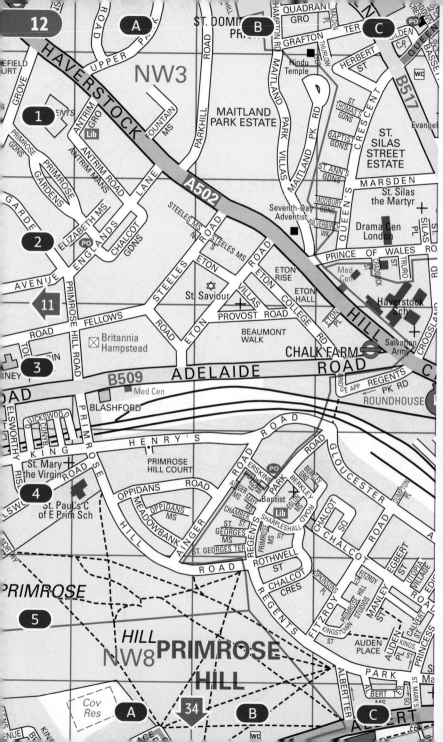

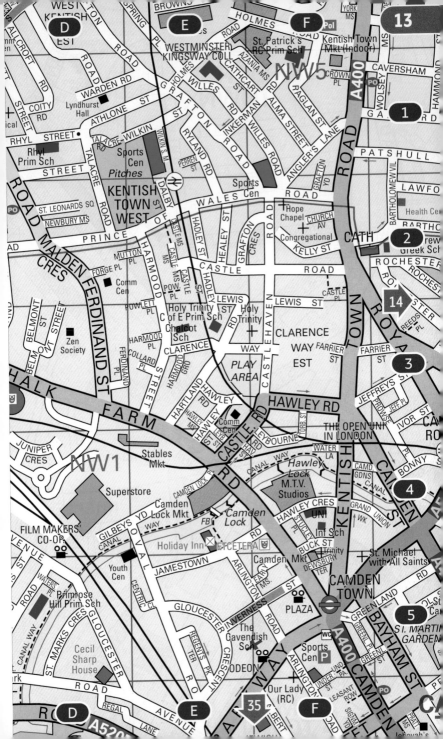

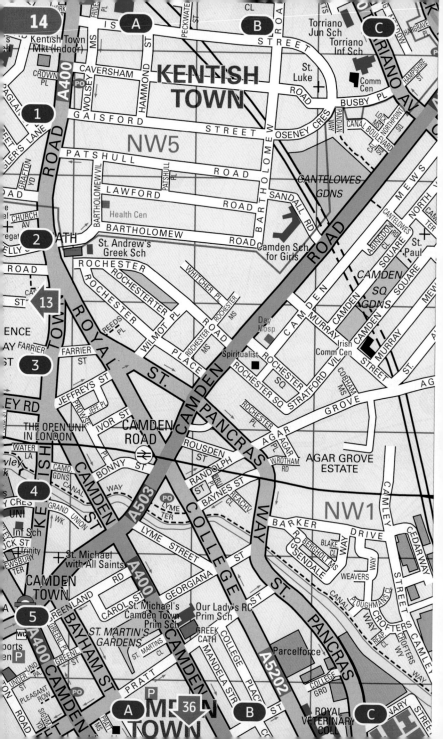

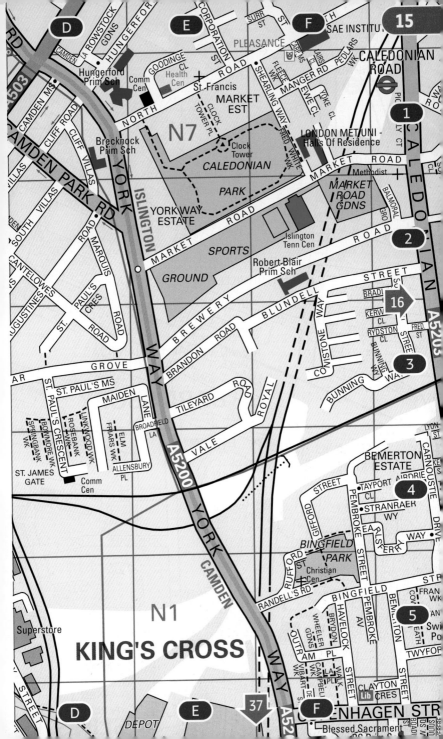

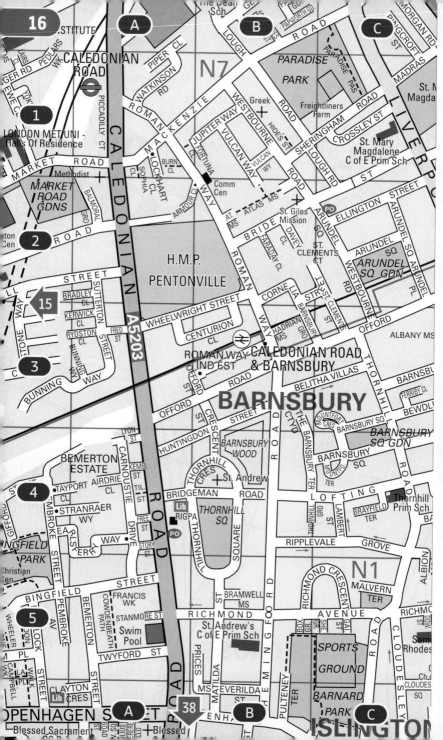

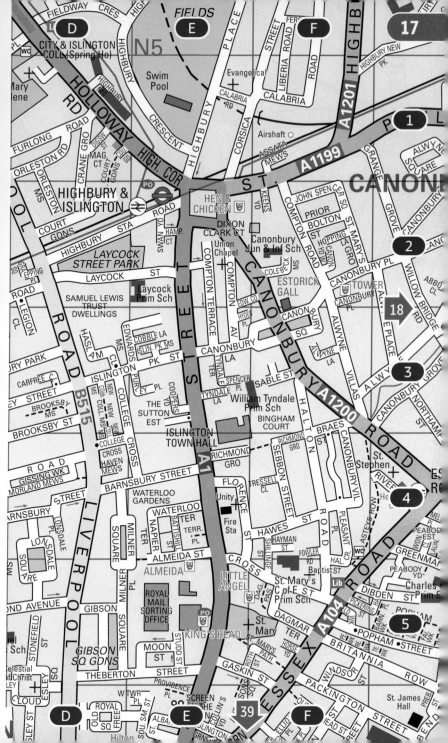

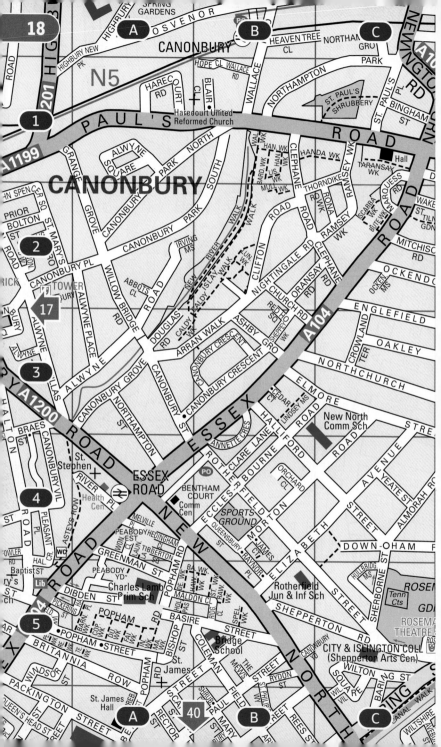

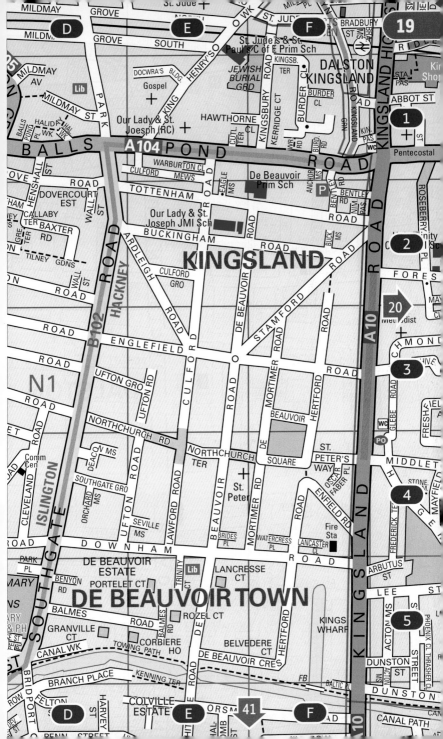

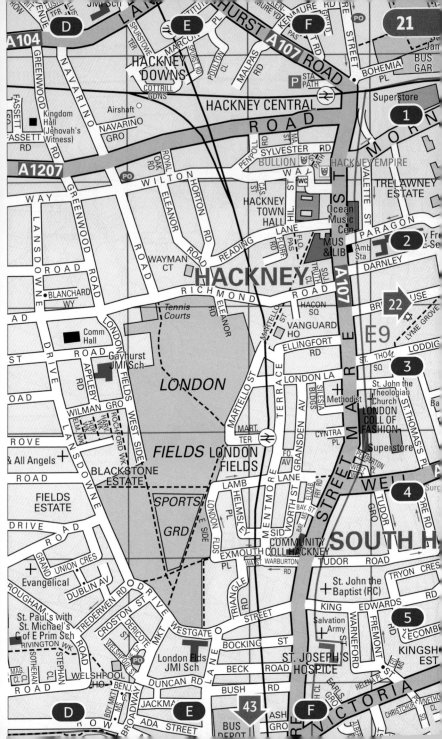

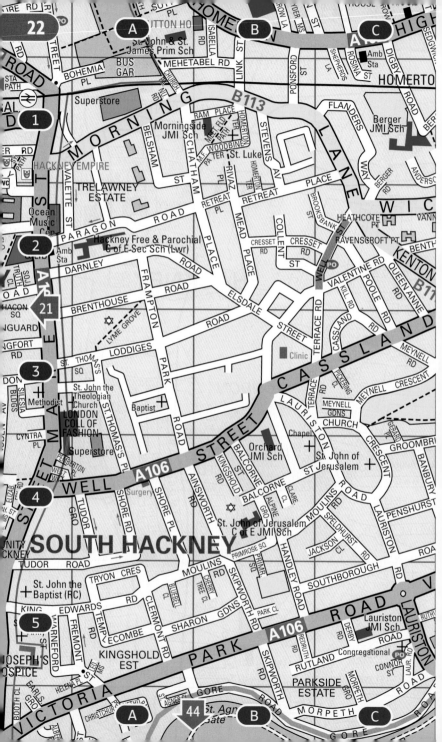

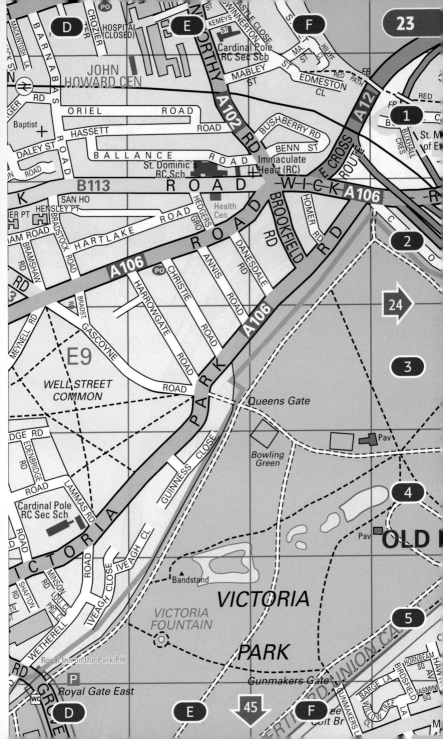

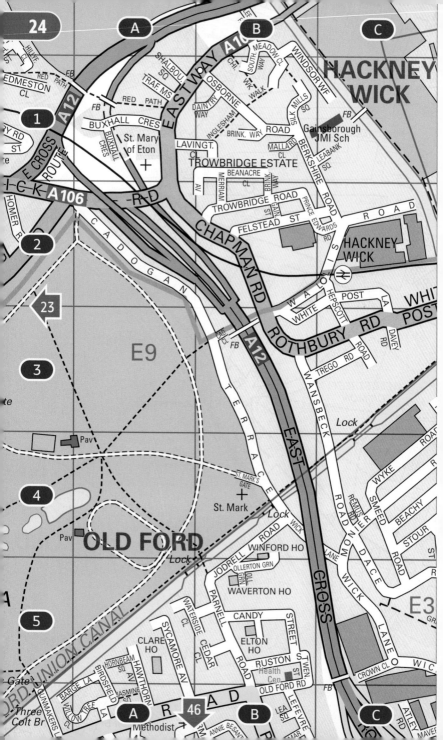

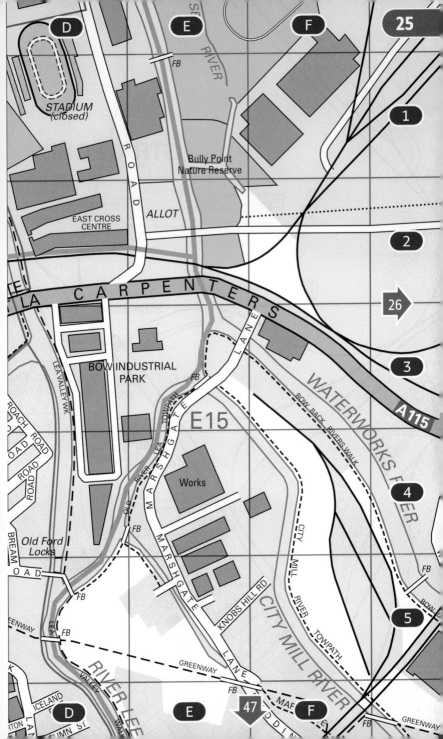

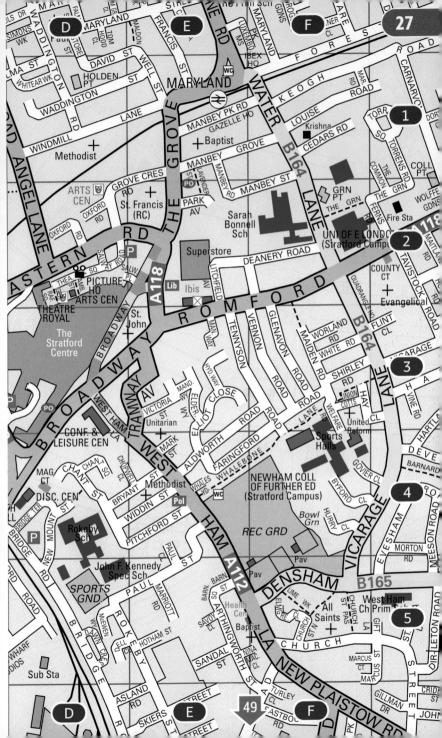

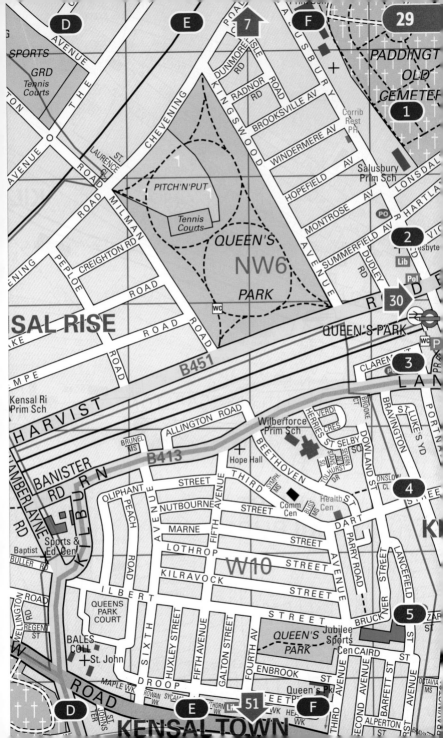

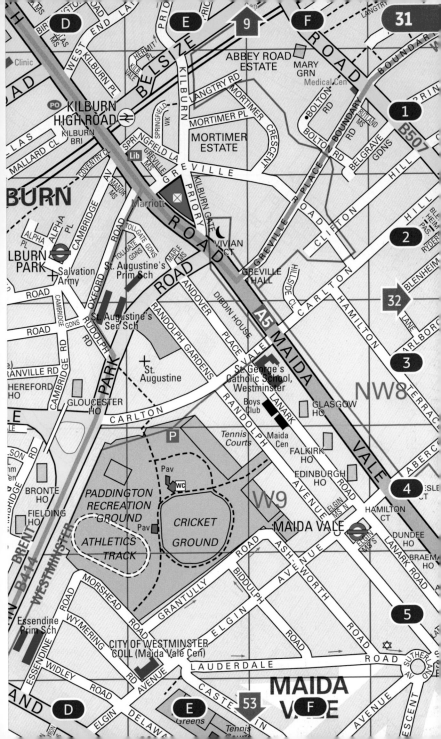

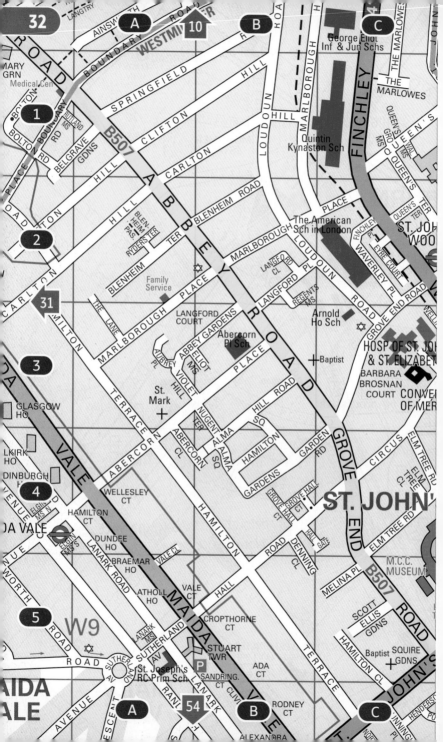

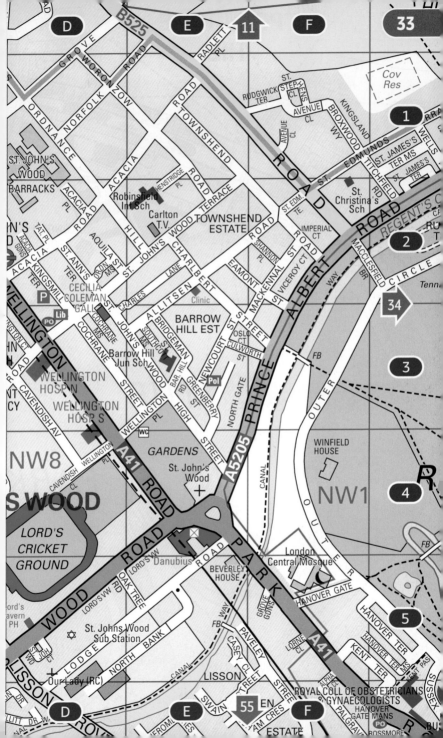

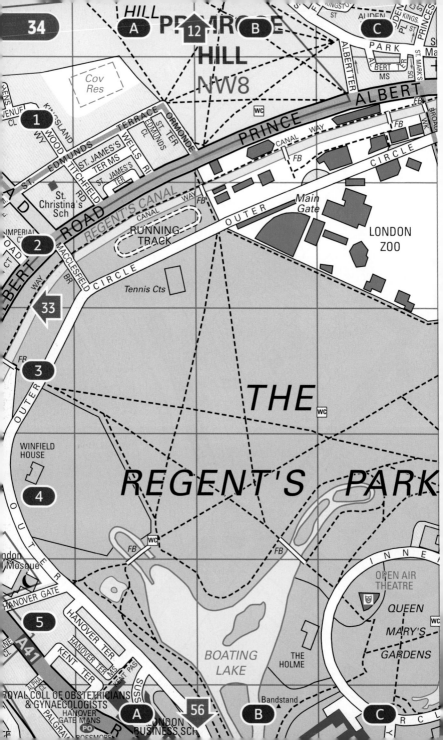

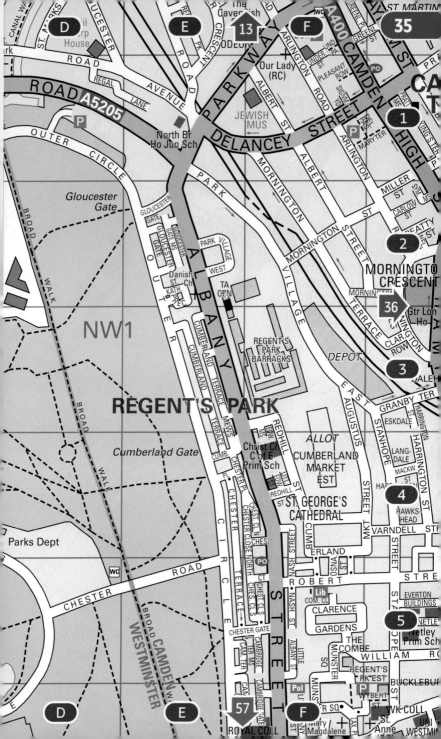

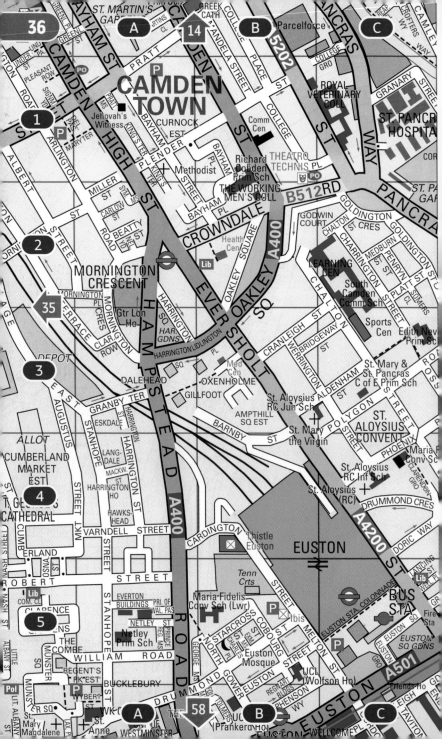

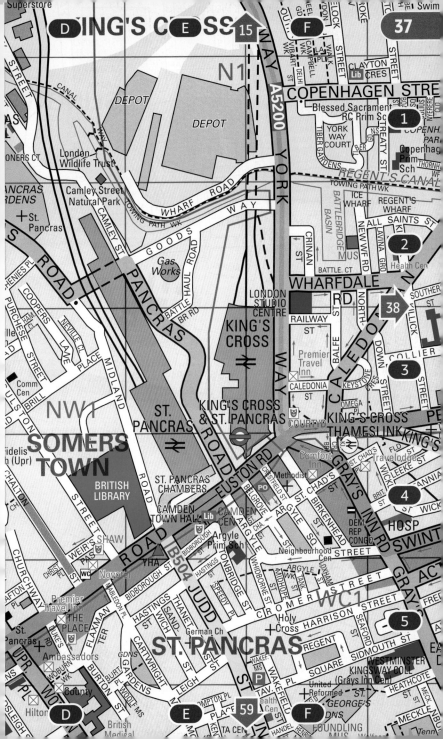

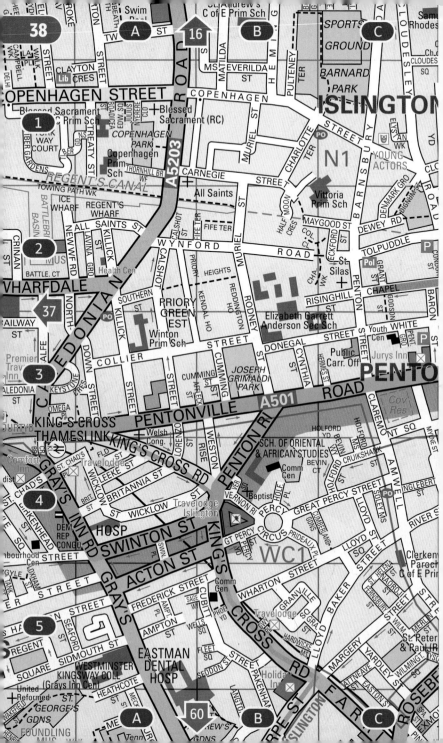

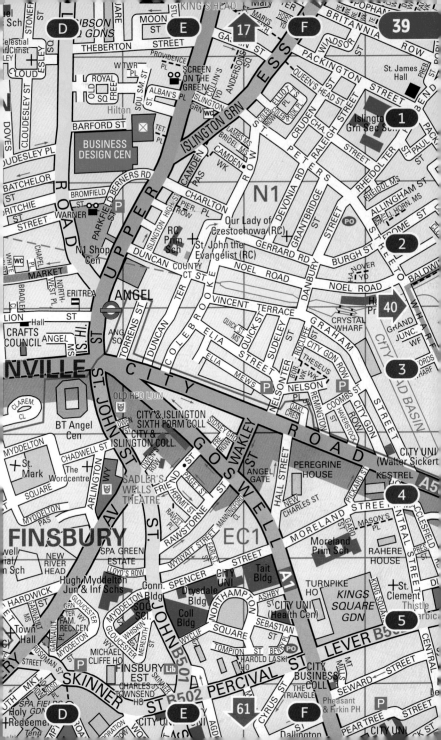

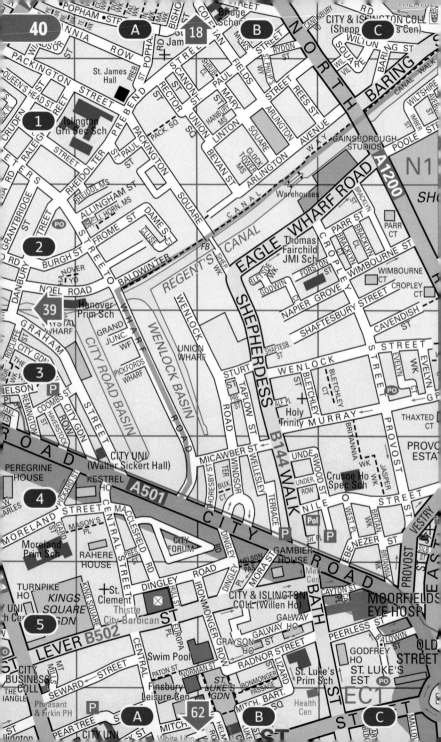

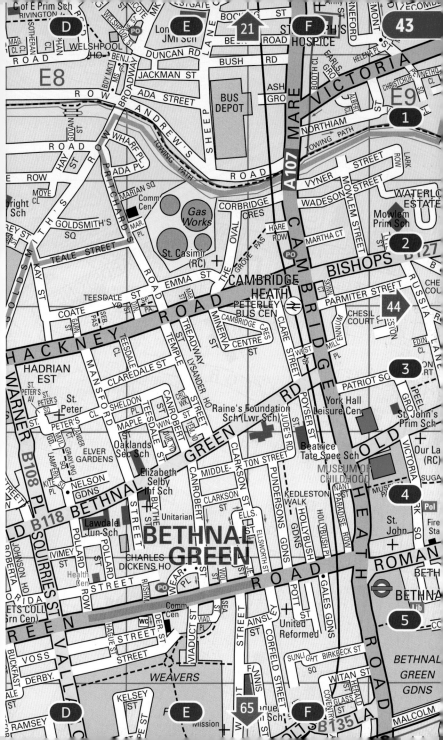

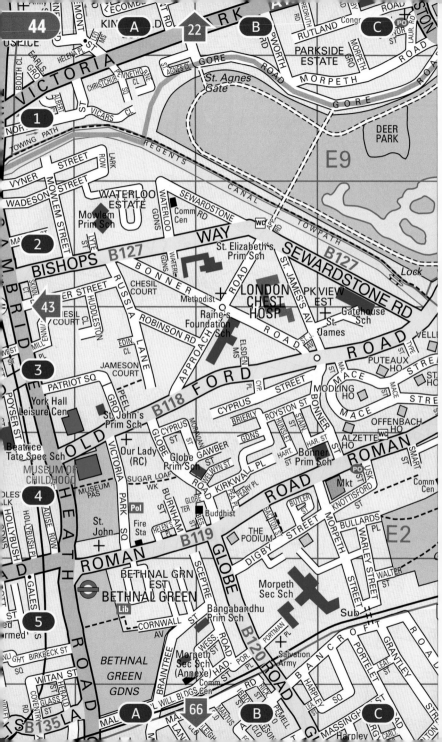

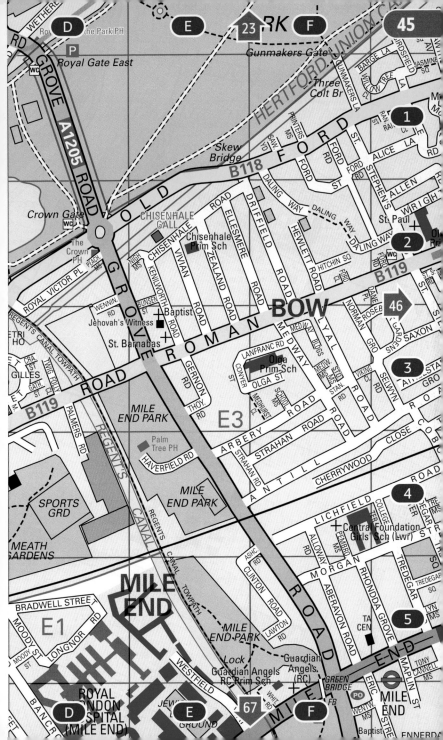

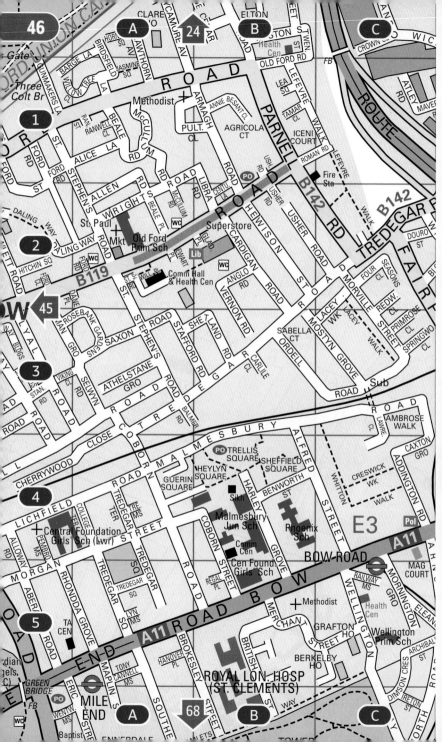

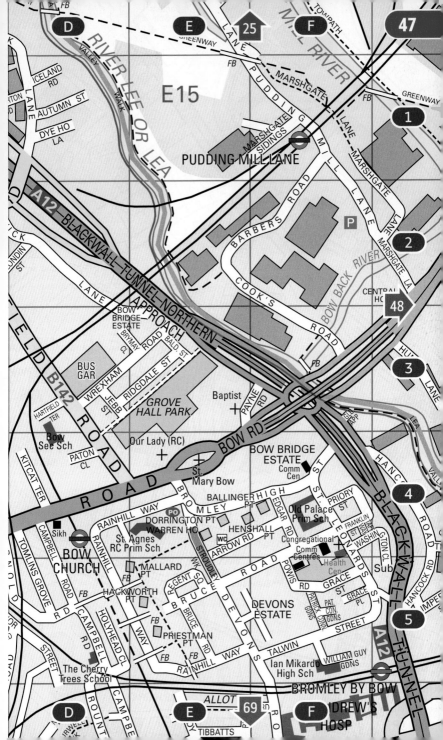

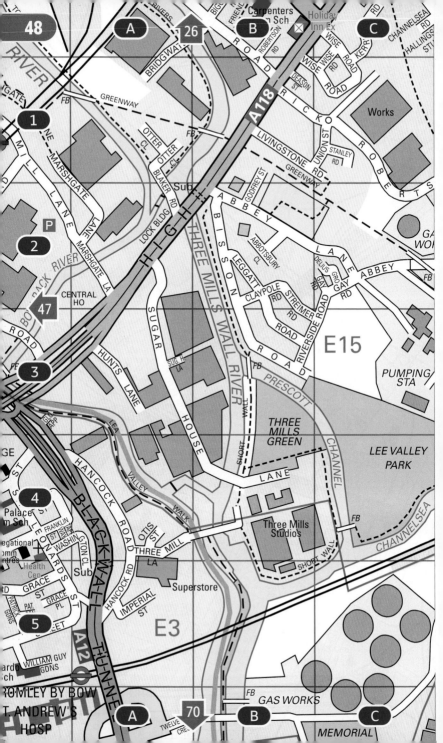

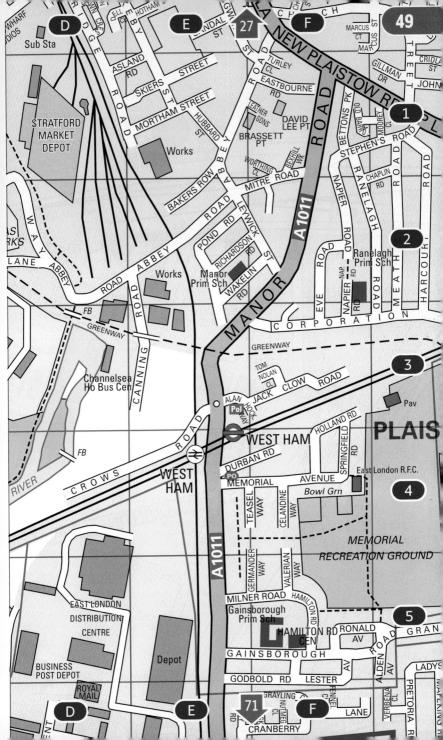

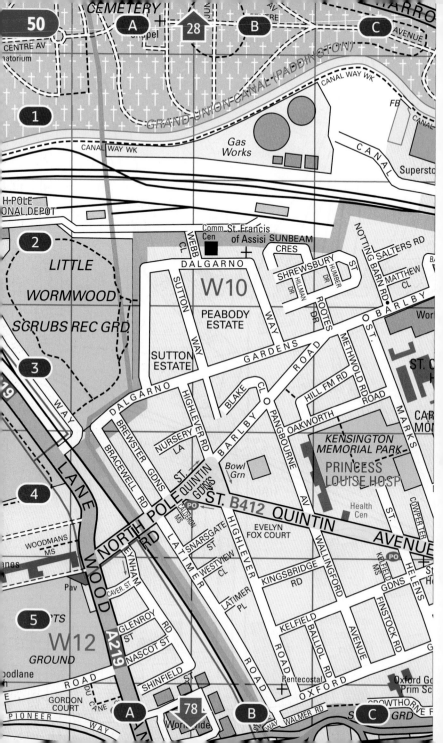

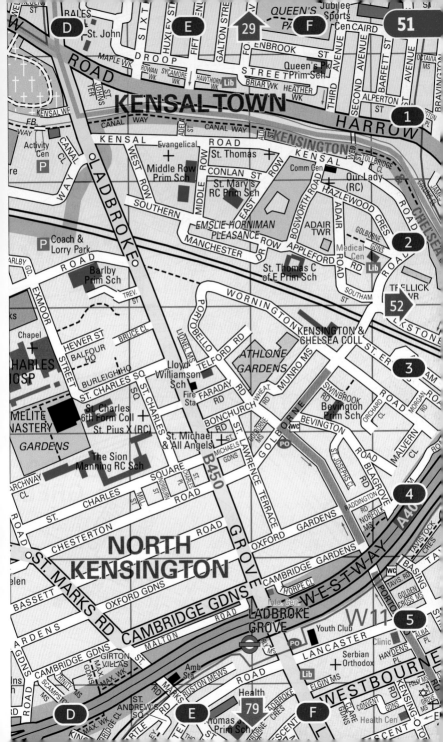

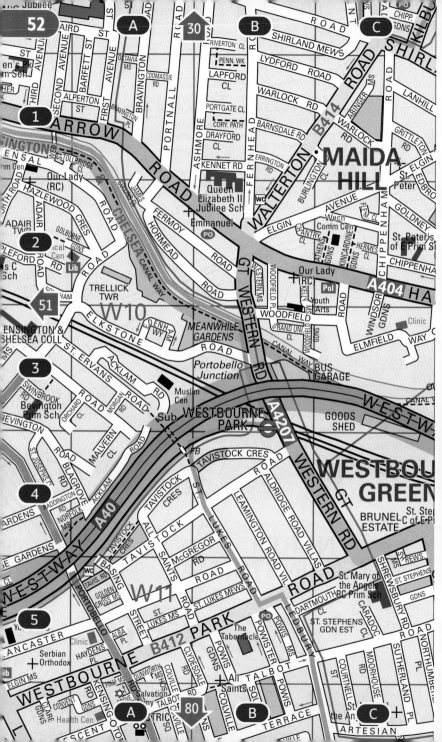

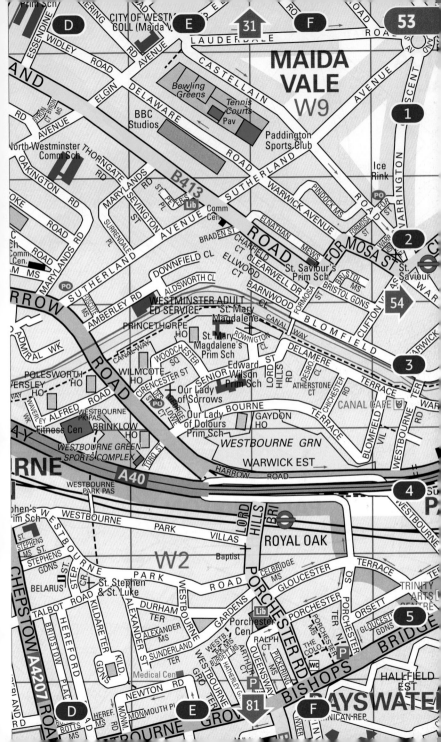

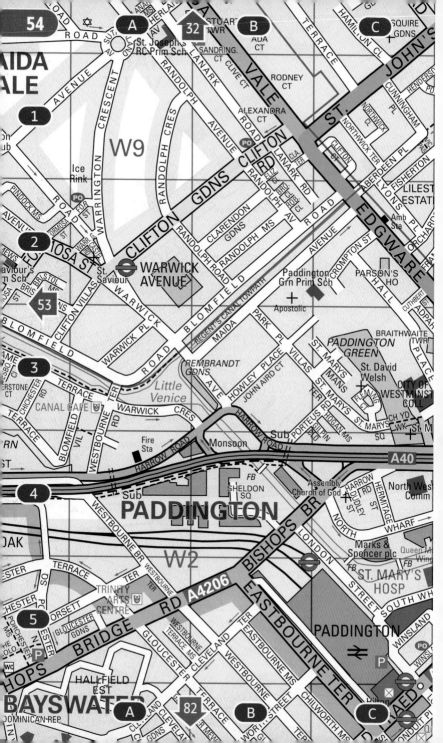

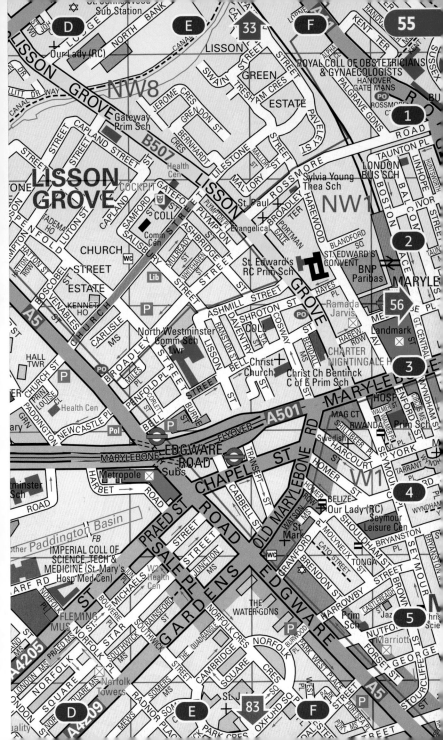

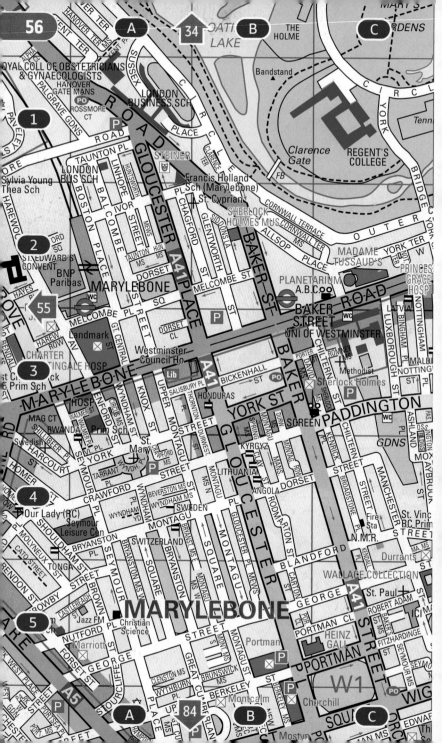

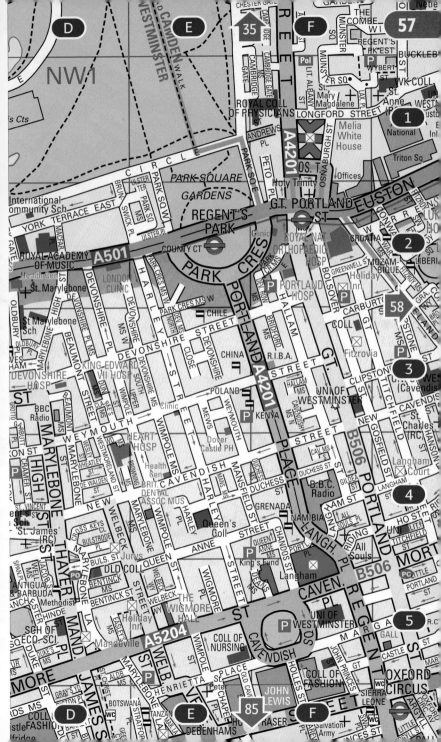

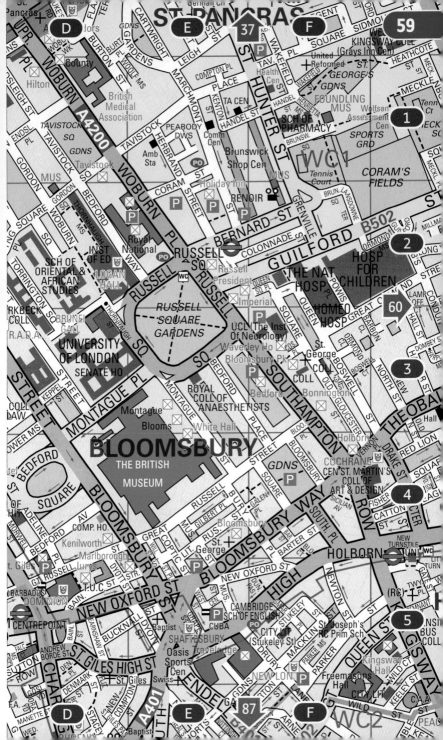

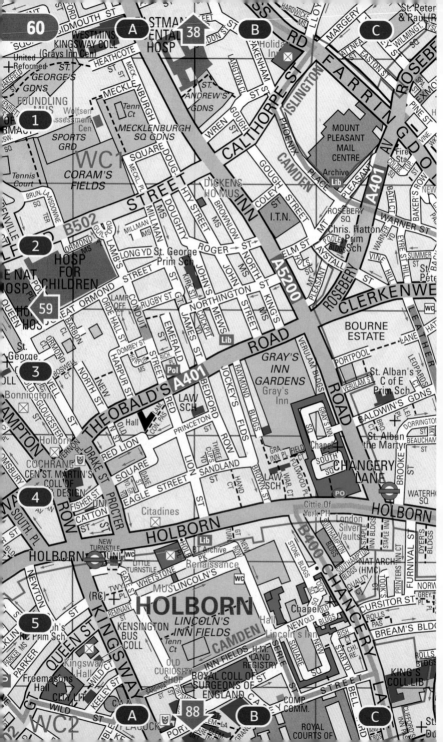

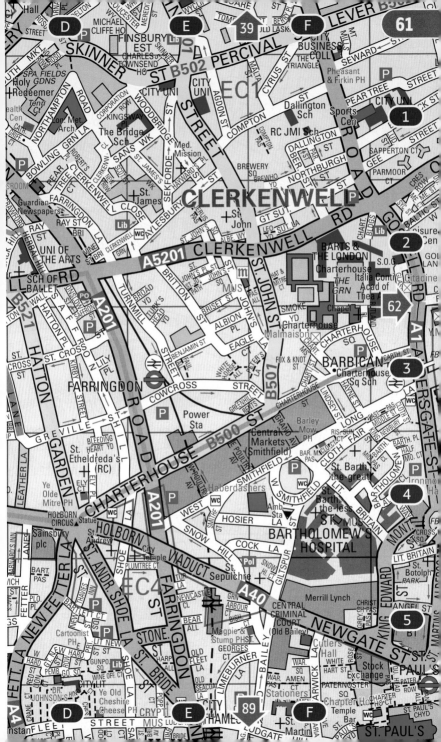

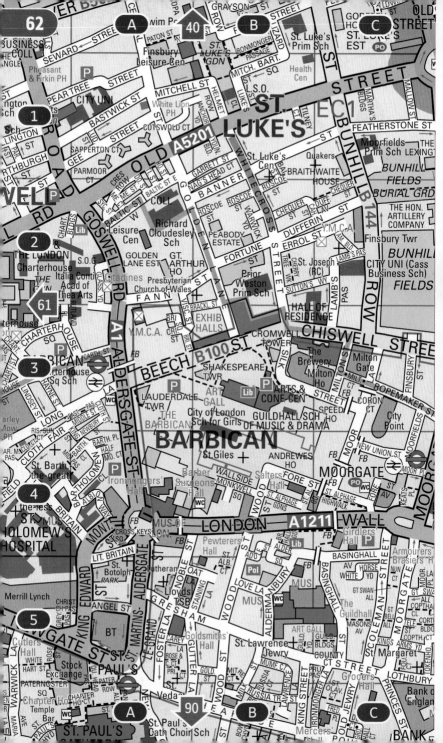

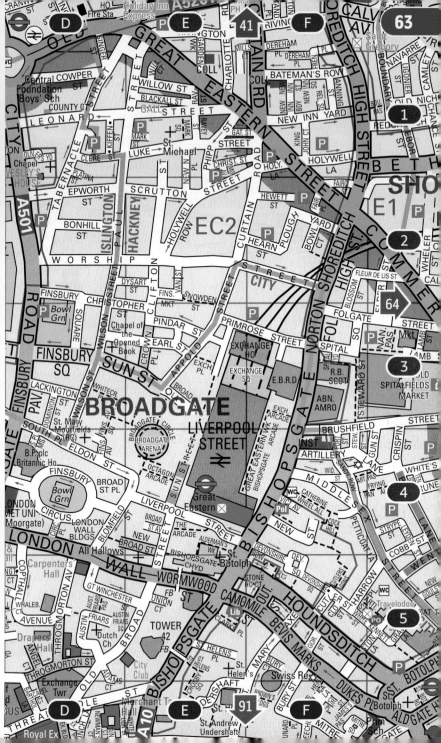

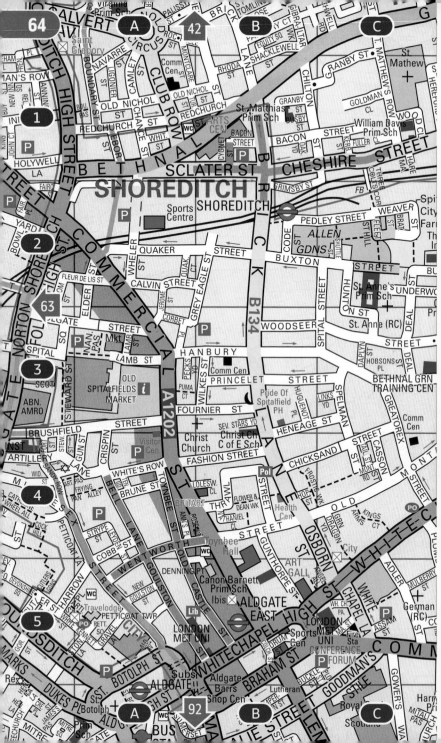

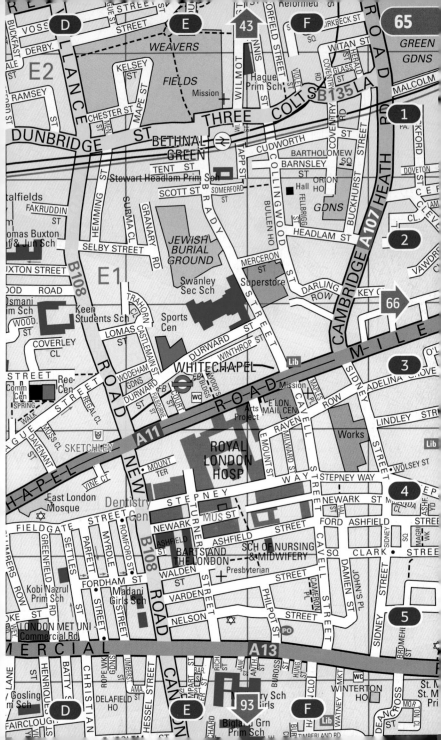

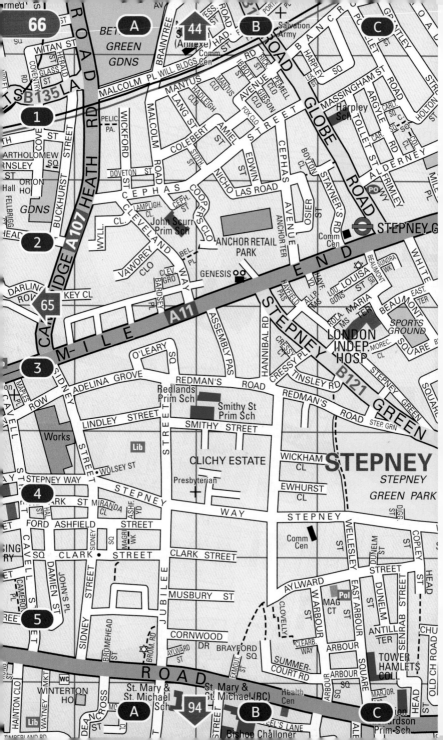

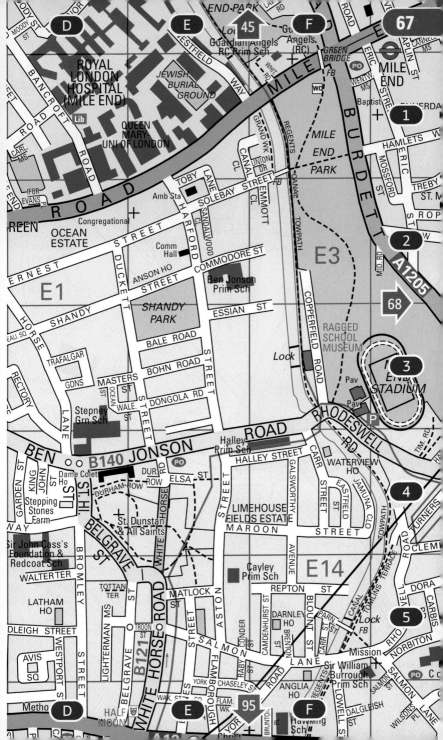

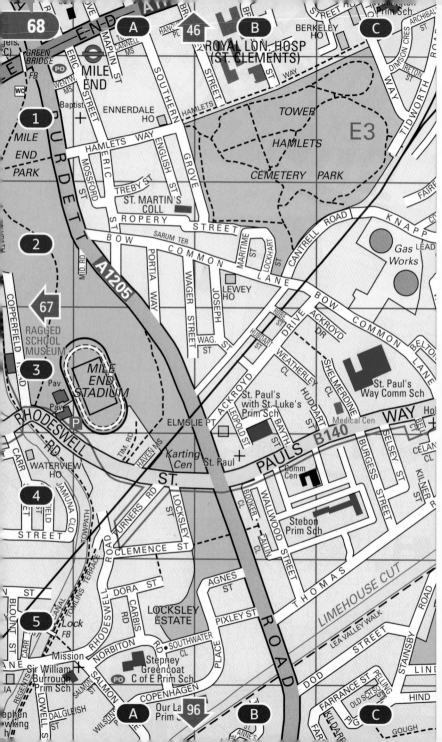

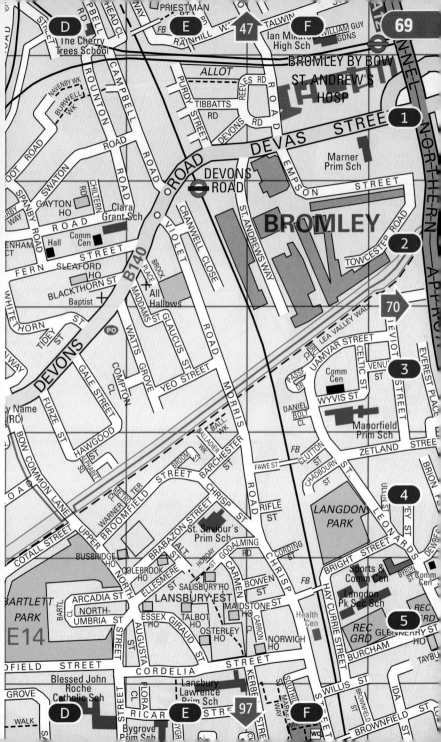

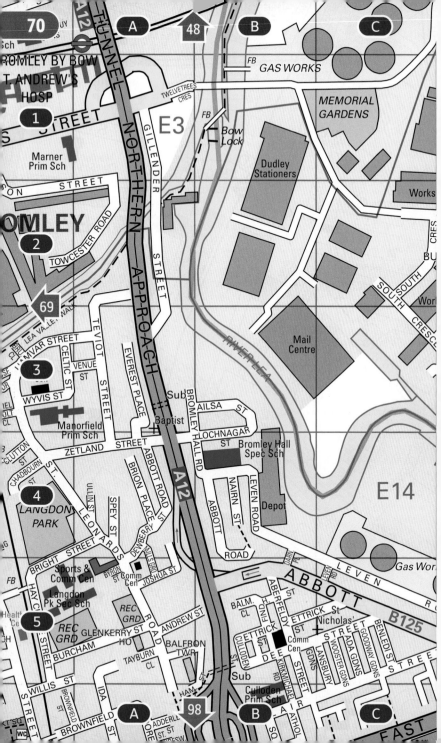

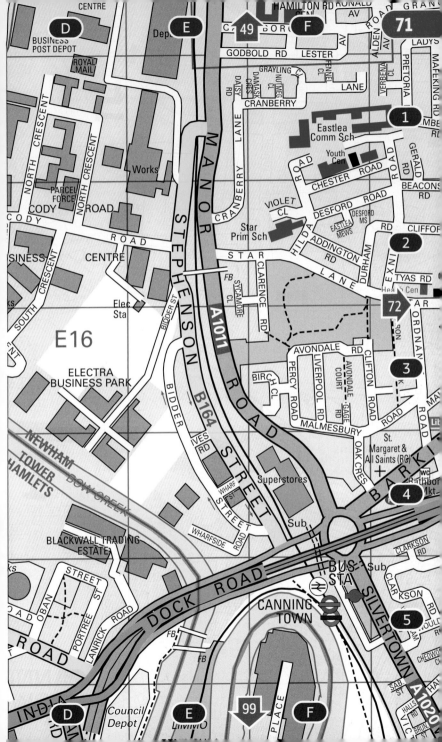

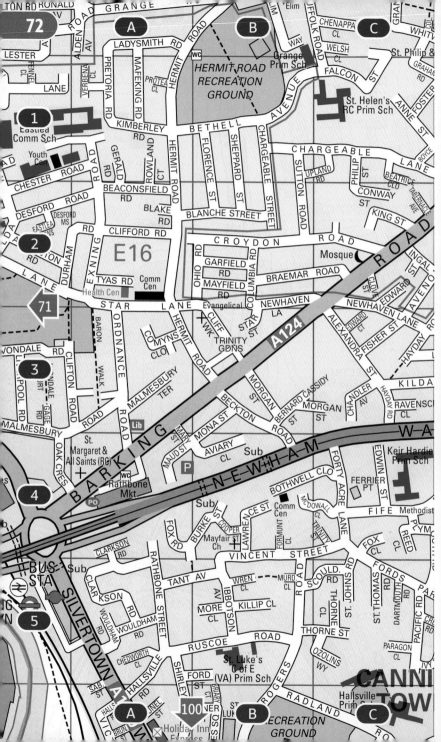

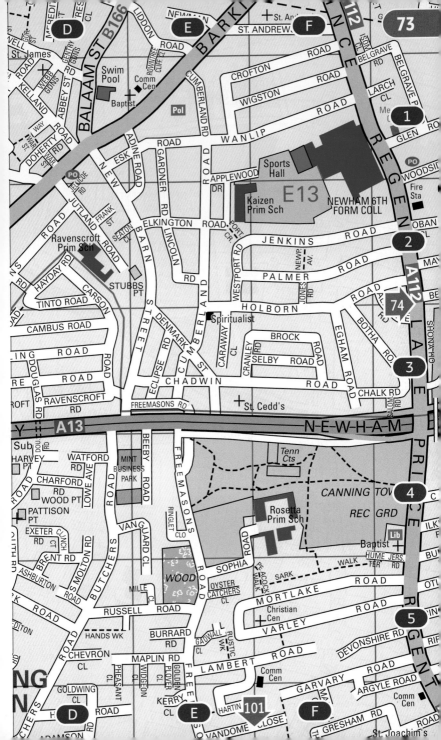

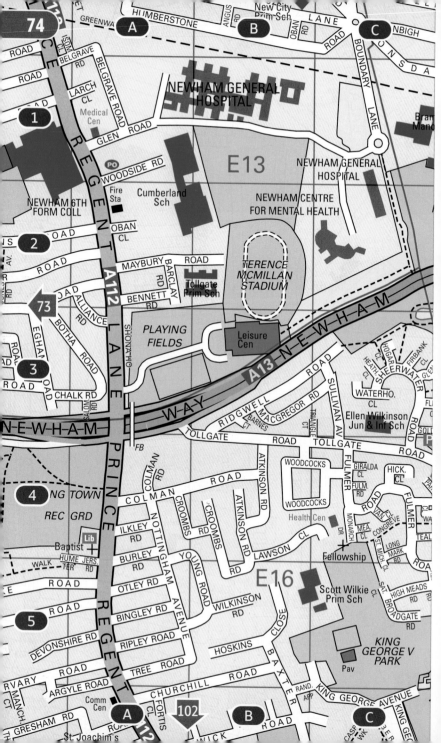

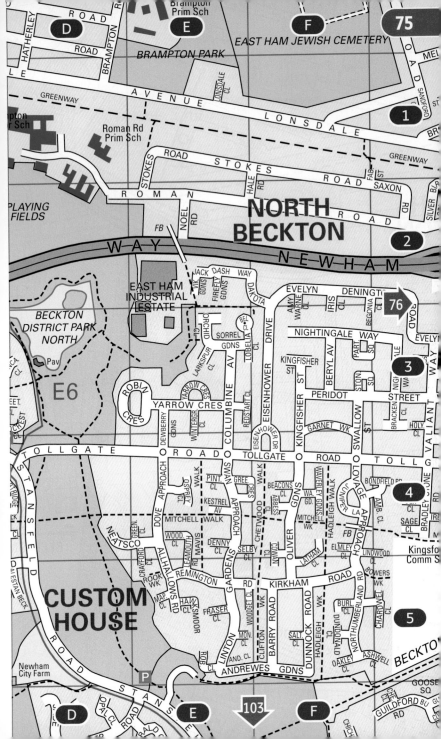

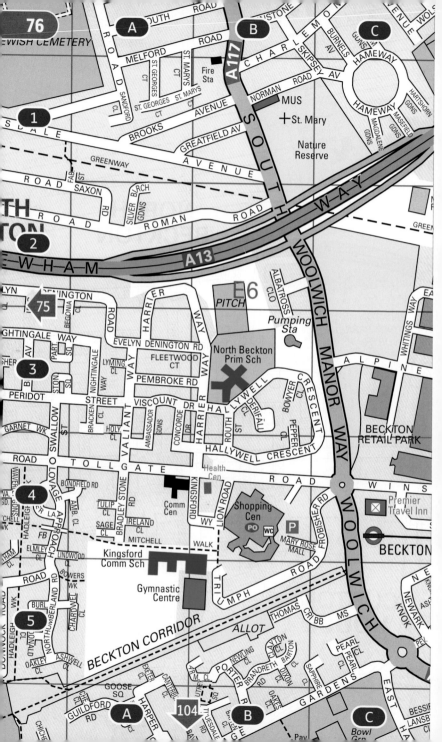

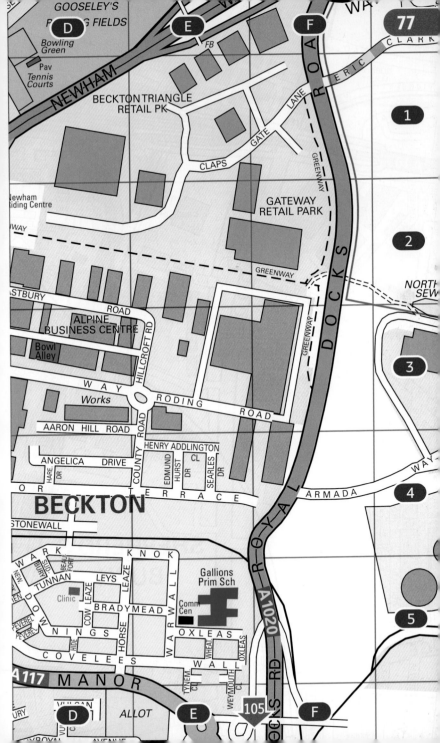

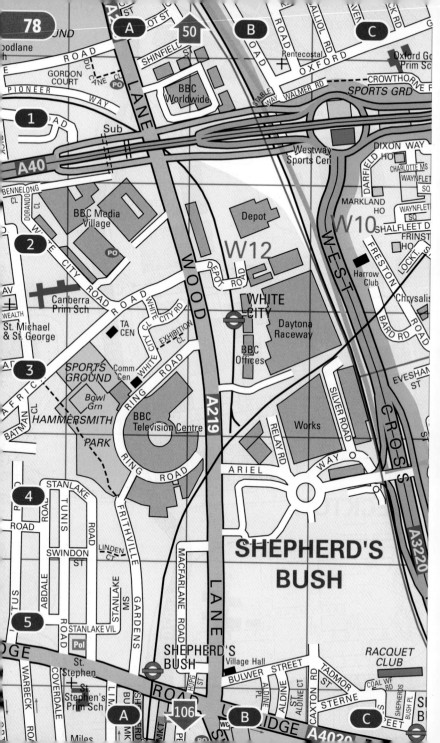

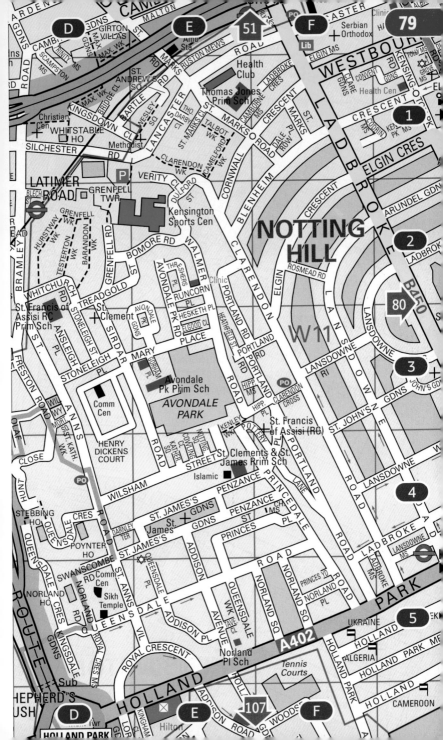

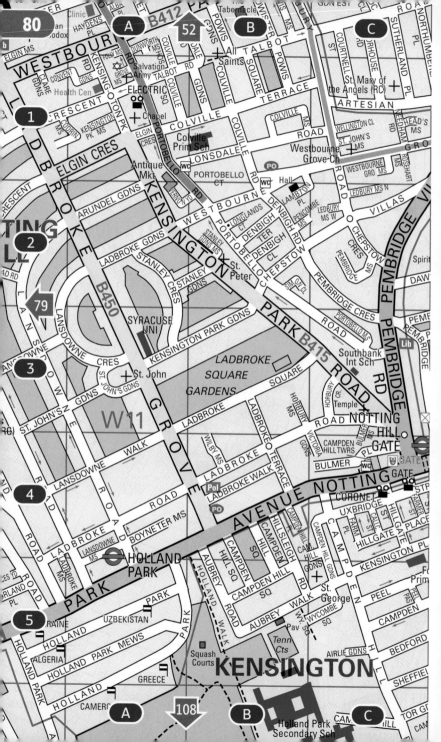

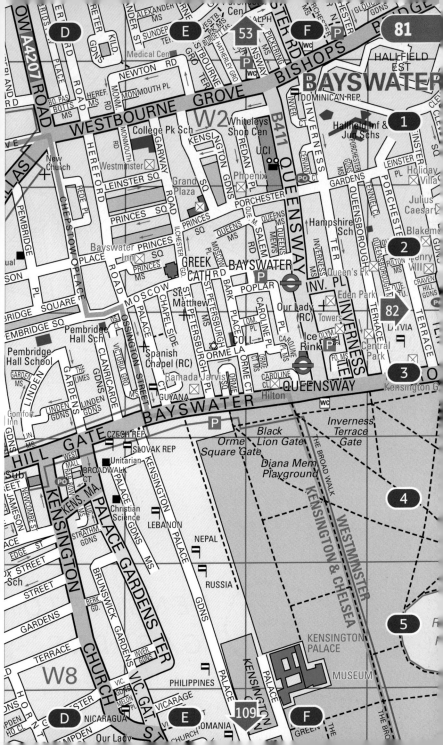

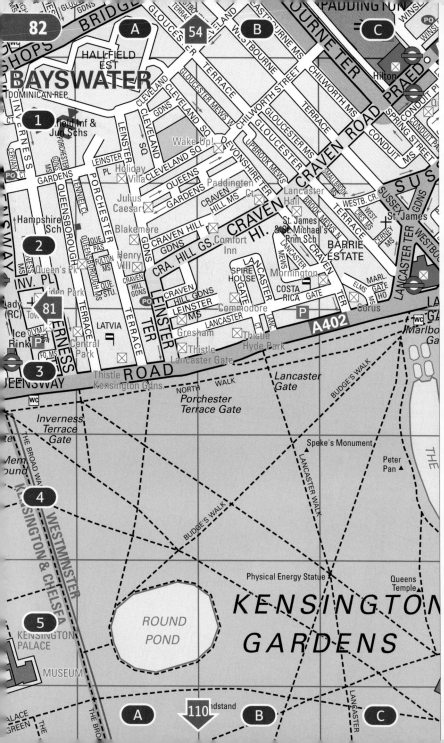

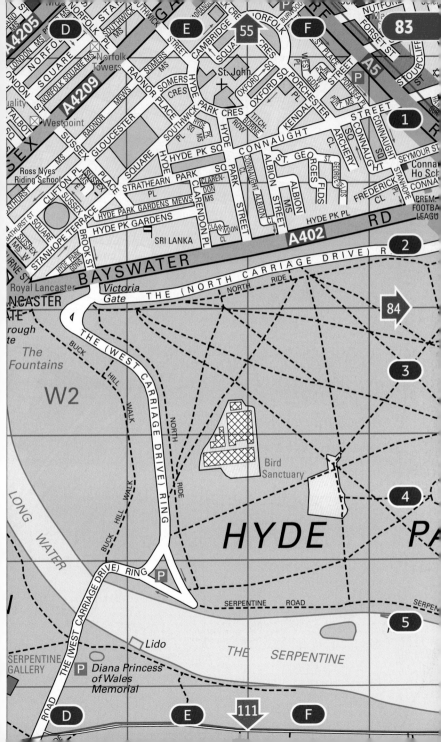

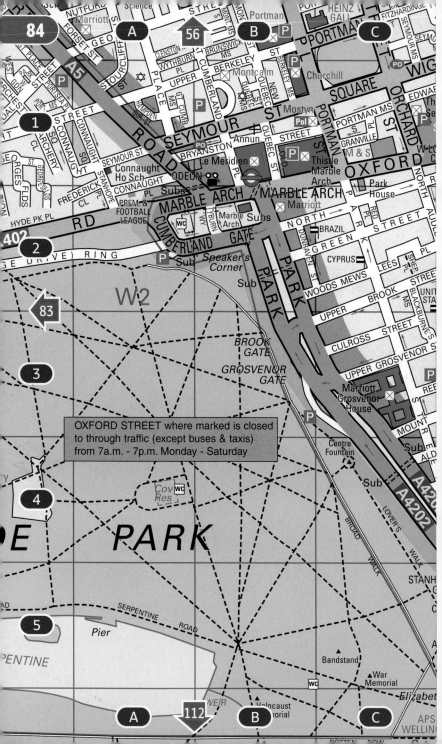

OXFORD STREET where marked is closed to through traffic (except buses & taxis) from 7a.m. - 7p.m. Monday - Saturday

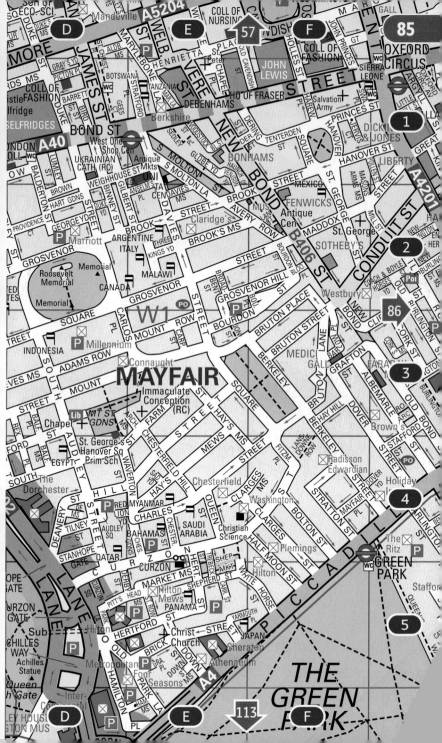

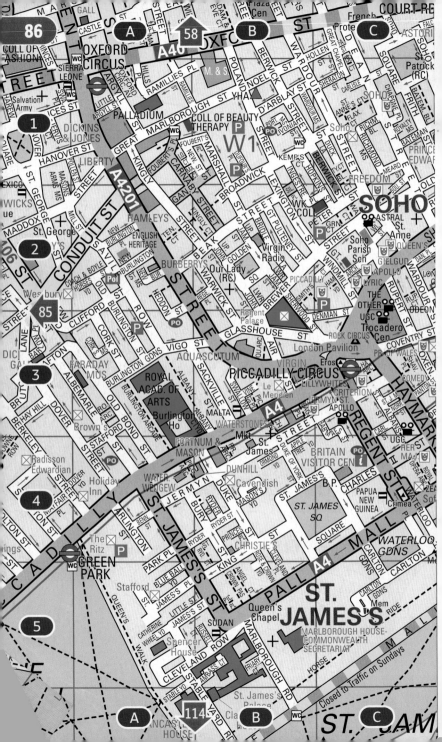

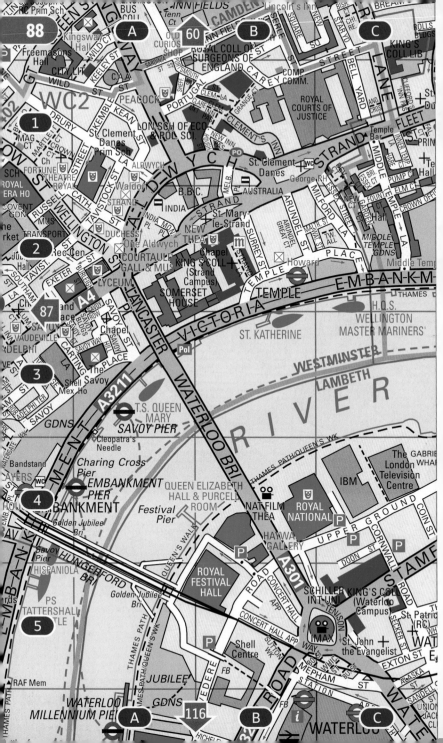

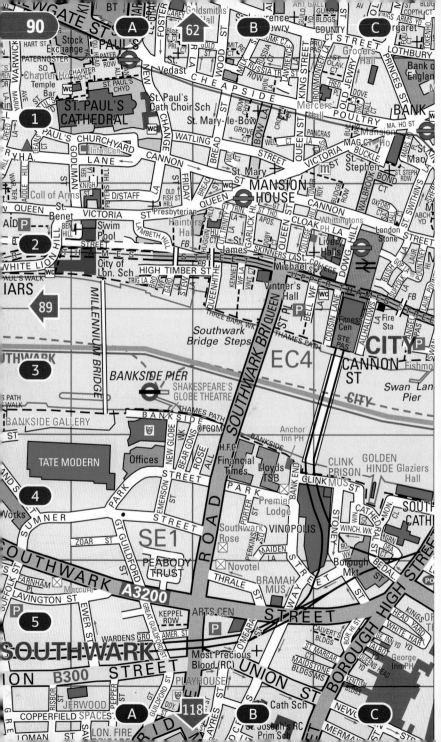

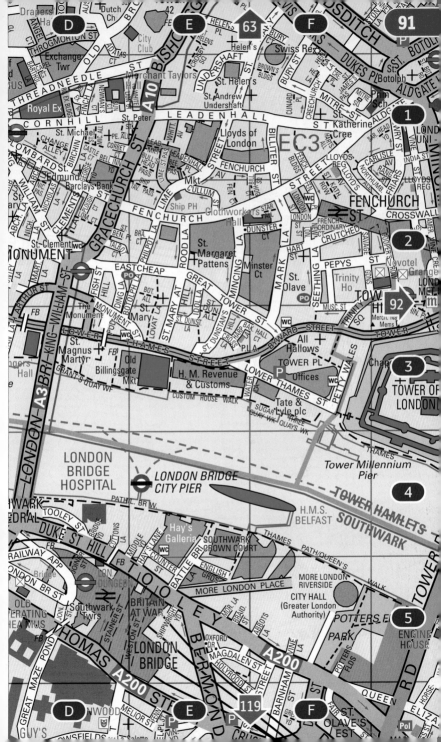

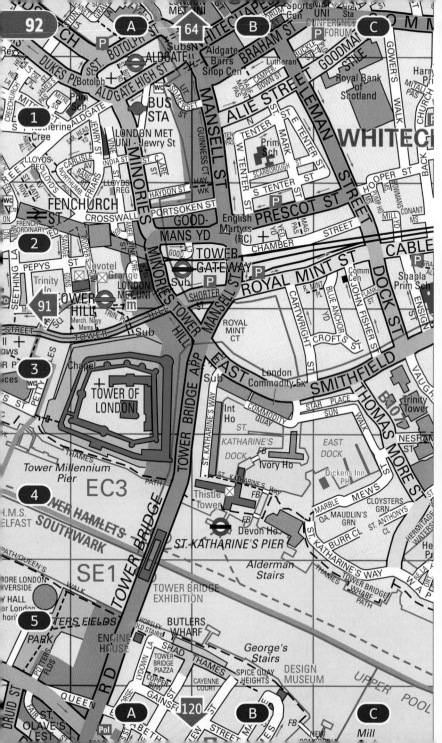

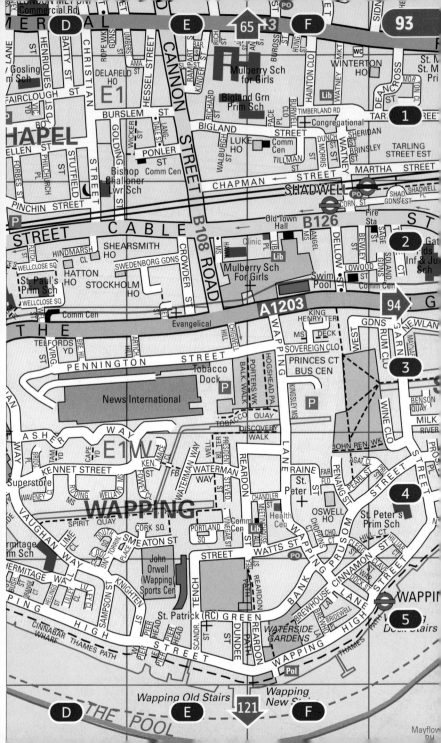

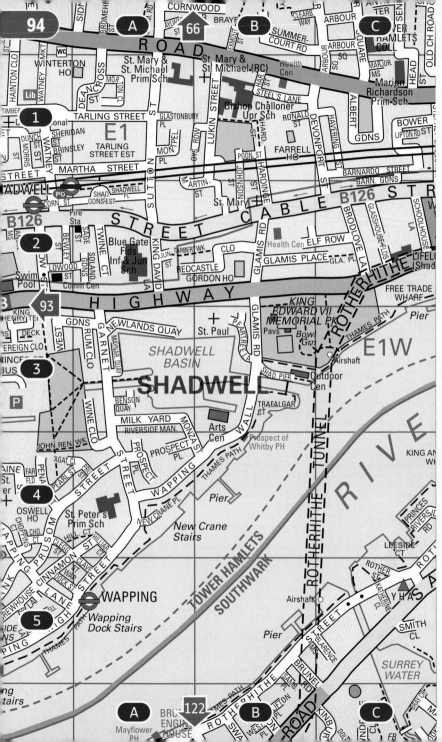

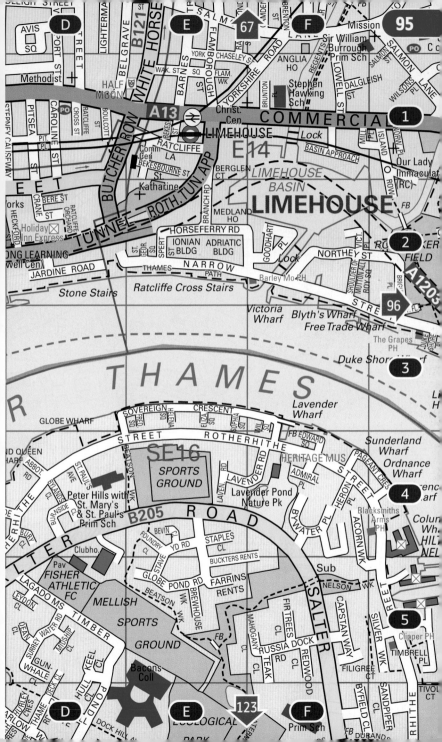

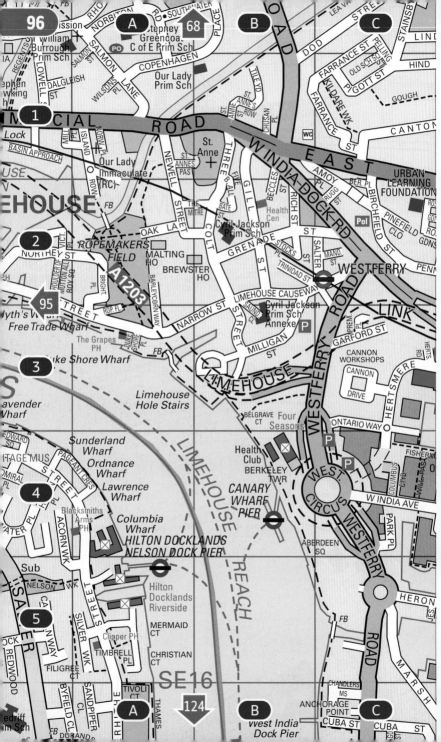

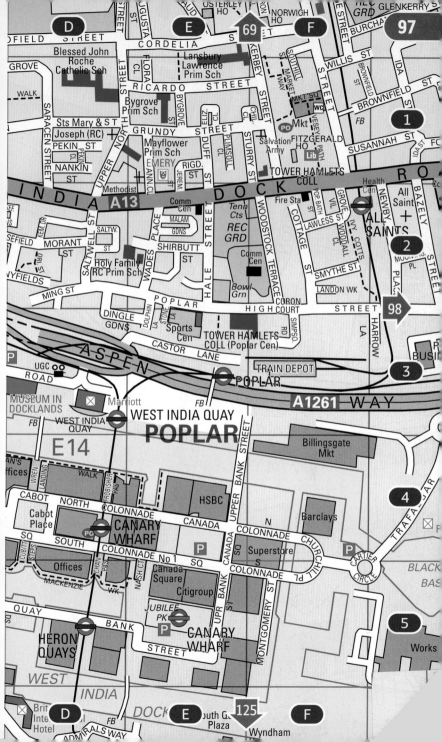

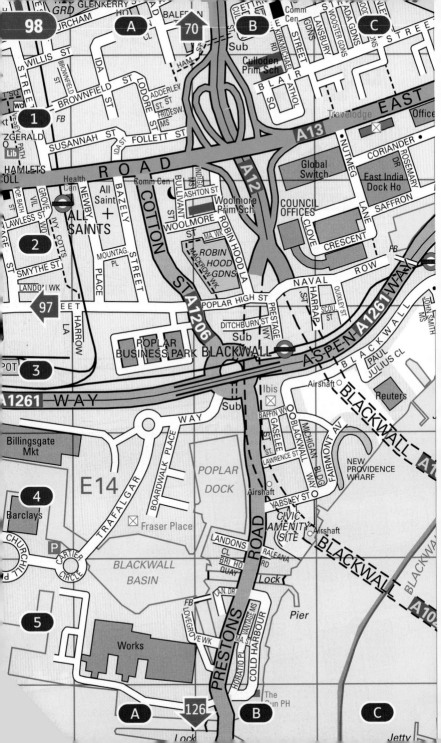

INDIA RD

LANRIC

Council
Depot

AV

OREGANO
DR

SORREL
LA

SILVOCEA WAY

LIMMO
PENINSULA
ECOLOGICAL
PARK

LEAMOUTH

ORCHARD   PLACE

ASPEN

AVENUE

E16

SWITCH HO HO

ELEKTRON HO

WAY

LOWER   LEA   CROSS

BLACKWALL WAY

EAST INDIA

WAY

PILGRIM
MS

EAST INDIA
DOCK BASIN

ORCHARD

BOW CREEK

NEWPORT AVENUE

JAMESTOWN WAY

NATURE
RESERVE

PLACE

Buly Wharf

Blackwall
Pier

Wo

Jetty

Thames
Whar

Blackwall
Beach

02

REACH TUNNEL

THAMES PATH/CYCLE PATH

Airy's
Point

SE10

MERIDIAN
GARDENS

The Dome
Redevelopment
(Open 2007)

Millennium
Pier

TUNNEL

DRAWDOCK
RD

ORDNANCE

GREENWICH

NORTH
GREENWICH

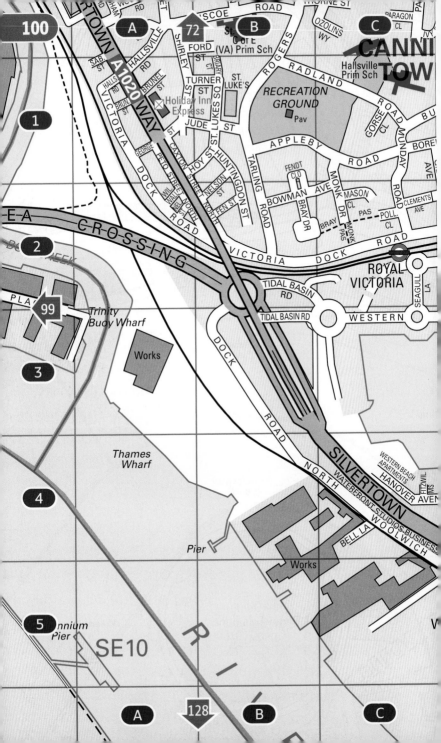

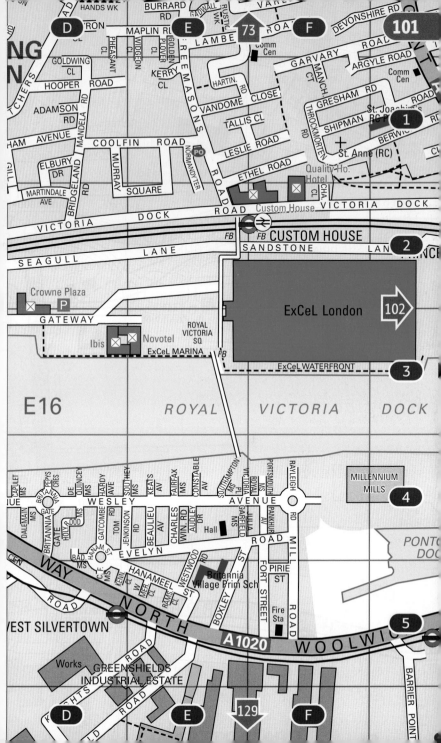

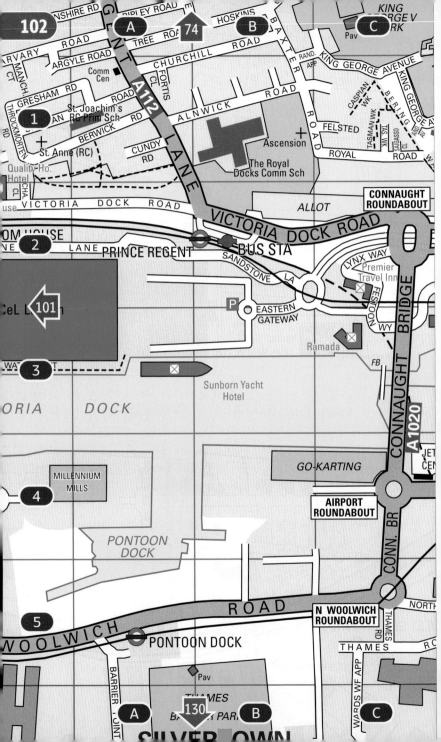

A | **B** | **C**

SHIRE RD
RIPLEY ROAD
HOSKINS
KING GEORGE V PARK
Pav

CHURCHILL
ROAD
TREE ROAD
74
BAXTER
RAND. APP
KING GEORGE AVENUE
KING GEORGE AV

ARVARY ROAD
ARGYLE ROAD
Comm Cen
FORTIS CL
ALNWICK
ROAD
CASPIAN WK
BERING WK
TASMAN WK
TAS. WK
GLASGOW RD
KING GEORGE AV

MANCH CT
GRESHAM RD
St. Joachim's RC Prim Sch
BERWICK
CUNDY RD
Ascension
FELSTED
ROYAL
ROAD

THROCKMORTEN RD
St. Anne (RC)
RD
The Royal Docks Comm Sch

Quality Ho. Hotel
VICTORIA DOCK ROAD
ALLOT
CONNAUGHT ROUNDABOUT

CHA. CL

1

OM HOUSE
VICTORIA DOCK ROAD

2 LANE PRINCE REGENT
BUS STA
SANDSTONE LA
LYNX WAY
Premier Travel Inn
FESTOON WY

CeL **101**
P EASTERN GATEWAY
Ramada
FB

3
WAT... ...T
Sunborn Yacht Hotel

...ORIA DOCK

CONNAUGHT BRIDGE
A1020

MILLENNIUM MILLS
GO-KARTING
JET CEN

4
AIRPORT ROUNDABOUT
CONN. BR

PONTOON DOCK

5
WOOLWICH ROAD
N WOOLWICH ROUNDABOUT
THAMES RD
NORTH

WOOLWICH
PONTOON DOCK
THAMES

BARRIER POINT
Pav
130
WARDS WF APP

A | **B** | **C**

THAMES BARRIER PARK

SILVER...OWN

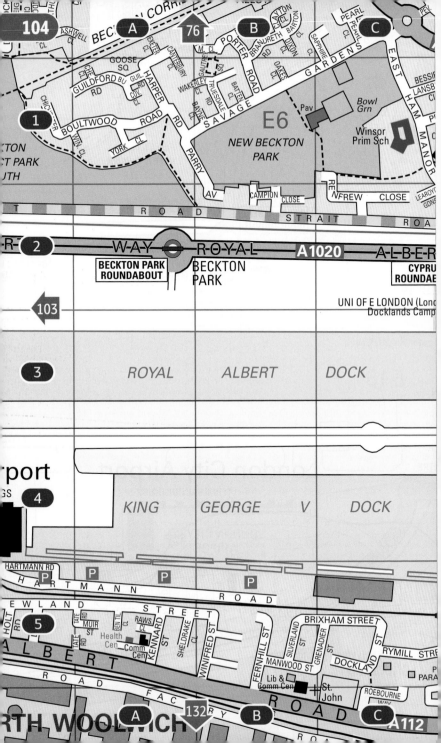

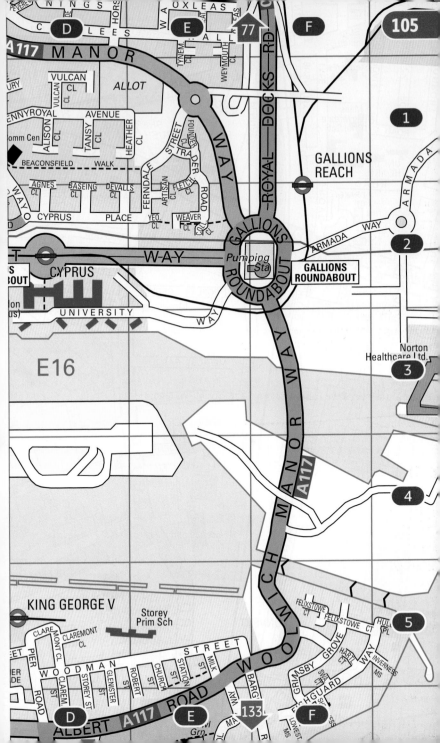

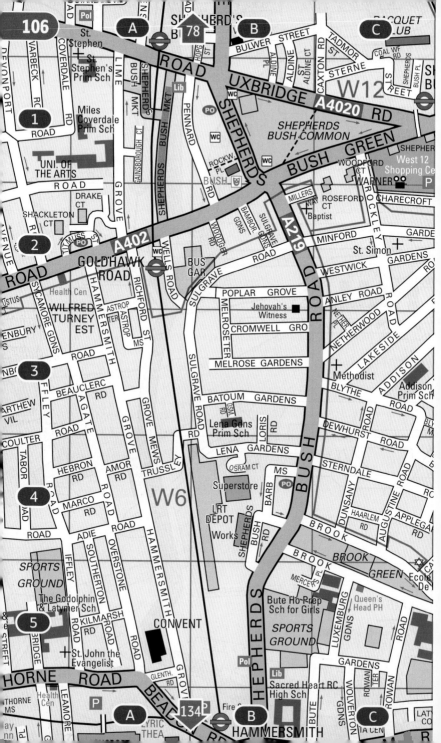

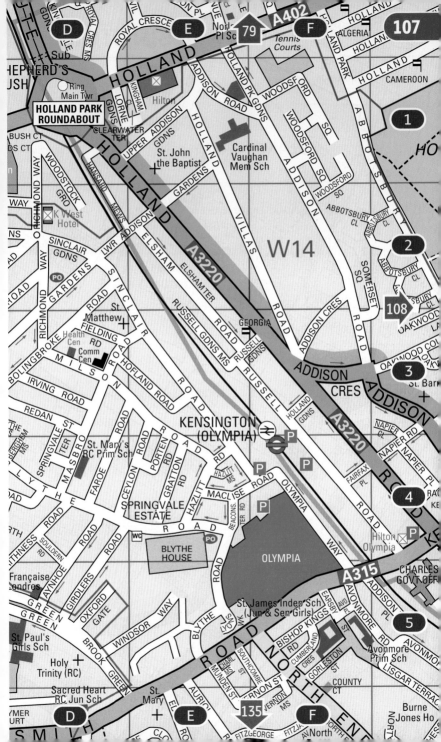

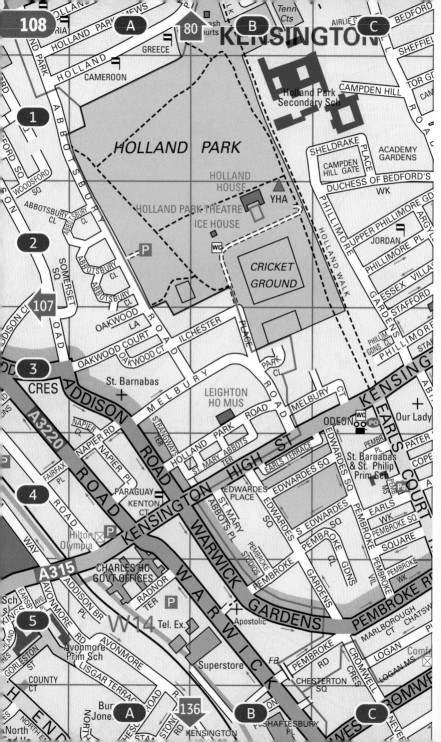

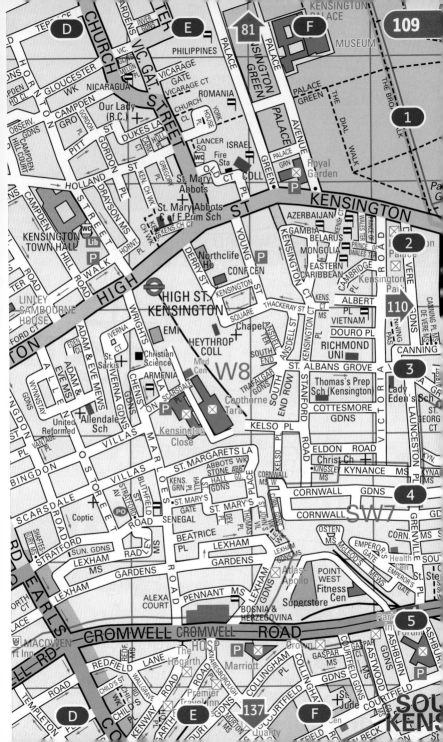

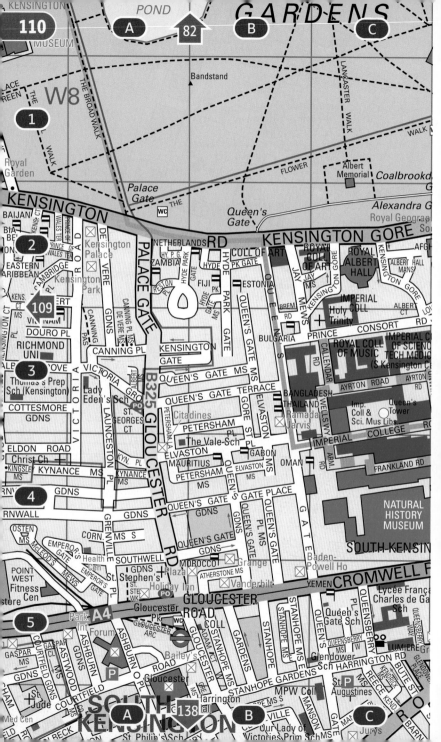

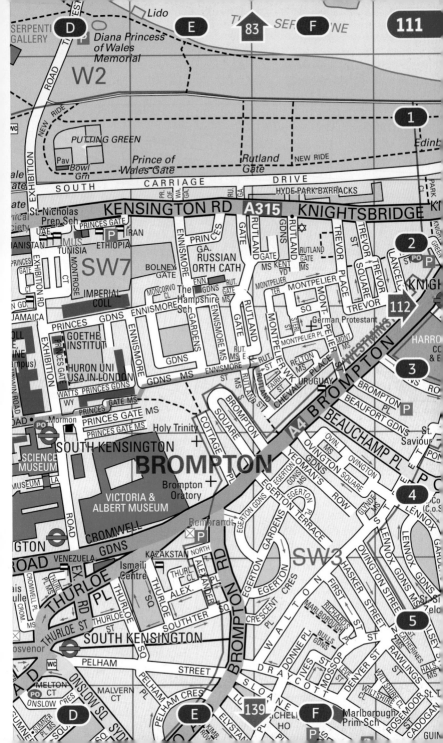

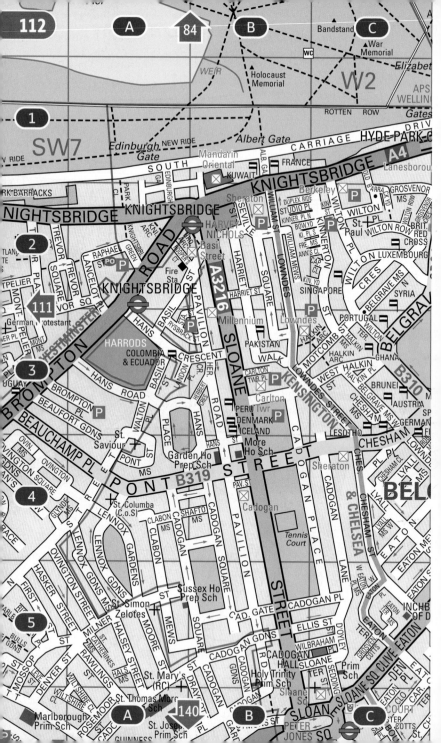

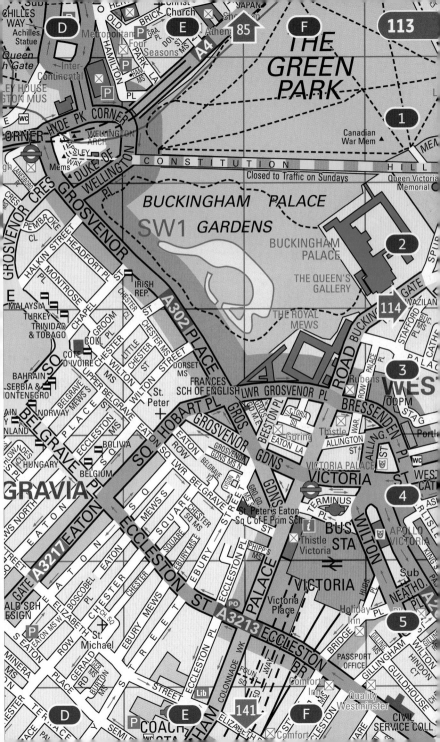

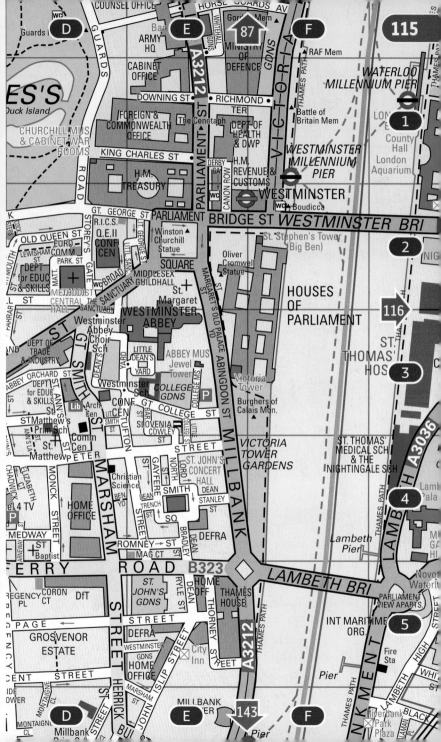

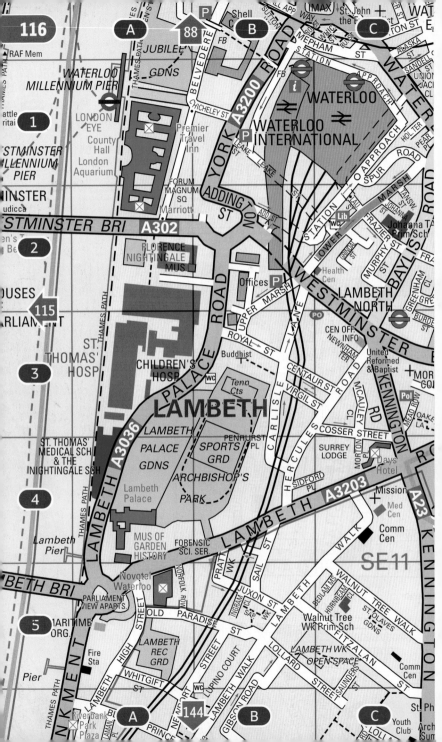

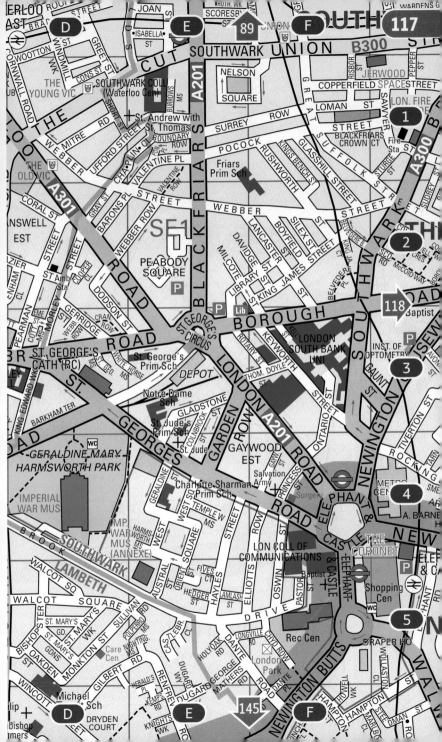

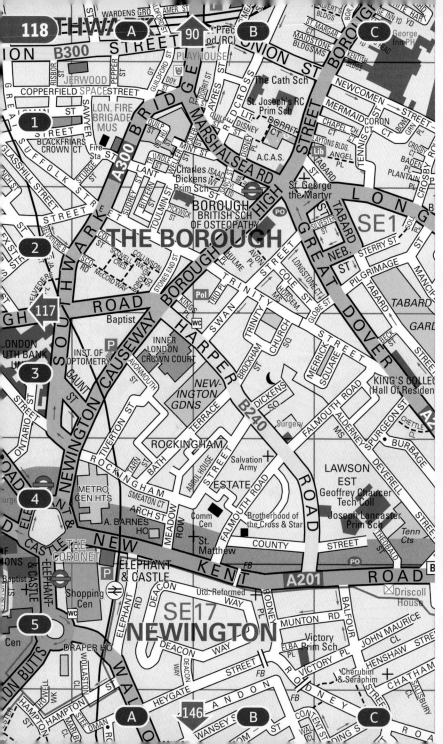

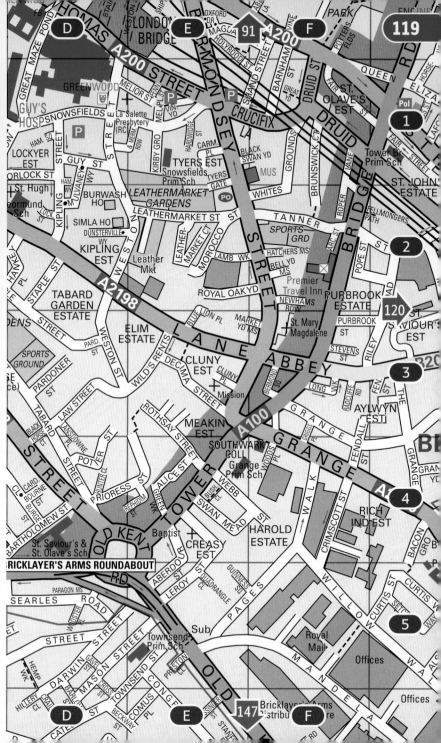

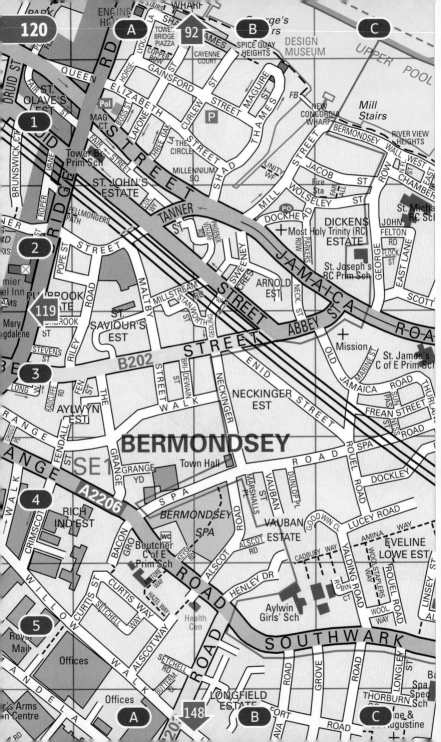

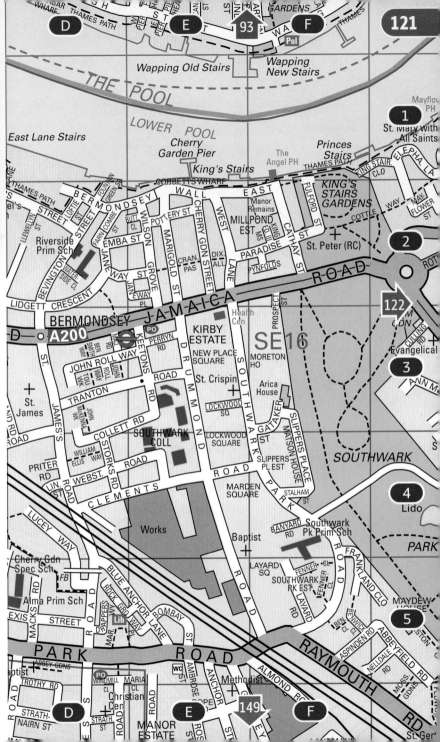

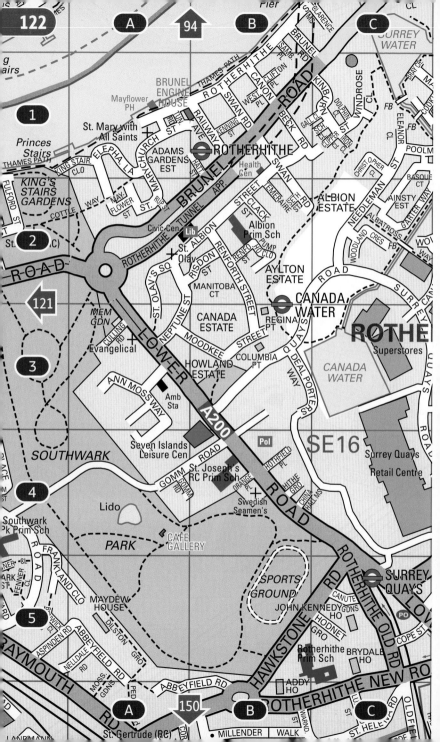

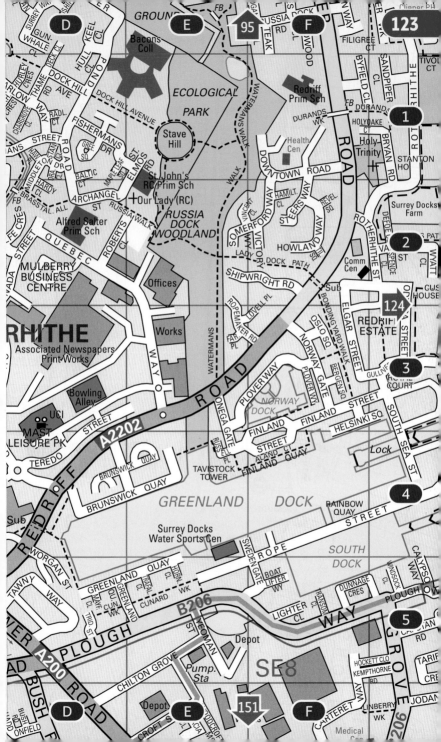

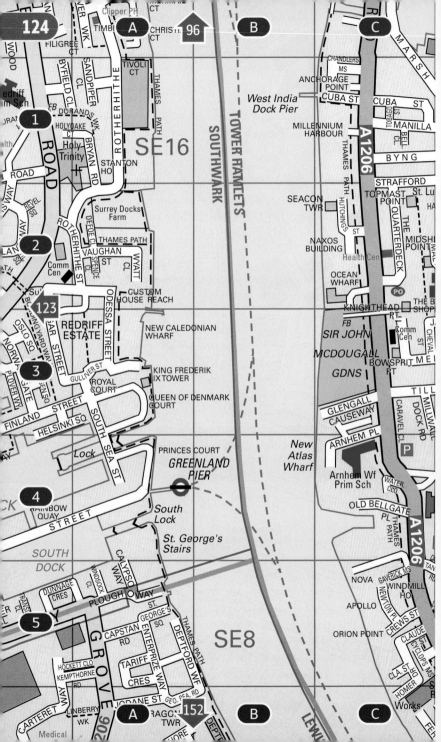

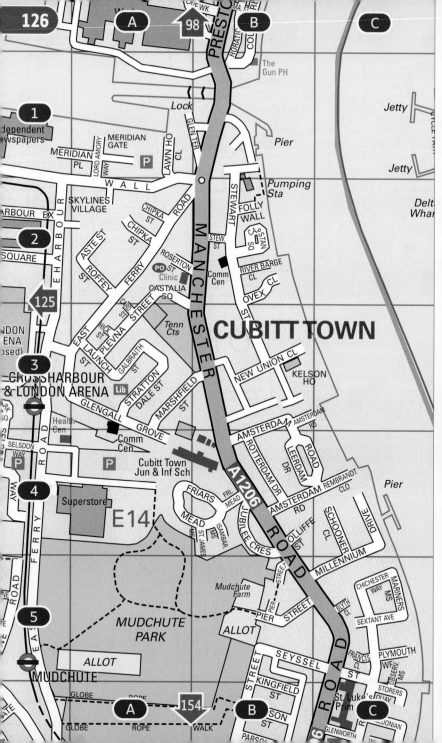

A **98** **B** **C**

1

Independent Newspapers

MERIDIAN GATE

MERIDIAN PL

LORD AMORY WAY

MERIDIAN WAY

LAWN HO CL

GLEN TER

Lock

HORATIO PL

COL

The Gun PH

Jetty

CYCLE PATH

Jetty

WALL

ROAD

Pier

Pumping Sta

Delta Wharf

SKYLINES VILLAGE

HARBOUR EX

2

SQUARE

CHIPKA ST

CHIPKA ST

ASTE ST

ROFFEY ST

FERRY

ROSERTON ST

PO Clinic

CASTALIA SQ

HIGH ST

CABIR ST

STREET

STEWART

STEW ST

FOLLY WALL

CAPSTAN SQ

RIVER BARGE CL

OVEX CL

Comm Cen

CUBITT TOWN

125

LONDON ARENA (closed)

EAST FERRY

LAUNCH ST

PLEVNA ST

GALBRAITH ST

STRATTON

DALE ST

Tenn Cts

MARSHFIELD ST

NEW UNION CL

KELSON HO

3

CROSSHARBOUR & LONDON ARENA

Lib

GLENGALL GROVE

Health Cen

Comm Cen

ROAD

AMSTERDAM

AMSTERDAM RD

ROTTERDAM DR

LEERDAM DR

ROAD

SELSDON WAY

P

WAY

ROAD

FERRY

4

Superstore

E14

Cubitt Town Jun & Inf Sch

P

FRIARS MEAD

FRI MEAD

ISAMBAR MS

ST JAMES

MS

ST MEAD MS

A1206

JUBILEE CRES

AMSTERDAM RD

OLLIFFE ST

REMBRANDT CLO

SCHOONER CL

MILLENNIUM DRIVE

MARINERS MS

Pier

CHICHESTER WAY MS

5

ROAD

EAST

MUDCHUTE PARK

ALLOT

Mudchute Farm

PIER STREET

ALLOT

PIER STREET

SEYSSEL STREET

BLYTH CL

SEXTANT AVE

FRANCIS CL

PLYMOUTH WF

TOBERY QUAY

STORERS QUAY

CALEDONIAN

MUDCHUTE

GLOBE

ROPE

A **154** **B** **C**

GLOBE

ROPE

WALK

STREET

KINGFIELD ST

SON ST

PARSON

ROAD

St Luke's Prim

GLENWORTH

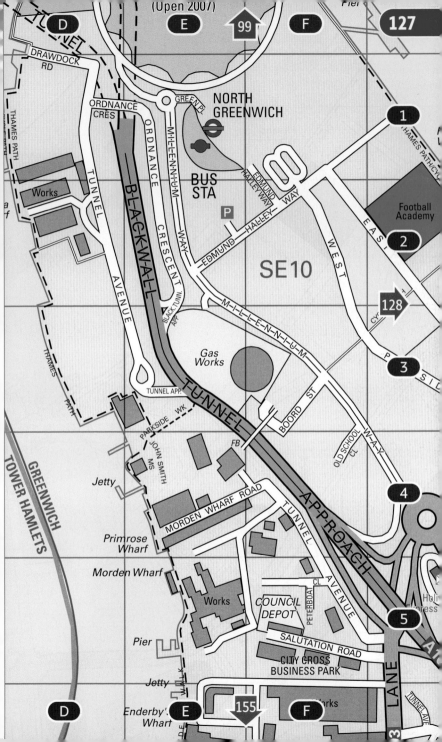

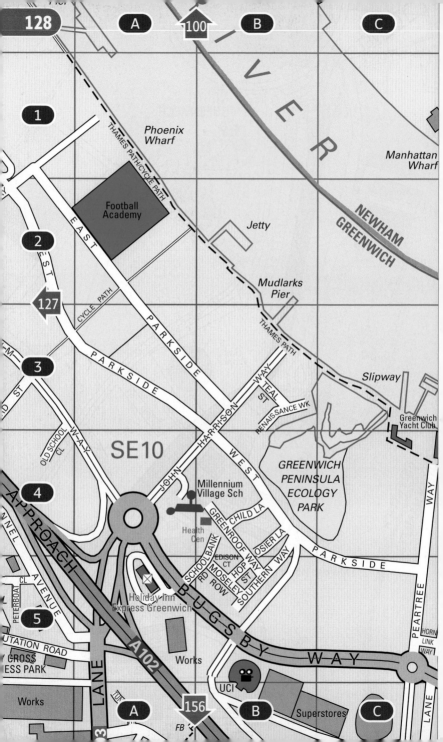

1

Phoenix Wharf

Manhattan Wharf

THAMES PATH/CYCLE PATH

Football Academy

EAST

2

127

Jetty

NEWHAM
GREENWICH

CYCLE PATH

PARKSIDE

Mudlarks Pier

THAMES PATH

3

PARKSIDE

Slipway

OLD SCHOOL WAY

OLD SCHOOL CL

HARRISON

WAY

TEAL ST

RENAISSANCE WK

Greenwich Yacht Club

SE10

WEST

4

JOHN

Millennium Village Sch

CHILD LA

GREENROOF WAY

OSIER LA

GREENWICH
PENINSULA
ECOLOGY
PARK

APPROACH

Health Cen

SCHOOL BANK RD

EDISON CT

MOSELEY ROW

HOP ST

SOUTHERN WAY

PARKSIDE

WAY

AVENUE

PETERBOAT CL

Holiday Inn Express Greenwich

PEARTREE

HORN LINK WAY

5

UTATION ROAD

CROSS
ESS PARK

A102

BUGSBY

Works

WAY

Works

LANE

TUN

UCI

FB

LANE

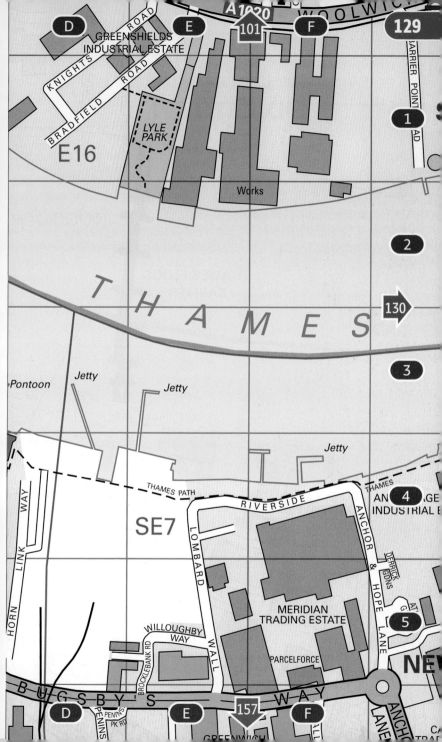

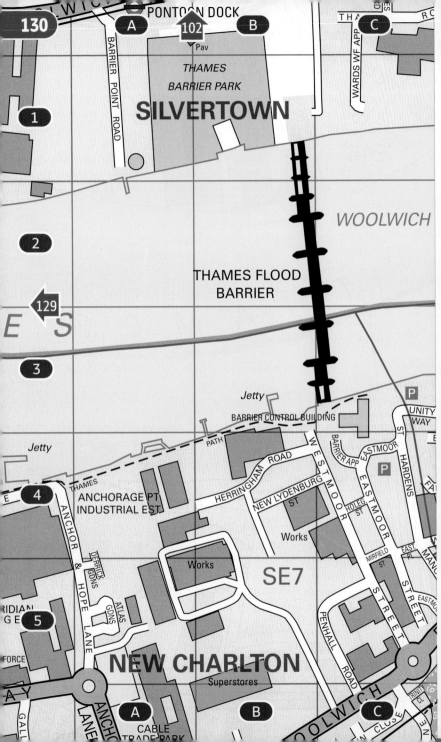

A PONTOON DOCK **B**

102

Pav

THAMES

BARRIER PARK

SILVERTOWN

C

WARDS WF APP

1

WOOLWICH

2

BARRIER POINT ROAD

THAMES FLOOD
BARRIER

129

3

Jetty

BARRIER CONTROL BUILDING

P

UNITY
WAY

Jetty

PATH

WESTMOOR

BARRIER APP

EASTMOOR

ST

HARDENS

4

THAMES

ANCHORAGE PT
INDUSTRIAL EST

HERRINGHAM ROAD

NEW LYDENBURG

ST

HOLEG
ST

EASTMOOR

FAR

ANCHOR &

DERRICK
GDNS

Works

MIRFIELD
ST

EAST
PL

MAN

Works

SE7

RIDIAN
GE

5

HOPE
LANE

ATLAS
GDNS

PENHALL
ROAD

STREET

EASTMOO

FORCE

NEW CHARLTON

Superstores

STREET

A

ANCHO

CABLE
TRADE PARK

B

C

WOOLWICH

TRINITY
CL

CLOSE

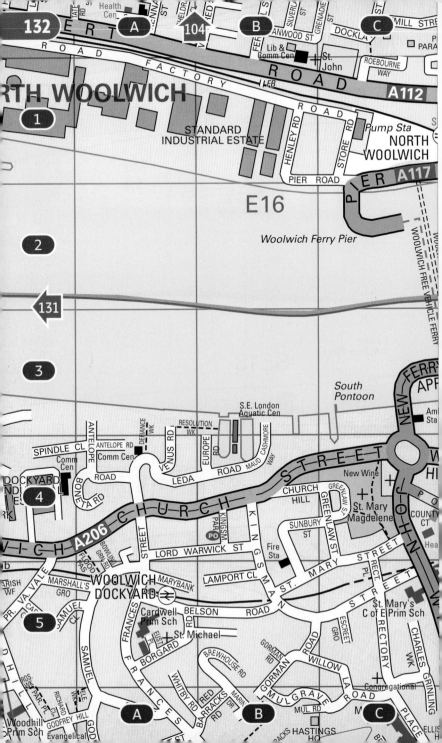

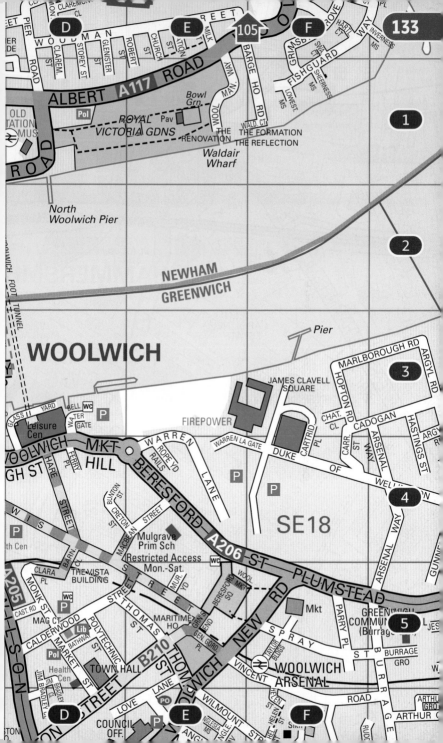

D **E** **105** **F**

CLAREMONT
CL
MAN
STREET
REET
GRIMSBY RD
HART CT
INVERNESS
WAY
MS

PIER
RDE
WOODMAN
CLAREM.
STOREY ST
GLENISTER ST
ROBERT ST
CHURCH ST
MILK ST
BARGE HO.
GRO VE
FISHGUARD
SHEERNESS MS
LOWEST.

ALBERT **A117** **ROAD**

OLD STATION MUS

Pol

Bowl Grn

WOOLMAN WAY

WALD CT

1

ROYAL VICTORIA GDNS
Pav
THE RENOVATION
THE FORMATION
THE REFLECTION

Waldair Wharf

ROAD

North Woolwich Pier

2

NEWHAM

GREENWICH

Pier

WOOLWICH

MARLBOROUGH RD
ARGYL RD

3

JAMES CLAVELL SQUARE

HOPTON RD
CHAT. CL
CADOGAN
ARSENAL
HASTINGS ST
ARGY
R

FIREPOWER

WARREN LA GATE
DUKE
CARTRID PL
CARR ST
OF

YARD
BELL ST
WC
TER WK
GATE
P

GLASS ST

Leisure Cen

WARREN
ROPE YD
RAILS

MKT HILL

BERESFORD

WAY
WELL
ON

WOOLWICH HIGH ST

HARE
STREET
FERRY PL

LANE

P

P

4

WIS

P

th Cen

A205

BUXTON ST
CRETON ST
MACBEAN ST

STREET

A206 **ST**

SE18

ARSENAL WAY

GUNNE

BARN CL
THE VISTA BUILDING

Mulgrave Prim Sch
Restricted Access
Mon.-Sat.
WC

WOOL
BERESFORD MKT

PLUMSTEAD

Mkt

PARRY PL

GREENWICH COMMUN (Burrage

5

CLARA PL
WC
P
CALDERWOOD
MAG CT
CAST. RD

MONK ST
MARKET ST
STREET
THOMAS ST
THOMAS
STREET
POLYTECHNIC
BATHWAY
Lib

MARITIME HO.
MUR. YD
BERESFORD SQ.
GEN END
GEN GORD PL

NEW RD

SPRAY
ST

BURRAGE GRO

JES

Pol
Health Cen
JIM BRADLEY CT
JIM BRADLEY
TOWN HALL
B210 ST

THOMPSON
LANE

TAYLOR BLDGS
VINCENT

WOOLWICH ARSENAL

ROAD

ARTHU GRO

W

D **E** **F**

COUNCIL OFF.
PO
P

LOVE LANE
WILMOUNT ST
ANGLESEA
NGLESEA MS
HELEN ST
St
ARTHUR ST
RUDE

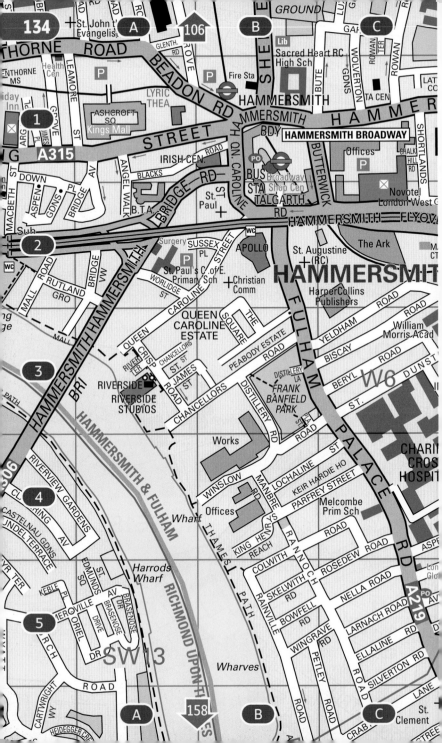

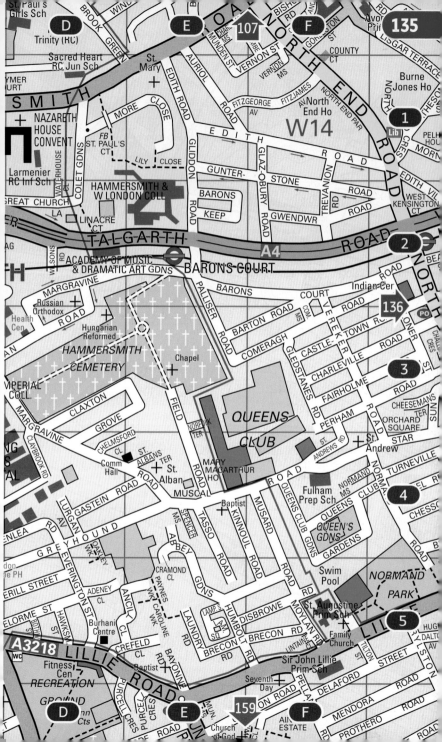

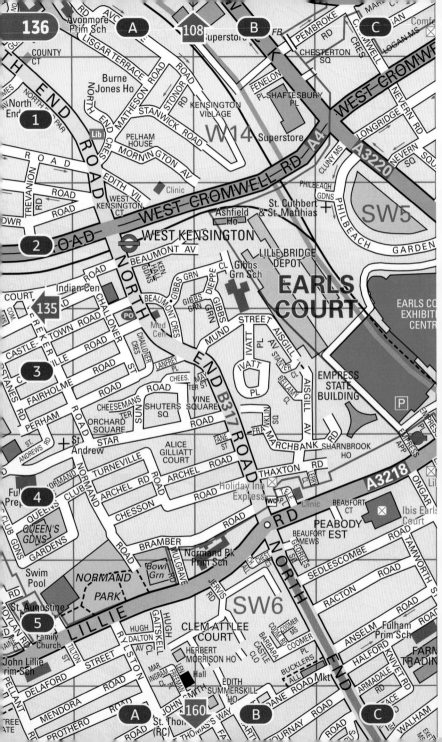

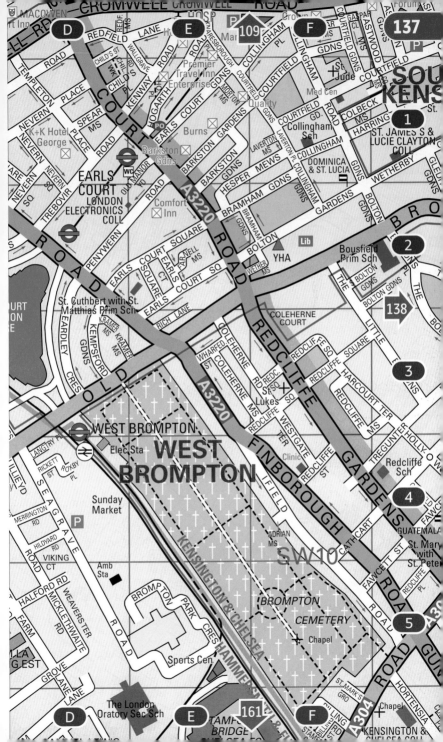

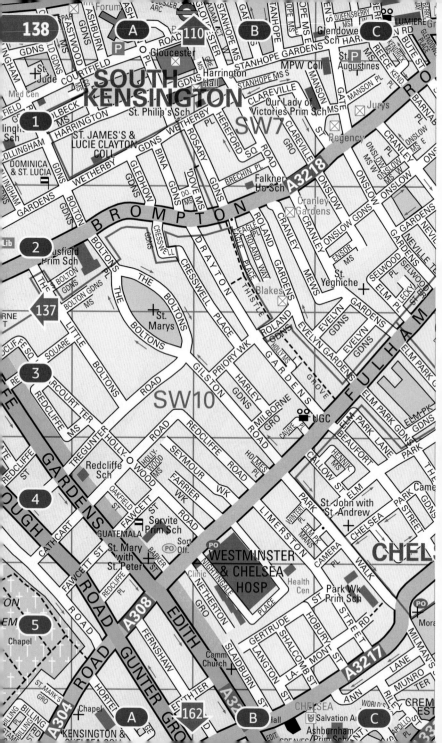

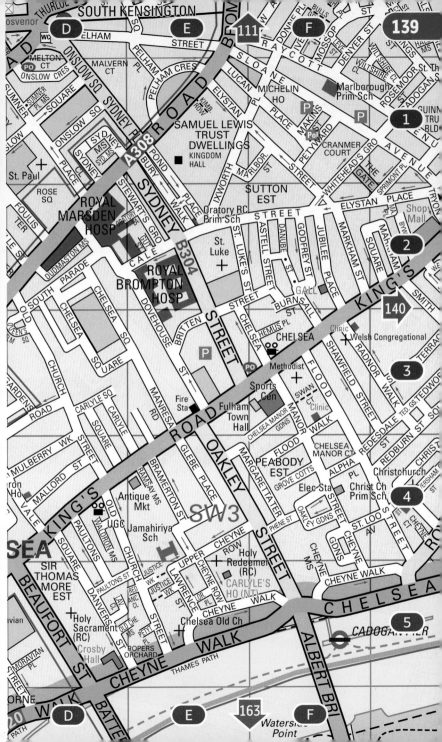

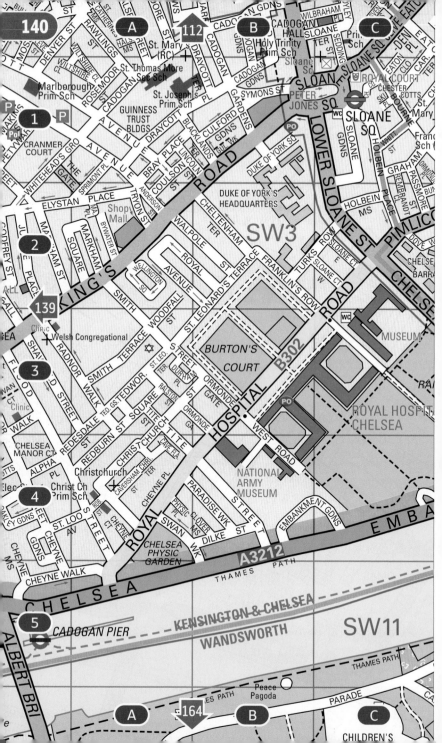

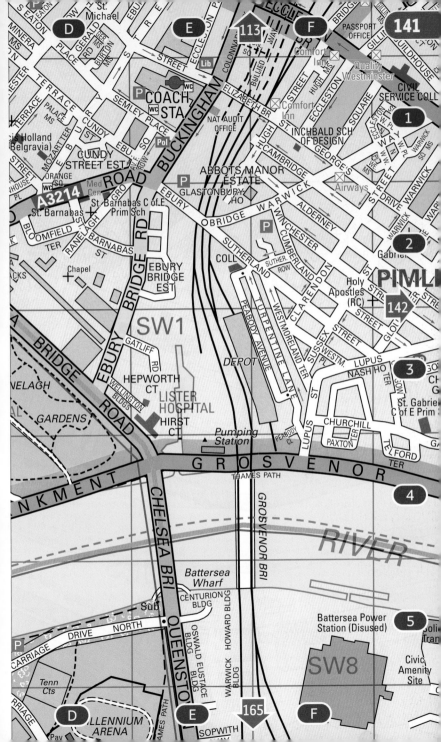

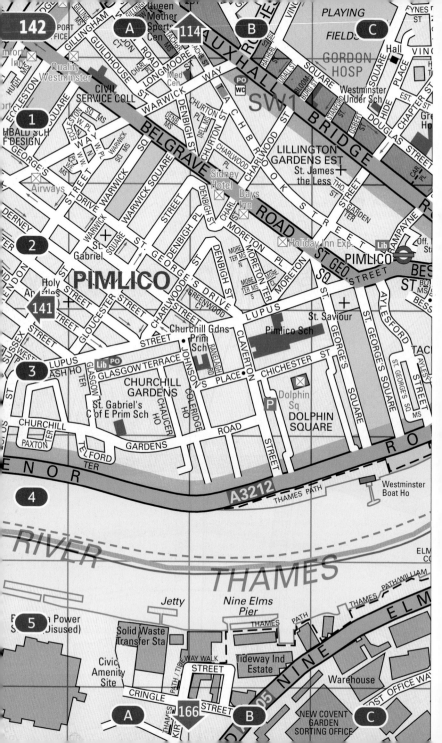

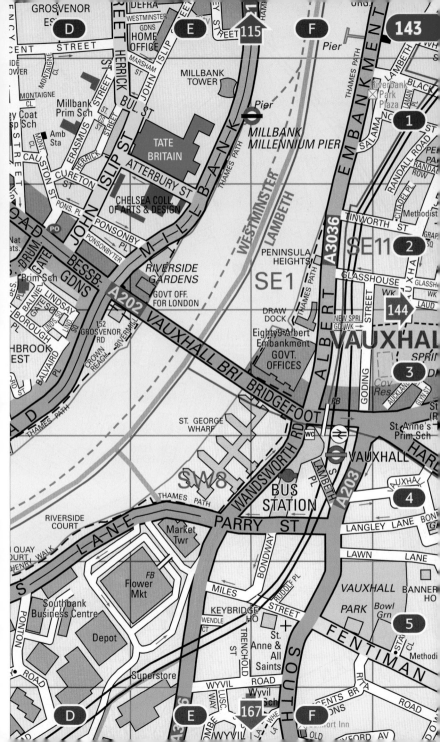

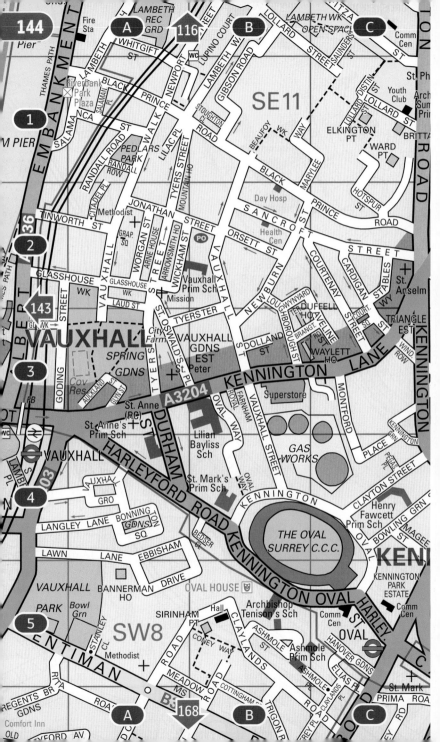

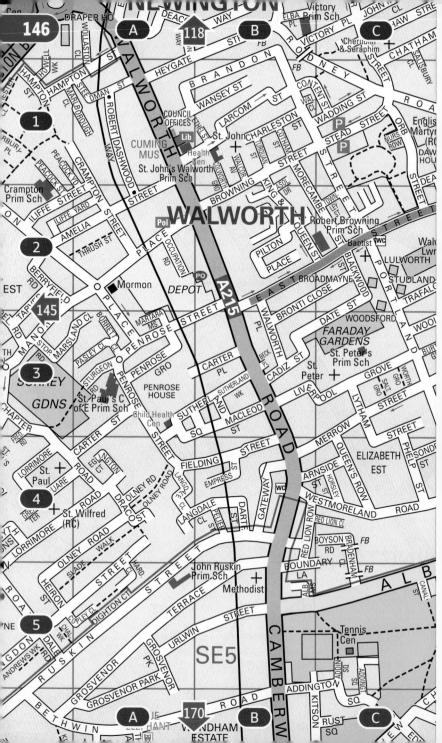

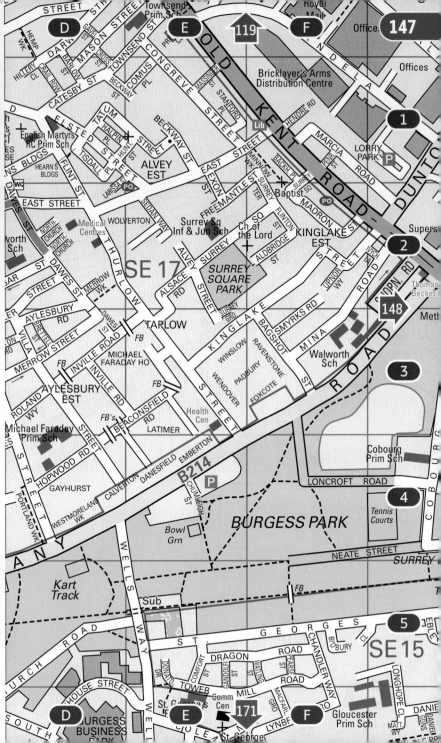

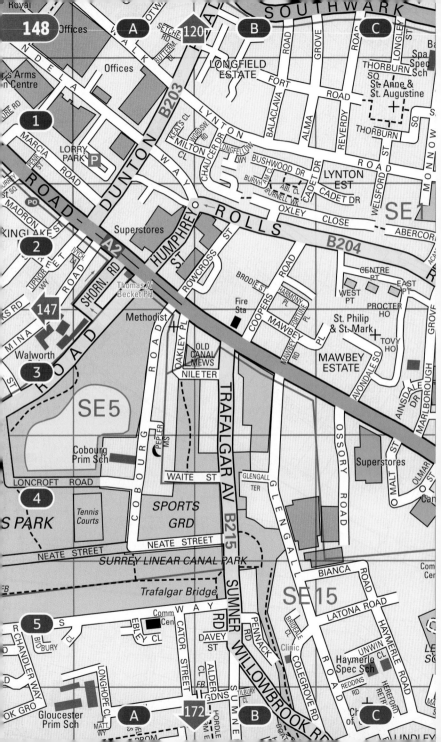

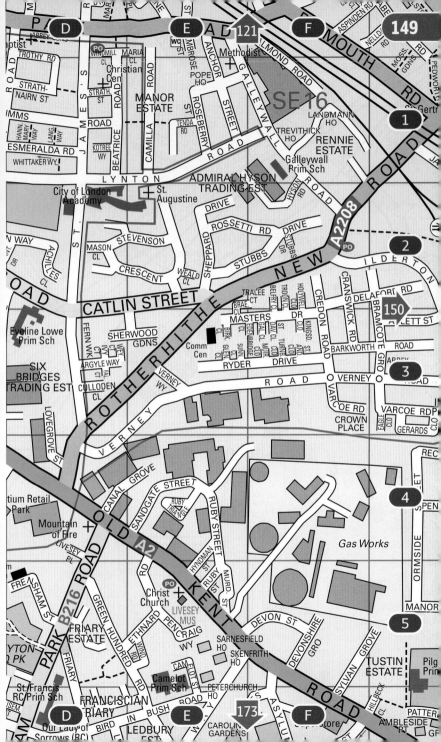

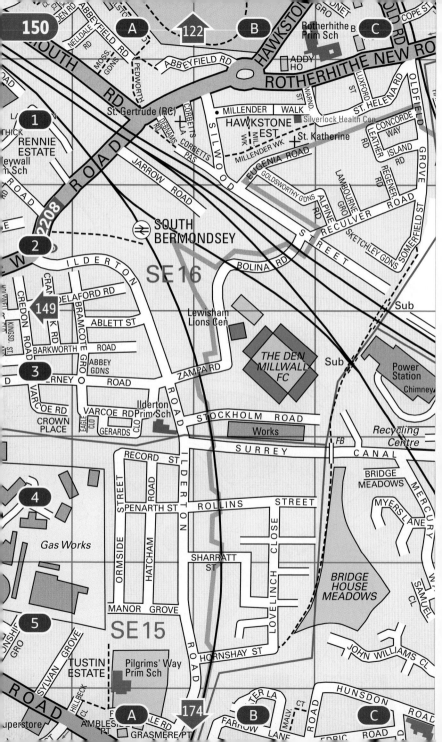

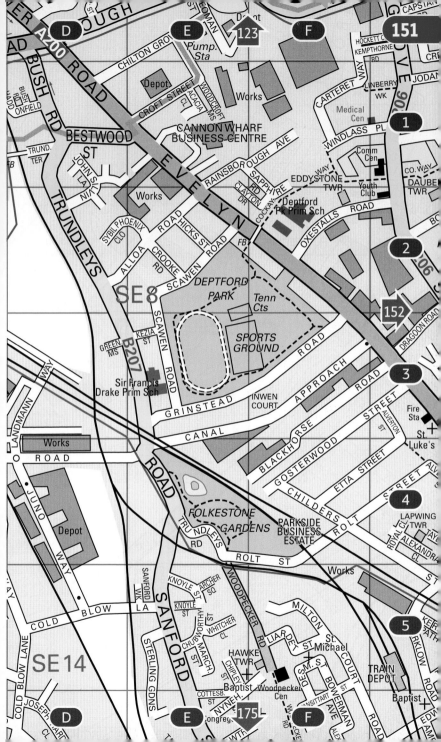

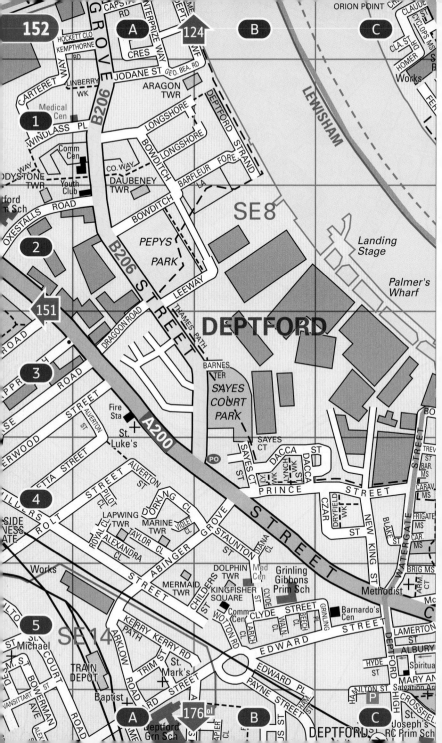

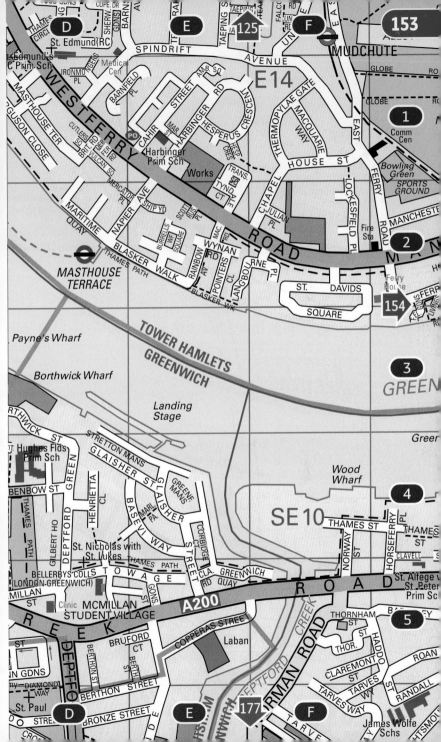

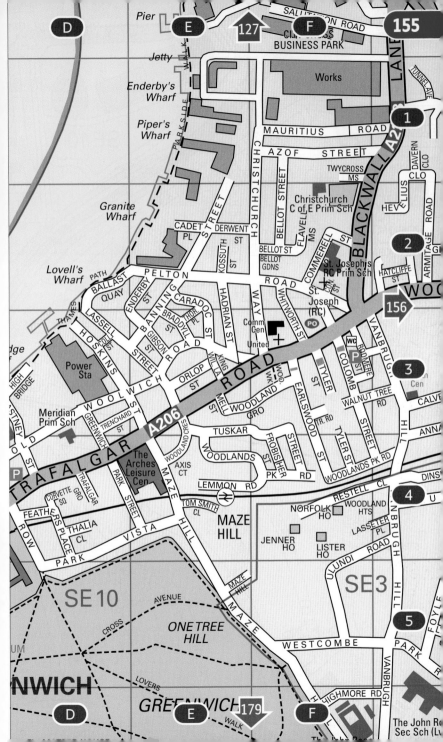

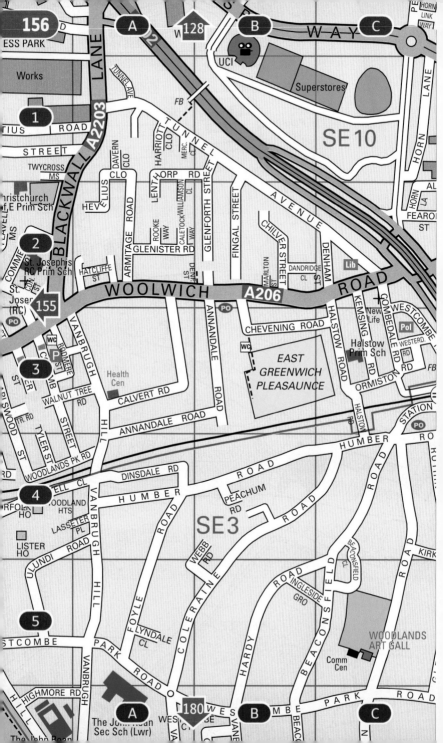

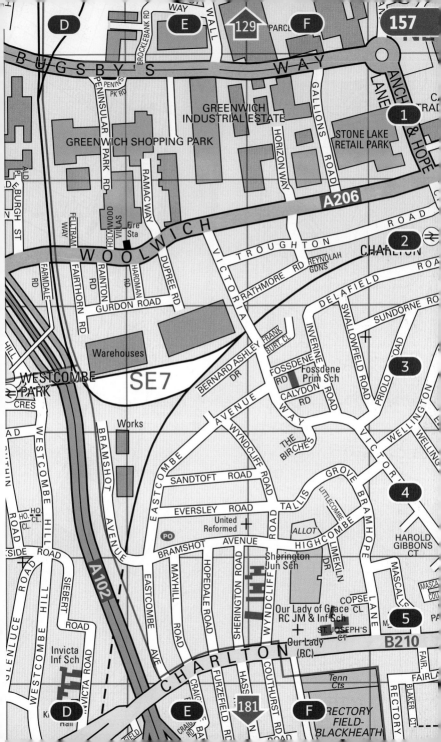

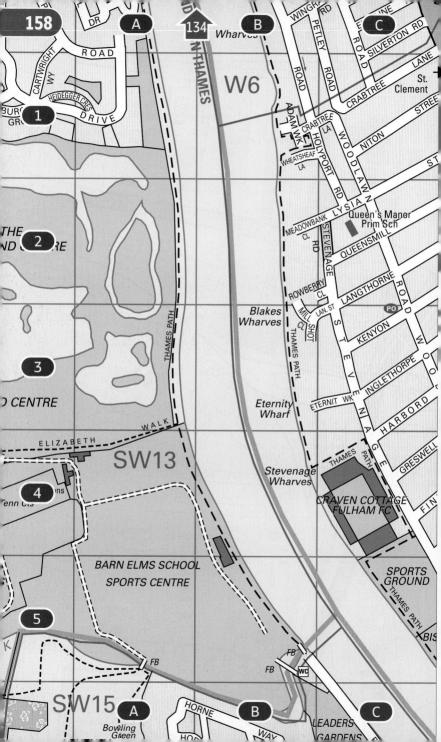

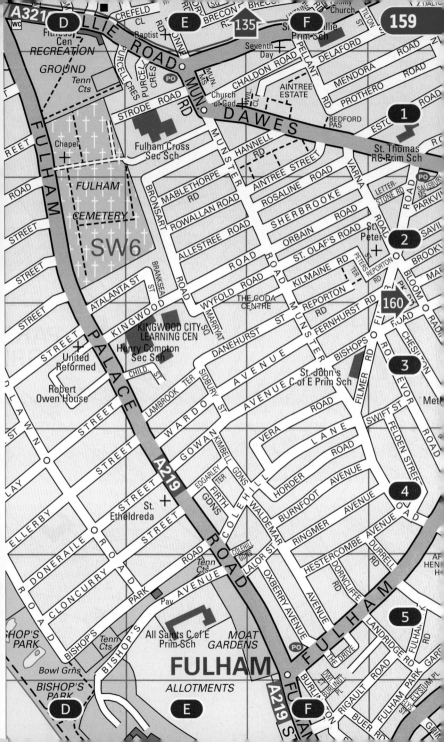

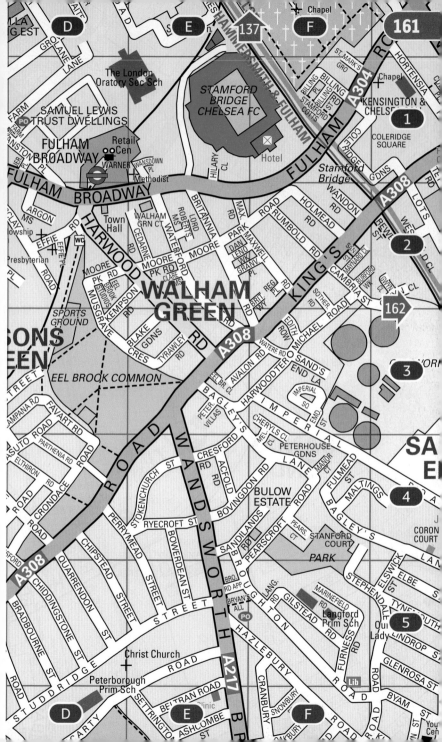

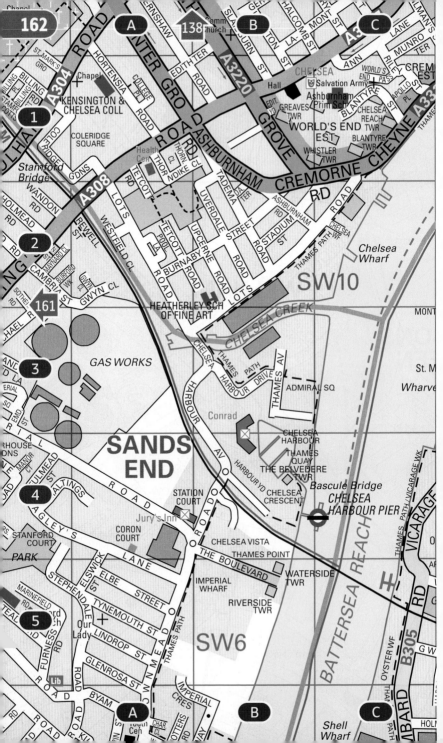

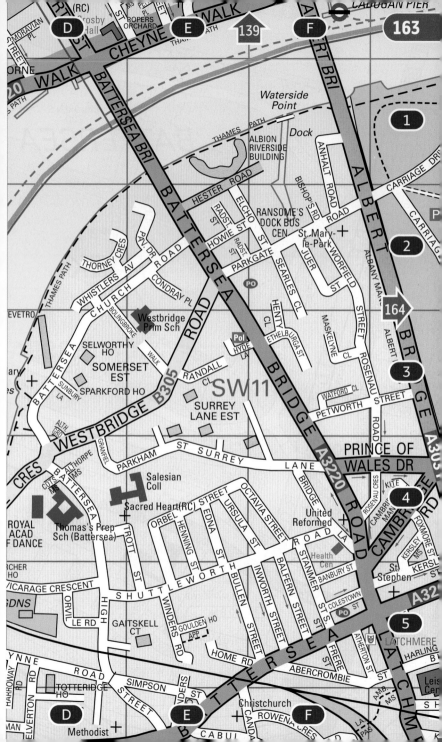

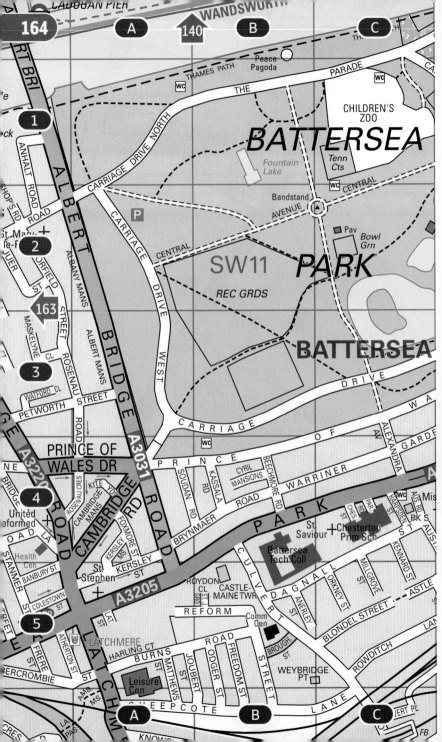

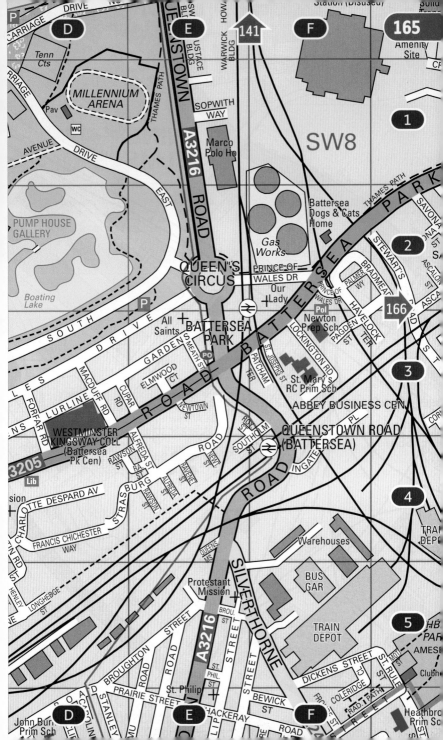

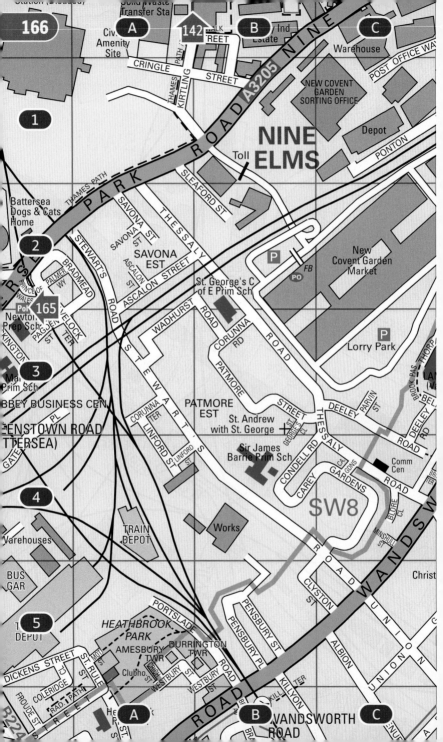

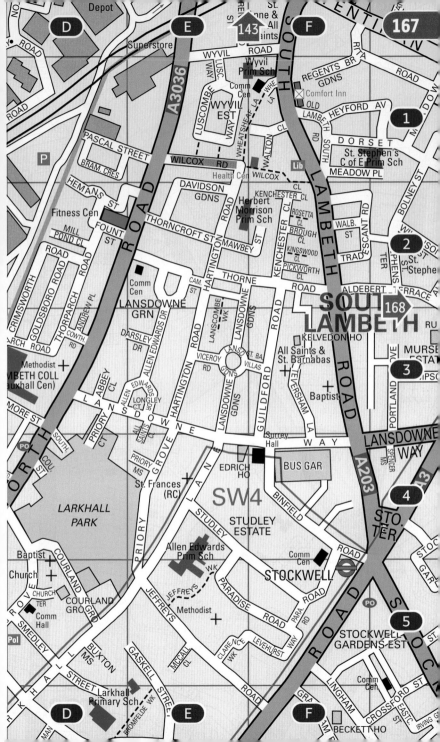

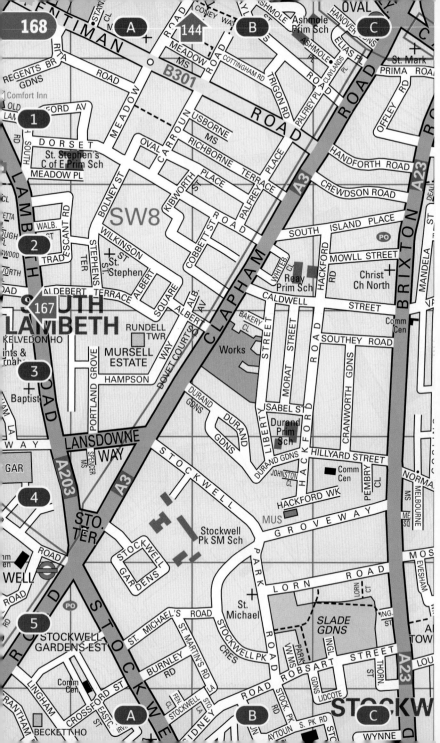

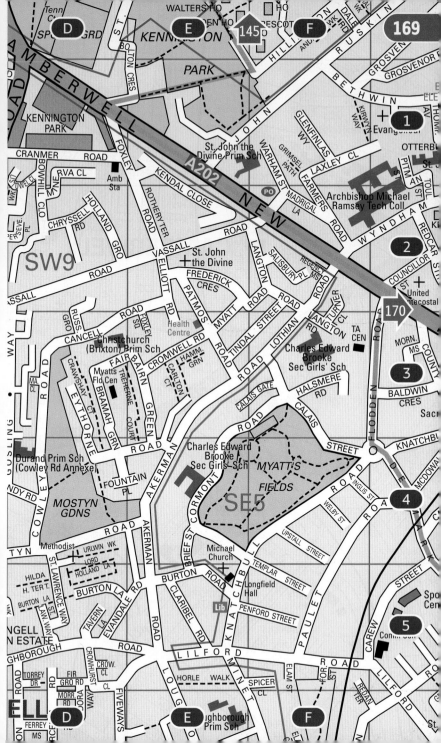

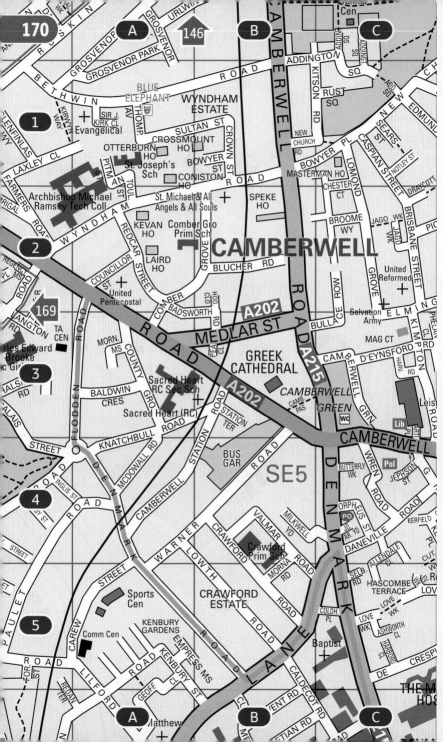

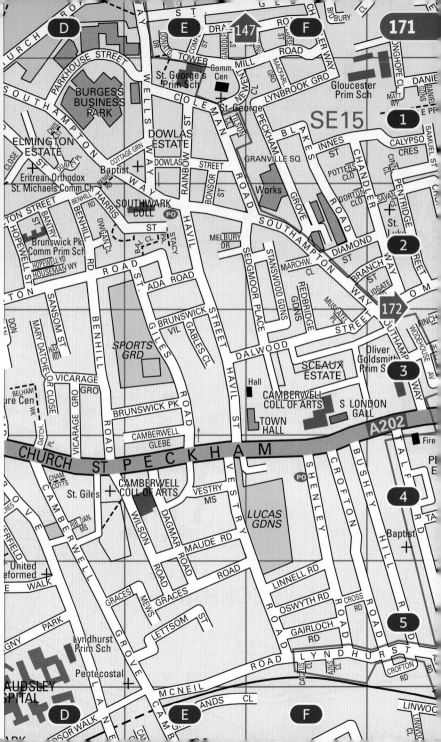

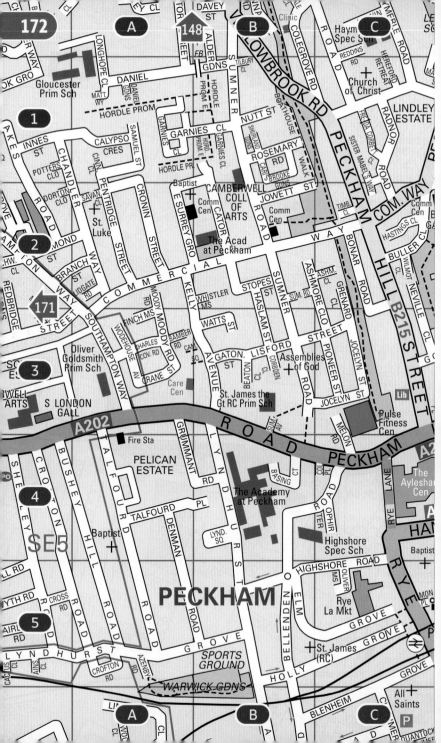

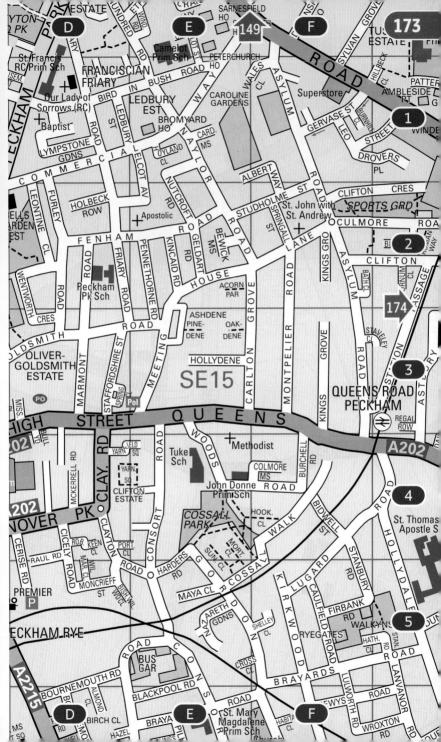

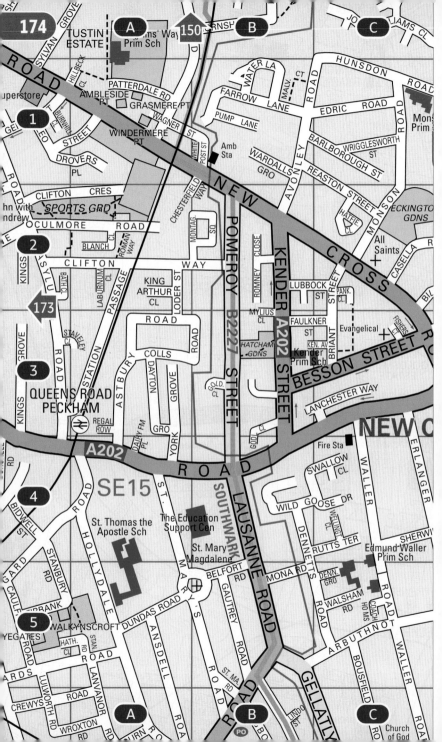

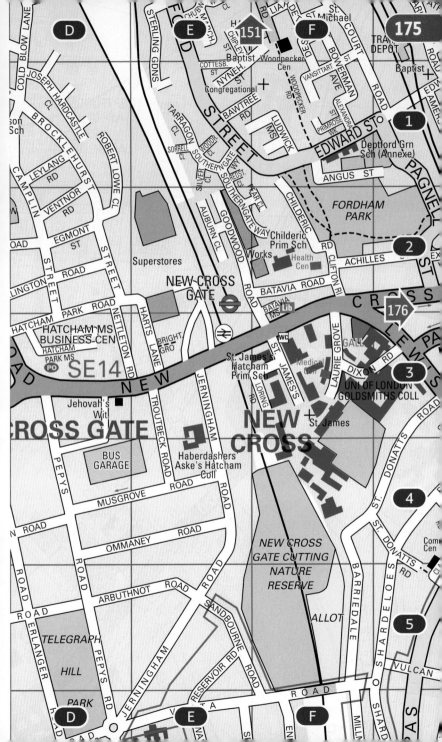

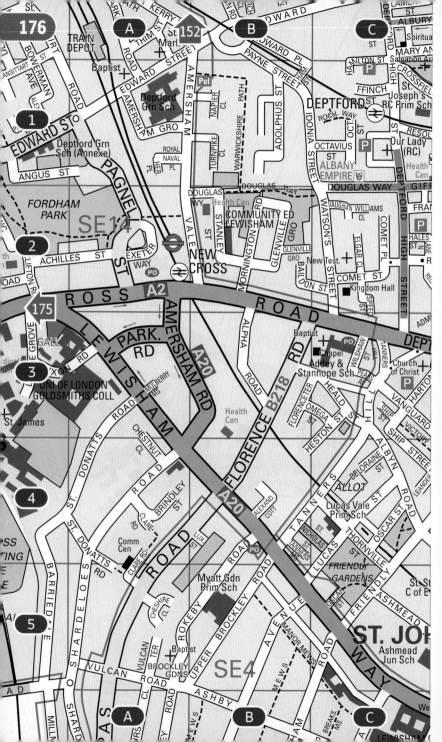

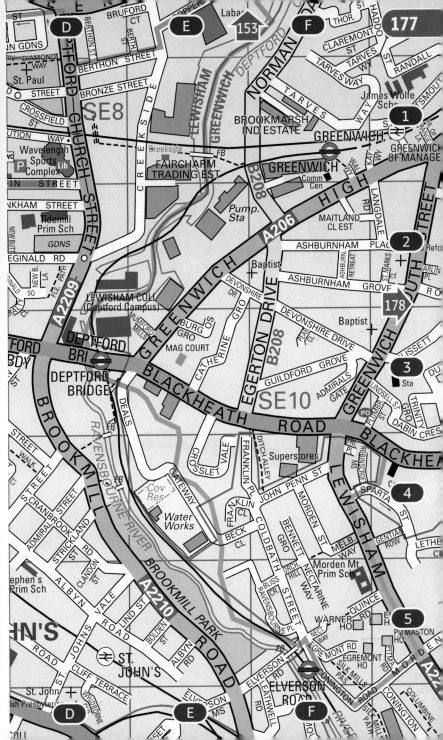

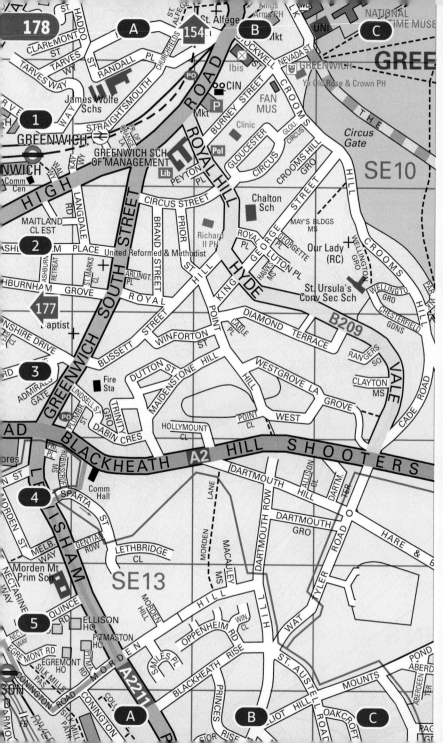

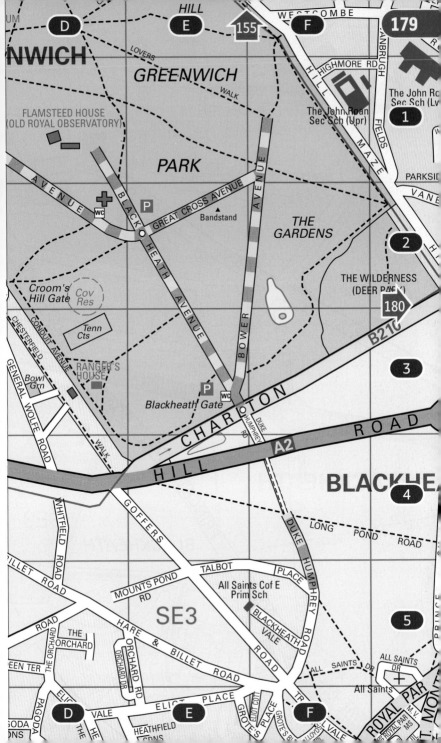

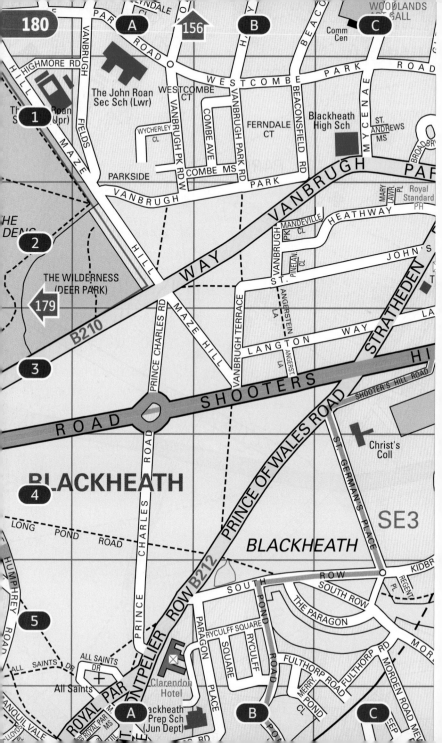

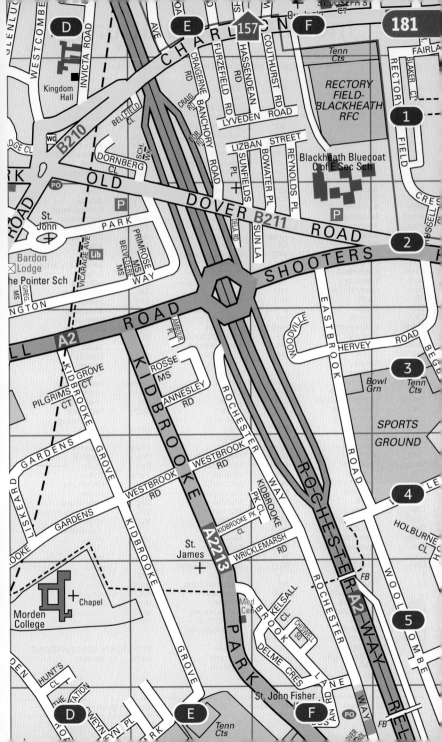

Index & abbreviations

The figures and letters following a name in the index indicate the Postal
District, page and map square where the name can be found.

Acad	Academy	Flds	Fields	Pk	Park
All	Alley	Fm	Farm	Pl	Place
Allot	Allotments	GM	Grant Maintained	Pol	Police
Amb	Ambulance	Gall	Gallery	Poly	Polytechnic
App	Approach	Gar	Garage	Prec	Precinct
Arc	Arcade	Gdn	Garden	Prep	Preparatory
Assoc	Association	Gdns	Gardens	Prim	Primary
Av	Avenue	Gen	General	Prom	Promenade
BUPA	British United	Govt	Government	Pt	Point
	Provident	Gra	Grange	Quad	Quadrant
	Association	Gram	Grammar	RC	Roman Catholic
Bdy	Broadway	Grd	Ground	Rd	Road
Bk	Bank	Grds	Grounds	Rds	Roads
Bldg	Building	Grn	Green	Rbt	Roundabout
Bldgs	Buildings	Grns	Greens	Rec	Recreation
Boul	Boulevard	Gro	Grove	Rehab	Rehabilitation
Bowl	Bowling	Gros	Groves	Res	Reservoir
Br	Bridge	Gt	Great	Ri	Rise
C of E	Church of	HQ	Headquarters	S	South
	England	Ho	House	SM	Secondary Mixed
Cath	Cathedral	Hos	Houses	Sch	School
Cem	Cemetery	Hosp	Hospital	Schs	Schools
Cen	Central, Centre	Hts	Heights	Sec	Secondary
Cft	Croft	Ind	Industrial	Sen	Senior
Cfts	Crofts	Indep	Independent	Shop	Shopping
Ch	Church	Inf	Infant(s)	Spec	Special
Chyd	Churchyard	Inst	Institute	Sq	Square
Cin	Cinema	Int	International	St	Street
Circ	Circus	JM	Junior Mixed	St.	Saint
Cl	Close	JMI	Junior Mixed &	Sta	Station
Co	County		Infant(s)	Sts	Streets
Coll	College	Jun	Junior	Sub	Subway
Comb	Combined	Junct	Junction	Swim	Swimming
Comm	Community	La	Lane	TA	Territorial Army
Comp	Comprehensive	Las	Lanes	TH	Town Hall
Conf	Conference	Lib	Library	Tech	Technical,
Cont	Continuing	Lit	Literary		Technology
Conv	Convent	Ln	Loan	Tenn	Tennis
Cor	Corner	Lo	Lodge	Ter	Terrace
Coron	Coroners	Lwr	Lower	Thea	Theatre
Cors	Corners	Mag	Magistrates	Trd	Trading
Cotts	Cottages	Mans	Mansions	Twr	Tower
Cov	Covered	Med	Medical	Twrs	Towers
Crem	Crematorium	Mem	Memorial	Uni	University
Cres	Crescent	Met	Metropolitan	Upr	Upper
Ct	Court	Mid	Middle	Vet	Veterinary
Cts	Courts	Mkt	Market	VA	Voluntary Aided
Ctyd	Courtyard	Mkts	Markets	VC	Voluntary
Dep	Depot	Ms	Mews		Controlled
Dept	Department	Mt	Mount	Vil	Villas
Dev	Development	Mus	Museum	Vil	Villa
Dr	Drive	N	North	Vw	View
Dws	Dwellings	NHS	National Health	W	West
E	East		Service	Wd	Wood
Ed	Education,	NT	National Trust	Wds	Woods
	Educational	Nat	National	Wf	Wharf
Elec	Electricity	Nurs	Nursery	Wk	Walk
Embk	Embankment	PH	Public House	Wks	Works
Est	Estate	PO	Post Office	Yd	Yard
Ex	Exchange	PRU	Pupil Referral		
Exhib	Exhibition		Unit		
FB	Footbridge	Par	Parade	POST TOWN ABBREVIATIONS	
FC	Football Club	Pas	Passage	Bark.	Barking
Fld	Field	Pav	Pavilion		

★ Place of interest   ⇌ Railway station   Ⓗ Hospital   ⊖ London Underground station

1 Canada Sq, E14.....97 E4

A

Aaron Hill Rd, E6 ......77 D3
Abbess Cl, E6 ....75 F4
Abbey Business Cen,
 SW8 ....165 F3
Abbey Cl, SW8 ......167 D3
Abbeyfield Rd,
 SE16..............122 A5
Abbey Gdns, NW8 ....32 A3
 SE16..............121 D5
 W6 ....135 E4
Abbey La, E15 ....48 B2
Abbey Orchard St,
 SW1..............115 D3
Abbey Rd, E15 ....49 D2
 NW6 ....9 E4
 NW8 ....32 A1
Abbey Rd Est, NW8...31 F1
Abbey St, E13........73 D1
 SE1 ....119 F3
Abbotsbury Cl, E15...48 B2
 W14 ....107 F2
Abbotsbury Rd,
 W14 ....107 F1
Abbots Cl, N1........18 A2
Abbots Gdns, W8....109 E4
Abbotshade Rd, SE16.95 D4
Abbots La, SE1.......91 F5
Abbots Manor Est,
 SW1 ....141 E1
Abbot's Pl, NW6 ......9 E5
Abbot St, E8 ....20 A1
Abbots Wk, W8 .....109 E4
Abbott Rd, E14 ......70 A4
Abchurch La, EC4 ....91 D2
Abchurch Yd, EC4 ....90 C2
Aberavon Rd, E3 .....45 F5
Abercorn Cl, NW8 ....32 A3
Abercorn Pl, NW8 ....32 A4
Sch Abercorn Pl Sch,
 NW8 ....32 B3
Abercorn Way, SE1 ..148 C2
Abercrombie St,
 SW11 ....163 F5
Aberdare Gdns, NW6...9 F4
Aberdeen Pl, NW8 ....54 C2
Aberdeen Sq, E14 ....96 B4
Aberdeen Ter, SE3 ..178 C5
Aberdour St, SE1 ....119 E5
Aberfeldy St, E14.....70 B5
Abingdon Cl, NW1 ....14 C2
 SE1 ....148 B2
Abingdon Rd, W8 ...108 C3
Abingdon St, SW1....115 E3
Abingdon Vil, W8 ...108 C4
Abinger Gro, SE8 ....152 A5
Abinger Ms, W9 .....52 C1
Ablett St, SE16 .....150 A3
Acacia Cl, SE8 .....151 E1

Acacia Gdns, NW8....33 D2
Acacia Pl, NW8 ......33 D2
Acacia Rd, NW8......33 D2
Sch Academy at Peckham,
 The, SE15 ....172 B4
 Annexe, SE15 .....172 B2
Academy Gdns, W8..108 C1
Acanthus Dr, SE1 ...148 C2
Acfold Rd, SW6 .....161 E4
Achilles Cl, SE1 .....149 D2
Achilles St, SE14 ....176 A2
Achilles Way, W1.....85 D5
Acklam Rd, W10 .....52 A4
Ackmar Rd, SW6 ....160 C4
Ackroyd Dr, E3.......68 B3
Acol Rd, NW6 ....9 D4
Acorn Par, SE15.....173 E2
Acorn Wk, SE16......95 F4
Acton Ms, E8 ....20 A5
Acton St, WC1 ....38 A5
Ada Ct, W9 ....32 B5
Ada Gdns, E14 ......70 C5
Adair Rd, W10 ......51 F2
Adair Twr, W10 ......51 F2
Adam & Eve Ct, W1 ...58 B5
Adam & Eve Ms, W8 .109 D3
Adam Ct, SW7 ......110 B5
Adams Ct, EC2 ....63 D5
Adams Gdns Est,
 SE16..............122 A1
Adamson Rd, E16 ...101 D1
 NW3 ....11 D3
Adams Row, W1 .....85 D3
Adam St, WC2 ....87 F3
Adam Wk, SW6 .....158 B1
Ada Pl, E2 ....43 D1
Ada Rd, SE5 ....171 E2
Ada St, E8...........43 E1
Adderley St, E14 .....98 A1
Sch Addey & Stanhope Sch,
 SE14..............176 C3
Addington Rd, E3 ....46 C4
 E16 ....71 F2
Addington Sq, SE5 ..170 B1
Addington St, SE1....116 B2
Addison Av, W11.....79 E4
Addison Br Pl, W14...108 A5
Addison Cres, W14 ..107 F3
Addison Gdns, W14 .106 C3
Addison Pl, W11 .....79 E5
Sch Addison Prim Sch,
 W14..............106 C3
Addison Rd, W14 ...108 A3
Addle Hill, EC4 ....89 F2
Addle St, EC2 ....62 B4
Addy Ho, SE16......150 B1
Adelaide Rd, NW3 ....11 D4
Adelaide St, WC2.....87 E3
Adela St, W10 ......51 E1
Adelina Gro, E1 .....66 A3
Adeline Pl, WC1 ......59 D4
Adelphi Ter, WC2.....87 F3
Adeney Cl, W6 .....135 D5
Adie Rd, W6 ....106 A4

Adine Rd, E13 ....73 E1
Adler St, E1..........64 C5
Admiral Hyson Trd Est,
 SE16..............149 E1
Admiral Pl, SE16 .....95 F4
Admirals Gate,
 SE10..............177 F3
Admiral Sq, SW10...162 B3
Admiral St, SE8 .....177 D4
Admirals Way, E14 ..125 D1
★ Admiralty Arch,
 SW1 ....87 D4
Admiralty Cl, SE8 ...176 C3
Admiral Wk, W9 .....53 D3
Adolphus St, SE8....176 B1
Adpar St, W2 ....54 C2
Adrian Ms, SW10 ...137 F4
Adriatic Bldg, E14 ...95 D1
Affleck St, N1 ....38 B3
★ Africa Cen, WC2 ...87 E2
Agar Gro, NW1.......14 B4
Agar Gro Est, NW1 ...14 C4
Agar Pl, NW1 ....14 B4
Agar St, WC2 ....87 E3
Agate Cl, E16 ......103 D1
Agate Rd, W6 ......106 A3
Agatha Cl, E1 ....93 F4
Agdon St, EC1 ......61 E1
Agnes Cl, E6 ....105 D1
Agnes St, E14 ....68 B5
Agricola Ct, E3 ......46 B1
Ailsa St, E14 ....70 B3
Ainger Ms, NW3 .....12 B4
Ainger Rd, NW3......12 A4
Ainsdale Dr, SE1 ....148 C3
Ainsley St, E2 ....43 F5
Ainsty Est, SE16 ....122 C2
Ainsworth Cl, SE15...171 F5
Ainsworth Rd, E9 ....22 A4
Ainsworth Way,
 NW8 ....10 A5
Aintree Est, SW6 ....159 F1
Aintree St, SW6 .....159 F2
Airdrie Cl, N1 ....16 A4
Airlie Gdns, W8 ......80 C5
Airport Rbt, E16 ....102 C4
Air St, W1 ....86 B3
Aisgill Av, W14 .....136 B3
Aitken Cl, E8.........20 C5
Akerman Rd, SW9...169 E4
Aland Ct, SE16......123 F3
Alan Hocken Way,
 E15 ....49 E3
Alaska St, SE1 ....88 C3
Albany, W1 ....86 A3
Albany Ctyd, W1 .....86 B3
Albany Mans, SW11.163 F2
Albany Ms, N1 ......17 D3
 SE5 ....146 B5
Albany Rd, SE5 ....146 C5

Albany St, NW1 ......35 E2
Alba Pl, W11........52 A5
Albatross Cl, E6 ......76 B2
Albatross Way,
  SE16.............122 C2
Albemarle St, W1 ....85 F3
Albemarle Way, EC1 ..61 D2
Alberta Est, SE17 ...145 F2
Alberta St, SE17 ....145 E2
Albert Av, SW8 ......168 A2
Albert Barnes Ho,
  SE1..............118 A4
Albert Br, SW3......139 F5
  SW11.............139 F5
Albert Br Rd, SW11..163 F5
Albert Cl, E9.........43 F1
Albert Ct, SW7......110 C2
Albert Embk, SE1 ...143 F3
Albert Gdns, E1 ......94 C1
Albert Gate, SW1 ...112 B1
Albert Hall Mans,
  SW7.............110 C2
Albert Mans, SW11..164 A3
★ Albert Mem,
  SW7.............110 C1
Albert Ms, W8 ......110 A3
Albert Pl, W8 ....109 F2
Albert Rd, E16 ......103 F5
  NW6..............30 B3
Albert Sq, SW8 .....168 A2
Albert St, NW1.......35 F1
Albert Ter, NW1......12 C5
Albert Ter Ms, NW1...34 C1
Albert Way, SE15 ...173 E1
Albion Av, SW8 .....166 C5
Albion Cl, W2........83 F2
Albion Dr, E8 ....20 A4
Albion Est, SE16 ....122 C2
Albion Ms, N1 ....16 C5
  NW6...............8 A3
  W2 ....83 F1
Albion Pl, EC1........61 E3
🅂 Albion Prim Sch,
  SE16.............122 B2
Albion Riverside Bldg,
  SW11.............163 F1
Albion Sq, E8 ....20 A4
Albion St, SE16 .....122 B2
  W2 ....83 F1
Albion Ter, E8........20 A4
Albion Way, EC1 .....62 A4
Albury St, SE8 ......152 C5
Albyn Rd, SE8 ......176 C4
Aldbridge St, SE17 ..147 F2
Aldburgh Ms, W1.....57 D5
Aldeburgh Pl, SE10 ..157 D1
Aldeburgh St, SE10..156 C2
Aldenham St, NW1 ...36 B3
Alder Cl, SE15 ......148 B5

Aldermanbury, EC2...62 B5
Aldermanbury Sq,
  EC2..............62 B4
Alderman's Wk, EC2 ..63 E4
Alderney Ms, SE1 ...118 C3
Alderney Rd, E1......66 C1
Alderney St, SW1 ...141 E2
Aldersgate St, EC1....62 A5
Aldershot Rd, NW6 ....8 B5
Alderson St, W10.....51 F1
Alderville Rd, SW6 ..160 B5
Aldford St, W1 ....84 C4
⊖ Aldgate 64 A5
Aldgate, EC3........92 A1
Aldgate Av, E1.......64 A5
Aldgate Barrs Shop Cen,
  E1 ....64 B5
⊖ Aldgate East 64 B5
Aldgate High St, EC3..92 A1
Aldine Ct, W12 .....106 B1
Aldine Pl, W12 ......78 B5
Aldine St, W12......106 B1
Aldington Rd, SE18..131 D4
Aldridge Rd Vil, W11..52 B4
Aldsworth Cl, W9 ....53 E2
Aldworth Rd, E15 ....27 E4
Aldwych, WC2 ....88 A2
Alestan Beck Rd, E16 .75 D5
Alexa Ct, W8 ....109 E5
★ Alexander Fleming ...
  Laboratory Mus,
  W2 ....55 D5
Alexander Ms, W2....53 E5
Alexander Pl, SW7...111 E5
Alexander Sq, SW3 ..111 E5
Alexander St, W2.....53 D5
Alexandra Av, SW11.164 C3
Alexandra Cl, SE8 ...152 A4
Alexandra Cotts,
  SE14.............176 B4
Alexandra Ct, W9 ....54 B1
Alexandra Pl, NW8 ...10 B5
Alexandra Rd, NW8..10 B5
Alexandra St, E16 ....72 C3
  SE14.............175 F1
Alexis St, SE16......120 C5
Alford Pl, N1.........40 B3
Alfreda St, SW11....165 E3
Alfred Ms, W1 ....58 C3
Alfred Pl, WC1 ......58 C3
Alfred Rd, W2........53 D3
🅂 Alfred Salter Prim Sch,
  SE16.............123 D2
Alfred St, E3 ....46 B3
Algernon Rd, NW6 ...30 C1
Alice Gilliatt Ct,
  W14.............136 A4
Alice La, E3..........46 A1
Alice St, SE1........119 E4
Alie St, E1 ....92 B1
Alison Cl, E6........105 D1
Allendale Cl, SE5 ...170 C5
🅂 Allendale Sch,
  W8 ....109 D3

Allen Edwards Dr,
  SW8 ....167 E3
🅂 Allen Edwards Prim Sch,
  SW4 ....167 E4
Allen Rd, E3 ....46 A2
Allensbury Pl, NW1 ...15 D4
Allen St, W8 ....109 D3
Allestree Rd, SW6 ..159 E2
Allgood St, E2........42 B3
Allhallows La, EC4 ....90 C3
★ All Hallows-on-the-Wall
  C of E Ch, EC2 .....63 D4
Allhallows Rd, E6 ....75 E4
Alliance Rd, E13 .....74 A2
Allingham Ms, N1 ....40 A2
Allingham St, N1.....40 A2
Allington Rd, W10....29 E4
Allington St, SW1 ...114 A4
Allison Cl, SE10 .....178 B4
Allitsen Rd, NW8.....33 E3
Alloa Rd, SE8 ....151 D2
Alloway Rd, E3.......45 F4
Allports Ms, E1 ......66 B2
🅃🅛🅡 All Saints 98 A2
All Saints Cl, SW8 ...167 E3
🅂 All Saints C of E Prim Sch,
  SE3 ....179 E5
  SW6 ....159 E5
All Saints Dr, SE3...179 F5
All Saints Rd, W11 ...52 A4
All Saints St, N1......38 A2
Allsop Pl, NW1 ......56 B2
🅂 All Souls C of E Prim Sch,
  W1 ....58 A4
All Souls Pl, W1 .....57 F4
Alma Gro, SE1 ......148 B1
🅂 Alma Prim Sch,
  SE16.............121 D5
Alma Sq, NW8 ....32 B4
Alma St, E15.........26 C1
  NW5..............13 F1
Almeida St, N1.......17 E4
Almond Rd, SE16 ...121 F5
Almorah Rd, N1......18 C4
Alnwick Rd, E16 ....102 A1
Alperton St, W10.....51 F1
Alphabet Sq, E3......69 D2
Alpha Cl, NW1 ....33 F5
Alpha Gro, E14......125 D2
Alpha Pl, NW6 ....31 D2
  SW3 ....139 F4
Alpha Rd, SE14 .....176 B3
Alpine Business Cen,
  E6 ....77 D3
Alpine Gro, E9 ....22 B4
Alpine Rd, SE16.....150 C2
Alpine Way, E6.......76 C3
Alsace Rd, SE17.....147 E2
Alscot Rd, SE1 ......120 B5
Alscot Way, SE1.....120 A5
Althorpe Gro, SW11 .163 D3
Althorpe Ms, SW11..163 D4
Alton St, E14 ....69 E4
Alverstone Rd, NW2 ...6 A3

★ Place of interest   ≷ Railway station   🄷 Hospital   ⊖ London Underground station

Alverton St, SE8 ....152 A3
Alvey Est, SE17 .....147 E1
Alvey St, SE17 ......147 E2
Alwyne La, N1 ....17 F3
Alwyne Pl, N1........18 A2
Alwyne Rd, N1 ....17 F3
Alwyne Sq, N1 ....18 A1
Alwyne Vil, N1 ....17 F3
Alzette Ho, E2 ....44 C4
Amazon St, E1 ....93 E1
Ambassador Gdns,
 E6 ....76 A4
Ambassador's Ct,
 SW1 ....86 B5
Ambassador Sq,
 E14...............153 E1
Ambergate St, SE17 .145 F2
Amberley Rd, W9 ....53 D3
Amber St, E15 ....27 D2
Amber Wf, E2........42 A1
Ambleside Pt, SE15..174 A1
Ambrosden Av, SW1..114 B4
Ambrose Cl, E6.......76 A4
Ambrose St, SE16 ...121 E5
Ambrose Wk, E3 .....46 C3
Amelia St, SE17 .....145 F2
Amen Cor, EC4.......89 F1
Amen Ct, EC4........61 F5
Sch American Sch in London,
 The, NW8.........32 C2
America Sq, EC3 .....92 A2
America St, SE1 ......90 A5
Amersham Gro,
 SE14..............176 A1
Amersham Rd, SE14..176 A2
Amersham Vale,
 SE14..............176 B1
Amesbury Twr, SW8..166 A5
Amiel St, E1 ....66 B1
Amina Way, SE16 ...120 C4
Amor Rd, W6 ....106 A4
Amoy Pl, E14 ....96 C1
Ampthill Sq Est, NW1..36 B3
Ampton Pl, WC1 .....38 A5
Ampton Yd, WC1 .....38 A5
Amsterdam Rd, E14..126 B4
Amwell St, EC1 ......38 C4
Amy Warne Cl, E6 ...75 F3
Anchorage Pt, E14 ..124 C1
Anchorage Pt Ind Est,
 SE7 ....130 A4
Anchor & Hope La,
 SE7 ....129 F4
Anchor Ms, N1 ......19 F2
Anchor Retail Pk, E1..66 B2
Anchor St, SE16.....121 E5
Anchor Ter, E1 ......66 B2
Anchor Yd, EC1 .....62 B1
Ancill Cl, W6 ....135 D5
Anderson Rd, E9 ....22 C1
Andersons Sq, N1 ...39 E1
Anderson St, SW3...140 A2
Andover Av, E16 ....102 C1
Andover Pl, NW6 ....31 E2

Andrew Borde St,
 WC2 ....59 D5
Andrewes Gdns, E6 ..75 E5
Andrewes Ho, EC2...62 B4
Andrew Pl, SW8.....167 D3
Andrews Cl, E6.......75 E5
Andrews Crosse,
 WC2 ....88 C1
Andrew's Rd, E8......43 E1
Andrew St, E14 ......70 A5
Andrews Wk, SE17 ..145 F5
Anerley St, SW11 ...164 B5
⊖ Angel 39 D2
Angel All, E1........64 B5
Angel Ct, EC2 ....63 D5
 SW1 ....86 B5
Angel Gate, EC1.....39 F4
Angelica Dr, E6 .....77 D4
Angel La, E15 ....27 D1
Angell Town Est,
 SW9 ....169 D5
Angel Ms, E1 ....93 F2
 N1................39 D3
Angel Pas, EC4......90 C3
Angel Pl, SE1 ....118 C1
Angel Sq, EC1 ....39 D3
Angel St, EC1 ....62 A5
Angel Wk, W6 ....134 A1
Angerstein La, SE3 ..180 B3
Angler's La, NW5 ....13 F2
Anglia Ho, E14.......95 F1
Anglo Rd, E3.........46 B2
Angrave Ct, E8 ......20 B5
Angrave Pas, E8......20 B5
Angus St, SE14 .....175 F1
Anhalt Rd, SW11....163 F1
Anley Rd, W14......106 C2
Annabel Cl, E14......97 E2
Anna Cl, E8..........20 B5
Annandale Rd, SE10..156 A3
Annesley Rd, SE3 ...181 E3
Anne St, E13.........72 C1
Annette Cres, E1.....18 B4
Annie Besant Cl, E3...46 B1
Anning St, EC2......63 F1
Annis Rd, E9.........23 E2
Ann La, SW10 ......162 C1
Ann Moss Way,
 SE16..............122 A3
Ann's Cl, SW1......112 B2
Ann's Pl, E1.........64 A4
Ansdell Rd, SE15...174 A5
Ansdell St, W8 ......109 F3
Ansdell Ter, W8 .....109 F3
Anselm Rd, SW6 ....136 C5
Ansleigh Pl, W11....79 D3
Anson Ho, E1 ....67 E2
Antelope Rd, SE18 ..132 A3
Anthony St, E1.......65 F5
Antill Rd, E3.........45 E4
Antill Ter, E1.........66 C5
Antrim Gro, NW3....12 A1
Antrim Mans, NW3...11 F1
Antrim Rd, NW3 .....12 A1

Apollo, E14.........124 C5
★ Apollo Hammersmith,
 W6 ....134 B2
Apollo Pl, SW10.....162 C1
★ Apollo Thea, W1 ...86 C2
★ Apollo Victoria Thea,
 SW1 ....114 A4
Apothecary St, EC4...89 E1
Appleby Rd, E8......21 D3
 E16...............100 B1
Appleby St, E2 ......42 A2
Appleford Rd, W10 ...51 F2
Applegarth Rd, W14..106 C4
Apple Tree Yd, SW1...86 B4
Applewood Dr, E13...73 E1
Appold St, EC2......63 E3
Approach Rd, E2 ....44 A3
★ Apsley Ho, Wellington
 Mus, W1 ....112 C1
Apsley Way, W1.....113 D1
Aquila St, NW8 .....33 D2
Aquinas St, SE1 .....89 D5
Aragon Twr, SE8 ....152 A1
Arbery Rd, E3........45 E4
Arbour Sq, E1 ....94 C1
Arbuthnot Rd,
 SE14..............174 C5
Arbutus St, E8 ......20 A5
Arcade, The, EC2 ....63 E4
Arcadia St, E14 .....69 D5
Archangel St, SE16 ...123 D2
Sch Archbishop Michael
 Ramsey Tech Coll,
 SE5 ....170 A2
Sch Archbishop Summers'
 C of E Prim Sch,
 SE11..............145 D1
Sch Archbishop Tenison's
 Sch, SE11 ....144 B5
Archel Rd, W14.....136 A4
Archer Ho, SW11....162 C5
Archer Sq, SE14.....151 E5
Archer St, W1........86 C2
Archery Cl, W2......83 F1
Arches, The, SW6 ...160 A5
 WC2 ....87 F4
Archibald Ms, W1 ...85 D3
Archibald St, E3.....46 C5
Archie St, SE1 ......119 F2
Coll Architectural Assoc
 Sch of Architecture,
 WC1 ....59 D4
Arch St, SE1 ....118 A4
Archway Cl, W10.....50 C4
Arden Cres, E14.....125 D5
Arden Est, N1........41 E3
Argon Ms, SW6 .....161 D2
Sch Argyle Prim Sch,
 WC1 ....37 E4

Argyle Rd, E1 ....66 C1
E16..............102 A1
Argyle Sq, WC1 ......37 F4
Argyle St, WC1 ......37 E4
Argyle Wk, WC1 .....37 F5
Argyle Way, SE16 ...149 D3
Argyll Rd, W8.......108 C2
Argyll St, W1 ....86 A1
Arica Ho, SE16......121 F3
Ariel Rd, NW6 ....8 C2
Ariel Way, W12 ......78 B4
Arklow Rd, SE14 ....152 A5
Arlington Av, N1 ....40 B1
Arlington Pl, SE10 ..178 A2
Arlington Rd, NW1 ...35 F1
Arlington Sq, N1 ....40 B1
Arlington St, SW1 ...86 A4
Arlington Way, EC1...39 D4
Armada Ct, SE8 .....152 C5
Armadale Rd, SW6 ..136 C5
Armada Way, E6 ....105 F2
Armagh Rd, E3.......46 B1
Armitage Rd, SE10 ..156 A2
Armour Cl, N7 ....16 A2
Armstrong Cl, E6 ....76 B5
Armstrong Rd, SW7 .110 C4
Arne Ho, SE11 ......144 A2
Arne St, WC2 ....87 F1
Arneway St, SW1 ...115 D4
Arnhem Pl, E14 .....124 C4
Sch Arnhem Wf Prim Sch,
E14..............124 C4
Arnold Circ, E2......42 A5
Arnold Est, SE1 .....120 B2
Sch Arnold Ho Sch,
NW8..............32 C3
Arnold Rd, E3........46 C4
Arnside St, SE17 ....146 B4
Arran Wk, N1 ....18 A3
Arrol Ho, SE1 ......118 A4
Arrow Rd, E3 ....47 E4
Arrowsmith Ho,
SE11..............144 A2
Artesian Rd, W2 .....80 C1
Arthingworth St, E15. 27 E5
Arthur Ct, W2 ....53 E5
Arthur Henderson Ho,
SW6..............160 A5
Arthur St, EC4 ....91 D3
Artichoke Hill, E1 ...93 E3
Artichoke Pl, SE5....170 C3
Artillery La, E1......63 F4
Artillery Pas, E1.....63 F4
Artillery Pl, SW1 ...114 C4
Artillery Row, SW1 ..114 C4
Artisan Cl, E6.......105 E2
Artizan St, E1.......63 F5
Arundel Gdns, W11...80 A2
Arundel Gt Ct, WC2...88 B2
Arundel Pl, N1 ......16 C2

Arundel Sq, N7.......16 C2
Arundel St, WC2 .....88 B2
Ascalon St, SW8 ....166 A2
Coll Ashbourne Indep 6th
Form Coll, W8.....109 E1
Ashbridge St, NW8 ...55 E2
Ashburn Gdns, SW7 .110 A5
Ashburnham Gro,
SE10..............177 F2
Ashburnham Pl,
SE10..............177 F2
Sch Ashburnham Prim Sch,
SW10............162 C1
Ashburnham Retreat,
SE10..............177 F2
Ashburnham Rd,
NW10..............28 A4
SW10............162 B2
Ashburn Pl, SW7 ....110 A5
Ashburton Rd, E16 ...73 D5
Ashby Gro, N1 ....18 B3
Ashby St, EC1........39 F5
Ashcroft Rd, E3 .....45 F4
Ashcroft Sq, W6......134 A1
Ashdene, SE15......173 E3
Ashdown Wk, E14...125 D5
Ashen, E6 ....76 C5
Ashentree Ct, EC4 ...89 D1
Asher Way, E1 ......93 D4
Ashfield St, E1 ......65 E4
Ashfield Yd, E1......66 A4
Ashford St, N1 ......41 E4
Ash Gro, E8.........43 E1
Ashington Rd, SW6..160 B5
Ashland Pl, W1......56 C3
Ashley Gdns, SW1 ..114 B4
Ashley Pl, SW1......114 A4
Sch Ashmead Jun Sch,
SE8..............176 C5
Ashmead Rd, SE8 ...176 C5
Ashmill St, NW1 .....55 E3
Ashmole Pl, SW8 ...144 C5
Sch Ashmole Prim Sch,
SW8..............144 B5
Ashmole St, SW8....144 B5
Ashmore Cl, SE15 ..172 B2
Ashmore Rd, W9 .....52 B1
Ashton St, E14......98 B2
Ashwell Cl, E6 ......75 F5
Ashwin St, E8........20 A1
Ashworth Cl, SE5 ...170 C5
Ashworth Rd, W9 ....31 F4
Aske St, N1..........41 E4
Asland Rd, E15......49 E1
Asolando Dr, SE17 ..146 B1
Aspenlea Rd, W6....134 C4
Aspen Way, E14......97 D3
Aspinden Rd, SE16 ..121 F5
Assam St, E1 ....64 C5
Assata Ms, N1 ....17 F1
Assembly Pas, E1....66 B3
Astbury Rd, SE15 ...174 A3
Astell St, SW3 ......139 F2
Aste St, E14 ....126 A2

Asteys Row, N1 ......17 F4
Astle St, SW11......164 C5
Aston St, E14........67 E5
Astrop Ms, W6......106 A3
Astrop Ter, W6......106 A3
Astwood Ms, SW7...110 A5
Asylum Rd, SE15 ...173 F1
Atalanta St, SW6....159 D3
Athelstane Gro, E3 ...46 A3
Athens Gdns, W9....52 C2
Atherstone Ct, W2 ...53 F3
Atherstone Ms,
SW7 ....110 B5
Atherton St, SW11 ..163 F5
Athlone St, NW5 .....13 D1
Atholl Ho, W9 ....32 A5
Athol Sq, E14........98 B1
Atkinson Rd, E16....74 B4
Atlas Gdns, SE7 .....130 A5
Atlas Ms, E8 ....20 B1
N7................16 B2
Atley Rd, E3 ....46 C1
Atterbury St, SW1...143 D1
Attneave St, WC1 ...38 C5
Aubrey Pl, NW8 .....32 A3
Aubrey Rd, W8.......80 B4
Aubrey Wk, W8 .....80 B5
Auburn Cl, SE14 ....175 E2
Auckland St, SE11...144 A3
Auden Pl, NW1.......12 C5
Audley Dr, E16......101 E4
Audley Sq, W1 ....85 D4
Audrey St, E2 ....42 C2
Augusta St, E14......69 E5
Augustine Rd, W14...106 C4
Augustus St, NW1....35 F3
Aulton Pl, SE11 .....145 D3
Auriol Rd, W14 .....135 E1
Austen Ho, NW6 .....30 C4
Austin Friars, EC2 ...63 D5
Austin Friars Pas, EC2. 63 D5
Austin Friars Sq, EC2 .63 D5
Austin Rd, SW11....164 C4
Austin St, E2 ....42 A5
Austral St, SE11.....117 E5
Autumn St, E3 ....47 D1
Avalon Rd, SW6.....161 E3
Avebury St, N1.......40 C1
Aveline St, SE11 ....144 C2
Ave Maria La, EC4 ...89 F1
Avenons Rd, E13 .....72 C2
Avenue, The, NW6.....7 E4
SE10..............178 C1
Avenue Cl, NW8......33 F1
Sch Avenue Prim Sch, The,
NW6 ....7 E4
Avenue Rd, NW3 ....10 C3
NW8 ....11 D4
Averill St, W6.......134 C5
Avery Fm Row, SW1. 141 D1
Avery Row, W1 ......85 E2
Aviary Cl, E16........72 B4
Avis Sq, E1 ....67 D5
Avondale Ct, E16.....71 F3

Avondale Pk Gdns,
W11 .... 79 E3
Sch Avondale Pk Prim Sch,
W11 .... 79 E3
Avondale Pk Rd, W11 . 79 E2
Avondale Rd, E16 .... 71 F3
Avondale Sq, SE1 ... 148 C3
Avonley Rd, SE14 ... 174 B2
Avonmore Pl, W14 ... 107 F5
Sch Avonmore Prim Sch,
W14 .... 107 F5
Avonmore Rd, W14 . 108 A5
Avonmouth St, SE1 . . 118 A3
Avon Pl, SE1 .... 118 B2
Axis Ct, SE10 .... 155 E4
Aybrook St, W1 ...... 56 C4
Aylesbury Est, SE17 . 147 D3
Aylesbury Rd, SE17. . 147 D3
Aylesbury St, EC1 .... 61 E2
Aylesford St, SW1 ... 142 C2
Aylesham Cen, The,
SE15 .... 172 C4
Aylestone Av, NW6 .... 6 C5
Aylton Est, SE16 .... 122 B2
Aylward St, E1 ...... 66 A3
Sch Aylwin Girls' Sch,
SE16 .... 120 B5
Aylwyn Est, SE1 .... 120 A3
Aynhoe Rd, W14 .... 107 D5
Ayres St, SE1 .... 118 B1
Ayrton Rd, SW7 ..... 110 C3
Azania Ms, NW5 ..... 13 E1
Azenby Rd, SE15 .... 172 A5
Azof St, SE10 .... 155 F1

B

Babmaes St, SW1 .... 86 B3
Bacchus Wk, N1...... 41 E3
Baches St, N1........ 41 D5
Back Ch La, E1 ...... 92 C2
Back Hill, EC1........ 60 C2
Backhouse Pl, SE17. . 147 F1
Bacon Gro, SE1 ..... 120 A4
Sch Bacon's Coll,
SE16 .... 123 E1
Bacon St, E1......... 64 B1
E2 .... 64 B1
Bacton St, E2 .... 44 B4
Baddow Wk, N1...... 18 A5
Baden Pl, SE1....... 118 C1
Badminton Ms, E16 . 101 D4
Badsworth Rd, SE5 . . 170 A2
Baffin Way, E14 ..... 98 B3
Bagley's La, SW6 .... 161 F4
Bagshot St, SE17.... 147 F3
Baildon St, SE8 ..... 176 B2
Bainbridge St, WC1 ... 59 D5
Baird St, EC1 .... 62 B1
Bakers Hall Ct, EC3 ... 91 F3
Baker's Ms, W1 ...... 56 C5
Baker's Rents, E2..... 42 A5

Bakers Row, E15 ..... 49 E2
Baker's Row, EC1..... 60 C2
⊖ Baker Street 56 B3
Baker St, NW1 ...... 56 B2
W1 .... 56 B3
Bakery Cl, SW9 ..... 168 B3
Balaam St, E13 ...... 73 D1
Balaclava Rd, SE1 ... 148 B1
Balcombe St, NW1 ... 56 A2
Balcorne St, E9....... 22 B4
Balderton St, W1..... 85 D1
Baldock St, E3 .... 47 E3
Baldwin Cres, SE5 ... 170 A3
Baldwin's Gdns, EC1 . . 60 C3
Baldwin St, EC1 ..... 40 C5
Baldwin Ter, N1...... 40 A2
Bale Rd, E1 .... 67 E3
Coll Bales Coll, W10..... 29 D5
Balfern St, SW11 .... 163 F4
Balfe St, N1 .... 37 F3
Balfour Ho, W10 ..... 51 D3
Balfour Ms, W1 ...... 85 D4
Balfour Pl, W1 .... 85 D3
Balfour St, SE17..... 118 C5
Balfron Twr, E14 ..... 70 A5
Balkan Wk, E1 .... 93 E3
Balladier Wk, E14 .... 69 E4
Ballance Rd, E9 ...... 23 D1
Ballast Quay, SE10 . . 155 D2
Ballinger Pt, E3 ...... 47 F4
Balliol Rd, W10 ...... 50 B5
Ballow Cl, SE5 ...... 171 E2
Balls Pond Pl, N1..... 19 D1
Balls Pond Rd, N1.... 19 D1
Balmer Rd, E3 .... 46 A3
Balmes Rd, N1....... 19 D5
Balmoral Gro, N7..... 16 A2
Balmore Cl, E14...... 70 B5
Balniel Gate, SW1 ... 143 D2
Baltic Ct, SE16...... 123 D1
Baltic Pl, N1 .... 41 F1
Baltic St E, EC1....... 62 A2
Baltic St W, EC1...... 62 A2
Balvaird Pl, SW1 .... 143 D3
Bamber Rd, SE15.... 172 A3
Bamborough Gdns,
W12 .... 106 B2
Banbury Ct, WC2..... 87 E2
Banbury Rd, E9 ...... 22 C4
Banbury St, SW11 ... 163 F5
Banchory Rd, SE3 ... 181 E1
Bancroft Rd, E1 ..... 44 B5
Sch Bangabandhu Prim Sch,
E2 .... 44 B5
Banister Rd, W10 .... 29 D4
⊖ Bank 90 C1
DLR Bank.............. 90 C1
Bank End, SE1 ...... 90 B4
★ Bank of England,
EC2 .... 90 C1
★ Bank of England Mus,
EC2 .... 91 D1
Bankside, SE1....... 90 A3
★ Bankside Gall, SE1 . 89 F3

Riv Bankside Pier 90 A3
Bank St, E14......... 97 D5
Bannerman Ho,
SW8 .... 144 A5
Banner St, EC1...... 62 B2
Banning St, SE10.... 155 E3
★ Banqueting Ho,
SW1 .... 87 E5
Bantry St, SE5 ...... 171 D2
Banyard Rd, SE16 ... 121 F4
Baptist Gdns, NW5 ... 12 C2
Barandon Wk, W11.... 79 D2
Barbara Brosnan Ct,
NW8 .... 32 C3
Barbara Castle Cl,
SW6 .... 136 B5
Barbers Rd, E15..... 47 E2
BARBICAN, EC2 ..... 62 A4
≋ Barbican 61 F3
⊖ Barbican 61 F3
★ Barbican Arts &
Conf Cen, EC2 .... 62 B3
Barb Ms, W6 .... 106 B4
Barbon Cl, WC1 ..... 59 F3
Barchester St, E14... 69 E4
Barclay Cl, SW6 .... 160 C2
Barclay Rd, E13 ..... 74 A2
SW6 .... 160 C2
Bard Rd, W10....... 78 C3
Bardsey Pl, E1 ...... 66 A2
Bardsey Wk, N1..... 18 B2
Bardsley La, SE10 ... 154 A5
Barfett St, W10 ..... 52 A1
Barfleur La, SE8..... 152 A1
Barford St, N1 ...... 39 D1
Barge Ho Rd, E16 ... 105 E5
Barge Ho St, SE1 ... 89 D4
Barge La, E3 .... 45 F1
Baring St, N1 .... 40 C1
Barkantine Shop Par,
The, E14 .... 124 C2
Barker Dr, NW1 ..... 14 B4
Barker St, SW10 ... 138 A4
Barkham Ter, SE1 ... 117 D3
Barking Rd, E16..... 72 A4
Bark Pl, W2.......... 81 E2
Barkston Gdns, SW5 . 137 E2
Barkworth Rd, SE16 . 149 F3
Barlborough St,
SE14 .... 174 B1
Barlby Gdns, W10 ... 50 C2
Sch Barlby Prim Sch,
W10 .... 51 D2
Barlby Rd, W10 ..... 50 C3
Barleycorn Way, E14. . 96 A2
Barley Mow Pas, EC1 . 61 F4
Barlow Pl, W1 .... 85 F3
Barlow Rd, NW6 ..... 8 B1
Barlow St, SE17..... 147 D1
Barnaby Pl, SW7 .... 138 C1

Barnard Cl, SE18 . . . . 133 D4
Barnardo Gdns, E1 . . . 94 C1
Barnardo St, E1 . . . . . . 94 C1
Barnard's Inn, EC1. . . . 61 D5
Barnby Sq, E15. . . . . . . 27 E5
Barnby St, E15 . . . . 27 E5
　NW1 . . . . 36 B3
Barnes Ct, E16 . . . . 74 B3
Barnes St, E14 . . . . 95 E1
Barnes Ter, SE8 . . . . . 152 B3
Barnet Gro, E2 . . . . 42 C4
Barnett St, E1. . . . . 65 E5
Barnfield Pl, E14 . . . . 153 D1
Barnham St, SE1. . . . . 119 F1
BARNSBURY, N1 . . . . . . 16 B3
Barnsbury Gro, N7. . . . 16 B2
Barnsbury Pk, N1 . . . . 16 C3
Barnsbury Rd, N1 . . . . 38 C2
Barnsbury Sq, N1 . . . . 16 C4
Barnsbury St, N1 . . . . . 16 C4
Barnsbury Ter, N1 . . . . 16 B4
Barnsdale Av, E14 . . . 125 D5
Barnsdale Rd, W9 . . . . 52 B1
Barnsley St, E1. . . . . . . 65 F1
Barnston Wk, N1 . . . . . 18 A5
Barnwood Cl, W9. . . . . 53 E2
Baroness Rd, E2. . . . . . 42 B4
⊖ Barons Court 135 D2
Barons Ct Rd, W14 . . 135 E2
Barons Keep, W14. . . 135 E2
Barons Pl, SE1 . . . . . . 117 D2
Baron St, N1. . . . . 38 C2
Baron Wk, E16. . . . . . . 72 A3
Barque Ms, SE8 . . . . . 152 C4
Barrett St, W1 . . . . 85 D1
Barriedale, SE14 . . . . 175 F5
Barrie Est, W2 . . . . 82 C2
Barrier App, SE7 . . . . 130 C4
Barrier Pt Rd, E16 . . . 102 A5
Barrow Hill Est, NW8 . 33 E3
Sch Barrow Hill Jun Sch,
　NW8 . . . . 33 E3
Barrow Hill Rd, NW8. . 33 E3
Barry Rd, E6 . . . . 75 F5
Barter St, WC1. . . . . . . 59 F4
Bartholomew Cl, EC1 . 62 A4
Bartholomew La, EC2 . 91 D1
Bartholomew Pl, EC1 . 62 A4
Bartholomew Rd,
　NW5 . . . . 14 B2
Bartholomew Sq, E1. . 65 F1
　EC1 . . . . 62 B1
Bartholomew St,
　SE1 . . . . 118 C4
Bartholomew Vil,
　NW5 . . . . 14 A2
Bartle Rd, W11 . . . . . . 79 D1
Bartlett Cl, E14 . . . . . . 69 D5
Bartlett Ct, EC4 . . . . . . 61 D5
Bartletts Pas, EC4 . . . . 61 D5

Barton Cl, E6 . . . . 76 B5
Barton Rd, W14 . . . . 135 E3
Barton St, SW1 . . . . . 115 E3
Baseing Cl, E6 . . . . . . 105 D2
Basevi Way, SE8 . . . . 153 E4
Basil St, SW3 . . . . 112 A3
Basin App, E14. . . . . . . 95 F1
Basing Ct, SE15 . . . . . 172 B4
Basinghall Av, EC2. . . . 62 C4
Basinghall St, EC2 . . . . 62 C5
Basing Ho Yd, E2 . . . . . 41 F4
Basing Pl, E2. . . . . 41 F4
Basing St, W11 . . . . . . 52 A5
Basire St, N1 . . . . 18 A5
Basque Ct, SE16 . . . . . 122 C2
Bassett Rd, W10 . . . . . 51 D5
Bastwick St, EC1 . . . . . 62 A1
Basuto Rd, SW6. . . . . 160 C4
Batavia Ms, SE14 . . . . 175 F2
Batavia Rd, SE14. . . . 175 F2
Batchelor St, N1 . . . . . 38 C2
Bateman Ho, SE17 . . 145 E5
Bateman's Bldgs, W1 . 86 C1
Bateman's Row, EC2. . 63 F1
Bate St, E14 . . . . 96 B2
Bath Cl, SE15 . . . . 173 F2
Bath Ct, EC1 . . . . 60 C2
Bath Pl, EC2 . . . . 41 E5
Bath St, EC1 . . . . 40 B5
Bath Ter, SE1 . . . . 118 A4
Bathurst Ms, W2 . . . . . 82 C2
Bathurst St, W2 . . . . . . 82 C2
Bathway, SE18 . . . . . 133 D5
Batoum Gdns, W6. . . 106 B3
Batten Cl, E6 . . . . 104 B1
BATTERSEA, SW11 . . 164 B3
Battersea Br, SW3. . . 163 D1
　SW11 . . . . 163 D1
Battersea Br Rd,
　SW11 . . . . 163 E2
Battersea Ch Rd,
　SW11 . . . . 163 D3
★ Battersea Dogs Home,
　SW8 . . . . 165 F2
Battersea High St,
　SW11 . . . . 163 D4
★ Battersea Park,
　SW11 . . . . 164 B1
⇌ Battersea Park . . . 165 E3
Battersea Pk Rd,
　SW8 . . . . 165 E3
Sch Battersea Tech Coll,
　SW11 . . . . 164 B4
Battishill St, N1 . . . . . . 17 E4
Battlebridge Ct, N1 . . . 37 F2
Battle Br La, SE1 . . . . . 91 E5
Battle Br Rd, NW1. . . . 37 E3
Batty St, E1 . . . . 65 D5
Bawtree Rd, SE14 . . . 175 E1
Baxendale St, E2 . . . . . 42 C4
Baxter Rd, E16 . . . . . . 74 B5
　N1. . . . . 19 D2
Bayford Ms, E8. . . . . . . 21 F4

Bayford Rd, NW10. . . . 28 C5
Bayford St, E8 . . . . 21 F4
Bayham Pl, NW1 . . . . . 36 A2
Bayham St, NW1. . . . . 36 A1
Bayley St, WC1. . . . . . . 58 C4
Baylis Rd, SE1 . . . . . . 116 C2
Bayne Cl, E6 . . . . 104 B1
Baynes Ms, NW3 . . . . . 11 D1
Baynes St, NW1 . . . . . . 14 B4
Bayonne Rd, W6 . . . . 135 E5
BAYSWATER, W2 . . . . 81 F1
⊖ Bayswater 81 E2
Bayswater Rd, W2. . . . 83 D2
Baythorne St, E3 . . . . . 68 B3
Bazely St, E14 . . . . 98 A2
Beachy Rd, E3 . . . . 24 C4
Beacons Cl, E6 . . . . 75 F4
Beaconsfield Cl, SE3 . 156 C4
Beaconsfield Rd, E16 . 72 B4
　SE3 . . . . 156 B5
　SE17 . . . . 147 D3
Beaconsfield Ter Rd,
　W14 . . . . 107 E4
Beaconsfield Wk, E6. 105 D1
　SW6 . . . . 160 B4
Beadon Rd, W6 . . . . . 134 B1
Beak St, W1 . . . . 86 B2
Beale Pl, E3. . . . . 46 A2
Beale Rd, E3. . . . . 46 A1
Beanacre Cl, E9 . . . . . . 24 B1
Bear All, EC4. . . . . 61 E5
Bear Gdns, SE1. . . . . . 90 A4
Bear La, SE1 . . . . 89 F4
Bear St, WC2 . . . . 87 D2
Beaton Cl, SE15. . . . . 172 B3
Beatrice Cl, E13 . . . . . 72 C1
Beatrice Pl, W8 . . . . . 109 E4
Beatrice Rd, SE1 . . . . 149 D1
Sch Beatrice Tate Spec
　Sch, E2 . . . . 43 F4
Beatson Wk, SE16 . . . 95 E4
Beatty St, NW1 . . . . . . 36 A2
Beauchamp Pl, SW3 . 111 F3
Beauchamp St, EC1. . . 60 C4
Beaufort, E6 . . . . 77 D5
Beaufort Ct, SW6 . . . 136 C4
Beaufort Gdns, SW3 . 111 F3
Beaufort Ms, SW6 . . . 136 B4
Beaufort St, SW3. . . . 139 D5
Beaufoy Wk, SE11. . . 144 B1
Beaulieu Av, E16. . . . 101 E4
Beaumont Av, W14 . . 136 A2
Beaumont Cres,
　W14 . . . . 136 A2
Beaumont Gro, E1. . . . 66 C2
Beaumont Ms, W1 . . . 57 F3
Beaumont Pl, W1 . . . . 58 B1
Beaumont Sq, E1. . . . . 66 C3
Beaumont St, W1 . . . . 57 F3
Beaumont Wk, NW3 . . 12 B3
Beccles St, E14. . . . . . . 96 B2
Beck Cl, SE13 . . . . 177 E4
Becket St, SE1 . . . . . . 118 C3
Beckford Pl, SE17 . . . 146 B3

Beck Rd, E8	21	E5
BECKTON, E6	77	D4
DLR Beckton	76	C4
DLR Beckton Park	104	B2
Beckton Pk Rbt, E16	104	A2
Beckton Retail Pk, E6	76	C3
Beckton Rd, E16	72	B3
Beckton Triangle Retail Pk, E6	77	E1
Beckway St, SE17	147	D1
Bedale St, SE1	90	C5
Bedford Av, WC1	59	D4
Bedfordbury, WC2	87	E2
Bedford Ct, WC2	87	E3
Bedford Gdns, W8	80	C5
Bedford Pas, SW6	159	F1
Bedford Pl, WC1	59	E3
Bedford Row, WC1	60	B3
Bedford Sq, WC1	59	D4
Bedford St, WC2	87	E2
Bedford Way, WC1	59	D2
Bedlam Ms, SE11	116	B5
Bedser Cl, SE11	144	B4
Beeby Rd, E16	73	E4
Beech Cl, SE8	152	B5
Beechmore Rd, SW11	164	B4
Beech St, EC2	62	A3
Beechwood Rd, E8	20	A1
Beehive Cl, E8	20	A3
Beehive Pas, EC3	91	E1
Beeston Pl, SW1	113	F4
Beethoven St, W10	29	F4
Begonia Cl, E6	75	F3
Bekesbourne St, E14	95	E1
Belfort Rd, SE15	174	B5
Belfry Cl, SE16	149	F2
Belgrave Ct, E14	96	B3
Belgrave Gdns, NW8	31	F1
Belgrave Ms N, SW1	112	C2
Belgrave Ms S, SW1	113	D3
Belgrave Ms W, SW1	112	C3
Belgrave Pl, SW1	113	D3
Belgrave Rd, E13	73	F1
SW1	142	A1
Belgrave Sq, SW1	112	C3
Belgrave St, E1	95	D1
Belgrave Yd, SW1	113	E4
BELGRAVIA, SW1	112	C4
Belgrove St, WC1	37	E4
Belham Wk, SE5	171	D3
Belitha Vil, N1	16	B3
Bellamy Cl, E14	124	C1
W14	136	B3
Bellenden Rd, SE15	172	B5
Coll Bellerbys Coll, SE8	153	D5
Bellevue Pl, E1	66	A2
Bellfield Cl, SE3	181	D1
Bellflower Cl, E6	75	E3
Bell Inn Yd, EC3	91	D1
Bell La, E1	64	A4
E16	100	C4
Bellmaker Ct, E3	68	C3

Bellot Gdns, SE10	155	F2
Bellot St, SE10	155	F2
Bells Gdn Est, SE15	172	C2
Bell St, NW1	55	E3
Bell Water Gate, SE18	133	D3
Bell Wf La, EC4	90	B2
Bell Yd, WC2	60	C5
Bell Yd Ms, SE1	119	F2
Belmont St, NW1	13	D3
Belmore St, SW8	166	C3
Belsham St, E9	22	A1
Belsize Av, NW3	11	D1
Belsize Gro, NW3	11	F1
Belsize La, NW3	10	C2
Belsize Ms, NW3	11	D1
BELSIZE PARK, NW3	11	E2
Belsize Pk, NW3	10	C2
Belsize Pk Gdns, NW3	11	D1
Belsize Pk Ms, NW3	11	D1
Belsize Pl, NW3	11	D1
Belsize Rd, NW6	10	B4
Belsize Sq, NW3	11	D1
Belsize Ter, NW3	11	D1
Belson Rd, SE18	132	A5
Belton Way, E3	68	C3
Belvedere Bldgs, SE1	117	F2
Belvedere Ct, N1	19	E5
Belvedere Ms, SE3	181	D2
Belvedere Pl, SE1	117	F2
Belvedere Rd, SE1	116	B1
Belvedere Twr, The, SW10	162	B4
Bembridge Cl, NW6	7	E3
Bemerton Est, N1	16	A4
Bemerton St, N1	16	A5
Benbow St, SE8	153	D4
Bendall Ms, NW1	55	F3
Benhill Rd, SE5	171	D2
Benjamin Cl, E8	43	D1
Benjamin St, EC1	61	E3
Sch Ben Jonson Prim Sch, E1	67	F2
Ben Jonson Rd, E1	67	D4
Benledi St, E14	70	C5
Bennet's Hill, EC4	89	F2
Bennett Gro, SE13	177	F4
Bennett Rd, E13	74	A2
Bennett St, SW1	86	A4
Bennetts Yd, SW1	115	D4
Benn St, E9	23	F1
Ben Smith Way, SE16	121	D3
Benson Quay, E1	94	A3
Bentham Ct, N1	18	B4
Bentham Rd, E9	22	C2
Ben Tillett Cl, E16	104	A5
Bentinck Ms, W1	57	D5
Bentinck St, W1	57	D5
Bentley Rd, N1	19	F2
Benwick Cl, SE16	121	F5
Benworth St, E3	46	B4
Benyon Rd, N1	19	D5

Sch Beormund Sch, SE1	119	D2
Berber Pl, E14	96	C2
Berens Rd, NW10	28	C5
Beresford Sq, SE18	133	E5
Beresford St, SE18	133	E4
Bere St, E1	95	D2
Bergen Sq, SE16	123	F3
Sch Berger JMI Sch, E9	22	C1
Berger Rd, E9	22	C1
Berghem Ms, W14	107	D4
Bergholt Ms, NW1	14	B4
Berglen Ct, E14	95	E1
Bering Wk, E16	102	C1
Berkeley Gdns, W8	81	D5
Berkeley Ho, E3	46	C5
Berkeley Ms, W1	56	B5
Berkeley Sq, W1	85	F3
Berkeley St, W1	85	F3
Berkeley Twr, E14	96	B4
Berkley Gro, NW1	12	B4
Berkley Rd, NW1	12	B4
Berkshire Rd, E9	24	B1
BERMONDSEY, SE1	120	A4
⊖ Bermondsey	121	D3
Bermondsey Sq, SE1	119	F3
Bermondsey St, SE1	91	E5
Bermondsey Wall E, SE16	121	D2
Bermondsey Wall W, SE16	120	C1
Bernard Ashley Dr, SE7	157	E3
Bernard Cassidy St, E16	72	B3
Bernard St, WC1	59	E2
Berners Ms, W1	58	B4
Berners Pl, W1	58	B5
Berners Rd, N1	39	D2
Berners St, W1	58	B4
Bernhardt Cres, NW8	55	E1
Berryfield Rd, SE17	145	F2
Berry Pl, EC1	39	F5
Berry St, EC1	61	F1
Berthon St, SE8	177	D1
Berwick Rd, E16	102	A1
Berwick St, W1	86	C1
Beryl Av, E6	75	F3
Beryl Rd, W6	134	C3
Bessborough Gdns, SW1	143	D2
Bessborough Pl, SW1	142	C2
Bessborough St, SW1	142	C2
Bessie Lansbury Cl, E6	104	C1
Besson St, SE14	174	B3
Bessy St, E2	44	B4
Bestwood St, SE8	151	D1

Bethell Av, E16 ......72 A1
BETHNAL GREEN, E2.. 43 E4
⇌ Bethnal Green.....65 E1
⊖ Bethnal Green.....44 A5
Bethnal Grn Est, E2..44 A5
Bethnal Grn Rd, E1 ...64 A1
  E2 ....64 A1
🏫 Bethnal Grn Tech Coll,
  E2 ....42 B5
🎓 Bethnal Grn Training Cen,
  E1 ....64 C3
Bethwin Rd, SE5 ....169 F1
Betterton St, WC2....87 E1
Bettons Pk, E15 ......49 F1
Betts St, E1..........93 E3
Bevan St, N1 ....40 B1
Bevenden St, N1 .....41 D4
Beverley Ho, NW8 ....33 E5
Beverston Ms, W1....56 A4
Bevin Cl, SE16 ....95 E4
Bevin Ct, WC1 ....38 B4
🏫 Bevington Prim Sch,
  W10 ....51 F3
Bevington Rd, W10...51 F3
Bevington St, SE16..121 D2
Bevin Way, WC1 .....38 C4
Bevis Marks, EC3.....63 F5
Bewdley St, N1 ......16 C3
Bewick Ms, SE15 ....173 E2
Bewley St, E1 ....93 F2
Bexhill Wk, E15 ......49 F1
Bianca Rd, SE15 .....148 C5
Bickenhall St, W1 ....56 B3
Bidborough St, WC1 ..37 E5
Bidbury Cl, SE15 ....147 F5
Bidder St, E16 ....71 E3
Biddulph Rd, W9 .....31 E5
Bidwell St, SE15 ....173 F4
★ Big Ben (St. Stephens
  Tower), SW1 ......115 F3
Biggerstaff Rd, E15 ...26 A5
🏫 Bigland Grn Prim Sch,
  E1 ....93 E1
Bigland St, E1........93 E1
Billing Pl, SW10.....161 F1
Billing Rd, SW10 ....161 F1
★ Billingsgate Mkt,
  E14 ....97 F4
Billing St, SW10.....161 F1
Billington Rd, SE14 ..174 C2
Billiter Sq, EC3 ......91 F1
Billiter St, EC3 ......91 F1
Billson St, E14 ......154 B1
Bina Gdns, SW5 .....138 A1
Binfield Rd, SW4 ....167 F4
Bingfield St, N1 ......15 F5
Bingham Ct, N1 ......17 F3
Bingham Pl, W1......56 C3
Bingham St, N1 ......18 C1
Bingley Rd, E16 ......74 A5

Binney St, W1 ....85 D2
Birch Cl, E16..........71 F3
Birches, The, SE7....157 F4
Birchfield St, E14.....96 C2
Birchington Rd, NW6 ..9 D5
Birchin La, EC3........91 D1
Birdcage Wk, SW1...114 B2
Bird in Bush Rd,
  SE15..............173 D1
Birdsfield La, E3......24 A5
Bird St, W1 ....85 D1
🎓 Birkbeck Coll, Main Bldg,
  WC1 ....59 D2
  Russell Sq, WC1 ...59 D3
Birkbeck St, E2.......43 F5
Birkdale Cl, SE16....149 E3
Birkenhead St, WC1 ..37 F4
Biscay Rd, W6 ......134 C3
🏫 Bishop Challoner Lwr Sch,
  E1 ....93 D1
🏫 Bishop Challoner Upr Sch,
  E1 ....94 B1
Bishop Kings Rd,
  W14..............107 F5
Bishop's Av, SW6....159 D5
Bishops Br, W2.......54 B5
Bishops Br Rd, W2....81 F1
Bishop's Ct, EC4......61 E5
  WC2 ....60 C5
Bishopsgate, EC2.....91 E1
Bishopsgate Arc, EC2 .63 F4
Bishopsgate Chyd,
  EC2 ....63 E4
🎓 Bishopsgate Inst,
  EC2 ....63 F4
Bishop's Pk, SW6....159 D5
Bishop's Pk Rd, SW6.159 D5
Bishops Rd, SW6 ....160 A2
Bishop's Rd, SW11 ..163 F1
Bishops Ter, SE11 ...117 D5
Bishop St, N1 ....18 A5
Bishops Way, E2 .....43 F2
Bishop Wilfred Wd Cl,
  SE15..............173 D5
Bisson Rd, E15.......48 B2
Bittern St, SE1 ......118 A2
Blackall St, EC2 ......63 E1
Blackbird Yd, E2......42 B4
Blackburne's Ms, W1..84 C2
Blackburn Rd, NW6....9 E2
⇌ Blackfriars 89 F2
⊖ Blackfriars 89 F2
Blackfriars Br, EC4....89 E2
  SE1 ....89 E2
Blackfriars Ct, EC4....89 E2
Black Friars La, EC4...89 E2
🛥 Blackfriars Millennium
  Pier 89 D2
Blackfriars Pas, EC4 ..89 E2
Blackfriars Rd, SE1 ..117 E2
BLACKHEATH, SE3...179 F4
★ Blackheath, SE3 ..180 B4
Blackheath Av,
  SE10..............179 D2

🏫 Blackheath Bluecoat
  C of E Sec Sch,
  SE3 ....181 F1
🏫 Blackheath High Sch,
  SE3 ....180 C1
Blackheath Hill,
  SE10..............177 F4
Blackheath Rd,
  SE10..............177 E3
Blackheath Vale,
  SE3 ....179 F5
Black Horse Ct, SE1..119 D3
Blackhorse Rd, SE8 ..151 F4
Blacklands Ter,
  SW3 ....140 A1
Black Prince Rd,
  SE1 ....144 A1
  SE11 ....144 B1
Blacks Rd, W6 ......134 A1
Blackstone Est, E8....21 D4
Black Swan Yd, SE1 ..119 E1
Blackthorn St, E3.....69 D2
🚈 Blackwall 98 B3
Blackwall La, SE10 ..155 F2
Blackwall Pier, E14 ...99 E3
Blackwall Trd Est,
  E14 ....71 D4
Blackwall Tunnel,
  E14 ....98 C3
Blackwall Tunnel App,
  SE10..............127 E2
Blackwall Tunnel Northern
  App, E3............47 D2
  E14 ....48 A4
Blackwall Way, E14...98 B3
Blackwood St, SE17 .146 C2
Blagrove Rd, W10 ....51 F4
Blair Cl, N1 ....18 B1
Blair St, E14 ....98 B1
Blake Cl, W10........50 B3
Blake Gdns, SW6 ....161 E3
Blake Rd, E16........72 A2
Blaker Rd, E15 ......48 A1
Blakes Rd, SE15 ....171 F1
Blake St, SE8 ....152 C4
Blanchard Way, E8 ...21 D2
Blanch Cl, SE15 ....174 A2
Blanche St, E16 ......72 A2
Blandford Sq, NW1 ...55 F2
Blandford St, W1.....56 B5
Blantyre St, SW10...162 C1
Blantyre Twr, SW10 .162 C1
Blashford, NW3 .....12 A3
Blasker Wk, E14 ....153 D2
Blechynden St, W10 ..79 D2
Bleeding Heart Yd,
  EC1 ....61 D4
Blenheim Cres, W11 ..79 E2
Blenheim Gdns, NW2 ..6 B1
Blenheim Pas, NW8 ..32 A2
Blenheim Rd, NW8 ...32 A2
Blenheim St, W1 .....85 E1
Blenheim Ter, NW8...32 A2

Sch Blessed John Roche Catholic Sch, The, E14 . . . . 97 D1
Sch Blessed Sacrament RC Prim Sch, N1 . . . . . . 38 A1
Bletchley Ct, N1 . . . . 40 C3
Bletchley St, N1 . . . . . . 40 B3
Bletsoe Wk, N1 . . . . . . 40 B2
Bliss Cres, SE13 . . . . . 177 F5
Blissett St, SE10 . . . . . 178 A3
Bliss Ms, W10 . . . . 29 F4
Blithfield St, W8 . . . . 109 E4
Blomfield Rd, W9 . . . . . 54 A3
Blomfield St, EC2 . . . . . 63 D4
Blomfield Vil, W2 . . . . . 53 F4
Blondel St, SW11 . . . . 164 C5
Blondin St, E3 . . . . 46 C2
Bloomburg St, SW1 . . 142 B1
Bloomfield Pl, W1 . . . . 85 F2
Bloomfield Ter, SW1 . 141 D2
Bloom Pk Rd, SW6 . . 160 A2
BLOOMSBURY, WC1 . . 59 D4
Bloomsbury Ct, WC1 . . 59 F4
Bloomsbury Pl, WC1 . . 59 F3
Bloomsbury Sq, WC1 . . . . 59 F4
Bloomsbury St, WC1 . . 59 D4
Bloomsbury Way, WC1 . . . . 59 E5
Blore Cl, SW8 . . . . 166 C4
Blore Ct, W1 . . . . 86 C1
Blossom St, E1 . . . . 63 F3
Blount St, E14 . . . . 67 F5
Blucher Rd, SE5 . . . . . 170 B2
Blue Anchor La, SE16 . . . . 121 D5
Blue Anchor Yd, E1 . . 92 C2
Blue Ball Yd, SW1 . . . . 86 A5
Bluebell Cl, E9 . . . . 22 A5
Sch Blue Gate Flds Inf & Jun Sch, E1 . . . . 94 A2
Bluelion Pl, SE1 . . . . . 119 E3
Blundell St, N7 . . . . . . 15 F3
Blyth Cl, E14 . . . . . . 126 C5
Blythe Ms, W14 . . . . . 107 D3
Blythe Rd, W14 . . . . . 107 E5
Blythe St, E2 . . . . 43 E4
Blyth's Wf, E14 . . . . 95 F3
Boadicea St, N1 . . . . . . 38 A1
Boardwalk Pl, E14 . . . . 98 A4
Boathouse Wk, SE15 . . . . 172 B1
Boat Lifter Way, SE16 . . . . 123 F5
Bocking St, E8 . . . . 21 E5
Bohemia Pl, E8 . . . . . . 21 F1
Bohn Rd, E1 . . . . 67 E3
Bolden St, SE8 . . . . . 177 E5
Bolina Rd, SE16 . . . . . 150 B2
Bolingbroke Rd, W14 . . . . 107 D3
Bolingbroke Wk, SW11 . . . . 163 D2
Bolney Gate, SW7 . . . 111 E2

Bolney St, SW8 . . . . . 168 A2
Bolsover St, W1 . . . . . . 57 F2
Bolt Ct, EC4 . . . . 89 D1
Bolton Cres, SE5 . . . . 145 D5
Bolton Gdns, NW10 . . 28 C3
SW5 . . . . 137 E2
Bolton Gdns Ms, SW10 . . . . 138 A2
Bolton Rd, NW8 . . . . . . 31 F1
Boltons, The, SW10 . 138 A2
Boltons Pl, SW5 . . . . . 138 A2
Bolton St, W1 . . . . 85 F4
Bombay St, SE16 . . . . 121 E5
Bomore Rd, W11 . . . . . 79 D2
Bonar Rd, SE15 . . . . . 172 C2
Bonchurch Rd, W10 . . 51 E3
Bond Ct, EC4 . . . . 90 C1
Bondfield Rd, E6 . . . . . 75 F4
Bonding Yd Wk, SE16 . . . . 123 F2
➡ Bond Street 85 D1
Bondway, SW8 . . . . . 143 F5
Boneta Rd, SE18 . . . . 132 A4
Bonhill St, EC2 . . . . . . 63 D2
Sch Bonner Prim Sch, E2 . . . . 44 C4
Bonner Rd, E2 . . . . 44 A2
Bonner St, E2 . . . . 44 B3
Bonnington Sq, SW8 . 144 A4
Bonny St, NW1 . . . . . . 14 A4
Bonsor St, SE5 . . . . . 171 E2
Booker Cl, E14 . . . . 68 B4
Book Ms, WC2 . . . . 87 D1
Boord St, SE10 . . . . . 127 F3
Booth Cl, E9 . . . . 43 F1
Booth's Pl, W1 . . . . 58 B4
Boot St, N1 . . . . 41 E5
Boreas Wk, N1 . . . . 39 F3
Boreham Av, E16 . . . . 100 C1
Borgard Rd, SE18 . . . 132 A5
➡ Borough 118 B2
BOROUGH, THE, SE1 . . . . 118 A2
Borough High St, SE1 . . . . 118 A2
★ Borough Mkt, SE1 . . 90 C5
Borough Rd, SE1 . . . . 117 E3
Borough Sq, SE1 . . . . 118 A2
Borrett Cl, SE17 . . . . . 146 A3
Borthwick St, SE8 . . . 152 C3
Boscobel Pl, SW1 . . . 113 D5
Boscobel St, NW8 . . . . 55 D2
Boss Ho, SE1 . . . . 120 A1
Boss St, SE1 . . . . 120 A1
Boston Pl, NW1 . . . . . . 56 A2
Boston St, E2 . . . . 42 C2
Bosun Cl, E14 . . . . . . 125 D1
Boswell Ct, WC1 . . . . . 59 F3
Boswell St, WC1 . . . . . 59 F3
Bosworth Rd, W10 . . . 51 F2
Botha Rd, E13 . . . . 74 A3
Bothwell Cl, E16 . . . . . 72 B4
Bothwell St, W6 . . . . 135 D5
Botolph All, EC3 . . . . . 91 E2

Botolph La, EC3 . . . . . 91 E2
Botts Ms, W2 . . . . 81 D1
Botts Pas, W2 . . . . . . 81 D1
Boulcott St, E1 . . . . . . 95 D1
Boulevard, The, SW6 . . . . 162 B4
Boultwood Rd, E6 . . . 103 F1
Boundary La, SE17 . . 146 B5
Boundary Pas, E2 . . . . 64 A1
Boundary Rd, NW8 . . . 31 D4
Boundary Row, SE1 . 117 E1
Boundary St, E2 . . . . . 42 A5
Bourchier St, W1 . . . . . 86 C2
Bourdon Pl, W1 . . . . . . 85 F2
Bourdon St, W1 . . . . . . 85 F2
Bourlet Cl, W1 . . . . 58 A4
Bourne Est, EC1 . . . . . 60 C3
Bourne St, SW1 . . . . . 140 C1
Bourne Ter, W2 . . . . . . 53 E3
Sch Bousfield Prim Sch, SW5 . . . . 138 A2
Sch Boutcher C of E Prim Sch, SE1 . . . . 120 A5
Bouverie Pl, W2 . . . . . . 55 D5
Bouverie St, EC4 . . . . . 89 D1
Bovingdon Rd, SW6 . 161 E4
BOW, E3 . . . . 45 F3
Bowater Pl, SE3 . . . . . 181 F5
Bowater Rd, SE18 . . . 131 D4
Bow Back Rivers Wk, E15 . . . . 25 F3
Bow Br Est, E3 . . . . . . 47 D3
DLR Bow Church 47 D4
Bow Chyd, EC4 . . . . . . 90 B1
Bow Common La, E3 . . 68 A2
Bowden St, SE11 . . . . 145 D3
Bowditch, SE8 . . . . . . 152 A2
Bowen St, E14 . . . . . . 69 F5
Bower Av, SE10 . . . . . 179 E3
Bowerdean St, SW6 . 161 E4
Bowerman Av, SE14 . 151 F5
Bower St, E1 . . . . 94 C1
Bowers Wk, E6 . . . . . . 75 F5
Bowfell Rd, W6 . . . . . 134 B5
Bowhill Cl, SW9 . . . . . 169 D1
Bow Ind Pk, E15 . . . . . 25 E3
Bowland Yd, SW1 . . . 112 B2
Bow La, EC4 . . . . 90 B1
Bowl Ct, EC2 . . . . 63 F2
Bowling Grn La, EC1 . . 61 D1
Bowling Grn Pl, SE1 . 118 C1
Bowling Grn Row, SE18 . . . . 132 A4
Bowling Grn St, SE11 . . . . 144 C4
Bowling Grn Wk, N1 . . 41 E4
Bowman Av, E16 . . . . 100 B2
Bowmans Ms, E1 . . . . 92 C2
Bowmore Wk, NW1 . . 15 D3
Bowness Cl, E8 . . . . . . 20 A2

⊖ Bow Road 46 B4
Bow Rd, E3..........46 B5
🏫 Bow Sec Sch, E3 ...47 D4
Bowsprit Pt, E14 ....124 C3
Bow St, WC2.........87 F1
Bowyer Cl, E6.......76 B3
Bowyer Pl, SE5......170 B1
Bowyer St, SE5 .....170 A1
Boxley St, E16 ......101 E5
Boxworth Gro, N1 ....16 B5
Boyce St, SE1 ....88 B5
Boyce Way, E13 ......72 C1
Boydell Ct, NW8 .....10 C4
Boyd St, E1 ....92 C1
Boyfield St, SE1 .....117 F2
Boyle St, W1.........86 A2
Boyne Ter Ms, W11 ...80 A4
Boyson Rd, SE17 ....146 C4
Boyton Cl, E1 ....66 B1
Brabant Ct, EC3.....91 E2
Brabazon St, E14....69 E5
Bracewell Rd, W10 ...50 A4
Bracken Cl, E6 ....76 A4
Brackley St, EC1.....62 A3
Bracklyn Cl, N1 .....40 C2
Bracklyn Ct, N1 .....40 C2
Bracklyn St, N1 .....40 C2
Bradbourne St, SW6 .161 D5
Braddyll St, SE10....155 E3
Bradenham Cl, SE17.146 C4
Braden St, W9 ....53 E2
Bradfield Rd, E16 ...129 D1
Bradiston Rd, W9 ....30 B4
Bradley Cl, N1 ....39 D2
N7.................15 F2
Bradley Stone Rd, E6 .76 A4
Bradmead, SW8.....165 F2
Bradstock Rd, E9 ....23 D2
Brad St, SE1 ....89 D5
Bradwell St, E1......45 D5
Bradymead, E6 ......77 D5
Brady St, E1 ....65 E2
Braemar Cl, SE16 ...149 E2
Braemar Rd, E13....72 B2
Braemer Ho, W9 .....32 A5
Braes St, N1 ....17 F3
Braganza St, SE17...145 E2
Braham St, E1 ....92 B1
Braidwood St, SE1....91 E5
Braintree St, E2 .....66 A1
Braithwaite Ho, EC1 ..62 B1
Braithwaite Twr, W2..54 C3
Bramah Grn, SW9 ...169 D3
★ Bramah Mus, SE1 ..90 B5
Bramber Rd, W14 ...136 A4
Bramcote Gro, SE16 .150 A2
Bramerton St, SW3..139 E4
Bramham Gdns, SW5 137 E2
Bramhope La, SE7...157 F4
Bramley Cres, SW8 ..167 D1

Bramley Rd, W10 ....79 D2
🏫 Brampton Manor Sch,
E6 ....75 D1
Brampton Rd, E6.....75 D1
Bramshaw Rd, E9 ....23 D2
Bramshot Av, SE7 ...157 D3
Bramwell Ms, N1.....16 B5
Branch Pl, N1 ....19 D5
Branch Rd, E14 ......95 E2
Branch St, SE15 .....171 E2
Brandon Est, SE17 ..145 F5
Brandon Rd, N7......15 E3
Brandon St, SE17 ...146 A1
Brandreth Rd, E6....76 B5
Brand St, SE10......178 A2
Brangton Rd, SE11 ..144 B3
Branksea St, SW6 ...159 E2
Bransdale Cl, NW6....9 D5
Brasenose Dr, SW13.134 A5
Brassett Pt, E15......49 F1
Brassey Rd, NW6 ......8 B1
Brass Tally All, SE16 .123 D2
Bratley St, E1 ....64 C2
Bravington Pl, W9 ....52 A1
Bravington Rd, W9 ...52 A1
Brawne Ho, SE17....145 F5
Bray, NW3 ....11 F3
Bray Cres, SE16 .....122 C1
Bray Dr, E16.........100 B2
Brayfield Ter, N1 .....16 C4
Brayford Sq, E1 ......66 B5
Bray Pas, E16........100 C2
Bray Pl, SW3........140 A1
Bread St, EC4 ....90 B1
Bream's Bldgs, EC4 ..60 C5
Bream St, E3........25 D4
Brechin Pl, SW7 .....138 B1
🏫 Brecknock Prim Sch,
N7.................15 D1
Brecon Rd, W6.......135 F5
Breezers Hill, E1......93 D3
Bremner Rd, SW7 ...110 B2
Brendon St, W1 ......55 F5
Brenthouse Rd, E9 ...22 A3
Brenton St, E14 .....67 F5
Brent Rd, E16........73 D5
Bressenden Pl, SW1 .113 F3
Brettell St, SE17 ....147 D3
Brewer's Grn, SW1 ..114 C3
Brewers Hall Gdns,
EC2.................62 B4
Brewer St, W1 ....86 B2
★ Brewery, The, EC1 .62 B3
Brewery Rd, N7 ......15 E3
Brewery Sq, EC1 .....61 F1
Brewhouse La, E1 ....93 F5
Brewhouse Rd,
SE18.............132 B5
Brewhouse Wk, SE16 .95 E5
Brewhouse Yd, EC1 ...61 F1
Brewster Gdns, W10 ..50 A3
Brewster Ho, E14 ....96 B2
Briant St, SE14 .....174 C3
Briar Wk, W10 ....51 E1

Briary Cl, NW3 ....11 E3
Briary Ct, E16 ....100 B1
Brick Ct, EC4.........88 C1
Brick La, E1..........64 B1
E2 ....42 B5
Bricklayer's Arms
Distribution Cen,
SE1 ....147 F1
Bricklayer's Arms Rbt,
SE1 ....118 C5
Brick St, W1 ....85 E5
Brideale Cl, SE15 ...148 B5
Bride Ct, EC4 ....89 E1
Bride La, EC4 ....89 E1
Bridel Ms, N1 ....39 E1
Brides Pl, N1.........19 E4
Bride St, N7 ....16 B2
Bridewain St, SE1 ...120 A3
Bridewell Pl, E1 ......93 F5
EC4 ....89 E1
Bridford Ms, W1.....57 F3
Bridge App, NW1.....12 C3
Bridge Cl, W10.......79 D1
Bridgefoot, SE1 .....143 E3
Bridge Ho Quay, E14..98 B5
Bridgeland Rd, E16 ..101 D2
Bridge La, SW11 ....163 F4
Bridgeman Rd, N1....16 A4
Bridgeman St, NW8 ..33 E3
Bridge Meadows,
SE14.............150 C4
Bridge Pl, SW1 .....113 F5
Bridgeport Pl, E1 ....93 D4
Bridge Rd, E15 ....27 D4
🏫 Bridge Sch, The,
EC1 ....61 E1
N1.................18 B5
Bridges Pl, SW6 .....160 B3
Bridge St, SW1......115 D2
Bridge Ter, E15.......27 D4
Bridge Vw, W6......134 A2
Bridgewater Sq, EC2 .62 A3
Bridgewater St, EC2 ..62 A3
Bridgeway St, NW1 ..36 B3
Bridge Yd, SE1 ....91 D4
Bridgwater Rd, E15...48 A1
Bridle La, W1 ....86 B2
Bridport Pl, N1.......41 D2
Bridport Ter, SW8 ...166 C4
Bridstow Pl, W2......53 D5
Brief St, SE5 ....169 E5
Brierly Gdns, E2.....44 B4
Brightlingsea Pl, E14..96 A2
Brighton Gro, SE14 ..175 E3
Bright St, E14........69 F4
Brig Ms, SE8........152 C5
Brill Pl, NW1.........37 D3
Brindley St, SE14....176 A4
Brinklow Ho, W2.....53 E3
Brinkworth Way, E9 ..24 B1
Brinsley St, E1 ....93 F1
Brinton Wk, SE1 .....89 E5
Brion Pl, E14.........70 A4
Brisbane St, SE5 ....170 C2

Briset St, EC1 . . . . 61 E3
Bristol Gdns, W9 . . . . . 53 F2
Bristol Ms, W9 . . . . 53 F2
★ Britain at War
　Experience, SE1 . . 91 E5
Britannia Gate, E16 . 101 D4
Britannia Rd, E14 . . . 153 D1
　SW6 . . . . 161 E2
Britannia Row, N1 . . . 17 F5
Britannia St, WC1 . . . 38 A4
Sch Britannia Village
　Prim Sch, E16 . . . . 101 E5
Britannia Wk, N1. . . . . 40 C4
Britannia Way, SW6 . 161 E2
★ British Dental Assoc
　Mus, W1. . . . . 57 E4
★ British Lib, NW1 . . 37 D4
★ British Med Assoc,
　WC1 . . . . 59 D1
★ British Mus, WC1 . . 59 E4
★ British Red Cross Mus &
　Archives, SW1. . . . 112 C2
Coll British Sch of Osteopathy,
　SE1 . . . . 118 B2
British St, E3 . . . . 46 B5
Brittany Pt, SE11. . . . 144 C1
Britten St, SW3 . . . . . 139 E3
Britton St, EC1 . . . . . . 61 E2
Brixham St, E16 . . . . 104 B5
Brixton Rd, SW9 . . . . 168 C2
Broadbent St, W1 . . . . 85 E2
Broadbridge Cl, SE3 . 180 C1
Broad Ct, WC2 . . . . 87 F1
Broadfield La, NW1. . . 15 E3
BROADGATE, EC2 . . . . 63 D3
Broadgate Circle, EC2. 63 E3
Broadgate Rd, E16 . . . 74 C5
Broadhurst Cl, NW6 . . 10 A2
Broadhurst Gdns, NW6. 9 E3
Broad La, EC2. . . . . 63 E3
Broadley St, NW8 . . . . 55 D3
Broadley Ter, NW1 . . . 55 F2
Broadmayne, SE17 . . 146 C2
Broad Sanctuary,
　SW1 . . . . 115 D2
Broadstone Pl, W1. . . . 56 C4
Broad St Av, EC2 . . . . . 63 E4
Broad St Pl, EC2 . . . . . 63 D4
Broad Wk, NW1 . . . . . . 35 E5
　W1 . . . . 84 C4
Broad Wk, The, W8 . . . 81 F3
Broadwalk Ct, W8 . . . . 81 D4
Broadwall, SE1. . . . . . . 89 D4
Broadway, E15. . . . . . . 27 D4
　SW1 . . . . 114 C3
Broadway Mkt, E8. . . . 43 D1
Broadway Mkt Ms,
　E8 . . . . 43 D1
Broadway Shop Cen,
　W6 . . . . 134 B1
Broadway Wk, E14 . . 125 D3
Broadwick St, W1 . . . . 86 B2
Broad Yd, EC1. . . . . 61 E2
Brocas Cl, NW3 . . . . . . 11 F3

Brockham St, SE1 . . . 118 B3
Brocklebank Rd, SE7. 157 E1
Brocklehurst St,
　SE14. . . . . 175 D1
Brockley Gdns, SE4 . . 176 A5
Brock Pl, E3 . . . . 69 E2
Brock Rd, E13. . . . . 73 F3
Brodie St, SE1 . . . . . . 148 B2
Brodlove La, E1 . . . . . . 94 C2
Broken Wf, EC4 . . . . . . 90 A2
Brokesley St, E3. . . . . . 46 A5
Broke Wk, E8 . . . . 20 B5
Bromehead Rd, E1. . . . 66 A5
Bromehead St, E1 . . . . 66 A5
Bromfield St, N1 . . . . . 39 D2
BROMLEY, E3. . . . . 69 F2
⬤ Bromley-by-Bow. . . 69 F1
Bromley Hall Rd, E14 . 70 A3
Sch Bromley Hall Spec Sch,
　E14. . . . . 70 B4
Bromley High St, E3 . . 47 E4
Bromley Pl, W1 . . . . . . 58 A3
Bromley St, E1 . . . . 67 D5
BROMPTON, SW3 . . . 111 E4
Brompton Arc, SW3 . . 112 A2
★ Brompton Oratory,
　SW7 . . . . 111 E4
Brompton Pk Cres,
　SW6 . . . . 137 E5
Brompton Pl, SW3. . . 111 F3
Brompton Rd, SW1. . 111 F3
　SW3 . . . . 111 E5
　SW7 . . . . 111 E3
Brompton Sq, SW3 . . 111 E3
Bromyard Ho, SE15. . 173 E1
BRONDESBURY, NW2. . 7 E3
⇌ Brondesbury 8 A3
Brondesbury Ct, NW2. . 6 C2
Brondesbury Ms, NW6 . 8 C4
BRONDESBURY PARK,
　NW6 . . . . 6 B4
⇌ Brondesbury Park. . . 7 E5
Brondesbury Pk, NW6. . 7 E4
Brondesbury Rd,
　NW6 . . . . 30 A2
Brondesbury Vil,
　NW6 . . . . 30 B2
Bronsart Rd, SW6 . . . 159 E2
Bronte Ho, NW6 . . . . . 31 D4
Bronti Cl, SE17. . . . . . 146 B3
Bronze St, SE8 . . . . . . 177 D1
Brook Dr, SE11 . . . . . . 117 D4
Brooke Ct, W10 . . . . . . 29 F3
Brooke's Ct, EC1. . . . . . 60 C3
Brookes Mkt, EC1 . . . . 61 D3
Brooke St, EC1 . . . . 60 C4
Brookfield Rd, E9. . . . . 23 F2
Brook Gate, W1 . . . . . . 84 B3
Brook Grn, W6 . . . . . . 107 D5
Brooklands Pas,
　SW8 . . . . 166 C3
Brook La, SE3. . . . . . . 181 F5
Brookmarsh Ind Est,
　SE10. . . . . 177 F1

Brook Ms N, W2. . . . . . 82 B2
Brookmill Rd, SE8 . . . 177 D3
Brooks Av, E6. . . . . 76 A1
Brooksbank St, E9. . . . 22 C2
Brooksby Ms, N1 . . . . . 17 D3
Brooksby St, N1 . . . . . . 17 D4
Brook's Ms, W1 . . . . . . 85 E2
Brook St, W1 . . . . 85 D2
　W2 . . . . 83 D2
Brooksville Av, NW6. . 29 F1
Brookville Rd, SW6 . . 160 A4
Broome Way, SE5 . . . 170 C2
Broomfield St, E14 . . . 69 D4
Broomhouse Rd,
　SW6 . . . . 160 C5
Brougham Rd, E8. . . . . 20 C5
Brougham St, SW11 . 164 B5
Brough Cl, SW8 . . . . . 167 F2
Broughton Rd, SW6 . 161 E4
Broughton Rd App,
　SW6 . . . . 161 E5
Broughton St, SW8. . 165 E5
Brownfield St, E14 . . . 97 F1
Brown Hart Gdns,
　W1 . . . . 85 D2
Browning Cl, W9 . . . . . 54 B2
Browning Ms, W1 . . . . 57 E4
Browning St, SE17 . . 146 B2
Brownlow Ms, WC1. . . 60 B2
Brownlow Rd, E8. . . . . 20 B5
Brownlow St, WC1 . . . 60 B4
Brown's Bldgs, EC3 . . 91 F1
Brown St, W1. . . . . 56 A5
Broxwood Way, NW8 . 33 F1
Bruce Cl, W10 . . . . 51 D3
Bruce Rd, E3. . . . . 47 E5
Bruckner St, W10 . . . . 29 F5
Bruford Ct, SE8 . . . . . 153 D5
Bruges Pl, NW1 . . . . . . 14 B4
★ Brunei Gall, WC1 . . 59 D3
★ Brunel Engine Ho,
　SE16. . . . . 122 A1
Brunel Est, W2. . . . . . . 52 C4
Brunel Ms, W10. . . . . . 29 F5
Brunel Rd, SE16. . . . . 122 A2
Brunel St, E16 . . . . . . 100 A1
Brune St, E1 . . . . 64 A4
Brunswick Ct, SE1. . . 119 F2
Brunswick Gdns, W8. . 81 D5
Brunswick Ms, W1 . . . 56 B5
Brunswick Pk, SE5. . . 171 D3
Sch Brunswick Pk Comm
　Prim Sch, SE5 . . . . 171 D2
Brunswick Pl, N1. . . . . 41 D5
　NW1. . . . . 57 D1
Brunswick Quay,
　SE16. . . . . 123 D4
Brunswick Shop Cen,
　WC1 . . . . 59 E1
Brunswick Sq, WC1 . . 59 F2

Brunswick Vil, SE5 . . 171 E3
Brunton Pl, E14 . . . . . . 95 F1
Brushfield St, E1 . . . . . . 63 F4
Brushwood Cl, E14 . . . 69 F3
Bruton La, W1 . . . . 85 F3
Bruton Pl, W1 . . . . 85 F3
Bruton St, W1 . . . . 85 F3
Bryan Rd, SE16 . . . . 124 A1
Bryan's All, SW6 . . . . 161 E5
Bryanston Ms E, W1 . 56 A4
Bryanston Ms W, W1 . 56 A4
Bryanston Pl, W1 . . . . . 56 A4
Bryanston Sq, W1 . . . . 56 A4
Bryanston St, W1 . . . . 84 A1
Bryant Ct, E2 . . . . 42 A2
Bryant St, E15 . . . . 27 D4
Brydale Ho, SE16 . . . . 122 C5
Brydges Pl, WC2 . . . . . . 87 E3
Brydon Wk, N1 . . . . . . 15 F5
Brymay Cl, E3 . . . . 47 D3
Brynmaer Rd, SW11 . 164 A4
Buckfast St, E2 . . . . 43 D5
Buck Hill Wk, W2 . . . . 83 D3
Buckhurst St, E1 . . . . . 65 F2
Buckingham Arc,
  WC2 . . . . 87 F3
Buckingham Gate,
  SW1 . . . . 114 A2
Buckingham Ms, N1 . . 19 F2
  SW1 . . . . 114 A3
★ Buckingham Palace,
  SW1 . . . . 113 F2
Buckingham Palace Rd,
  SW1 . . . . 141 E1
Buckingham Pl,
  SW1 . . . . 114 A3
Buckingham Rd, N1 . . 19 E2
Buckingham St, WC2 . 87 F3
Buckland Cres, NW3 . . 10 C3
Buckland St, N1 . . . . . 41 D3
Bucklebury, NW1 . . . . 58 A1
Bucklers All, SW6 . . . 136 B5
Bucklersbury, EC4 . . . . 90 C1
Bucklersbury Pas,
  EC4 . . . . 90 C1
Buckle St, E1 . . . . 64 B5
Buckley Rd, NW6 . . . . . . 8 B4
Buckley St, SE1 . . . . . . 88 C5
Bucknall St, WC2 . . . . . 59 D5
Buck St, NW1 . . . . 13 F4
Buckters All, SE16 . . 95 E5
Budge Row, EC4 . . . . . . 90 C2
Budge's Wk, W2 . . . . . . 82 A4
Bugsby's Way, SE7 . . 157 D1
  SE10 . . . . 128 A5
🎓 Building Crafts Coll,
  E15 . . . . 26 C4
Bulinga St, SW1 . . . . . 143 D1
Bullace Row, SE5 . . . . 170 B3
Bullards Pl, E2 . . . . 44 C4

Bullen Ho, E1 . . . . 65 F2
Bullen St, SW11 . . . . . 163 E5
Buller Cl, SE15 . . . . . . 172 C2
Buller Rd, NW10 . . . . . 29 D5
Bullied Way, SW1 . . . 141 F1
Bull Inn Ct, WC2 . . . . . 87 F3
Bullivant St, E14 . . . . . 98 A1
Bulls Gdns, SW3 . . . . . 111 F5
Bull's Head Pas, EC3 . . 91 E1
Bull Yd, SE15 . . . . 173 D4
Bulmer Ms, W11 . . . . . 80 C4
Bulmer Pl, W11 . . . . . . 80 C4
Bulow Est, SW6 . . . . . 161 F4
Bulstrode Pl, W1 . . . . . 57 D4
Bulstrode St, W1 . . . . . 57 D5
Bulwer St, W12 . . . . . . 78 B5
Bunhill Row, EC1 . . . . . 62 C1
Bunhouse Pl, SW1 . . . 140 C2
Bunning Way, N7 . . . . . 15 F3
Bunsen St, E3 . . . . 45 E2
Bunton St, SE18 . . . . . 133 D4
Buonaparte Ms,
  SW1 . . . . 142 C2
Burbage Cl, SE1 . . . . . 118 C4
🎓 Burbage JMI Sch,
  N1 . . . . 41 E2
Burcham St, E14 . . . . . 69 F5
Burchell Rd, SE15 . . . 173 F4
Burder Cl, N1 . . . . 19 F1
Burder Rd, N1 . . . . 19 F1
🎓 Burdett Coutts C of E
  Prim Sch, SW1 . . . 114 C4
Burdett Ms, NW3 . . . . 11 D1
  W2 . . . . 53 E5
Burdett Rd, E3 . . . . 67 F1
  E14 . . . . 67 F1
Burdett St, SE1 . . . . . . 116 C3
Burford Rd, E15 . . . . . . 26 C4
Burford Wk, SW6 . . . . 161 F2
Burgess Business Pk,
  SE5 . . . . 171 D1
Burgess St, E14 . . . . . . 68 C4
Burge St, SE1 . . . . 119 D4
Burgh St, N1 . . . . 39 F2
Burgon St, EC4 . . . . . . 89 F1
Burgos Gro, SE10 . . . . 177 E3
Burke St, E16 . . . . 72 B4
Burleigh Ho, W10 . . . . 51 D3
Burleigh St, WC2 . . . . . 88 A2
Burley Rd, E16 . . . . 74 A4
Burlington Arc, W1 . . 86 A3
Burlington Cl, E6 . . . . . 75 F5
  W9 . . . . 52 B2
Burlington Gdns, W1 . 86 A3
Burlington Rd, SW6 . 159 F5
Burnaby St, SW10 . . 162 A2
Burne Jones Ho,
  W14 . . . . 136 A1
Burnell Wk, SE1 . . . . . 148 B2
Burness Cl, N7 . . . . 16 A1
Burne St, NW1 . . . . 55 E3
Burney St, SE10 . . . . . 178 B1
Burnfoot Av, SW6 . . . 159 F4
Burnham, NW3 . . . . . . 11 E3

Burnham Cl, SE1 . . . . 148 B1
Burnham St, E2 . . . . . . 44 A4
Burnhill Cl, SE15 . . . . 173 F1
Burnley Rd, SW9 . . . . 168 A5
Burnsall St, SW3 . . . . 139 F2
Burnside Cl, SE16 . . . . 95 D4
Burns Rd, SW11 . . . . . 164 A5
Burnthwaite Rd,
  SW6 . . . . 160 B2
Buross St, E1 . . . . 65 F5
Burrard Rd, E16 . . . . . . 73 E5
Burr Cl, E1 . . . . 92 C4
Burrell St, SE1 . . . . 89 E4
Burrells Wf Sq, E14 . . 153 E2
Burrows Ms, SE1 . . . . 117 E1
Burrows Rd, NW10 . . . 28 A4
Burslem St, E1 . . . . 93 D1
Burton Gro, SE17 . . . . 146 C3
Burton La, SW9 . . . . . 169 D5
Burton Ms, SW1 . . . . 141 D1
Burton Pl, WC1 . . . . . . 37 D5
Burton Rd, NW6 . . . . . . 8 B4
  SW9 . . . . 169 E5
Burton St, WC1 . . . . . . 37 D5
Burwash Ho, SE1 . . . . 119 D2
Burwell Cl, E1 . . . . 93 F1
Burwell Wk, E3 . . . . . . 69 D1
Burwood Pl, W2 . . . . . 55 F5
Bury Cl, SE16 . . . . 95 D4
Bury Ct, EC3 . . . . 63 F5
Bury Pl, WC1 . . . . 59 E4
Bury St, EC3 . . . . 91 F1
  SW1 . . . . 86 A4
Bury Wk, SW3 . . . . . . 139 E1
Busbridge Ho, E14 . . . 69 D5
Busby Pl, NW5 . . . . 14 C1
Busby St, E2 . . . . 64 B1
Bushbaby Cl, SE1 . . . . 119 E4
Bushberry Rd, E9 . . . . 23 F1
Bush Ct, W12 . . . . 107 D1
Bushell St, E1 . . . . 93 D5
Bushey Hill Rd, SE5 . . 171 F4
Bush La, EC4 . . . . 90 C2
Bush Rd, E8 . . . . 43 E1
  SE8 . . . . 123 D5
Bushwood Dr, SE1 . . 148 B1
★ Business Design Cen,
  N1 . . . . 39 E2
Butcher Row, E1 . . . . . 95 D2
  E14 . . . . 95 D2
Butchers Rd, E16 . . . . 73 D5
Bute Gdns, W6 . . . . . . 134 C1
🎓 Bute Ho Prep Sch
  for Girls, W6 . . . . . 106 C5
Bute St, SW7 . . . . 110 C5
Bute Wk, N1 . . . . 18 C2
Butler Pl, SW1 . . . . . . 114 C3
Butler St, E2 . . . . 44 B4
Butlers Wf, SE1 . . . . . . 92 B5
Butterfield Cl, SE16 . 121 E2
Butterfield Sq, E6 . . . 104 A1
Butterfly Wk, SE5 . . . 170 C4
Buttermere Cl, SE1 . . 120 A5
Buttermere Wk, E8 . . . 20 B2

Butterwick, W6 . . . . . 134 B1
Buttesland St, N1 . . . . 41 D4
Buxhall Cres, E9 . . . . . . 24 A1
Buxted Rd, E8 . . . . 20 A3
Buxton Cl, N1 . . . . . . 40 B4
Buxton Ms, SW4 . . . . 167 D5
Buxton St, E1 . . . . 64 B2
Byfield Cl, SE16 . . . . . 123 F1
Byford Cl, E15 . . . . 27 F4
Sch Bygrove Prim Sch,
    E14 . . . . 97 E1
Bygrove St, E14 . . . . . . 97 E1
Bylands Cl, SE16 . . . . . 95 D4
Byng Pl, WC1 . . . . 58 C2
Byng St, E14 . . . . 124 C1
Byron Cl, E8 . . . . 20 C5
Byron Ct, W9 . . . . 53 D1
Byron Ms, W9 . . . . 53 D1
Byron St, E14 . . . . 70 A5
Byward St, EC3 . . . . . . 91 F3
Bywater Pl, SE16 . . . . . 95 F4
Bywater St, SW3 . . . . 140 A2
Bywell Pl, W1 . . . . 58 A4

C

Cabbell St, NW1 . . . . . . 55 E4
Cable Pl, SE10 . . . . . . 178 B3
Cable St, E1 . . . . 92 C2
Cabot Pl, E14 . . . . 97 D4
Cabot Sq, E14 . . . . 97 D4
Cactus Cl, SE15 . . . . . 171 F5
Cadbury Way, SE16 . . 120 B4
Cadell Cl, E2 . . . . 42 B3
Cade Rd, SE10 . . . . . . 178 C3
Cadet Dr, SE1 . . . . 148 B2
Cadet Pl, SE10 . . . . . . 155 E2
Cadiz St, SE17 . . . . . . 146 B3
Cadogan Cl, E9 . . . . 24 B3
Cadogan Gdns, SW3 . 112 B5
Cadogan Gate, SW1 . 112 B5
Cadogan La, SW1 . . . 112 C4
Riv Cadogan Pier 139 F5
Cadogan Pl, SW1 . . . . 112 B3
Cadogan Rd, SE18 . . . 133 F3
Cadogan Sq, SW1 . . . 112 B4
Cadogan St, SW3 . . . . 140 A1
Cadogan Ter, E9 . . . . . . 24 A2
Cahill St, EC1 . . . . 62 B2
Cahir St, E14 . . . . 153 E1
Caird St, W10 . . . . 29 F5
Caithness Rd, W14 . . 106 C5
Calabria Rd, N5 . . . . . . 17 C1
Calais Gate, SE5 . . . . 169 E3
Calais St, SE5 . . . . 169 F3
Caldecot Rd, SE5 . . . . 170 B5
Calderon Pl, W10 . . . . . 50 A4
Calderwood St,
    SE18 . . . . 133 D5
Caldwell St, SW9 . . . . 168 B2
Caldy Wk, N1 . . . . 18 A3
Caleb St, SE1 . . . . 118 A1

⊖ Caledonian Road . . 15 F1
Caledonian Rd, N1 . . . 37 F3
    N7 . . . . 16 A1
⇌ Caledonian Road &
    Barnsbury 16 B3
Caledonian Sq, NW1 . . 14 C1
Caledonian Wf,
    E14 . . . . 154 C1
Caledonia St, N1 . . . . . 37 F3
Cale St, SW3 . . . . 139 E2
Caletock Way, SE10 . 156 A2
Callaby Ter, N1 . . . . 19 D2
Callcott Rd, NW6 . . . . . . 8 A4
Callcott St, W8 . . . . 80 C4
Callendar Rd, SW7 . . 110 C3
Callingham Cl, E14 . . . 68 B4
Callow St, SW3 . . . . . 138 B4
Calshot St, N1 . . . . 38 C1
Calthorpe St, WC1 . . . . 60 B1
Calvert Av, E2 . . . . 41 F5
Calverton, SE5 . . . . . . 147 D4
Sch Calverton Prim Sch,
    E16 . . . . 103 D1
Calvert Rd, SE10 . . . . 156 A3
Calvert's Bldgs, SE1 . . 90 C5
Calvert St, NW1 . . . . . . 12 C5
Calvin St, E1 . . . . 64 A2
Calydon Rd, SE7 . . . . 157 F3
Calypso Cres, SE15 . . 172 A1
Calypso Way, SE16 . . 124 A4
CAMBERWELL, SE5 . . 170 B2
Camberwell Ch St,
    SE5 . . . . 170 C4
Uni Camberwell Coll of Arts,
    Peckham Rd, SE5 . 171 F3
    Sumner Rd, SE15 . 172 B1
    Wilson Rd, SE5 . . . 171 E4
Camberwell Glebe,
    SE5 . . . . 171 E4
Camberwell Grn,
    SE5 . . . . 170 C3
Camberwell Gro,
    SE5 . . . . 171 D4
Camberwell New Rd,
    SE5 . . . . 144 C5
Camberwell Pas,
    SE5 . . . . 170 B3
Camberwell Rd,
    SE5 . . . . 146 B5
Camberwell Sta Rd,
    SE5 . . . . 170 A4
Camborne Ms, W11 . . 79 F1
Cambria St, SW6 . . . . 161 F2
Cambridge Av, NW6 . . 31 D2
Cambridge Circ,
    WC2 . . . . 87 D1
Cambridge Cres, E2 . . . 43 E3
Cambridge Gdns,
    NW6 . . . . 31 D2
    W10 . . . . 51 F5
Cambridge Gate,
    NW1 . . . . 35 F5
Cambridge Gate Ms,
    NW1 . . . . 35 F5

⇌ Cambridge Heath . . 43 E2
Cambridge Heath Rd,
    E1 . . . . 65 F3
    E2 . . . . 65 F3
Cambridge Mans,
    SW11 . . . . 164 A4
Cambridge Pl, W8 . . . 109 F2
Cambridge Rd, NW6 . . 30 C4
    SW11 . . . . 164 A4
Coll Cambridge Sch of English,
    The, WC2 . . . . 59 F5
Cambridge Sq, W2 . . . . 55 E5
Cambridge St, SW1 . . 141 F1
Cambridge Ter, NW1 . . 35 F5
Cambridge Ter Ms,
    NW1 . . . . 35 F5
Cambus Rd, E16 . . . . . 73 D3
Camden Gdns, NW1 . . 13 F4
Camden High St,
    NW1 . . . . 13 F5
Camdenhurst St, E14 . 67 F5
★ Camden Lock Mkt &
    Waterbuses, NW1 . 13 E4
Camden Lock Pl,
    NW1 . . . . 13 E4
Camden Ms, NW1 . . . . 14 B3
🏥 Camden Ms Day Hosp,
    NW1 . . . . 14 B3
Camden Pk Rd, NW1 . . 14 C1
Camden Pas, N1 . . . . . 39 E1
⇌ Camden Road 14 A4
Camden Rd, N7 . . . . . . 14 A4
    NW1 . . . . 14 C1
Sch Camden Sch for Girls,
    NW5 . . . . 14 B2
Camden Sq, NW1 . . . . 14 C3
    SE15 . . . . 172 A3
Camden St, NW1 . . . . . 14 A5
Camden Ter, NW1 . . . . 14 C2
CAMDEN TOWN,
    NW1 . . . . 36 A1
⊖ Camden Town 13 F5
Camden Wk, N1 . . . . . 39 E1
Camelford Wk, W11 . . 79 E1
Camellia St, SW8 . . . . 167 E2
Sch Camelot Prim Sch,
    SE15 . . . . 149 E5
Camelot St, SE15 . . . 149 E5
Camel Rd, E16 . . . . . . 103 D4
Camera Pl, SW10 . . . . 138 C5
Sch Cameron Ho,
    SW3 . . . . 139 D4
Cameron Pl, E1 . . . . . . 65 F5
Camerton Cl, E8 . . . . . 20 B2
Camilla Rd, SE16 . . . . 149 E1
Camlet St, E2 . . . . 64 A1
Camley St, NW1 . . . . . . 37 D2
★ Camley St Natural Pk,
    NW1 . . . . 37 D2
Camomile St, EC3 . . . . 63 E5

Campana Rd, SW6 ..160 C3
Campbell Rd, E3 .....47 D4
Campbell Wk, N1...15 F5
Campden Gro, W8...109 D1
Campden Hill, W8...108 C1
Campden Hill Ct,
  W8 ....109 D1
Campden Hill Gdns,
  W8 ....80 B4
Campden Hill Gate,
  W8 ....108 C1
Campden Hill Pl, W11.80 B4
Campden Hill Rd,
  W8 ....109 D2
Campden Hill Sq, W8 .80 B5
Campden Hill Twrs,
  W11 ....80 C4
Campden Ho Cl, W8 .108 C1
Campden St, W8 .....80 C5
Camperdown St, E1 ..92 B1
Campion Cl, E6 .....104 B2
Camplin St, SE14....175 D1
Cam Rd, E15.........26 C5
Canada Est, SE16 ...122 B3
Canada Sq, E14 .....97 E4
Canada St, SE16 ....122 C2
⊖ Canada Water....122 B2
Canal App, SE8 .....151 E3
Canal Boul, NW1 .....14 C1
Canal Cl, E1 ....67 E1
  W10 ....51 D1
Canal Gro, SE15 ....149 D4
Canal Path, E2 ......42 A1
Canal St, SE5 ....146 C5
Canal Wk, N1 ....19 D5
Canal Way, N1 ......40 B2
  NW1 ....33 F4
  NW8 ....33 E5
  W2 ....53 F3
  W9 ....52 B3
  W10 ....52 B3
Canal Way Wk, W10 ..50 C1
⊖ Canary Wharf 97 E5
🚄 Canary Wharf 97 D4
🚢 Canary Wharf Pier .96 B4
Cancell Rd, SW9 ....169 D3
Candover St, W1 .....58 A4
Candy St, E3 ....24 B5
Canfield Gdns, NW6 ..10 A2
Canfield Pl, NW6 .....10 A2
Canning Pas, W8.....110 A3
Canning Pl, W8 .....110 A3
Canning Pl Ms, W8 ..110 A2
Canning Rd, E15 .....49 E3
CANNING TOWN, E16.72 C5
⇌ Canning Town.....71 F5
⊖ Canning Town.....71 F5
🚄 Canning Town.....71 F5
Cannon Dr, E14 ......96 C3
⇌ Cannon Street.....90 C3

⊖ Cannon Street.....90 C3
Cannon St, EC4 ......90 A1
Cannon St Rd, E1....65 E5
Cannon Wf Business Cen,
  SE8 ....151 E1
Cannon Workshops,
  E14 ....96 C3
🏫 Canon Barnett Prim Sch,
  E1 ....64 B5
Canon Beck Rd,
  SE16.............122 B1
CANONBURY, N1.....17 F2
Canonbury Cres, N1 ..18 A3
Canonbury Gro, N1 ...18 A3
🏫 Canonbury Jun & Inf Sch,
  N1 ....17 F2
Canonbury La, N1....17 E3
Canonbury Pk N, N1 ..18 A3
Canonbury Pk S, N1 ..18 A2
Canonbury Pl, N1 ....17 F2
Canonbury Rd, N1....17 E2
Canonbury Sq, N1....17 F3
Canonbury St, N1 ....18 A3
Canonbury Vil, N1....17 F3
Canonbury Yd, N1....18 C5
Canonbury Yd W,
  N1 ....17 F2
Canon Row, SW1 ....115 E2
Canon St, N1 ....40 A1
Canrobert St, E2 .....43 E4
Cantelowes Rd, NW1 .15 D2
Canterbury Cl, E6 ....76 A5
Canterbury Pl, SE17 .145 F1
Canterbury Rd, NW6 .30 C3
Canterbury Ter, NW6 .30 C2
Cantium Retail Pk,
  SE1 ....148 C4
Canton St, E14.......96 C1
Cantrell Rd, E3.......68 B2
Canute Gdns, SE16 ..122 C5
Capel Ct, EC2 ....91 D1
Capener's Cl, SW1 ...112 C2
Cape Yd, E1..........93 D4
Capital Coll (CIFE)
  London Sch of Insurance,
  WC1 ....60 A3
Capland St, NW8 ....55 D1
Capper St, WC1 .....58 B2
Capstan Rd, SE8 ....124 A5
Capstan Sq, E14 ....126 B2
Capstan Way, SE16...95 F5
Capulet Ms, E16 ....101 D4
Caradoc Cl, W2 ......52 C5
Caradoc St, SE10....155 E2
Caravel Cl, E14 .....124 C3
Caravel Ms, SE8.....152 C4
Caraway Cl, E13......73 E3
Carbis Rd, E14 ......68 A5
Carburton St, W1 ....57 F3
Cardale St, E14 .....126 A3
Cardigan Rd, E3......46 B2
Cardigan St, SE11 ..144 C2
Cardinal Bourne St,
  SE1 ....119 D4

🏫 Cardinal Pole RC Sec Sch,
  Annexe, E9........23 D4
🏫 Cardinal Vaughan
  Mem Sch, W14 ...107 E1
Cardine Ms, SE15 ...173 E1
Cardington St, NW1 .36 A4
🏫 Cardwell Prim Sch,
  SE18.............132 A5
Carew St, SE5 ......169 F5
Carey Gdns, SW8 ...166 C4
Carey La, EC2 ....62 A5
Carey Pl, SW1.......142 C1
Carey St, WC2 ......88 B1
Carfree Cl, N1.......17 D3
Carisbrooke Gdns,
  SE15.............172 B1
Carlile Cl, E3........46 B3
Carlisle Av, EC3 .....91 F1
Carlisle La, SE1 .....116 B4
Carlisle Ms, NW8....55 D3
Carlisle Pl, SW1 ....114 A4
Carlisle Rd, NW6 .....7 E5
Carlisle St, W1 ....86 C1
Carlisle Wk, E8......20 A2
Carlos Pl, W1 ....85 D3
Carlow St, NW1 ......36 A2
Carlton Ct, SW9.....169 E3
Carlton Gdns, SW1 ..86 C5
Carlton Gro, SE15 ..173 E3
Carlton Hill, NW8 ....32 A1
Carlton Ho Ter, SW1 ..86 C5
Carlton Sq, E1 ....66 C1
Carlton St, SW1 ......86 C3
Carlton Twr Pl,
  SW1 ....112 B3
Carlton Vale, NW6....31 D3
🏫 Carlton Vale Inf Sch,
  NW6 ....30 B4
Carlyle Ms, E1 ....67 D1
★ Carlyle's Ho, SW3 .139 E5
Carlyle Sq, SW3 .....139 D3
Carmarthen Pl, SE1..119 E1
Carmel Ct, W8 ......109 E1
Carmelite St, EC4 ....89 D2
Carmen St, E14 ......69 E5
Carnaby St, W1 ......86 A1
Carnegie St, N1 ......38 A1
Carnoustie Dr, N1....16 A4
Caroline Cl, W2 ......81 F3
Caroline Gdns, SE15 .173 E1
Caroline Pl, W2 ......81 F2
Caroline Pl Ms, W2 ..81 F3
Caroline St, E1 ......95 D1
Caroline Ter, SW1 ...140 C1
Caroline Wk, W6 ....135 E5
Carol St, NW1 ....14 A5
🏫 Carpenters Prim Sch,
  E15 ....26 B5
Carpenters Rd, E15...25 D2
Carpenter St, W1.....85 E3
Carr Gro, SE18 ......131 F5
Carriage Dr E, SW11 .164 C1
Carriage Dr N, SW11 .141 D5
Carriage Dr S, SW11 .164 A3

Carriage Dr W,
SW11 . . . . 164 A2
Carriage St, SE18 . . . . 133 F4
Carrick Ms, SE8 . . . . . 152 C4
Carrington St, W1 . . . . 85 E5
Carron Cl, E14 . . . . . . 69 F5
Carroun Rd, SW8 . . . . 168 A1
Carr St, E14 . . . . 67 F5
Carson Rd, E16 . . . . . . 73 D2
Carteret St, SW1 . . . . 114 C2
Carteret Way, SE8 . . . 151 F1
Carter La, EC4 . . . . . . 89 F1
Carter Pl, SE17 . . . . . 146 B3
Carter St, SE17 . . . . . 146 A4
Carthusian St, EC1 . . . 62 A3
Cartier Circle, E14 . . . 97 F5
Carting La, WC2 . . . . . 87 F3
Carton St, W1 . . . . 56 B5
Cartridge Pl, SE18 . . . 133 F4
Cartwright Gdns,
WC1 . . . . 37 E5
Cartwright St, E1 . . . . . 92 B2
Casella Rd, SE14 . . . . 174 C2
Casey Cl, NW8 . . . . 33 E5
Caspian St, SE5 . . . . . 170 C1
Caspian Wk, E16 . . . . 102 C3
Cassidy Rd, SW6 . . . . 160 C2
Cassilis Rd, E14 . . . . . 125 D2
Cassland Rd, E9 . . . . . . 22 B3
Casson St, E1 . . . . 64 C4
Castalia Sq, E14 . . . . . 126 A2
Castellain Rd, W9 . . . . 54 A2
Casterbridge, NW6 . . . . 9 F5
Casterton St, E8 . . . . . 21 F2
Castile Rd, SE18 . . . . 133 D5
Castle Baynard St,
EC4 . . . . 89 F2
Castlebrook Cl,
SE11 . . . . 117 E5
Castle Ct, EC3 . . . . 91 D1
Castlehaven Rd, NW1 . 13 E4
Castle La, SW1 . . . . . . 114 B3
Castlemaine Twr,
SW11 . . . . 164 B5
Castlemain St, E1 . . . . 65 E3
Castle Ms, NW1 . . . . . . 13 E2
Castle Pl, NW1 . . . . 13 E2
Castlereagh St, W1 . . . 56 A5
Castle Rd, NW1 . . . . . . 13 E2
Castletown Rd,
W14 . . . . 135 F3
Castle Yd, SE1 . . . . 89 F4
Castor La, E14 . . . . 97 E3
Catesby St, SE17 . . . . 147 D1
Cathay St, SE16 . . . . . 121 F2
Cathcart Rd, SW10 . . 137 F4
Cathcart St, NW5 . . . . 13 E1
Cathedral Piazza,
SW1 . . . . 114 A4
Sch Cathedral Sch of St.
Saviours & St. Mary
Overie C of E, The,
SE1 . . . . 118 B1
Cathedral St, SE1 . . . . . 90 C4

Catherine Griffiths Ct,
EC1 . . . . 61 D1
Catherine Gro, SE10 . 177 E3
Catherine Pl, SW1 . . . 114 A3
Catherine St, WC2 . . . . 88 A2
Catherine Wheel All,
E1 . . . . 63 F4
Catherine Wheel Yd,
SW1 . . . . 86 A5
Catlin St, SE16 . . . . . . 149 D3
Cator St, SE15 . . . . . . 148 A5
Cato St, W1 . . . . 55 F4
Catton St, WC1 . . . . . . 60 A4
Caulfield Rd, SE15 . . . 173 F5
Causton St, SW1 . . . . 143 D1
Cavaye Pl, SW10 . . . . 138 B3
Cavell St, E1 . . . . 65 F3
Cavendish Av, NW8 . . . 33 D3
NW8 . . . . 33 D4
Coll Cavendish Coll,
WC1 . . . . 58 C3
Cavendish Ct, EC3 . . . . 63 F5
Cavendish Ms N, W1 . . 57 F3
Cavendish Ms S, W1 . . 57 F4
Cavendish Pl, NW2 . . . . 7 D2
W1 . . . . 57 F5
Cavendish Rd, NW6 . . . 7 F4
Sch Cavendish Sch, The,
NW1 . . . . 13 F5
Cavendish Sq, W1 . . . . 57 F5
Cavendish St, N1 . . . . . 40 C3
Caversham Flats,
SW3 . . . . 140 A4
Caversham Rd, NW5 . . 14 A1
Caversham St, SW3 . . 140 A4
Caverswall St, W12 . . . 50 A5
Caxton Gro, E3 . . . . 46 C4
Caxton Rd, W12 . . . . . 106 C1
Caxton St, SW1 . . . . . 114 B3
Caxton St N, E16 . . . . 100 A4
Cayenne Ct, SE1 . . . . . . 92 B5
Sch Cayley Prim Sch,
E14 . . . . 67 E5
Cayton Pl, EC1 . . . . 40 C5
Cayton St, EC1 . . . . 40 C5
Cecil Ct, WC2 . . . . 87 D3
★ Cecilia Coleman Gall,
NW8 . . . . 33 D2
★ Cecil Sharp Ho,
NW1 . . . . 13 D5
Cedar Cl, E3 . . . . 24 B5
Cedar Ct, N1 . . . . 18 B3
Cedarne Rd, SW6 . . . 161 E2
Cedars Rd, E15 . . . . 27 F1
Cedar Way, NW1 . . . . . 14 C4
Celandine Cl, E14 . . . . 68 C4
Celandine Dr, E8 . . . . . 20 B3
Celandine Way, E15 . . 49 F4
Celbridge Ms, W2 . . . . 53 F5
Celtic St, E14 . . . . 69 F3
★ Cenotaph, The,
SW1 . . . . 115 E1
Centaur St, SE1 . . . . . 116 B3

Central Av, SW11 . . . 164 A2
★ Central Criminal Ct
(Old Bailey), EC4 . . . 61 F5
Sch Central Foundation
Boys' Sch, EC2 . . . . . 63 D1
Sch Central Foundation
Girls' Sch,
Lwr Sch, E3 . . . . 45 F4
Upr Sch, E3 . . . . 46 B5
Uni Central St. Martins
Coll of Art & Design,
WC1 . . . . 60 A4
Back Hill Site, EC1 . . 61 D2
Catton St Site,
WC1 . . . . 60 A4
Charing Cross Rd Site,
WC2 . . . . 87 D1
Coll Central Sch of Ballet,
EC1 . . . . 61 D2
Coll Central Sch of Speech &
Drama, NW3 . . . . . . 10 C3
Central St, EC1 . . . . . . 40 A5
Centre Av, W10 . . . . . . 28 B5
Centre Pt, SE1 . . . . . . 148 C2
Centrepoint, WC1 . . . . 59 D5
Centre St, E2 . . . . 43 E3
Centric Cl, NW1 . . . . . . 13 E5
Centurion Bldg,
SW8 . . . . 141 E5
Centurion Cl, N7 . . . . . 16 A3
Centurion La, E3 . . . . . 46 B2
Cephas Av, E1 . . . . 66 B1
Cephas St, E1 . . . . 66 A2
Cerise Rd, SE15 . . . . . 173 D4
Cerney Ms, W2 . . . . 82 C2
Cervantes Ct, W2 . . . . 81 F1
Cester St, E2 . . . . 42 C1
Ceylon Rd, W14 . . . . . 107 D4
Chadbourn St, E14 . . . 69 F4
Chadwell St, EC1 . . . . 39 D4
Chadwick St, SW1 . . . 115 D4
Chadwin Rd, E13 . . . . 73 E3
Chagford St, NW1 . . . . 56 A2
Chalbury Wk, N1 . . . . . 38 B2
Chalcot Cres, NW1 . . . 12 B5
Chalcot Gdns, NW3 . . . 12 A2
Chalcot Rd, NW1 . . . . . 12 C4
Sch Chalcot Sch, NW1 . . 13 E3
Chalcot Sq, NW1 . . . . . 12 C4
Chaldon Rd, SW6 . . . 159 E1
● Chalk Farm 12 B3
Chalk Fm Rd, NW1 . . . 12 C3
Chalk Hill Rd, W6 . . . 134 C1
Chalk Rd, E13 . . . . 73 F3
Challoner Cres,
W14 . . . . 136 A3
Challoner St, W14 . . . 136 A2
Chalmers Wk, SE17 . . 145 F5
Chaloner Ct, SE1 . . . . 118 C1
Chalton St, NW1 . . . . . 37 D4

Chamberlain Cotts,
SE5 . . . . 171 D4
Chamberlain St, NW1 . 12 B4
Chamberlayne Rd,
NW10 . . . . 28 C4
Chambers St, SE16 . . 120 C1
Chamber St, E1 . . . . . . 92 B2
Chambord St, E2 . . . . . 42 B5
Chancellor Pas, E14 . . 97 D5
Chancellor Rd, W6 . 134 A3
Chancellors St, W6 . 134 A3
Chancel St, SE1 . . . . . . 89 E4
⊖ Chancery Lane 60 C4
Chancery La, WC2 . . . . 60 C5
Chance St, E1 . . . . 64 A1
E2 . . . . 64 A1
Chandler Av, E16 . . . . . 72 C3
Chandlers Ms, E14 . . 124 C1
Chandler St, E1 . . . . . . 93 F4
Chandler Way, SE15 . 171 F1
Chandos Pl, WC2 . . . . . 87 E3
Chandos St, W1 . . . . . . 57 F4
Change All, EC3 . . . . . . 91 D1
Channelsea Ho Business
Cen, E15 . . . . 49 D3
Channelsea Rd, E15 . 26 C5
Chantry Cl, W9 . . . . . . 52 B2
Chantry St, N1 . . . . 39 F1
Chant Sq, E15 . . . . 27 D4
Chant St, E15 . . . . 27 D4
Chapel Ct, SE1 . . . . . . 118 C1
Chapel Ho St, E14 . . . 153 F2
Chapel Mkt, N1 . . . . . . 38 C2
Chapel Pl, EC2 . . . . 41 E5
N1 . . . . 39 D2
W1 . . . . 85 E1
Chapel Side, W2 . . . . . 81 E2
Chapel St, NW1 . . . . . . 55 E4
SW1 . . . . 113 D3
Chaplin Cl, SE1 . . . . . 117 D1
Chaplin Rd, E15 . . . . . . 49 F2
Chapman Rd, E9 . . . . . 24 B2
Chapman St, E1 . . . . . . 93 E2
Chapone Pl, W1 . . . . . . 86 C1
Chapter Ho Ct, EC4 . . . 90 A1
Chapter Rd, SE17 . . . 145 F3
Chapter St, SW1 . . . . 142 C1
Chardwell Cl, E6 . . . . . . 76 A5
Charecroft Way,
W12 . . . . 106 C2
Charfield Ct, W9 . . . . . 53 E2
Charford Rd, E16 . . . . . 73 D4
Chargeable La, E13 . . . 72 B1
Chargeable St, E16 . . . 72 B1
Chargrove Cl, SE16 . . 123 D1
⇌ Charing Cross 87 E4
⊖ Charing Cross 87 E4
Charing Cross, SW1 . . 87 E4
🏥 Charing Cross Hosp,
W6 . . . . 134 C4

Charing Cross Rd,
WC2 . . . . 59 D5
Charlbert St, NW8 . . . . 33 E2
Charlemont Rd, E6 . . 76 B1
Charles Coveney Rd,
SE15 . . . . 172 A3
Charles Dickens Ho,
E2 . . . . 43 E5
🏫 Charles Dickens Prim Sch,
SE1 . . . . 118 A2
🏫 Charles Edward Brooke
C of E Sec Girls' Sch,
Lwr Sch, SE5 . . . . . 169 E4
Upr Sch, SW9 . . . . . 169 F3
Charles Flemwell Ms,
E16 . . . . 101 D5
Charles Grinling Wk,
SE18 . . . . 132 C5
Charles La, NW8 . . . . . 33 D3
Charles Pl, NW1 . . . . . . 36 B5
Charles II St, SW1 . . . . 86 C4
Charles Sq, N1 . . . . 41 D5
Charles St, W1 . . . . 85 E4
Charleston St, SE17 . 146 B1
Charles Townsend Ho,
EC1 . . . . 61 E1
Charles Whincup Rd,
E16 . . . . 101 E4
Charleville Rd, W14 . 135 F3
Charlotte Despard Av,
SW11 . . . . 165 D4
Charlotte Ms, W1 . . . . 58 B3
W10 . . . . 78 C5
W14 . . . . 107 E5
Charlotte Pl, SW1 . . . 142 A1
W1 . . . . 58 B4
Charlotte Rd, EC2 . . . . 63 E1
🏫 Charlotte Sharman
Prim Sch, SE11 . . . 117 E4
Charlotte St, W1 . . . . . 58 B3
Charlotte Ter, N1 . . . . . 38 B1
Charlton Pl, N1 . . . . . . 39 E2
Charlton Rd, SE3 . . . . 181 E1
SE7 . . . . 181 E1
🏫 Charlton Sch,
SE10 . . . . 178 B2
Charlton Way, SE3 . . 179 E4
Charlwood Pl, SW1 . . 142 B1
Charlwood St, SW1 . . 142 B1
Charnwood Gdns,
E14 . . . . 125 D5
Charrington St, NW1 . 36 C2
★ Chartered Insurance
Institutes Mus, EC2
(Aldermanbury) 62 B5
★ Charterhouse, EC1 . 61 F3
Charterhouse Bldgs,
EC1 . . . . 61 F2
Charterhouse Ms,
EC1 . . . . 61 F3
Charterhouse Sq, EC1 . 61 F3
🏫 Charterhouse Sq Sch,
EC1 . . . . 62 A3
Charterhouse St, EC1 . 61 D4

Charteris Rd, NW6 . . . 30 B1
🏥 Charter Nightingale
Hosp, NW1 . . . . 55 F3
Chart St, N1 . . . . 41 D4
Chaseley St, E14 . . . . . 95 E1
Chatham Cl, SE18 . . . 133 F3
Chatham Pl, E9 . . . . . . 22 A1
Chatham St, SE17 . . . 118 C5
Chatsworth Ct, W8 . . 108 C5
Chatsworth Rd, NW2 . . 7 E2
Chaucer Dr, SE1 . . . . . 148 B1
Chaucer Ho, SW1 . . . 142 A3
Chauntler Cl, E16 . . . 101 F2
Cheapside, EC2 . . . . . . 90 B1
Chedworth Cl, E16 . . . 72 A5
Cheesemans Ter,
W14 . . . . 136 A3
Chelmsford Cl, E6 . . . 104 A1
W6 . . . . 135 D4
Chelmsford Sq,
NW10 . . . . 28 A1
CHELSEA, SW3 . . . . . . 138 C4
🏥 Chelsea & Westminster
Hosp, SW10 . . . . . 138 B5
★ Chelsea Antique Mkt,
SW3 . . . . 139 D4
Chelsea Br, SW1 . . . 141 E4
SW8 . . . . 141 E4
Chelsea Br Rd, SW1 . 140 C2
🎓 Chelsea Coll of Art &
Design, SW1 . . . . 143 E2
Chelsea Cres, SW10 . 162 B4
Chelsea Embk, SW3 . 139 F5
★ Chelsea FC, SW6 . . 161 E1
Chelsea Harbour,
SW10 . . . . 162 B4
Chelsea Harbour Dr,
SW10 . . . . 162 B3
🚢 Chelsea Harbour Pier .
162 . . . . C4
Chelsea Manor Ct,
SW3 . . . . 139 F4
Chelsea Manor Gdns,
SW3 . . . . 139 E4
Chelsea Manor St,
SW3 . . . . 139 E3
Chelsea Pk Gdns,
SW3 . . . . 138 C4
★ Chelsea Physic Gdn,
SW3 . . . . 140 A4
Chelsea Reach Twr,
SW10 . . . . 162 C1
Chelsea Sq, SW3 . . . . 139 D2
Chelsea Vista, SW6 . . 162 B4
Chelsea Wf, SW10 . . . 162 C2
Cheltenham Ter,
SW3 . . . . 140 B2
Chenies Ms, WC1 . . . . 58 C2
Chenies Pl, NW1 . . . . . 36 C2
Chenies St, WC1 . . . . . 58 C3
Cheniston Gdns, W8 . 109 E3
Chepstow Cres, W11 . . 80 C2
Chepstow Pl, W2 . . . . . 81 D2
Chepstow Rd, W2 . . . . 53 D5

Chepstow Vil, W11 . . .80 B2
Chequer St, EC1 . . . . . .62 B2
Cherbury Ct, N1 . . . . . .41 D3
Cherbury St, N1 . . . . . .41 D3
Sch Cherry Gdn Spec Sch,
   SE16 . . . . .121 D5
Cherry Gdn St, SE16 .121 E2
Cherry Tree Cl, E9 . . . .22 B5
Sch Cherry Trees Sch, The,
   E3 . . . . .47 D5
Cherry Tree Wk, EC1 . .62 B2
Cherrywood Cl, E3 . . . .45 F4
Cheryls Cl, SW6 . . . . .161 F3
Chesham Cl, SW1 . . .112 C4
Chesham Ms, SW1 . . .112 C3
Chesham Pl, SW1 . . .112 C4
Chesham St, SW1 . . .112 C4
Cheshire Cl, SE4 . . . . .176 A5
Cheshire Ct, EC4 . . . . .89 D1
Cheshire St, E2 . . . . . . .64 B1
Chesil Ct, E2 . . . . .43 F3
Chesilton Rd, SW6 . .160 A3
Chesney St, SW11 . . .164 C3
Chesson Rd, W14 . . .136 A4
Chester Cl, SW1 . . . . .113 D2
Chester Cl N, NW1 . . . .35 F4
Chester Cl S, NW1 . . . .35 F5
Chester Cotts, SW1 . .140 C1
Chester Ct, NW1 . . . . .35 F4
   SE5 . . . . .170 B2
Chesterfield Gdns,
   SE10 . . . . .178 C2
   W1 . . . . .85 E4
Chesterfield Hill, W1 . .85 E3
Chesterfield St, W1 . . .85 E4
Chesterfield Wk,
   SE10 . . . . .179 D3
Chesterfield Way,
   SE15 . . . . .174 A2
Chester Gate, NW1 . . .35 E5
Chester Ms, SW1 . . . .113 E3
Chester Pl, NW1 . . . . .35 E4
Chester Rd, E16 . . . . . .71 F1
   NW1 . . . . .35 D5
Chester Row, SW1 . . .140 C1
Chester Sq, SW1 . . . .113 E5
Chester Sq Ms, SW1 .113 E4
Chester St, E2 . . . . .65 D1
   SW1 . . . . .113 D3
Chester Ter, NW1 . . . .35 E4
Sch Chesterton Prim Sch,
   SW11 . . . . .164 C4
Chesterton Rd, W10 . .51 D4
Chesterton Sq, W8 . .108 B5
Chester Way, SE11 . .145 D1
Chestnut All, SW6 . . .136 B5
Chestnut Cl, SE14 . . .176 A4
Chestnut Ct, SW6 . . .136 B4
Chettle Cl, SE1 . . . . . .118 C3
Chetwood Wk, E6 . . . .75 F4
Cheval Pl, SW7 . . . . . .111 F3
Cheval St, E14 . . . . . .124 C3
Chevening Rd, NW6 . .29 E1
   SE10 . . . . .156 B3

Chevron Cl, E16 . . . . . .73 D5
Cheyne Ct, SW3 . . . . .140 A4
Cheyne Gdns, SW3 . .139 F4
Cheyne Ms, SW3 . . . .139 F4
Cheyne Pl, SW3 . . . . .140 A4
Cheyne Row, SW3 . . .139 E5
Cheyne Wk, SW3 . . . .139 F5
   SW10 . . . . .162 A5
Chicheley St, SE1 . . . .116 B1
Chichester Cl, E6 . . . .103 F1
Chichester Rents,
   WC2 . . . . .60 C5
Chichester Rd, NW6 . .30 C3
   W2 . . . . .53 F3
Chichester St, SW1 . .142 B3
Chichester Way,
   E14 . . . . .126 C5
Chicksand St, E1 . . . . .64 B4
Chiddingstone St,
   SW6 . . . . .161 D5
Chigwell Hill, E1 . . . . . .93 E3
Chilcot Cl, E14 . . . . . . .97 F1
Sch Childeric Prim Sch,
   SE14 . . . . .175 F2
Childeric Rd, SE14 . . .175 F2
Childerley St, SW6 . .159 E3
Childers St, SE8 . . . . .151 F4
Child La, SE10 . . . . . .128 B4
Child's Pl, SW5 . . . . . .137 D1
Child's St, SW5 . . . . . .137 D1
Child's Wk, SW5 . . . .137 D1
Chiltern Rd, E3 . . . . . . .69 D2
Chiltern St, W1 . . . . . . .56 C3
Chilton Gro, SE8 . . . . .151 D1
Chilton St, E2 . . . . .64 B1
Chilver St, SE10 . . . . .156 B2
Chilworth Ms, W2 . . . .82 B1
Chilworth St, W2 . . . . .82 B1
China Hall Ms, SE16 .122 B4
★ Chinatown,
   W1 (Gerrard St) 86 C2
Ching Ct, WC2 . . . . . . .87 E1
Chipka St, E14 . . . . . .126 A2
Chipley St, SE14 . . . .151 E5
Chippenham Gdns,
   NW6 . . . . .30 C5
Chippenham Ms, W9 .52 C2
Chippenham Rd, W9 . .52 C2
Chipstead St, SW6 . .161 D4
Sch Chisenhale Prim Sch,
   E3 . . . . .45 E2
Chisenhale Rd, E3 . . . .45 E2
Chisledon Wk, E9 . . . .24 B1
Chiswell Sq, SE3 . . . .181 F5
Chiswell St, EC1 . . . . .62 B3
   SE5 . . . . .171 D1
Chitty St, W1 . . . . .58 B3
Choppins Ct, E1 . . . . . .93 F4
Chopwell Cl, E15 . . . . .27 D4
Chrisp St, E14 . . . . . . .69 E4
Christchurch Av,
   NW6 . . . . .7 F3
Sch Christ Ch Bentinck C of E
   Prim Sch, NW1 . . . .55 F3

Sch Christchurch (Brixton)
   C of E Prim Sch,
   SW9 . . . . .169 D3
Sch Christ Ch Brondesbury
   C of E Prim Sch,
   NW6 . . . . .8 A4
Sch Christ Ch C of E
   Prim Sch, NW1 . . . .35 F4
   SE10 . . . . .155 F2
   SW3 . . . . .140 A4
Sch Christ Ch C of E Sch,
   E1 . . . . .64 B3
Christchurch Ct,
   NW6 . . . . .7 E3
Christ Ch Pas, EC1 . . . .61 F5
Christchurch Sq, E9 . . .44 A1
Christchurch St,
   SW3 . . . . .140 A4
Christchurch Ter,
   SW3 . . . . .140 A4
Christchurch Way,
   SE10 . . . . .155 F1
Christian Ct, SE16 . . . .96 A5
Christian St, E1 . . . . . .65 D5
Christie Rd, E9 . . . . . . .23 E2
Coll Christie's Ed, W1 . .57 F3
Christina St, EC2 . . . . .63 E1
Christopher Cl,
   SE16 . . . . .122 C1
Sch Christopher Hatton
   Prim Sch, EC1 . . . . .60 C2
Christopher Pl, NW1 . .37 D5
Christopher's Ms,
   W11 . . . . .79 F4
Christopher St, EC2 . . .63 D2
Sch Christ's Coll,
   SE3 . . . . .180 C1
Chryssell Rd, SW9 . . .169 D2
Chubworthy St,
   SE14 . . . . .151 E5
Chudleigh Rd, NW6 . . .6 B4
Chudleigh St, E1 . . . . .66 C5
Chumleigh St, SE5 . . .147 E4
Church Av, NW1 . . . . .13 F2
Church Cl, W8 . . . . . . .109 E1
Church Cres, E9 . . . . . .22 C3
Church Entry, EC4 . . . .89 F1
Churchfields, SE10 . .154 A5
Church Hill, SE18 . . . .132 B4
Churchill Gdns, SW1 .142 A3
Sch Churchill Gdns
   Prim Sch, SW1 . . .142 B3
Churchill Gdns Rd,
   SW1 . . . . .141 F3
★ Churchill Mus & Cabinet
   War Rooms, SW1 .115 D2
Churchill Pl, E14 . . . . .97 F4
Churchill Rd, E16 . . . . .74 B5
Church Pl, SW1 . . . . . .86 B3
Church Rd, N1 . . . . . . .18 B2

Church St, E15 . . . . 27 F5
  E16 . . . . 105 E5
  NW8 . . . . 55 D3
  W2 . . . . 55 D3
Church St Est, NW8 . . 55 D2
Church St N, E15 . . . . . 27 F5
Church St Pas, E15 . . . 27 F5
Church Ter, SW8 . . . . 167 D5
Churchway, NW1 . . . . 37 D4
Churchwell Path, E9 . . 22 A1
Churchyard Row,
  SE11 . . . . 117 F5
Church Yd Wk, W2 . . . 54 C3
Churton Pl, SW1 . . . . 142 B1
Churton St, SW1 . . . . 142 B1
Chusan Pl, E14 . . . . 96 B1
Cicely Rd, SE15 . . . . 173 D4
Cinnabar Wf, E1 . . . . . 93 D5
Cinnamon Cl, SE15 . . 172 A1
Cinnamon St, E1 . . . . . 93 F5
Circle, The, SE1 . . . . 120 A1
Circus Ms, W1 . . . . . . 56 A3
Circus Pl, EC2 . . . . 63 D4
Circus Rd, NW8 . . . . . . 32 C4
Circus Space, N1 . . . . 41 E5
Circus St, SE10 . . . . . 178 A2
Cirencester St, W2 . . . 53 E3
Citadel Pl, SE11 . . . . . 144 A2
City & Guilds of London
  Art Sch, SE11 . . . . 145 D3
City & Islington Coll,
  Cen for Applied Sciences,
  EC1 . . . . 39 E4
  Shepperton Arts Cen,
  N1 . . . . 18 C5
  Spring Ho, N7 . . . . . . 17 D1
  Willen Ho, EC1 . . . . . 40 B5
City & Islington 6th Form
  Coll, EC1 . . . . 39 E4
City Business Coll,
  EC1 . . . . 39 F5
City Coll, The, N1 . . 40 C4
City Cross Business Pk,
  SE10 . . . . 127 F5
City Forum, EC1 . . . . . 40 A4
City Gdn Row, N1 . . . . 39 F3
City Learning Cen,
  NW10 . . . . 28 C1
City Lit, Bolt Ct Cen,
  EC4 . . . . 89 D1
  Keeley Ho, WC2 . . . . 88 A1
  Stukeley St, WC2 . . . 59 F5
City Mill River Towpath,
  E15 . . . . 25 E3
City of London Acad,
  The, SE1 . . . . 149 D2
City of London Sch,
  EC4 . . . . 90 A2
City of London
  Sch for Girls, EC2 . . 62 B3

★ City of Westminster
  Archives Cen, SW1 115 D3
City of Westminster Coll,
  NW8 . . . . 55 E2
  Cosway St Cen,
  NW1 . . . . 55 F3
  Maida Vale Cen,
  W9 . . . . 31 E5
  Paddington Grn Cen,
  W2 . . . . 54 C3
  Queens Pk Cen,
  W9 . . . . 30 C5
City Pt, EC2 . . . . 62 C3
City Rd, EC1 . . . . 39 E3
City Thameslink . . . 89 E1
City Uni, Cass
  Business Sch, EC1 . . 62 C2
  College Bldg, EC1 . . 39 E5
  Drysdale Bldg,
  EC1 . . . . 39 E5
  Gloucester Bldg,
  EC1 . . . . 39 E5
  Halls of Res & Saddlers
  Sports Cen, EC1 . . . 62 A1
  Health Cen, EC1 . . . 39 F5
  Innovation Cen,
  EC1 . . . . 39 E5
  Social Sciences Bldg,
  EC1 . . . . 39 E5
  Tait Bldg, EC1 . . . . . 39 E5
  Uni Bldg, EC1 . . . . . . 39 E5
  Walmsley Bldg,
  EC1 . . . . 61 E1
  Walter Sickert Hall,
  N1 . . . . 40 A4
City Uni - Inns of Ct
  Sch of Law,
  Atkin Bldg, WC1 . . . 60 B3
  Gray's Inn Pl, WC1 . . 60 B4
  Princeton St, WC1 . 60 B3
City Uni -
  St.Bartholomew Sch of
  Nursing & Midwifery,
  E1 . . . . 65 F4
Civil Service Coll,
  SW1 . . . . 142 A1
Clabon Ms, SW1 . . . . 112 A4
Clack St, SE16 . . . . . . 122 B2
Claire Pl, E14 . . . . 125 D3
Clandon St, SE8 . . . . . 177 D5
Clanricarde Gdns, W2 . 81 D3
Clapham Rd, SW9 . . . 168 B3
Claps Gate La, E6 . . . . . 77 E1
Clara Grant Sch,
  E3 . . . . 69 D2
Clara Pl, SE18 . . . . 133 D5
Claredale St, E2 . . . . . 43 D3
Clare Gdns, W11 . . . . . 79 F1
Clare Ho, E3 . . . . 24 A5
Clare La, N1 . . . . 18 B4
Clare Mkt, WC2 . . . . . 88 A1
Clare Ms, SW6 . . . . . 161 E2
Claremont Cl, E16 . . . 105 D5
  N1 . . . . 39 D3

Claremont Rd, W9 . . . . 29 F3
Claremont Sq, N1 . . . . 38 C3
Claremont St, E16 . . . 105 D5
  SE10 . . . . 153 F3
Clarence Gdns, NW1 . . 35 F5
★ Clarence Ho,
  SW1 . . . . 114 B1
Clarence Ms, SE16 . . . . 94 C5
Clarence Rd, E16 . . . . . 71 F2
  NW6 . . . . 8 A4
  SE8 . . . . 153 E5
Clarence Ter, NW1 . . . . 56 B1
Clarence Wk, SW4 . . . 167 E5
Clarence Way, NW1 . . 13 E4
Clarence Way Est,
  NW1 . . . . 13 F3
Clarendon Cl, E9 . . . . . 22 B4
  W2 . . . . 83 E2
Clarendon Cross,
  W11 . . . . 79 F3
Clarendon Gdns, W9 . . 54 B2
Clarendon Gro, NW1 . . 36 C4
Clarendon Ms, W2 . . . . 83 E1
Clarendon Pl, W2 . . . . . 83 E2
Clarendon Rd, W11 . . . 79 E2
Clarendon St, SW1 . . 141 F3
Clarendon Ter, W9 . . . . 54 B1
Clarendon Wk, W11 . . 79 E1
Clare Rd, SE14 . . . . . . 176 A4
Clare St, E2 . . . . 43 F2
Clareville Gro, SW7 . . 138 B1
Clareville St, SW7 . . . 138 B1
Clarges Ms, W1 . . . . . . 85 E4
Clarges St, W1 . . . . 85 F4
Claribel Rd, SW9 . . . . 169 E5
Clarissa St, E8 . . . . 42 A1
Clarke's Ms, W1 . . . . . . 57 D3
Clarkson Rd, E16 . . . . . 72 A5
Clarkson Row, NW1 . . 36 A3
Clarkson St, E2 . . . . 43 E4
Clarks Pl, EC2 . . . . 63 E5
Clark St, E1 . . . . 65 F4
Claude St, E14 . . . . . . 124 C5
Clavell St, SE10 . . . . . 154 A4
Claverton St, SW1 . . . 142 B3
Clave St, E1 . . . . 94 A5
Claxton Gro, W6 . . . . 135 D3
Claybrook Rd, W6 . . . 135 D4
Claylands Pl, SW8 . . . 168 C1
Claylands Rd, SW8 . . 144 B5
Claypole Rd, E15 . . . . . 48 B2
Clay St, W1 . . . . 56 B4
Clayton Cl, E6 . . . . 76 B5
Clayton Cres, N1 . . . . . 37 F1
Clayton Dr, SE8 . . . . . 151 E2
Clayton Ms, SE10 . . . 178 C3
Clayton Rd, SE15 . . . . 173 D4
Clayton St, SE11 . . . . 144 C4
Clearbrook Way, E1 . . . 66 B5
Clearwater Ter,
  W11 . . . . 107 D1
Clearwell Dr, W9 . . . . . 53 E2
Cleaver Sq, SE11 . . . . 145 D2
Cleaver St, SE11 . . . . 145 D2

Clegg St, E1 .... 93 F4
Clem Attlee Ct, SW6 . 136 A5
Clemence St, E14..... 68 A4
Clement Cl, NW6 ...... 6 B4
Clements Av, E16 ... 100 C2
Clement's Inn, WC2... 88 B1
Clement's Inn Pas,
  WC2 .... 88 B1
Clements La, EC4..... 91 D2
Clements Rd, SE16 .. 121 D4
Clennam St, SE1 .... 118 B1
Clenston Ms, W1..... 56 A5
★ Cleopatra's Needle,
  WC2 .... 88 A4
Clephane Rd, N1 ..... 18 C2
Clere St, EC2......... 63 D1
CLERKENWELL, EC1 .. 61 E2
Clerkenwell Cl, EC1.. 61 D1
Clerkenwell Grn, EC1 . 61 D2
Sch Clerkenwell Parochial
  C of E Prim Sch,
  EC1 .... 38 C4
Clerkenwell Rd, EC1 .. 60 C2
Clermont Rd, E9 ..... 22 A5
Cleveland Gdns, W2 .. 82 A1
Cleveland Gro, E1 .... 66 A2
Cleveland Ms, W1 .... 58 A3
Cleveland Pl, SW1 .... 86 B4
Cleveland Rd, N1..... 19 D4
Cleveland Row, SW1.. 86 A5
Cleveland Sq, W2..... 82 A1
Cleveland St, W1 ..... 58 A2
Cleveland Ter, W2 .... 54 B5
Cleveland Way, E1.... 66 A2
Cleveley Cl, SE7 ..... 131 D5
Cleve Rd, NW6 .... 9 D3
Clichy Est, E1 .... 66 B4
Clifford Gdns,
  NW10.............. 28 A3
Clifford Rd, E16 ..... 72 A2
Clifford's Inn Pas,
  EC4 .... 88 C1
Clifford St, W1 .... 86 A3
Cliff Rd, NW1 .... 15 D1
Cliff Ter, SE8......... 177 D5
Cliff Vil, NW1 .... 15 D1
Cliff Wk, E6 .... 72 B3
Clifton Ct, NW8 ...... 54 C1
Clifton Cres, SE15 .. 173 F2
Clifton Est, SE15 .... 173 D4
Clifton Gdns, W9 ..... 54 A2
Clifton Gro, E8 ...... 20 C1
Clifton Hill, NW8 ..... 32 A1
Clifton Pl, SE16 ..... 122 B1
  W2 .... 83 D2
Clifton Ri, SE14 ..... 175 F2
Clifton Rd, E16....... 71 F3
  N1................ 18 B2
  W9 .... 54 B1
Clifton St, EC2 .... 63 E3
Clifton Vil, W9 .... 53 F3
Clifton Wk, E6 ...... 75 F5
Clifton Way, SE15 ... 174 A2
Clinch Ct, E16 .... 73 D4

Clinger Ct, N1........ 41 E1
★ Clink Prison Mus,
  SE1 .... 90 C4
Clink St, SE1......... 90 B4
Clinton Rd, E3 .... 45 E5
Clipper Cl, SE16 ..... 122 C1
Clipstone Ms, W1 .... 58 A2
Clipstone St, W1 ..... 57 F3
Clive Ct, W9 .... 54 B1
Cliveden Pl, SW1 .... 112 C5
Cloak La, EC4........ 90 B2
★ Clockmakers Company
  Collection, The,
  Guildhall Lib, EC2 .. 62 B5
Clock Twr Ms, N1..... 40 B1
Clock Twr Pl, N7...... 15 E1
Cloncurry St, SW6... 159 D5
Clonmel Rd, SW6 ... 160 B2
Cloth Ct, EC1 .... 61 F4
Cloth Fair, EC1....... 61 F4
Clothier St, E1 .... 63 F5
Cloth St, EC1 .... 62 A3
Cloudesley Pl, N1..... 38 C1
Cloudesley Rd, N1.... 16 C5
Cloudesley Sq, N1 ... 38 C1
Cloudesley St, N1 .... 39 D1
Clove Cres, E14 ..... 98 B2
Clovelly Way, E1...... 66 B5
Clover Ms, SW3 ..... 140 A4
Clove St, E13 .... 72 C2
Cloysters Grn, E1..... 92 C4
Club Row, E1 .... 64 A1
  E2 .... 64 A1
Clunbury St, N1 ...... 41 D3
Cluny Est, SE1 ...... 119 E3
Cluny Ms, SW5....... 136 C1
Cluny Pl, SE1 .... 119 E3
Cluse Ct, N1 .... 40 A2
Clutton St, E14 ...... 69 F4
Clydesdale Rd, W11 .. 52 B5
Clyde St, SE8 .... 152 B5
Clyston St, SW8..... 166 C5
Coach & Horses Yd,
  W1 .... 85 F2
Coach Ho Ms, SE14.. 174 C5
Coal Wf Rd, W12..... 78 C5
Coate St, E2......... 43 D3
Cobbett St, SW8 .... 168 A2
Cobble La, N1........ 17 E3
Cobb St, E1 .... 64 A4
Cobham Ms, NW1 .... 14 C3
Coborn Rd, E3 .... 46 A3
Coborn St, E3 .... 46 B4
Sch Cobourg Prim Sch,
  SE5 .... 148 A4
Cobourg Rd, SE5 .... 148 A4
Cobourg St, NW1..... 36 B5
Coburg Cl, SW1 ..... 114 B5
Cochrane Ms, NW8 ... 33 D3
Cochrane St, NW8.... 33 D3
Cockayne Way, SE8.. 151 F2
Cock Hill, E1......... 63 F4
Cock La, EC1......... 61 E4
Cockpit Steps, SW1.. 115 D2

Cockpit Yd, WC1 ..... 60 B3
Cockspur Ct, SW1 ... 87 D4
Cockspur St, SW1 ... 87 D4
Coda Cen, The, SW6 . 159 F2
Code St, E1 .... 64 B2
Codling Cl, E1........ 93 D4
Codrington Ms, W11.. 79 F1
Cody Rd, E16 .... 71 D2
Cody Rd Business Cen,
  E16............... 71 D2
Coin St, SE1 .... 88 C4
Coity Rd, NW5....... 13 D1
Coke St, E1 .... 64 C5
Colas Ms, NW6........ 9 D5
Colbeck Ms, SW7.... 137 F1
Colchester St, E1..... 64 B5
Coldbath Sq, EC1..... 60 C1
Coldbath St, SE13... 177 F5
Cold Blow La, SE14.. 151 D5
Cold Harbour, E14.... 98 B5
Coldharbour Pl, SE5 . 170 C5
Colebeck Ms, N1 ..... 17 F2
Colebert Av, E1 ...... 66 A1
Colebrooke Pl, N1 .... 39 F1
Colebrooke Row, N1 .. 39 E3
Colebrook Ho, E14.... 69 E5
Coleby Path, SE5 .... 171 D2
Colegrove Rd, SE15 .. 148 B5
Coleherne Ct, SW5 .. 137 F3
Coleherne Ms, SW10 137 E3
Coleherne Rd, SW10. 137 E3
Colehill Gdns, SW6 .. 159 E4
Colehill La, SW6 ..... 159 E4
Coleman Flds, N1 .... 18 B5
Coleman Rd, SE5 .... 171 E1
Coleman St, EC2 ..... 62 C5
Coleraine Rd, SE3 ... 156 A5
Coleridge Gdns, NW6 . 10 A4
  SW10 .... 161 F1
Coleridge Ho, SW1 .. 142 A3
Coleridge Sq, SW10. 162 A1
Colestown St, SW11. 163 F5
Cole St, SE1 .... 118 B2
Colet Gdns, W14.... 135 D2
Coley St, WC1........ 60 B2
★ Coliseum, The,
  WC2 .... 87 E3
Collard Pl, NW1 ..... 13 E3
College App, SE10... 154 B5
College Cres, NW3.... 10 C2
College Cross, N1..... 17 D4
College Gro, NW1 .... 36 C1
College Hill, EC4 ..... 90 B2
College Ms, SW1 .... 115 E3
★ College of Arms,
  EC4 .... 89 F2
Coll College of Law, The,
  WC1 .... 58 C3
Coll College of N W London,
  Kilburn Cen, NW6 ... 8 C5

Sch College Pk Sch, W2. 81 E1
College Pl, NW1 ..... 36 B1
SW10 .... 162 A1
College Rd, NW10 .... 28 A3
College St, EC4 ...... 90 B2
College Ter, E3 ...... 46 A4
Collent St, E9 .... 22 B2
Collett Rd, SE16 .... 121 D4
Collier Cl, E6 .... 105 E2
Collier St, N1 .... 38 A3
Collingham Gdns,
  SW5 .... 137 F1
H Collingham Gdns Hosp,
  SW5 .... 137 F1
Collingham Pl, SW5 . 137 E1
Collingham Rd, SW5. 109 F5
Sch Collingham Sch,
  SW5 .... 137 F1
Collington St, SE10.. 155 D3
Collingwood St, E1 ... 65 F1
Collinson St, SE1 .... 118 A3
Collinson Wk, SE1 ... 118 A2
Collin's Yd, N1 .... 39 E1
Colls Rd, SE15 ...... 174 A3
Collyer Pl, SE15 ..... 172 C4
Colman Rd, E16 ...... 74 A4
Colmar Cl, E1 .... 66 C1
Colmore Ms, SE15 ... 173 F4
Colnbrook St, SE1 ... 117 E4
Colombo St, SE1 ..... 89 E5
Colomb St, SE10 .... 155 F3
Colonnade, WC1 ..... 59 E4
Colonnades, The, W2. 53 F5
Colonnade Wk, SW1 . 141 E1
Columbia Pt, SE16 .. 122 B3
Sch Columbia Prim Sch,
  E2 .... 42 B4
Columbia Rd, E2 ..... 42 A4
E13 .... 72 B3
Columbine Av, E6 .... 75 E4
Columbus Ctyd, E14 . 96 C4
Colville Est, N1 ...... 41 E1
Colville Gdns, W11 .. 80 B1
Colville Hos, W11 .... 52 A5
Colville Ms, W11 ..... 80 B1
Colville Pl, W1 .... 58 B4
Sch Colville Prim Sch,
  W11 .... 80 B1
Colville Rd, W11 ..... 80 B1
Colville Sq, W11 ..... 80 A1
Colville Ter, W11 ..... 80 A1
Colwith Rd, W6 ..... 134 B5
Colworth Gro, SE17 . 146 B1
Colyer Cl, N1 .... 38 A2
Combe, The, NW1 .... 35 F5
Combe Av, SE3 ...... 180 B1
Combedale Rd,
  SE10 .... 156 C2
Combe Ms, SE3 ..... 180 A1
Comber Gro, SE5 .... 170 A3

Sch Comber Gro Prim Sch,
  SE5 .... 170 A2
Comeragh Ms, W14 . 135 F2
Comeragh Rd, W14.. 135 E3
Comet Pl, SE8 ...... 176 C2
Comet St, SE8 ...... 176 C2
Comfort St, SE15 ... 147 E5
Commercial Rd, E1 ... 64 C5
E14 .... 95 F1
Commercial St, E1.... 64 A2
Commercial Way,
  SE15 .... 172 A2
Commerell St, SE10 . 155 F2
Commodity Quay, E1 . 92 B3
Commodore St, E1 ... 67 E2
Common, The, E15 ... 27 F1
Coll Community Coll Hackney,
  London Flds, E8... 21 F4
  Shoreditch Campus,
  N1 .... 41 F4
Coll Community Ed Lewisham,
  Mornington Cen,
  SE8 .... 176 B2
Compayne Gdns,
  NW6 .... 9 E3
Compton Av, N1 ..... 17 E2
Compton Cl, E3 ..... 69 D3
NW1 .... 35 F5
Compton Pas, EC1... 61 F1
Compton Pl, WC1 .... 59 E1
Compton Rd, N1 ..... 17 F2
NW10 .... 28 C5
Compton St, EC1 .... 61 E1
Compton Ter, N1..... 17 E2
Comus Pl, SE17 ..... 147 E1
Comyns Cl, E16 ..... 72 A3
Conant Ms, E1 .... 92 C2
Concert Hall App,
  SE1 .... 88 B5
Concorde Dr, E6..... 76 A3
Concorde Way,
  SE16 .... 150 C1
Condell Rd, SW8 ... 166 B4
Conder St, E14...... 67 E5
Condray Pl, SW11 .. 163 E2
Conduit Av, SE10 ... 179 D3
Conduit Ct, WC2 .... 87 E2
Conduit Ms, W2..... 82 C1
Conduit Pas, W2 .... 82 C1
Conduit Pl, W2...... 82 C1
Conduit St, W1 ..... 85 F2
Coney Way, SW8 ... 144 B5
★ Conference Forum, The,
  E1 .... 64 C5
Congreve St, SE17... 119 E5
Congreve Wk, E16... 74 C4
Coniger Rd, SW6 ... 160 C5
Conington Rd, SE13 . 177 F5
Conistone Way, N7... 15 F3
Coniston Ho, SE5 ... 170 A1
Conlan St, W10 ..... 51 E1
Conley St, SE10 .... 155 F2
Connaught Br, E16.. 102 C5
Connaught Cl, W2... 83 E1

Sch Connaught Ho Sch,
  W2 .... 84 A1
Connaught Pl, W2... 84 A2
Connaught Rd, E16.. 103 D4
Connaught Rbt, E16. 102 C2
Connaught Sq, W2 ... 84 A1
Connaught St, W2... 83 E1
Connor St, E9........ 22 C5
Consort Rd, SE15 ... 173 E5
Cons St, SE1........ 117 D1
Constable Av, E16... 101 E4
Constance St, E16... 103 E5
Constitution Hill,
  SW1 .... 113 E1
Content St, SE17.... 146 B1
Convent Gdns, W11 .. 79 F1
Sch Convent of Jesus & Mary
  RC Inf Sch, NW2 .... 6 A2
Conway Ms, W1...... 58 A2
Conway St, E13 ...... 72 C2
W1 .... 58 A2
Conybeare, NW3 ..... 11 F3
Conyer St, E3 .... 45 E3
Cookham Cres,
  SE16 .... 122 C1
Cook's Rd, E15....... 47 E2
Cooks Rd, SE17 ..... 145 E4
Coolfin Rd, E16 ..... 101 E1
Coomassie Rd, W9 ... 52 A1
Coombs St, N1 ...... 39 F3
Coomer Ms, SW6... 136 B5
Coomer Pl, SW6.... 136 B5
Coomer Rd, SW6... 136 B5
Cooper Cl, SE1 ..... 117 D2
Coopers Cl, E1 ...... 66 A2
Coopers La, NW1.... 37 D2
Coopers Rd, SE1 ... 148 B3
Cooper's Row, EC3 ... 92 A2
Cooper St, E16...... 72 B4
Coopers Yd, N1 ..... 17 E3
Copeland Dr, E14 ... 125 D5
Copenhagen Pl, E14 .. 96 A1
Sch Copenhagen Prim Sch,
  N1 .... 38 A1
Copenhagen St, N1... 37 F1
Cope Pl, W8 .... 108 C4
Cope St, SE16....... 122 C5
Copford Wk, N1 ..... 18 A5
Copley Cl, SE17 ..... 145 F5
Copley St, E1 .... 66 C4
Copperas St, SE8 ... 153 E5
Copperfield Rd, E3 ... 67 F3
Copperfield St, SE1 .. 117 F1
Copper Row, SE1..... 92 A5
Copse Cl, SE7 ...... 157 F5
Copthall Av, EC2 ..... 63 D5
Copthall Bldgs, EC2... 62 C5
Copthall Cl, EC2..... 62 C5
Copthall Ct, EC2 ..... 62 C5
Coptic St, WC1....... 59 E4
Coral St, SE1 ...... 117 D2
Coram St, WC1....... 59 D2
Corbden Cl, SE15.... 172 B3
Corbet Ct, EC3 .... 91 D1

Corbet Pl, E1. . . . . **64** A3
Corbetts La, SE16 . . . **150** A1
Corbetts Pas, SE16 . . . **150** A1
Corbidge Ct, SE8 . . . . . . **153** E4
Corbiere Ho, N1. . . . . . . **19** E5
Corbridge Cres, E2. . . . . **43** E2
Corby Way, E3 . . . . **68** C2
Cordelia St, E14. . . . . . **69** E5
Cording St, E14 . . . . . . **69** F4
Ⓤ Cordwainers at London
  Coll of Fashion,
  EC1. . . . . **62** A2
Cord Way, E14. . . . . . . **125** D3
Corfield St, E2 . . . . . . **43** F5
Coriander Av, E14. . . . . **98** C1
Cork Sq, E1 . . . . **93** E4
Cork St, W1 . . . . **86** A3
Cork St Ms, W1 . . . . . . **86** A3
Corlett St, NW1. . . . . . . **55** E3
Cormont Rd, SE5. . . . . **169** E4
Cornelia St, N7. . . . . . . **16** B2
Corner Ho St, WC2 . . . **87** E4
Cornhill, EC3 . . . . **91** D1
Cornish Ho, SE17 . . . **145** E5
Cornwall Av, E2 . . . . . . **44** A5
Cornwall Cres, W11 . . . **79** E2
Cornwall Gdns, SW7 . **109** F4
Cornwall Gdns Wk,
  SW7. . . . . **109** F4
Cornwall Ms S, SW7 . **110** A4
Cornwall Ms W,
  SW7 . . . . **109** F4
Cornwall Rd, SE1. . . . . **88** C4
Cornwall Sq, SE11. . . **145** E2
Cornwall St, E1 . . . . . . **93** F2
Cornwall Ter, NW1 . . . **56** B2
Cornwall Ter Ms,
  NW1. . . . . **56** B2
Cornwood Dr, E1. . . . . **66** A5
Coronet St, N1. . . . . . . **41** E5
Corporation Row,
  EC1. . . . . **61** D1
Corporation St, E15 . . **49** F3
Corsham St, N1 . . . . . . **41** D5
Corsica St, N5 . . . . **17** E1
Cortayne Rd, SW6. . . . **160** B5
Corunna Rd, SW8 . . . **166** B3
Corunna Ter, SW8. . . . **166** A3
Corvette Sq, SE10 . . . **155** D4
Coryton Path, W9 . . . . **52** B1
Cosmo Pl, WC1. . . . . . . **59** F3
Cossall Wk, SE15. . . . **173** E5
Cosser St, SE1 . . . . . . **116** C3
Cosway St, NW1 . . . . . **55** F3
Cotall St, E14. . . . . **69** D4
Cotham St, SE17. . . . . **146** B1
Cotleigh Rd, NW6 . . . . . **8** C3
Cotswold Ct, EC1. . . . . **62** A1
Cotswold Ms, SW11 . **163** D4
Cottage Grn, SE5. . . . **171** D1
Cottage Pl, SW3. . . . . **111** E3
Cottage St, E14 . . . . . . **97** F2
Cottesbrook St,
  SE14. . . . . **175** E1

Cottesloe Ms, SE1 . . . **117** D3
Cottesmore Gdns,
  W8. . . . . **109** F3
Cottingham Rd,
  SW8 . . . . **144** B5
Cottington St,
  SE11. . . . . **145** D2
Cottle Way, SE16. . . . **121** F2
Cottons Gdns, E2. . . . . **41** F4
Cottons La, SE1 . . . . . . **91** D4
Cotton St, E14 . . . . **98** A2
Cottrill Gdns, E8 . . . . . **21** E1
Coulson St, SW3 . . . . **140** A2
Councillor St, SE5 . . . **170** A2
Counter St, SE1 . . . . . . **91** E5
County Gro, SE5 . . . . **170** A3
★ County Hall, SE1 . **116** A1
County Rd, E6 . . . . **77** E4
County St, SE1. . . . . . . **118** B4
Courland Gro, SW8 . . **167** D4
Courland Gro Hall,
  SW8 . . . . **167** D5
Courland St, SW8 . . . **167** D4
★ Courtauld Inst of Art,
  WC2 . . . . **88** A2
★ Court Dress Collection,
  Kensington Palace,
  W8 . . . . **81** F5
Courtenay Sq, SE11 . . **144** C3
Courtenay St, SE11. . **144** C2
Courtfield Gdns,
  SW5 . . . . **109** F5
Courtfield Ms, SW5. . **138** A1
Courtfield Rd, SW7 . . **137** F1
Court Gdns, N7 . . . . . . **17** D2
Courtnell St, W2 . . . . **52** C5
Court St, E1 . . . . **65** E3
Courtyard, The, N1 . . **16** B3
Cousin La, EC4 . . . . **90** C3
Couthurst Rd, SE3. . . **157** F5
Covelees Wall, E6 . . . **77** D5
★ Covent Garden,
  WC2 . . . . **87** F2
⊖ Covent Garden . . . **87** E2
Coventry Cl, E6 . . . . . **104** A1
  NW6 . . . . **31** D1
Coventry Rd, E1. . . . . . **65** F1
  E2. . . . . **65** F1
Coventry St, W1 . . . . . **86** C3
Coverdale Rd, NW2 . . . . **7** D3
Coverley Cl, E1. . . . . . . **65** D3
Cowan Cl, E6 . . . . **75** F4
Cowcross St, EC1. . . . . **61** E3
Cowdenbeath Path,
  N1. . . . . **16** A5
Cow Leaze, E6 . . . . **77** D5
Cowley Rd, SW9 . . . . **169** D4
Cowley St, SW1 . . . . . **115** E3
Cowling Cl, W11 . . . . . **79** E3
Cowper St, EC2 . . . . . . **63** D1
Cowper Ter, W10. . . . . **50** C4
Cowthorpe Rd, SW8 . **167** D3
Coxson Way, SE1. . . . **120** A2
Crabtree Cl, E2. . . . . . . **42** A2

Crabtree La, SW6 . . . **158** C1
Craddock St, NW5 . . . . **12** C2
★ Crafts Council, N1 . **39** D3
Craigerne Rd, SE3 . . . **181** E1
Craigs Ct, SW1 . . . . **87** E4
Craik Ct, NW6 . . . . **30** B3
Crail Row, SE17. . . . . **147** D1
Cramer St, W1 . . . . **57** D4
Cramond Cl, W6 . . . . **135** E5
Ⓢ Crampton Prim Sch,
  SE17. . . . . **145** F2
Crampton St, SE17 . . **146** A1
Cranberry La, E16 . . . . **71** E2
Cranbourne Pas,
  SE16. . . . . **121** E2
Cranbourn St, WC2 . . **87** D2
Cranbrook Rd, SE8 . . **177** D4
Cranbrook St, E2 . . . . . **45** D3
Cranbury Rd, SW6. . . **161** F5
Crane Ct, EC4 . . . . **89** D1
Crane Gro, N7 . . . . **17** D1
Crane St, SE10 . . . . . . **154** C3
  SE15. . . . . **172** A3
Cranfield Row, SE1 . . **117** D3
Cranford St, E1. . . . . . . **95** D2
Cranhurst Rd, NW2. . . . **6** B1
Cranleigh St, NW1. . . . **36** B3
Cranley Gdns, SW7 . . **138** B2
Cranley Ms, SW7 . . . . **138** B2
Cranley Pl, SW7. . . . . **138** C1
Cranley Rd, E13. . . . . . **73** E3
Cranmer Ct, SW3. . . . **139** F1
Cranmer Rd, SW9 . . . **169** D1
Cranston Est, N1 . . . . . **41** D3
Cranswick Rd, SE16 . **149** F2
Cranwell Cl, E3. . . . . . . **69** E2
Cranwood St, EC1. . . . **40** C5
Cranworth Gdns,
  SW9 . . . . **168** C4
Craven Hill, W2 . . . . . . **82** B2
Craven Hill Gdns, W2 . **82** A2
Craven Hill Ms, W2 . . **82** B2
Craven Pas, WC2 . . . . . **87** E4
Craven Rd, W2. . . . . . . **82** B2
Craven St, WC2 . . . . . . **87** E4
Craven Ter, W2 . . . . . . **82** B2
Crawford Est, SE5 . . . **170** B5
Crawford Ms, W1. . . . . **56** A4
Crawford Pas, EC1. . . . **60** C2
Crawford Pl, W1. . . . . . **55** F5
Ⓢ Crawford Prim Sch,
  SE5. . . . . **170** B4
Crawford Rd, SE5 . . . **170** B4
Crawford St, W1 . . . . . **56** A4
Crawshay Ct, SW9. . . **169** D3
Crayford Cl, E6. . . . . . . **75** E5
Creasy Est, SE1 . . . . . **119** E4
Crediton Rd, E16 . . . . . **73** D5
  NW10. . . . . **28** C1
Credon Rd, SE16 . . . . **149** F2

Creechurch La, EC3 . . 91 F1
Creechurch Pl, EC3 . . 91 F1
Creed La, EC4 . . . . 89 C1
Creek Rd, SE8. . . . . . . 152 C5
  SE10. . . . . 152 C5
Creekside, SE8 . . . . . . 177 E2
Crefeld Cl, W6 . . . . . . 135 D5
Creighton Rd, NW6 . . . 29 D2
Cremer St, E2 . . . . 42 A3
Cremorne Est,
  SW10 . . . . 162 C1
Cremorne Rd, SW10. 162 B2
Crescent, EC3 . . . . 92 A2
Crescent Arc, SW10 . . 162 C1
Crescent Pl, SW3 . . . . 111 E5
Crescent Row, EC1 . . . 62 A2
Crescent St, N1 . . . . . . 16 B3
Cresford Rd, SW6 . . . 161 E4
Cresset Rd, E9 . . . . . . 22 B2
Cresswell Gdns,
  SW5 . . . . 138 A2
Cresswell Pl, SW10 . . 138 A2
Cressy Ct, E1 . . . . 66 B3
Cressy Pl, E1 . . . . 66 B3
Crestfield St, WC1 . . . 37 F4
Creswick Wk, E3 . . . . . 46 C5
Creton St, SE18 . . . . . 133 D4
Crewdson Rd, SW9 . . 168 C2
Crews St, E14 . . . . 124 C5
Crichton St, SW8 . . . . 166 A5
Cricketers Ct, SE11 . . 145 E1
Crimscott St, SE1 . . . 119 F4
Crimsworth Rd,
  SW8 . . . . 167 D3
Crinan St, N1 . . . . 37 F2
Cringle St, SW8 . . . . . 166 A1
Cripplegate St, EC2 . . . 62 A3
Crispin St, E1 . . . . 64 A4
Crisp Rd, W6 . . . . 134 A3
Cristowe Rd, SW6 . . . 160 B5
Crofters Way, NW1 . . . 14 C5
Crofton Rd, E13. . . . . . 73 E1
  SE5 . . . . 171 F4
Crofts St, E1 . . . . 92 C3
Croft St, SE8. . . . . 151 E1
Crogsland Rd, NW1 . . . 12 C3
Cromer St, WC1 . . . . . . 37 F5
Crompton St, W2 . . . . . 54 C2
Cromwell Cres,
  SW5 . . . . 108 C5
Cromwell Gdns,
  SW7 . . . . 111 D4
Cromwell Gro, W6. . . 106 B3
🏥 Cromwell Hosp, The,
  SW5 . . . . 109 E5
Cromwell Ms, SW7 . . 111 D5
Cromwell Pl, SW7 . . . 111 D5
Cromwell Rd, SW5 . . 109 D5
  SW7 . . . . 110 C5
  SW9 . . . . 169 E3

Cromwell Twr, EC2 . . . 62 B3
Crondace Rd, SW6 . . 161 D4
Crondall Ct, N1 . . . . . . 41 E3
Crondall St, N1. . . . . . . 41 D3
Cronin St, SE15 . . . . . 172 A2
Crooke Rd, SE8 . . . . . 151 E2
Crookham Rd, SW6. . 160 A4
Croombs Rd, E16. . . . . 74 A4
Crooms Hill, SE10 . . . 178 B1
Crooms Hill Gro,
  SE10. . . . . 178 B1
Cropley Ct, N1 . . . . 40 C2
Cropley St, N1 . . . . 40 C2
Cropthorne Ct, W9 . . . 32 B5
Crosby Ct, SE1 . . . . . . 118 C1
Crosby Row, SE1 . . . . 118 C2
Crosby Sq, EC3 . . . . . . 91 E1
Crosby Wk, E8 . . . . 20 A2
Cross Av, SE10 . . . . . . 155 D5
Cross Cl, SE15 . . . . . . 173 E5
Crossfield Rd, NW3 . . . 11 D2
Crossfield St, SE8 . . . 176 C1
🚇 Crossharbour & London
  Arena 125 F3
Cross Keys Cl, W1 . . . 57 D4
Cross Keys Sq, EC1 . . 62 A4
Cross La, EC3 . . . . 91 E3
Crosslet St, SE17 . . . . 119 D5
Crosslet Vale, SE10 . . 177 E4
Crossley St, N7 . . . . . . 16 C1
Crossmount Ho,
  SE5 . . . . 170 A1
Cross Rd, SE5 . . . . 171 F5
Cross St, N1 . . . . 17 E5
Crosswall, EC3 . . . . 92 A2
Croston St, E8 . . . . 21 D5
Crowder St, E1. . . . . . . 93 E2
Crowhurst Cl, SW9 . . 169 D5
Crowland Ter, N1. . . . . 18 C3
Crown Cl, E3. . . . . 24 C5
  NW6 . . . . 9 E1
Crown Ct, EC2 . . . . 90 B1
  WC2 . . . . 87 F1
Crowndale Rd, NW1 . . 36 A2
Crown Office Row,
  EC4 . . . . 88 C2
Crown Pas, SW1 . . . . . 86 B5
Crown Pl, EC2. . . . . 63 E3
  NW5 . . . . 13 F1
  SE16. . . . . 149 F3
Crown Reach, SW1 . . 143 D3
Crown St, SE5 . . . . 170 B1
Crown Wks, E2. . . . . . . 43 E3
Crows Rd, E15 . . . . 49 D4
Crowthorne Rd, W10 . 78 C1
Croxley Rd, W9 . . . . . . 30 B5
Croydon Rd, E13 . . . . . 72 B2
Crucifix La, SE1 . . . . . 119 E1
Cruden Ho, SE17 . . . . 145 E5
Cruden St, N1. . . . . 39 F1
Cruikshank St, WC1 . . 38 C4
🏫 Crusoe Ho Spec Sch,
  N1. . . . . 40 C4
Crutched Friars, EC3. . 91 F2

Crystal Wf, N1 . . . . 39 F3
Cuba St, E14 . . . . 124 C1
Cubitt Steps, E14. . . . . 97 D4
Cubitt St, WC1 . . . . 38 A5
Cubitts Yd, WC2. . . . . . 87 F2
CUBITT TOWN, E14 . . 126 B3
🏫 Cubitt Town
  Jun & Inf Sch, E14 . 126 B4
Cudworth St, E1 . . . . . 65 F1
Cuff Pt, E2. . . . . 42 A4
Culford Gdns, SW3 . . 140 B1
Culford Gro, N1 . . . . . . 19 E2
Culford Ms, N1. . . . . . . 19 E1
Culford Rd, N1 . . . . 19 E3
Culling Rd, SE16 . . . . 122 A3
Culloden Cl, SE16 . . . 149 D3
🏫 Culloden Prim Sch,
  E14. . . . . 98 B1
Culloden St, E14 . . . . . 70 B5
Cullum St, EC3 . . . . 91 E2
Culmore Rd, SE15 . . . 173 F2
Culross St, W1 . . . . 84 C3
Culvert Rd, SW11 . . . 164 B4
Culworth St, NW8. . . . 33 E3
Cumberland Cl, E8. . . . 20 A2
Cumberland Cres,
  W14 . . . . 107 F5
Cumberland Gdns,
  WC1 . . . . 38 B4
Cumberland Gate,
  W1 . . . . 84 A2
Cumberland Mkt,
  NW1 . . . . 35 F4
Cumberland Mkt Est,
  NW1 . . . . 35 F4
Cumberland Mills Sq,
  E14 . . . . 154 C2
Cumberland Pl, NW1 . 35 E4
Cumberland Rd, E13. . 73 E3
🏫 Cumberland Sch,
  E13 . . . . 74 A1
Cumberland St,
  SW1 . . . . 141 F2
Cumberland Ter,
  NW1 . . . . 35 E3
Cumberland Ter Ms,
  NW1 . . . . 35 E3
★ Cuming Mus,
  SE17. . . . . 146 A1
Cumming St, N1 . . . . . 38 A3
Cunard Pl, EC3 . . . . 91 F1
Cunard Wk, SE16. . . . 123 D5
Cundy Rd, E16 . . . . . . 102 A1
Cundy St, SW1. . . . . . 141 D1
Cundy St Est, SW1. . . 141 D1
Cunningham Pl, NW8 . 54 C1
Cupar Rd, SW11 . . . . 165 D3
Cureton St, SW1 . . . . 143 D1
Curlew St, SE1 . . . . . . 120 A1
Curnock Est, NW1 . . . . 36 A1
Cursitor St, EC4 . . . . . . 60 C5
Curtain Rd, EC2 . . . . . . 63 E2
Curtis St, SE1 . . . . 120 A5
Curtis Way, SE1 . . . . . 120 A5

Curzon Gate, W1 . . . . . **85** D5
Curzon Sq, W1 . . . . **85** D5
Curzon St, W1 . . . . **85** D5
CUSTOM HOUSE, E16 . **75** D5
⇌ Custom House . . . **101** F2
🚈 Custom House
   for ExCeL **101** F2
Custom Ho Reach,
   SE16 . . . . **124** A2
Custom Ho Wk, EC3 . . **91** E3
Cut, The, SE1 . . . . . . **117** D1
Cuthbert St, W2 . . . . . **54** C3
Cuthill Wk, SE5 . . . . . **170** C4
Cutlers Gdns, E1 . . . . **63** F5
Cutlers Sq, E14 . . . . . **153** D1
Cutlers Ter, N1 . . . . . . **19** E1
Cutler St, E1 . . . . **63** F5
★ Cutty Sark, SE10 . **154** A4
🚈 Cutty Sark for Maritime
   Greenwich **154** A5
Cutty Sark Gdns,
   SE10 . . . . **154** B4
Cyclops Ms, E14 . . . . **124** C5
Cygnet St, E1 . . . . **64** B1
Cynthia St, N1 . . . . . . **38** B3
Cyntra Pl, E8 . . . . **21** F4
Cypress Pl, W1 . . . . . . **58** B2
🚈 Cyprus **105** D2
Cyprus Pl, E2 . . . . . . **44** B3
   E6 . . . . **105** D2
Cyprus Rbt, E16 . . . . . **104** C2
Cyprus St, E2 . . . . **44** A3
🏫 Cyril Jackson Prim Sch,
   E14 . . . . **96** B2
   Annexe, E14 . . . . . . **96** B3
Cyril Mans, SW11 . . . **164** B4
Cyrus St, EC1 . . . . **61** F1
Czar St, SE8 . . . . **152** C4

D

Dabin Cres, SE10 . . . . **178** A3
Dacca St, SE8 . . . . . . **152** B4
Dace Rd, E3 . . . . **24** C4
Dacre St, SW1 . . . . . . **114** C3
Dagmar Gdns,
   NW10 . . . . **28** C3
Dagmar Pas, N1 . . . . . . **17** F5
Dagmar Rd, SE5 . . . . **171** E4
Dagmar Ter, N1 . . . . . . **17** F5
Dagnall St, SW11 . . . **164** B5
Daintry Way, E9 . . . . . . **24** A1
Dairy Fm Pl, SE15 . . . **174** A4
Daisy Rd, E16 . . . . **71** E1
Dakota Gdns, E6 . . . . . **75** F2
Dalby St, NW5 . . . . **13** E2
Daleham Ms, NW3 . . . **11** D1
Dalehead, NW1 . . . . . . **36** A3
Dalemain Ms, E16 . . . **101** D4
Dale Rd, SE17 . . . . . . **145** F5
Dale Row, W11 . . . . . . **79** F1
Daley St, E9 . . . . **23** D1

Dalgarno Gdns, W10 . . **50** A3
Dalgarno Way, W10 . . **50** A2
Dalgleish St, E14 . . . . . **95** F1
Daling Way, E3 . . . . **45** F1
🏫 Dallington Sch,
   EC1 . . . . **61** F1
Dallington St, EC1 . . . **61** F1
DALSTON, E8 . . . . **20** C3
⇌ Dalston Kingsland . **19** F1
Dalston La, E8 . . . . **20** A1
Dalwood St, SE5 . . . . **171** E3
Damask Cres, E16 . . . . **71** F1
Damer Ter, SW10 . . . **162** B2
Dame St, N1 . . . . **40** A2
Damien St, E1 . . . . **65** F5
Danbury St, N1 . . . . . . **39** F2
Dancer Rd, SW6 . . . . **160** A4
Dandridge Cl, SE10 . . **156** B2
Danehurst St, SW6 . . **159** E3
Dane Pl, E3 . . . . **46** A2
Danesdale Rd, E9 . . . . **23** F2
Danesfield, SE5 . . . . . **147** E4
Dane St, WC1 . . . . **60** A4
Daneville Rd, SE5 . . . **170** C4
Daniel Bolt Cl, E14 . . . **69** F3
Daniel Gdns, SE15 . . . **172** A1
Dan Leno Wk, SW6 . . **161** E2
Dansey Pl, W1 . . . . **86** C2
Dante Pl, SE11 . . . . . . **117** F5
Dante Rd, SE11 . . . . . **117** E5
Danube St, SW3 . . . . **139** F2
Danvers St, SW3 . . . . **139** D5
Daplyn St, E1 . . . . **64** C3
D'Arblay St, W1 . . . . . . **86** B1
Darfield Way, W10 . . . **78** C2
Darlan Rd, SW6 . . . . . **160** B2
Darling Row, E1 . . . . . . **65** F2
Darnaway Pl, E14 . . . . **70** B4
Darnley Ho, E14 . . . . . **67** F5
Darnley Rd, E9 . . . . **21** F2
Darnley Ter, W11 . . . . . **79** D4
Darsley Dr, SW8 . . . . **167** D3
Dartford St, SE17 . . . **146** B4
Dartmoor Wk, E14 . . . **125** D5
Dartmouth Cl, W11 . . **52** B5
Dartmouth Gro,
   SE10 . . . . **178** B4
Dartmouth Hill,
   SE10 . . . . **178** B4
Dartmouth Rd, E16 . . . **72** C5
   NW2 . . . . **6** C1
Dartmouth Row,
   SE10 . . . . **178** B5
Dartmouth St, SW1 . **114** C2
Dartmouth Ter,
   SE10 . . . . **178** C4
Dart St, W10 . . . . **29** F4
Darwin St, SE17 . . . . **119** D5
Datchelor Pl, SE5 . . . **171** D4
Date St, SE17 . . . . . . **146** C3
Daubeney Twr, SE8 . . **152** A1
Davenant St, E1 . . . . . **65** D4
Daventry St, NW1 . . . **55** E3
Davern Cl, SE10 . . . . . **156** A1

Davey Cl, N7 . . . . **16** B2
Davey Rd, E9 . . . . **24** C3
Davey St, SE15 . . . . . **148** B5
Davidge St, SE1 . . . . . **117** E2
David Lee Pt, E15 . . . . **49** F1
David Ms, W1 . . . . **56** B3
Davidson Gdns,
   SW8 . . . . **167** E2
David St, E15 . . . . **27** D1
🎓 Davies Laing & Dick
   Indep Coll, W1 . . . **57** D5
Davies Ms, W1 . . . . . . **85** E2
Davies St, W1 . . . . **85** E2
Dawes Ho, SE17 . . . . **147** D1
Dawes Rd, SW6 . . . . . **159** E1
Dawes St, SE17 . . . . . **147** D2
Dawlish Rd, NW2 . . . . . . **7** D1
Dawn Cres, E15 . . . . . . **27** D5
Dawson Pl, W2 . . . . **80** C2
Dawson St, E2 . . . . **42** B3
Dayton Gro, SE15 . . . **174** A3
Deacon Ms, N1 . . . . . . **19** D4
Deacon Way, SE17 . . **118** A5
Deal Porters Way,
   SE16 . . . . **122** B3
Deals Gateway,
   SE10 . . . . **177** D3
Deal St, E1 . . . . **64** C3
Deal Wk, SW9 . . . . . . **168** C2
Dean Bradley St,
   SW1 . . . . **115** E4
Dean Cl, SE16 . . . . **95** D5
Deancross St, E1 . . . . **94** A1
Deanery Ms, W1 . . . . . **85** D4
Deanery Rd, E15 . . . . . **27** E2
Deanery St, W1 . . . . . . **85** D4
Dean Farrar St, SW1 . **114** C3
Dean Rd, NW2 . . . . **6** A2
Dean Ryle St, SW1 . . **115** E5
Deans Bldgs, SE17 . . **146** C1
Deans Ct, EC4 . . . . **89** F1
Deans Ms, W1 . . . . **57** F5
Dean Stanley St,
   SW1 . . . . **115** E4
Dean St, W1 . . . . **58** C5
Dean's Yd, SW1 . . . . . **115** D3
Dean Trench St,
   SW1 . . . . **115** E4
Deason St, E15 . . . . . . **48** B1
De Beauvoir Cres, N1 . **19** E5
De Beauvoir Est, N1 . . **19** D5
🏫 De Beauvoir Prim Sch,
   N1 . . . . **19** F2
De Beauvoir Rd, N1 . . **19** E3
De Beauvoir Sq, N1 . . **19** F4
DE BEAUVOIR TOWN,
   N1 . . . . **19** D5
Debnams Rd, SE16 . . **150** A1
Decima St, SE1 . . . . . **119** E3
Deck Cl, SE16 . . . . . . **123** D1

De Crespigny Pk,
SE5 . . . . 170 C5
Deeley Rd, SW8 . . . . . 166 C3
Deerhurst Rd, NW2 . . . . 7 D2
Dee St, E14 . . . . 70 B5
Defiance Wk, SE18 . . 132 A4
Defoe Cl, SE16 . . . . . . 124 A2
Defoe Ho, EC2 . . . . 62 B3
Delacourt Rd, SE3 . . . 181 E2
Delafield Ho, E1 . . . . . . 93 D1
Delafield Rd, SE7 . . . 157 F2
Delaford Rd, SE16 . . . 149 F2
Delaford St, SW6 . . . . 159 F1
Delamere Ter, W2 . . . . 53 F3
Delancey Pas, NW1 . . . 35 F1
Delancey St, NW1 . . . . 35 E1
De Laune St, SE17 . . . 145 E3
Delaware Rd, W9 . . . . . 53 E1
Delhi St, N1 . . . . 37 F1
Delius Gro, E15 . . . . . . 48 C2
Dell Cl, E15 . . . . 27 D5
Dellow St, E1 . . . . 93 F2
Dell's Ms, SW1 . . . . . . 142 B1
Delme Cres, SE3 . . . . 181 F5
Deloraine St, SE8 . . . 176 C4
Delorme St, W6 . . . . . 134 C5
Delta St, E2 . . . . 42 C4
Delverton Rd, SE17 . . 145 F3
Delvino Rd, SW6 . . . . 160 C4
Denbigh Cl, W11 . . . . . 80 B2
Denbigh Ms, SW1 . . . 142 A1
Denbigh Pl, SW1 . . . . 142 A2
Denbigh Rd, W11 . . . . 80 B2
Denbigh St, SW1 . . . . 142 A1
Denbigh Ter, W11 . . . . 80 B2
Denford St, SE10 . . . . 156 A2
Dengie Wk, N1 . . . . . . 18 A5
Denham St, SE10 . . . 156 C2
Denholme Rd, W9 . . . . 30 B4
Denman Rd, SE15 . . . 172 A4
Denman St, W1 . . . . . . 86 C3
Denmark Gro, N1 . . . . 38 C2
Denmark Hill, SE5 . . . 170 C4
Denmark Pl, WC2 . . . . 59 D5
Denmark Rd, NW6 . . . 30 B3
SE5 . . . . 170 A4
Denmark St, E13 . . . . . 73 E3
WC2 . . . . 87 D1
Denne Ter, E8 . . . . 42 B1
Dennetts Gro, SE14 . 174 C5
Dennetts Rd, SE14 . . 174 B4
Denning Cl, NW8 . . . . 32 B4
Denning Pt, E1 . . . . . . 64 A5
Dennington Pk Rd,
NW6 . . . . 9 D1
Dennison Pt, E15 . . . . 26 B4
Denny Cl, E6 . . . . 75 E4
Denny Cres, SE11 . . . 145 D1
Denny St, SE11 . . . . . 145 D2
Densham Rd, E15 . . . . 27 F5

Denyer St, SW3 . . . . . 139 F1
★ Department for
Environment, Food &
Rural Affairs (D.E.F.R.A.),
SW1 . . . . 87 E4
★ Department for Transport
(D.f.T.), SW1 . . . . . 115 D3
★ Department of Health &
Dept for Work & Pensions
(D.W.P.), SW1 . . . . . 115 E1
Depot Rd, W12 . . . . . . 78 B2
DEPTFORD, SE8 . . . . 152 B3
⇌ Deptford 176 C1
⊞ Deptford Bridge . . 177 D3
Deptford Br, SE8 . . . 177 D3
Deptford Bdy, SE8 . . 176 C3
Deptford Ch St, SE8 . 177 D3
Deptford Ferry Rd,
E14 . . . . 153 D1
Deptford Grn, SE8 . . 153 D5
⊞ Deptford Grn Sch,
SE14 . . . . 176 A1
Annexe, SE14 . . . 175 F1
Deptford High St,
SE8 . . . . 152 C5
⊞ Deptford Pk Prim Sch,
SE8 . . . . 151 F2
Deptford Strand,
SE8 . . . . 152 B1
Deptford Wf, SE8 . . . 124 A5
De Quincey Ms,
E16 . . . . 101 D4
Derby Gate, SW1 . . . 115 E1
Derby Rd, E9 . . . . 22 C5
Derbyshire St, E2 . . . . 43 D5
Derby St, W1 . . . . 85 D5
Dereham Pl, EC2 . . . . 41 F5
Dericote St, E8 . . . . . . 21 D5
Derifall Cl, E6 . . . . 76 B3
Dering St, W1 . . . . 85 E1
Derrick Gdns, SE7 . . 130 A5
Derry St, W8 . . . . 109 E2
Derwent St, SE10 . . . 155 E2
Desborough Cl, W2 . . 53 F3
Desborough St, W2 . . 53 E3
Desford Ms, E16 . . . . . 71 F2
Desford Rd, E16 . . . . . 71 F2
★ Design Mus, SE1 . . 92 B5
Desmond St, SE14 . . 151 F5
Devalls Cl, E6 . . . . . . 105 D2
Devas St, E3 . . . . 69 F1
De Vere Gdns, W8 . . . 110 A2
Deverell St, SE1 . . . . 118 C4
De Vere Ms, W8 . . . . . 110 A3
Devereux Ct, WC2 . . . 88 C1
Devizes St, N1 . . . . . . 41 D1
Devonia Rd, N1 . . . . . 39 F2
Devonport St, E1 . . . . 94 C1
Devons Est, E3 . . . . . . 47 F5
Devonshire Cl, W1 . . . 57 E3
Devonshire Dr,
SE10 . . . . 177 E2
Devonshire Gro,
SE15 . . . . 149 F5

⊞ Devonshire Hosp,
W1 . . . . 57 D3
Devonshire Ms N, W1 . 57 E3
Devonshire Ms S, W1 . 57 E3
Devonshire Ms W, W1 57 E2
Devonshire Pl, W1 . . . 57 D2
W8 . . . . 109 E4
Devonshire Pl Ms, W1 . 57 D2
Devonshire Rd, E16 . . . 73 F5
Devonshire Row, EC2 . 63 F4
Devonshire Row Ms,
W1 . . . . 57 F2
Devonshire Sq, EC2 . . 63 F5
Devonshire St, W1 . . . 57 D3
Devonshire Ter, W2 . . 82 B1
⊞ Devons Road 69 E1
Devons Rd, E3 . . . . . . 69 D3
Devon St, SE15 . . . . . 149 F5
De Walden St, W1 . . . 57 D4
Dewberry Gdns, E6 . . . 75 E3
Dewberry St, E14 . . . . 70 A4
Dewey Rd, N1 . . . . 38 C2
Dewhurst Rd, W14 . . 106 C3
Dewsbury Ter, NW1 . . 13 F5
D'Eynsford Rd, SE5 . . 170 C3
Diadem Ct, W1 . . . . . . 86 C1
Dial Wk, The, W8 . . . . 109 F1
Diamond St, SE15 . . . 171 F2
Diamond Ter, SE10 . . 178 B3
Diamond Way, SE8 . . 176 C1
Diana Cl, SE8 . . . . 152 B4
★ Diana Princess of Wales
Mem, W2 . . . . 83 D5
Dibden St, N1 . . . . 17 F5
Dibdin Ho, W9 . . . . . . 31 E2
Dickens Est, SE1 . . . . 120 C2
SE16 . . . . 120 C2
Dickens Ho, NW6 . . . . 30 C4
★ Dickens Ho Mus,
WC1 . . . . 60 B2
Dickens Sq, SE1 . . . . 118 B3
Dickens St, SW8 . . . . 165 F5
Dieppe Cl, W14 . . . . . 136 B2
Digby St, E2 . . . . 44 B5
Diggon St, E1 . . . . 66 C4
Dighton Ct, SE5 . . . . . 146 A5
Dignum St, N1 . . . . . . 38 C2
Digswell St, N7 . . . . . . 17 D1
Dilke St, SW3 . . . . 140 B4
Dilston Gro, SE16 . . . 122 A5
Dimson Cres, E3 . . . . . 68 C1
Dingle Gdns, E14 . . . . 97 D3
Dingley Pl, EC1 . . . . . . 40 B5
Dingley Rd, EC1 . . . . . 40 A5
Dinmont St, E2 . . . . . . 43 E2
Dinsdale Rd, SE3 . . . . 156 A4
Disbrowe Rd, W6 . . . 135 E5
Discovery Wk, E1 . . . . 93 E3
Disney Pl, SE1 . . . . . . 118 B1
Disney St, SE1 . . . . . . 118 B1
Diss St, E2 . . . . 42 A4
Distaff La, EC4 . . . . . . 90 A2
Distillery La, W6 . . . . 134 B3
Distillery Rd, W6 . . . . 134 B3

Distin St, SE11	144	C1
Ditch All, SE10	177	F4
Ditchburn St, E14	98	B3
Dixon Clark Ct, N1	17	E2
Dixon Cl, E6	76	B5
Dixon Ho, W10	78	C1
Dixon Rd, SE14	175	F3
Dixon's All, SE16	121	E2
Dobson Cl, NW6	10	C4
Doby Ct, EC4	90	B2
Dockers Tanner Rd,		
E14	124	C4
Dockhead, SE1	120	B2
Dock Hill Av, SE16	123	D1
Dockland St, E16	104	C5
Dockley Rd, SE16	120	C4
Dock Rd, E16	100	B3
Dockside Rd, E16	102	C3
Dock St, E1	92	C2
Dockyard Ind Est,		
SE18	131	F4
★ Doctor Johnson's Ho,		
EC4	89	D1
Docwra's Bldgs, N1	19	E1
Doddington Gro,		
SE17	145	E4
Doddington Pl,		
SE17	145	E4
Dodson St, SE1	117	D2
Dod St, E14	68	C5
Doherty Rd, E13	73	D1
Dolben St, SE1	89	E5
Dolland St, SE11	144	B3
Dolphin Cl, SE16	122	C1
Dolphin La, E14	97	E3
Dolphin Sq, SW1	142	B3
Dolphin Twr, SE8	152	B5
Dombey St, WC1	60	A3
★ Dome, The, SE10	99	E5
Domingo St, EC1	62	A1
Dominion St, EC2	63	D3
★ Dominion Thea,		
W1	59	D5
Donaldson Rd, NW6	30	B1
Donato Dr, SE15	147	E5
Doneraile St, SW6	159	D5
Dongola Rd, E1	67	E3
Donne Pl, SW3	111	F5
Don Phelan Cl, SE5	171	D3
Doon St, SE1	88	C5
Doran Wk, E15	26	B4
Dora St, E14	68	A5
Doria Rd, SW6	160	B5
Doric Way, NW1	36	C4
Dorking Cl, SE8	152	A4
Dorman Way, NW8	10	C5
Dornberg Cl, SE3	181	D1
Dornberg Rd, SE3	181	E1
Dorncliffe Rd, SW6	159	F5
Dorney, NW3	11	F3
Dorrington Pt, E3	47	E4
Dorrington St, EC1	60	C3
Dorrit St, SE1	118	B1

Dorset Bldgs, EC4	89	E1
Dorset Cl, NW1	56	A3
Dorset Est, E2	42	B4
Dorset Ms, SW1	113	E3
Dorset Pl, E15	26	C1
Dorset Ri, EC4	89	E1
Dorset Rd, SW8	167	F1
Dorset Sq, NW1	56	A2
Dorset St, W1	56	B4
Dorton Cl, SE15	171	F2
Doughty Ms, WC1	60	A2
Doughty St, WC1	60	A1
Douglas Path, E14	154	B2
Douglas Rd, E16	73	D4
N1	18	A3
NW6	8	A5
Douglas St, SW1	142	C1
Douglas Way, SE8	176	B2
Doulton Ms, NW6	9	F1
Douro Pl, W8	109	F3
Douro St, E3	46	C2
Douthwaite Sq, E1	93	D4
Dove App, E6	75	E4
Dove Ct, EC2	90	C1
Dovehouse St, SW3	139	E2
Dove Ms, SW5	138	A1
Dovercourt Est, N1	19	D2
Dove Rd, N1	18	C1
Dove Row, E2	42	C1
Dover St, W1	85	F3
Dover Yd, W1	86	A4
Doves Yd, N1	39	D1
Dovet Ct, SW8	168	A3
Doveton St, E1	66	A1
Dove Wk, SW1	140	C2
Dowgate Hill, EC4	90	C2
Dowland St, W10	29	F4
Dowlas Est, SE5	171	E1
Dowlas St, SE5	171	E1
Downfield Cl, W9	53	E2
Downham Rd, N1	18	C4
Downings, E6	77	D5
Downing St, SW1	115	E1
Down St, W1	85	E5
Down St Ms, W1	85	E5
Downtown Rd,		
SE16	123	F1
Dowrey St, N1	16	C5
Doyce St, SE1	118	A1
D'Oyley St, SW1	112	C5
Draco St, SE17	146	A4
Dragon Rd, SE15	147	E5
Dragoon Rd, SE8	152	A3
Drake Cl, SE16	123	D1
Drake Ct, W12	106	A2
Drakes Ctyd, NW6	8	B3
Drake St, WC1	60	A4
🅂🅒🅗 Drama Cen London,		
NW5	12	C2
Draper Ho, SE1	117	F5
Drappers Way,		
SE16	121	D5
Drawdock Rd, SE10	99	D5
Draycott Av, SW3	111	F5

Draycott Cl, SE5	170	C2
Draycott Ms, SW6	160	B5
Draycott Pl, SW3	140	A1
Draycott Ter, SW3	112	B5
Drayford Cl, W9	52	B1
Drayson Ms, W8	109	D2
Drayton Gdns,		
SW10	138	B2
🅂🅒🅗 Drew Prim Sch,		
E16	103	E5
Drew Rd, E16	103	E5
Driffield Rd, E3	45	F2
Drive, The, SW6	159	F5
Droop St, W10	51	E1
Drovers Pl, SE15	173	F1
Druid St, SE1	119	F1
Drummond Cres,		
NW1	36	C4
Drummond Gate,		
SW1	143	D2
Drummond Rd,		
SE16	121	E3
Drummond St,		
NW1	58	A1
Drum St, E1	64	B5
Drury La, WC2	87	F1
Dryden Ct, SE11	145	D1
Dryden St, WC2	87	F1
Dryfield Wk, SE8	152	C4
Drysdale Pl, N1	41	F4
Drysdale St, N1	41	F5
Dublin Av, E8	21	D5
Ducal St, E2	42	B5
Du Cane Cl, W12	78	A1
Duchess Ms, W1	57	F4
Duchess of Bedford's		
Wk, W8	108	C2
Duchess St, W1	57	F4
Duchy St, SE1	89	D4
Duckett St, E1	67	E3
Duck La, W1	86	C1
Dudley Rd, NW6	30	A2
Dudley St, W2	54	C4
Dudmaston Ms,		
SW3	139	D2
Duffell Ho, SE11	144	B2
Dufferin Av, EC1	62	C2
Dufferin St, EC1	62	B2
Duff St, E14	97	E1
Dufour's Pl, W1	86	B1
Dugard Way, SE11	117	E5
Duke Humphrey Rd,		
SE3	179	F3
Duke of Wellington Av,		
SE18	133	F4
Duke of Wellington Pl,		
SW1	113	D1
Duke of York Sq,		
SW3	140	B1

Duke of York St,
SW1 . . . . 86 B4
Duke Shore Pl, E14 . . . 96 A3
Duke Shore Wf, E14 . . 96 A3
Dukes La, W8 . . . . 109 D1
Duke's Ms, W1 . . . . 57 D5
Dukes Pl, EC3 . . . . 91 F1
Duke's Rd, WC1 . . . . . . 37 D5
Duke St, SW1 . . . . 86 B4
W1 . . . . 57 D5
Duke St Hill, SE1 . . . . . 91 D4
Duke's Yd, W1 . . . . 85 D2
Dulford St, W11 . . . . . . 79 E2
Dumpton Pl, NW1 . . . 12 C4
Dunbridge St, E2 . . . . . 65 D1
Duncannon St, WC2 . . 87 E3
Duncan Rd, E8 . . . . 21 E5
Duncan St, N1 . . . . 39 E2
Duncan Ter, N1 . . . . . . 39 E3
Dunch St, E1 . . . . 93 F1
Dundas Rd, SE15 . . . . 174 A5
Dundee Ho, W9 . . . . . 32 A4
Dundee St, E1 . . . . 93 E5
Dundonald Cl, E6 . . . . . 75 F5
Dundonald Rd,
NW10 . . . . 28 C1
Dunelm St, E1 . . . . 66 C5
Dunloe St, E2 . . . . 42 A3
Dunlop Pl, SE16 . . . . . 120 B4
Dunmore Pt, E2 . . . . . . 42 A5
Dunmore Rd, NW6 . . . 29 E1
Dunmow Wk, N1 . . . . . 18 A5
Dunnage Cres, SE16 . 123 F5
Dunnock Rd, E6 . . . . . 75 F5
Dunns Pas, WC1 . . . . . 59 F5
Dunraven St, W1 . . . . . 84 B2
Dunsany Rd, W14 . . . 106 C4
Dunstable Ms, W1 . . . . 57 D3
Dunster Ct, EC3 . . . . . . 91 E2
Dunster Gdns, NW6 . . . . 8 B3
Dunsterville Way,
SE1 . . . . 119 D2
Dunston Rd, E8 . . . . . . 42 A1
Dunston St, E8 . . . . 20 A5
Dunton Rd, SE1 . . . . . 148 A2
Dunworth Ms, W11 . . 52 A5
Duplex Ride, SW1 . . . 112 B2
Dupree Rd, SE7 . . . . . 157 E2
Durand Gdns, SW9 . . 168 B3
[Sch] Durand Prim Sch,
SW9 . . . . 168 B3
Cowley Rd Annexe,
SW9 . . . . 169 D4
Durands Wk, SE16 . . 123 F1
Durant St, E2 . . . . 42 C4
Durban Rd, E15 . . . . . . 49 E4
Durfey Pl, SE5 . . . . . . 171 D1
Durham Ho St, WC2 . . 87 F3
Durham Pl, SW3 . . . . 140 A3
Durham Rd, E16 . . . . . 71 F2

Durham Row, E1 . . . . . 67 D4
Durham St, SE11 . . . . 144 A3
Durham Ter, W2 . . . . . 53 E5
Durham Yd, E2 . . . . 43 E4
Durnford St, SE10 . . . 154 B5
Durrell Rd, SW6 . . . . . 160 A5
Durrington Twr,
SW8 . . . . 166 B5
Durward St, E1 . . . . . . 65 E3
Durweston Ms, W1 . . . 56 B3
Durweston St, W1 . . . . 56 B3
Dutton St, SE10 . . . . . 178 A3
Dwight Ct, SW6 . . . . . 159 F5
Dye Ho La, E3 . . . . 47 D1
Dyer's Bldgs, EC1 . . . . 60 C4
Dyne Rd, NW6 . . . . 7 F4
Dynham Rd, NW6 . . . . . 8 C3
Dyott St, WC1 . . . . 59 E5
Dysart St, EC2 . . . . 63 E2

E

Eagle Cl, SE16 . . . . . . 150 A3
Eagle Ct, EC1 . . . . 61 E3
Eagle Ms, N1 . . . . 19 E2
Eagle Pl, SW1 . . . . 86 B3
SW7 . . . . 138 B2
Eagle St, WC1 . . . . 60 A4
Eagle Wf Rd, N1 . . . . . . 40 B2
Eamont St, NW8 . . . . . 33 E2
Eardley Cres, SW5 . . . 137 D3
Earlham St, WC2 . . . . . 87 D1
EARLS COURT, SW5 . 136 B2
⊖ Earls Court 137 D1
★ Earls Court Exhib Cen,
SW5 . . . . 136 C2
Earls Ct Gdns, SW5 . . 137 E1
Earls Ct Rd, SW5 . . . . 109 D5
W8 . . . . 109 D5
Earls Ct Sq, SW5 . . . . 137 E2
Earlsferry Way, N1 . . . 15 F4
Earlsmead Rd, NW10 . 28 A4
Earls Ter, W8 . . . . 108 B4
Earlstoke St, EC1 . . . . . 39 E4
Earlston Gro, E9 . . . . . . 43 F1
Earl St, EC2 . . . . 63 E3
Earls Wk, W8 . . . . 108 C4
Earlswood St, SE10 . . 155 F3
Early Ms, NW1 . . . . 13 F5
Earnshaw St, WC2 . . . 59 D5
Earsby St, W14 . . . . . 107 F5
Easley's Ms, W1 . . . . . . 57 D5
East Arbour St, E1 . . . . 66 C5
Eastbourne Ms, W2 . . . 54 B5
Eastbourne Rd, E15 . . 49 F1
Eastbourne Ter, W2 . . . 54 B5
Eastbrook Rd, SE3 . . . 181 F2
Eastbury Rd, E6 . . . . . . 76 C2
Eastbury Ter, E1 . . . . . . 66 C2
Eastcastle St, W1 . . . . 58 A5
Eastcheap, EC3 . . . . . . 91 D2
Eastcombe Av, SE7 . . 157 E4

East Cross Cen, E15 . . . 25 D2
East Cross Route, E3 . . 24 B3
E9 . . . . 23 F2
Eastern Gateway,
E16 . . . . 102 B3
East Ferry Rd, E14 . . . 125 F5
Eastfield St, E14 . . . . . 67 F4
East Ham Ind Est,
E6 . . . . 75 E2
East Ham Manor Way,
E6 . . . . 76 C5
East Harding St, EC4 . . 61 D5
[DLR] East India 99 D2
East India Dock Rd,
E14 . . . . 96 B1
East La, SE16 . . . . 120 C2
[Sch] Eastlea Comm Sch,
E16 . . . . 71 F1
Eastlea Ms, E16 . . . . . . 71 F2
[H] Eastman Dental Hosp,
WC1 . . . . 38 A5
Eastmoor Pl, SE7 . . . . 130 C4
Eastmoor St, SE7 . . . . 130 C4
East Mt St, E1 . . . . 65 F3
Eastney St, SE10 . . . . 154 C3
Easton St, WC1 . . . . . . 38 C5
East Parkside, SE10 . 128 A2
East Pas, EC1 . . . . 61 F3
East Pier, E1 . . . . 93 E5
East Pt, SE1 . . . . 148 C2
East Poultry Av, EC1 . . 61 E4
East Rd, N1 . . . . 40 C5
East Row, W10 . . . . 51 E2
East Smithfield, E1 . . . 92 B3
East St, SE17 . . . . 146 B2
East Surrey Gro,
SE15 . . . . 172 A2
East Tenter St, E1 . . . . 92 B1
Eastway, E9 . . . . 24 A1
Eaton Cl, SW1 . . . . . . 140 C1
Eaton Gate, SW1 . . . . 112 C5
Eaton La, SW1 . . . . . . 113 F4
Eaton Ms N, SW1 . . . . 112 C5
Eaton Ms S, SW1 . . . . 113 D5
Eaton Ms W, SW1 . . . . 113 D5
Eaton Pl, SW1 . . . . . . 112 C4
Eaton Row, SW1 . . . . 113 E4
Eaton Sq, SW1 . . . . . . 113 E3
Eaton Ter, SW1 . . . . . 112 C5
Eaton Ter Ms, SW1 . . 112 C5
Ebbisham Dr, SW8 . . 144 A4
Ebenezer Ho, SE11 . . 145 D1
Ebenezer St, N1 . . . . . . 40 C4
Ebley Cl, SE15 . . . . . . 148 A5
Ebor St, E1 . . . . 64 A1
Ebury Br, SW1 . . . . . . 141 E2
Ebury Br Est, SW1 . . . 141 E2
Ebury Br Rd, SW1 . . . 141 D3
Ebury Ms, SW1 . . . . . 113 D5
Ebury Ms E, SW1 . . . . 113 E5
Ebury Sq, SW1 . . . . . . 141 D1
Ebury St, SW1 . . . . . . 113 E5
Ecclesbourne Rd, N1 . . 18 B4
Eccleston Br, SW1 . . . 113 F5

★ Place of interest ⇌ Railway station [H] Hospital ⊖ London Underground station

Eccleston Ms, SW1 ..113 D4
Eccleston Pl, SW1 ...113 E5
Eccleston Sq, SW1...141 F1
Eccleston Sq Ms,
  SW1 ....142 A1
Eccleston St, SW1....113 E4
Eckford St, N1 ....38 C2
Eclipse Rd, E13 ......73 E3
Sch Ecole Française de
  Londres, W6 .....107 D5
Edbrooke Rd, W9.....52 C1
Eddiscombe Rd,
  SW6 ....160 B5
Eddystone Twr, SE8 .151 F1
Edenbridge Cl, SE16 .149 F3
Edenbridge Rd, E9....23 D4
Eden Cl, W8 ....109 D3
Edenham Way, W10 ..52 A3
Edgarley Ter, SW6...159 E4
Edgar Rd, E3.........47 F4
Edge St, W8 ....81 D4
✚ Edgware Road.....55 E4
Edgware Rd, W2 .....55 F5
Edinburgh Cl, E2 .....44 A3
Edinburgh Gate,
  SW1 ....112 A1
Edinburgh Ho, W9....31 F4
Edison Ct, SE10 .....128 B5
Edis St, NW1........12 C5
Edith Gro, SW10 ....138 A5
Sch Edith Neville Prim Sch,
  NW1 ....36 C3
Edith Rd, W14 ....135 E1
Edith Row, SW6 ....161 F3
Edith St, E2.........42 C2
Edith Summerskill Ho,
  SW6 ....136 B5
Edith Ter, SW10.....162 A1
Edith Vil, W14 ....136 A1
Edith Yd, SW10 .....162 B1
Edmeston Cl, E9 .....23 F1
Edmund Halley Way,
  SE10 ....127 E2
Edmund Hurst Dr, E6 .77 E4
Edmund St, SE5.....170 C1
Sch Edmund Waller Prim Sch,
  SE14 ....174 C5
Edna St, SW11......163 E4
Edrich Ho, SW4 .....167 F4
Edric Rd, SE14 ......174 C1
Sch Education Support Cen,
  The, SE15 ....174 B4
Edward Ct, E16 ......72 C3
Edwardes Pl, W8 ....108 B4
Edwardes Sq, W8 ...108 C3
Edward Ms, NW1.....35 F3
Edward Pl, SE8......152 B5
Edwards Cotts, N1 ...17 E2
Edwards Ms, N1......17 D3
  W1 ....84 C1
Edward Sq, N1 ....38 A1
  SE16 ....95 F4
Edward St, E16 ......72 C2
  SE8 ....176 A1

SE14 ....175 F1
Sch Edward Wilson Prim Sch,
  W2 ....53 E3
Edwin St, E1.........66 B1
  E16 ....72 C4
Eel Brook Cl, SW6 ...161 E3
Eel Brook Studios,
  SW6 ....161 D2
Effie Pl, SW6........161 D2
Effie Rd, SW6 ....161 D2
Egbert St, NW1 ......12 C5
Egeremont Rd, SE13 .177 F5
Egerton Cres, SW3 ..111 F5
Egerton Dr, SE10....177 E3
Egerton Gdns, NW10 .28 A1
  SW3 ....111 E4
Egerton Gdns Ms,
  SW3 ....111 F4
Egerton Pl, SW3.....111 F4
Egerton Ter, SW3 ...111 F4
Egham Rd, E13 ......73 F3
Eglington Ct, SE17 ..146 A4
Eglon Ms, NW1 ......12 B4
Egmont St, SE14.....175 D2
Egremont Ho, SE13..177 F5
Eisenhower Dr, E6....75 D4
Elam St, SE5........169 F5
Elba Pl, SE17 ....118 B5
Elbe St, SW6........162 A5
Elcho St, SW11 .....163 E2
Elcot Av, SE15 ......173 E1
Elderflower Way,
  E15 ....27 E3
Elder St, E1..........64 A3
Elder Wk, N1 ....17 F5
Eldon Rd, W8.......109 F4
Eldon St, EC2 ....63 D4
Eleanor Cl, SE16 ....122 C1
Eleanor Rd, E8 ......21 E2
Eleanor St, E3........46 C5
Electra Business Pk,
  E16 ....71 D3
Elektron Ho, E14 .....99 D2
⇌ Elephant & Castle. 118 A5
✚ Elephant & Castle. 118 A5
Elephant & Castle,
  SE1 ....117 F4
Elephant La, SE16...122 A1
Elephant Rd, SE17 ..118 A5
Elf Row, E1 ....94 B2
Elgar Cl, SE8........176 C2
Elgar St, SE16......123 F3
Elgin Av, W9........31 E5
Elgin Cres, W11 .....80 A1
Elgin Ms, W11 ....79 F1
Elgin Ms N, W9.......31 F4
Elgin Ms S, W9 ....31 F4
Elgood Cl, W11......79 E3
Elia Ms, N1 ....39 E3
Elias Pl, SW8 ....144 C5
Elia St, N1 ....39 E3
Elim Est, SE1 ....119 E3
Eliot Ms, NW8 ....32 B3

Elizabeth Av, N1 .....18 B5
Elizabeth Br, SW1 ...141 E1
Elizabeth Cl, E14 .....97 E1
  W9 ....54 B1
Elizabeth Ct, SW1 ...115 D4
Elizabeth Est, SE17..146 C4
Elizabeth Fry Rd, E8 ..21 F4
Sch Elizabeth Garrett
  Anderson Sec Sch,
  N1 ....38 B2
Elizabeth Ms, NW3 ...11 F2
Sch Elizabeth Selby Inf Sch,
  E2 ....43 D4
Elizabeth Sq, SE16....95 E3
Elizabeth St, SW1 ...113 D5
Elkington Pt, SE11 ...144 C1
Elkington Rd, E13 ....73 E2
Elkstone Rd, W10 ....52 A3
Ellaline Rd, W6 .....134 C5
Ellen St, E1 ....93 D1
Sch Ellen Wilkinson Jun &
  Inf Sch, E6 ....74 C3
Ellerby St, SW6 .....159 D4
Ellesmere Rd, E3 .....45 E2
Ellesmere St, E14.....69 E5
Ellingfort Rd, E8 .....21 F3
Ellington St, N7 ......16 C2
Elliot Cl, E15.........27 E4
Elliott Rd, SW9 .....169 E2
Elliott's Pl, N1 ....39 F1
Elliott Sq, NW3 ......11 F3
Elliotts Row, SE11...117 E5
Ellison Ho, SE13 ....178 A5
Ellis St, SW1........112 B5
Ellsworth St, E2......43 E4
Ellwood Ct, W9 ......53 E2
Elmbridge Wk, E8 ....21 D3
Elm Ct, EC4..........88 C2
Elmfield Way, W9 ....52 C3
Elm Friars Wk, NW1 ..15 D4
Elmgreen Cl, E15 .....27 F5
Elm Gro, SE15 ......172 B5
Elmington Est, SE5 ..171 D1
Elmington Rd, SE5 ..170 C3
Elmley Cl, E6 ....75 F4
Elmore St, N1........18 B3
Elm Pk Gdns, SW10..138 C3
Elm Pk La, SW3 .....138 C3
Elm Pk Mans, SW10 .138 B4
Elm Pk Rd, SW3 ....138 C4
Elm Pl, SW7 ....138 C2
Elm Quay Ct, SW8...142 C4
Elmslie Pt, E3........68 A3
Elms Ms, W2........82 C2
Elmstone Rd, SW6 ..160 C3
Elm St, WC1 ....60 B2
Elm Tree Cl, NW8 ....32 C4
Elm Tree Rd, NW8 ...32 C4
Elmwood Ct, SW11..165 E3
Elnathan Ms, W9.....53 F2

Elrington Rd, E8......20 C2
Elsa St, E1 ....67 E4
Elsdale St, E9 ....22 B3
Elsden Ms, E2........44 B3
Elsham Rd, W14 .....107 E2
Elsham Ter, W14 .....107 E2
Elsted St, SE17......147 D1
Elswick St, SW6 .....162 A5
Elsworthy Ri, NW3 ...11 F3
Elsworthy Rd, NW3...11 F4
Elsworthy Ter, NW3 ..11 F4
Elthiron Rd, SW6....161 D4
Elton Ho, E3 ....24 B5
Elvaston Ms, SW7 ...110 B3
Elvaston Pl, SW7 ....110 A4
Elver Gdns, E2 ....43 D4
Elverson Rd, SE8 ....177 F5
Elverton St, SW1 ....114 C5
Elvis Rd, NW2.........6 A1
Elwin St, E2 ....42 C4
Ely Ct, EC1 ....61 D4
Ely Pl, EC1 ....61 D4
Elystan Pl, SW3 .....139 F2
Elystan St, SW3 .....139 E1
Elystan Wk, N1 ......38 C1
⊖ Embankment 87 F4
Embankment Gdns,
   SW3 ....140 B4
🚣 Embankment Pier . 88 A4
Embankment Pl, WC2. 87 F4
Emba St, SE16 ......121 D2
Emberton, SE5.......147 E4
Emden St, SW6 .....161 F3
Emerald Cl, E16.....103 E1
Emerald St, WC1 .....60 A3
Emerson St, SE1......90 A4
Emery Hill St, SW1 . 114 B4
Emery St, SE1 ......117 D3
Emma St, E2.........43 E2
Emmott Cl, E1 ....67 F2
Emperor's Gate,
   SW7 ....109 F4
Empire Wf Rd, E14 . .154 C1
Empress App, SW6 . 136 C3
Empress Ms, SE5 ....170 A5
Empress Pl, SW6 ....136 C3
Empress St, SE17....146 B4
Empson St, E3 ....69 F1
Enbrook St, W10 .....29 F5
Endell St, WC2 ......59 E5
Enderby St, SE10....155 D3
Endsleigh Gdns,
   WC1 ....58 C1
Endsleigh Pl, WC1 ...59 D1
Endsleigh St, WC1...58 C1
Enfield Rd, N1 ......19 F4
Enford St, W1.......56 A3
Englands La, NW3...12 A2
Englefield Rd, N1....18 C2
English Grds, SE1.....91 E5

🏫 English Martyrs RC
   Prim Sch, E1 ......92 B1
   SE17............147 D1
English St, E3 ....68 A1
Enid St, SE16 ....120 B3
Ennerdale Ho, E3.....68 A1
Ennismore Gdns,
   SW7 ....111 E2
Ennismore Gdns Ms,
   SW7 ....111 E3
Ennismore Ms, SW7 . 111 E3
Ennismore St, SW7 . . 111 E3
Ensign St, E1 ....92 C2
Ensor Ms, SW7.......138 C2
Enterprize Way, SE8. 124 A5
Epirus Ms, SW6 .....160 C1
Epirus Rd, SW6 .....160 B1
Epping Cl, E14......125 D5
Epping Pl, N1 ....17 D2
Epple Rd, SW6 .....160 B3
Epworth St, EC2 .....63 D2
Equity Sq, E2 ....42 B5
Erasmus St, SW1....143 D1
Eresby Pl, NW6........8 C4
Eric Clarke La, Bark.
   IG11 ....77 F1
Eric St, E3 ....68 A1
Erlanger Rd, SE14 ...175 D5
Ernest St, E1.........67 D2
★ Eros, W1..........86 C3
Errington Rd, W9.....52 B1
Errol St, EC1 ....62 B2
Erskine Ms, NW3 .....12 B4
Erskine Rd, NW3 .....12 B4
Escreet Gro, SE18 ...132 C5
Eskdale, NW1........36 A3
Esk Rd, E13..........73 D1
Esmeralda Rd, SE1 . . 149 D1
Esmond Rd, NW6 .....30 B1
🏫 Essendine Prim Sch,
   W9 ....31 D5
Essendine Rd, W9 ....53 D1
Essex Ct, EC4 ....88 C1
Essex Ho, E14........69 E5
🚉 Essex Road 18 A4
Essex Rd, N1 ....18 A4
Essex St, WC2........88 C2
Essex Vil, W8 ....108 C2
Essian St, E1.........67 E3
Estcourt Rd, SW6 ....160 A1
Esterbrooke St, SW1. 142 C1
★ Estorick Collection of
   Modern Italian Art,
   N1...............17 F2
Eternit Wk, SW6 .....158 B3
Ethelburga St,
   SW11 ....163 F3
Ethel Rd, E16.......101 E1
Ethel St, SE17 ......146 A1
Ethnard Rd, SE15 ...149 E5
Eton Av, NW3........11 E3
Eton Coll Rd, NW3...12 B2
Eton Ct, NW3........11 D3
Eton Garages, NW3...11 F2

Eton Hall, NW3 ......12 B2
Eton Pl, NW3 ....12 C3
Eton Ri, NW3 ....12 B2
Eton Rd, NW3 ....12 A3
Eton Vil, NW3 ....12 B2
Etta St, SE8 ....151 F4
Ettrick St, E14 ....70 B5
Eugenia Rd, SE16 ...150 B1
Europa Pl, EC1 ......40 A5
Europe Rd, SE18 ...132 B4
Eustace Bldg, SW8 . .141 E5
Eustace Pl, SE18 ...132 A5
Eustace Rd, SW6 ...160 C1
⊖ Euston 36 B4
⊖ Euston 36 B4
Euston Gro, NW1....36 C5
Euston Rd, N1 ....37 E4
   NW1 ....57 F2
⊖ Euston Square.....58 B1
Euston Sq, NW1.....36 C5
Euston Sta Colonnade,
   NW1 ....36 C5
Euston St, NW1 ......58 B1
Euston Twr, NW1.....58 A1
Evandale Rd, SW9...169 D5
Evans Cl, E8 ....20 B2
🏥 Evelina Children's Hosp,
   SE1 ....116 A3
Eveline Lowe Est,
   SE16 ....120 C4
🏫 Eveline Lowe Prim Sch,
   SE1 ....149 D3
Evelyn Ct, N1 ....40 C3
Evelyn Denington Rd,
   E6 ....75 F2
Evelyn Fox Ct, W10...50 B4
Evelyn Gdns, SW7 ...138 C3
Evelyn Rd, E16......101 E4
Evelyn St, SE8 ......151 F4
Evelyn Wk, N1 ....40 C3
Evelyn Yd, W1 ....58 C5
Everest Pl, E14.......70 A3
Evergreen Sq, E8 ....20 A3
Everilda St, N1.......38 B1
Everington St, W6...135 D4
Eve Rd, E15 ....49 F3
Eversholt St, NW1...36 B2
Eversley Rd, SE7....157 E4
Everton Bldgs, NW1 . . 36 A5
Evesham St, W11 ....78 C3
Evesham Wk, SE5 ...170 C5
   SW9 ....168 C4
Ewart Pl, E3 ....46 A2
Ewe Cl, N7 ....15 F1
Ewer St, SE1 ....90 A5
Ewhurst Cl, E1 ....66 B4
Excel Ct, WC2........87 D3
★ ExCeL London,
   E16..............101 F2
ExCeL Marina, E16 . .101 E3
ExCeL Waterfront,
   E16..............101 F3
Exchange Arc, EC2....63 F3
Exchange Ct, WC2....87 F3

Exchange Pl, EC2 . . . . . **63** E3
Exchange Sq, EC2 . . . . . **63** E3
Exeter Cl, E6 . . . . **76** A5
Exeter Ms, NW6 . . . . **9** E2
  SW6 . . . . **160** C1
Exeter Rd, E16 . . . . **73** D4
  NW2 . . . . **7** F2
Exeter St, WC2 . . . . **87** F2
Exeter Way, SE14 . . . **176** A2
Exhibition Cl, W12 . . **78** A3
Exhibition Rd,
  SW7 . . . . **111** D2
Exmoor St, W10 . . . . . . **51** D2
Exmouth Mkt, EC1 . . . **60** C1
Exmouth Ms, NW1 . . . **36** B5
Exmouth Pl, E8 . . . . . . **21** E4
Exmouth St, E1 . . . . . . **66** B5
Exning Rd, E16 . . . . **72** A2
Exon St, SE17 . . . . **147** E2
Exton St, SE1 . . . . **88** C5
Eynham Rd, W12 . . . . . **50** A4
Eyre Ct, NW8 . . . . **32** C2
Eyre St Hill, EC1 . . . . . **60** C2
Eythorne Rd, SW9 . . . **169** D3
Ezra St, E2 . . . . **42** B4

F

Fabian Rd, SW6 . . . . . **160** B1
Fabian St, E6 . . . . **75** F2
Factory Rd, E16 . . . . . **103** D5
Fairbairn Grn, SW9 . . **169** D3
Faircharm Trd Est,
  SE8 . . . . **177** E1
Fairchild Pl, EC2 . . . . . **63** F2
Fairchild St, EC2 . . . . . **63** F2
Fairclough St, E1 . . . . . **93** D1
Fairfax Ms, E16 . . . . . **101** E4
Fairfax Pl, NW6 . . . . . . **10** B4
  W14 . . . . **107** F4
Fairfax Rd, NW6 . . . . . **10** B4
Fairfield Rd, E3 . . . . . . **46** C2
Fairfoot Rd, E3 . . . . **68** C2
Fairford Ho, SE11 . . . **145** D1
Fairhazel Gdns, NW6 . . . **9** F2
Fairholme Rd, W14 . . **135** F3
Fairholt St, SW7 . . . . **111** F3
Fairmont Av, E14 . . . . **98** C4
Fairstead Wk, N1 . . . . **18** A5
Fair St, SE1 . . . . **119** F1
Fairthorn Rd, SE7 . . . **157** D2
Fakruddin St, E1 . . . . **65** D2
Falconberg Ct, W1 . . . **59** D5
Falconberg Ms, W1 . . **58** C5
Falcon Ct, EC4 . . . . **88** C1
Falcon St, E13 . . . . **72** C1
Falcon Way, E14 . . . . **125** F5
Falkirk Ho, W9 . . . . **31** F4
Falkirk St, N1 . . . . **41** F3
Sch Falkner Ho Sch,
  SW7 . . . . **138** B1
Fallow Ct, SE16 . . . . . **149** D3

Falmouth Rd, SE1 . . . **118** B3
★ Family Records Cen,
  Public Record Office,
  EC1 . . . . **39** D5
Fane St, W14 . . . . **136** B4
★ Fan Mus, SE10 . . . **178** B1
Fann St, EC1 . . . . **62** A2
  EC2 . . . . **62** A2
Fanshaw St, N1 . . . . . . **41** E4
Faraday Cl, N7 . . . . **16** B2
★ Faraday Mus, W1 . . **86** A3
Faraday Rd, W10 . . . . . **51** E3
Faraday Way, SE18 . . **130** C4
Fareham St, W1 . . . . . . **58** C5
Faringford Rd, E15 . . . **27** E4
Farm Cl, SW6 . . . . **161** D1
Farmdale Rd, SE10 . . **157** D2
Farmers Rd, SE5 . . . . **169** F1
Farmer St, W8 . . . . **80** C4
Farm La, SW6 . . . . . . **137** D5
Farm La Trd Cen,
  SW6 . . . . **136** C5
Farm Pl, W8 . . . . **80** C4
Farm St, W1 . . . . **85** E3
Farncombe St, SE16 . **121** D2
Farnell Ms, SW5 . . . . **137** E2
Farnham Pl, SE1 . . . . . **89** F5
Farnham Royal,
  SE11 . . . . **144** B3
Faroe Rd, W14 . . . . . . **107** D4
Farrance St, E14 . . . . . **96** B1
Farrell Ho, E1 . . . . **94** B1
Farrier St, NW1 . . . . . . **13** F1
Farrier Wk, SW10 . . . **138** A4
⇌ Farringdon **61** D3
⊖ Farringdon **61** D3
Farringdon La, EC1 . . . **61** D2
Farringdon Rd, EC1 . . **60** C1
Farringdon Rents, SE16 . . **95** E5
Farrins Rents, SE16 . . **95** E5
Farrow La, SE14 . . . . **174** B1
Farrow Pl, SE16 . . . . . **123** E3
Farthingale Wk, E15 . . **26** C4
Farthing All, SE1 . . . . **120** C2
Farthing Flds, E1 . . . . . **93** F4
Fashion St, E1 . . . . **64** A4
Fassett Rd, E8 . . . . **21** D1
Fassett Sq, E8 . . . . **20** C1
Faulkner's All, EC1 . . . **61** E3
Faulkner St, SE14 . . . **174** B3
Faunce St, SE17 . . . . **145** E4
Favart Rd, SW6 . . . . . **161** D3
Fawcett St, SW10 . . . **138** A4
Fawe St, E14 . . . . **69** F4
Fearon St, SE10 . . . . . **156** C2
Feathers Pl, SE10 . . . **155** D4
Featherstone St, EC1 . **62** C1
Felden St, SW6 . . . . . **160** A3
Felixstowe Ct, E16 . . **105** F5
Fellbrigg St, E1 . . . . . . **65** F2
Fellmongers Path,
  SE1 . . . . **119** F2
Fellows Ct, E2 . . . . **42** A3
Fellows Rd, NW3 . . . . . **11** D3

Felltram Way, SE7 . . . **157** D2
Felstead Gdns, E14 . . **154** A3
Felstead St, E9 . . . . **24** B2
Felsted Rd, E16 . . . . . **102** C1
Felton St, N1 . . . . **41** D1
Fenchurch Av, EC3 . . . **91** E1
Fenchurch Bldgs, EC3 . **91** F1
Fenchurch Pl, EC3 . . . . **91** F2
⇌ Fenchurch Street . . **91** F2
Fenchurch St, EC3 . . . . **91** E2
Fen Ct, EC3 . . . . **91** E2
Fendall St, SE1 . . . . . **119** F4
Fendt Cl, E16 . . . . **100** B1
Fenelon Pl, W14 . . . . **136** B1
Fenham Rd, SE15 . . . **173** D2
Fennel Cl, E16 . . . . **71** F1
Fenner Cl, SE16 . . . . . **121** F5
Fenning St, SE1 . . . . . **119** E1
Fen St, E16 . . . . **100** B2
Fentiman Rd, SW8 . . . **143** F5
Fenton Cl, E8 . . . . **20** B1
Ferdinand Pl, NW1 . . . **13** D3
Ferdinand St, NW1 . . . **13** D2
Ferguson Cl, E14 . . . . **152** C1
Fermoy Rd, W9 . . . . . . **52** A2
Fern Cl, N1 . . . . **41** E2
Ferndale Ct, SE3 . . . . **180** B1
Ferndale St, E6 . . . . . **105** E2
Fernhead Rd, W9 . . . . . **30** B4
Fernhill St, E16 . . . . . **104** B5
Fernhurst Rd, SW6 . . **159** F3
Fernleigh Cl, W9 . . . . . **30** B4
Fernsbury St, WC1 . . . **38** C5
Fernshaw Rd, SW10 . **138** A5
Fern St, E3 . . . . **69** D2
Fern Wk, SE16 . . . . . . **149** D3
Ferranti Cl, SE18 . . . . **131** D4
Ferriby Cl, N1 . . . . **16** C3
Ferrier Pt, E16 . . . . **72** C4
Ferry Pl, SE18 . . . . . . **133** D4
Ferry St, E14 . . . . **154** A2
Festoon Way, E16 . . . **102** C2
Fetter La, EC4 . . . . **89** D1
Ffinch St, SE8 . . . . **176** C1
Field Ct, WC1 . . . . **60** B4
Fieldgate St, E1 . . . . . . **65** D4
Fielding Ho, NW6 . . . . **31** D4
Fielding Rd, W14 . . . . **107** D3
Fielding St, SE17 . . . . **146** A4
Field Rd, W6 . . . . **135** E3
Fields Est, E8 . . . . **21** D4
Field St, WC1 . . . . **38** A4
Fife Rd, E16 . . . . **72** C4
Fife Ter, N1 . . . . **38** B2
Fifth Av, W10 . . . . **29** E5
Filigree Ct, SE16 . . . . . **95** F5
Filmer Rd, SW6 . . . . . **160** A3
Finborough Rd,
  SW10 . . . . **137** E4
Finch La, EC3 . . . . **91** D1

Finchley Pl, NW8 . . . . . 32 C2
⊖ Finchley Road 10 A1
Finchley Rd, NW3 . . . . 10 A1
 NW8 . . . . 32 C1
Finch Ms, SE15 . . . . 172 A3
Findhorn St, E14 . . . . . 70 B5
Fingal St, SE10 . . . . . 156 B2
Finland Quay, SE16 . . 123 F4
Finland St, SE16 . . . . 123 F3
Finlay St, SW6 . . . . . 158 C4
Finnis St, E2 . . . . 43 F5
FINSBURY, EC1 . . . . . . 39 D4
Finsbury Av, EC2 . . . . . 63 D4
Finsbury Av Sq, EC2 . . 63 D4
Finsbury Circ, EC2 . . . 63 D4
Finsbury Est, EC1 . . . . . 39 D5
Finsbury Mkt, EC2 . . . 63 E2
Finsbury Pavement,
 EC2 . . . . 63 D3
Finsbury Sq, EC2 . . . . 63 D3
Finsbury St, EC2 . . . . . 62 C3
Finsbury Twr, EC1 . . . 62 C2
Finstock Rd, W10 . . . . 50 C5
Firbank Cl, E16 . . . . . . 74 C3
Firbank Rd, SE15 . . . . 173 F5
Firefly Gdns, E6 . . . . . 75 E2
★ Firepower, SE18 . . 133 E3
Fir Gro Rd, SW9 . . . . 169 D5
First Av, W10 . . . . 52 A1
First St, SW3 . . . . 111 F5
Firth Gdns, SW6 . . . . 159 E4
Fir Trees Cl, SE16 . . . . . 95 F5
Fishermans Dr,
 SE16 . . . . 123 D1
Fisherman's Wk,
 E14 . . . . 96 C4
Fishers Ct, SE14 . . . . . 174 C3
Fisher St, E16 . . . . 72 C3
 WC1 . . . . 59 F4
Fisherton St, NW8 . . . 54 C2
Fishguard Way, E16 . 133 F1
Fish St Hill, EC3 . . . . . 91 D2
Fitzalan St, SE11 . . . . 116 C5
Fitzgeorge Av, W14 . . 135 E2
Fitzgerald Ho, E14 . . . 97 F1
Fitzhardinge St, W1 . . 56 C5
Fitzjames Av, W14 . . . 135 F1
Fitzmaurice Pl, W1 . . . 85 F4
Fitzroy Ct, W1 . . . . . . 58 B2
Fitzroy Ms, W1 . . . . . . 58 A2
Fitzroy Rd, NW1 . . . . 12 B5
Fitzroy Sq, W1 . . . . . . 58 A2
Fitzroy St, W1 . . . . . . 58 A2
Fitzroy Yd, NW1 . . . . . 12 C5
Fitzwilliam Ms, E16 . 100 C4
Five Bell All, E14 . . . . . 96 B1
Fives Ct, SE11 . . . . . . 117 E5
Fiveways Rd, SW9 . . . 169 D5
Flamborough St,
 E14 . . . . 67 E5

Flamborough Wk,
 E14 . . . . 95 E1
★ Flamsteed Ho Mus,
 SE10 . . . . 179 D1
Flanders Way, E9 . . . . 22 C1
Flank St, E1 . . . . 92 C2
Flavell Ms, SE10 . . . . 155 F2
Flaxman Ct, W1 . . . . . 86 C1
Flaxman Ter, WC1 . . . . 37 D5
Fleece Wk, N7 . . . . . . 15 F1
Fleet Sq, WC1 . . . . . . 38 A5
Fleet St, EC4 . . . . 88 C1
Fleet St Hill, E1 . . . . . 64 C2
Fleetwood Cl, E16 . . . 74 C3
Fleetwood Ct, E6 . . . . 76 A3
Fleming Cl, W9 . . . . . . 52 C2
Fleming Ct, W2 . . . . . . 54 C3
Fleming Rd, SE17 . . . 145 F4
Fletcher Cl, E6 . . . . . 105 E2
Fletcher Path, SE8 . . . 177 D2
Fletcher St, E1 . . . . . . 93 D2
Fleur de Lis St, E1 . . . 63 F2
Flinton St, SE17 . . . . 147 F2
Flint St, SE17 . . . . . . 147 D1
Flitcroft St, WC2 . . . . . 59 D5
Flockton St, SE16 . . . 120 C2
Flodden Rd, SE5 . . . 170 A4
Flood Pas, SE18 . . . . . 132 A4
Flood St, SW3 . . . . . 139 F3
Flood Wk, SW3 . . . . . 139 F4
Flora Cl, E14 . . . . 97 E1
Floral St, WC2 . . . . . . 87 E2
★ Florence Nightingale
 Mus, SE1 . . . . 116 A2
Florence Rd, SE14 . . . 176 B4
Florence St, E16 . . . . . 72 B1
 N1 . . . . 17 E4
Florence Ter, SE14 . . . 176 B3
Florfield Pas, E8 . . . . . 21 F2
Florfield Rd, E8 . . . . . 21 F2
Florida St, E2 . . . . 42 C5
Flower & Dean Wk,
 E1 . . . . 64 B4
Flower Wk, The,
 SW7 . . . . 110 A2
Foley St, W1 . . . . 58 A4
Folgate St, E1 . . . . 63 F3
Follett St, E14 . . . . . . 98 A1
Folly Ms, W11 . . . . . . 80 A1
Folly Wall, E14 . . . . . . 126 B2
Forbes St, E1 . . . . 93 D1
Ford Cl, E3 . . . . 45 F2
Fordham St, E1 . . . . . 65 D5
Fordingley Rd, W9 . . . 30 B5
Ford Rd, E3 . . . . 46 A2
Fords Pk Rd, E16 . . . . 72 C5
Ford Sq, E1 . . . . 65 F4
Ford St, E3 . . . . 45 F1
 E16 . . . . 72 B5
★ Foreign & Commonwealth
 Office, SW1 . . . . . . 115 E1
Foreign St, SE5 . . . . . 169 F5
Foreshore, SE8 . . . . . . 152 B1
Forest Cl, NW6 . . . . 7 E4

Forest Gro, E8 . . . . . . 20 A2
Forest La, E15 . . . . . . 27 F1
Fore St, EC2 . . . . 62 B4
Fore St Av, EC2 . . . . . . 62 C4
Forest Rd, E8 . . . . 20 A2
Forfar Rd, SW11 . . . . 165 D3
Forge Pl, NW1 . . . . 13 D2
Formation, The,
 E16 . . . . 133 E1
Formosa St, W9 . . . . . 54 A2
Formunt Cl, E16 . . . . . 72 B4
Forset St, W1 . . . . 55 F5
Forston St, N1 . . . . . . 40 C2
Forsyth Gdns,
 SE17 . . . . 145 F4
Fortescue Av, E8 . . . . . 21 F4
Fortis Cl, E16 . . . . 102 A1
★ Fortnum & Mason,
 W1 . . . . 86 A4
Fort Rd, SE1 . . . . 148 B1
Fort St, E1 . . . . 63 F4
 E16 . . . . 101 F5
Fortuna Cl, N7 . . . . . . 16 B1
Fortune Pl, SE1 . . . . . 148 B3
Fortune St, EC1 . . . . . . 62 B2
Forty Acre La, E16 . . . 72 C4
Forum Magnum Sq,
 SE1 . . . . 116 A1
Fosbury Ms, W2 . . . . . 81 F3
Foscote Ms, W9 . . . . . 53 D2
🅂 Fossdene Prim Sch,
 SE7 . . . . 157 F3
Fossdene Rd, SE7 . . . 157 F3
Foster La, EC2 . . . . 62 A5
Foster Rd, E13 . . . . . . 72 C1
Foubert's Pl, W1 . . . . . 86 A1
Foulis Ter, SW7 . . . . . 139 D2
Founder Cl, E6 . . . . . 105 E1
Founders Ct, EC2 . . . . . 62 C5
★ Foundling Mus,
 WC1 . . . . 59 F1
Foundry Cl, SE16 . . . . 95 E4
Foundry Ms, NW1 . . . 58 B1
Fountain Ct, EC4 . . . . 88 C2
Fountain Grn Sq,
 SE16 . . . . 121 D1
Fountain Ms, NW3 . . . 12 A1
Fountain Pl, SW9 . . . 169 D4
Fountain Sq, SW1 . . . 113 E5
Fount St, SW8 . . . . . . 167 D2
Fournier St, E1 . . . . . . 64 A3
Four Seasons Cl, E3 . . 46 C2
Fourth Av, W10 . . . . . 29 E5
Fowey Cl, E1 . . . . 93 E4
Fowler Rd, N1 . . . . 17 F4
Fox & Knot St, EC1 . . . 61 F3
Fox Cl, E1 . . . . 66 B1
 E16 . . . . 72 C4
Foxcote, SE5 . . . . 147 F3
Foxley Rd, SW9 . . . . . 169 D1
Foxley Sq, SW9 . . . . . 169 E3
Foxmore St, SW11 . . . 164 A4
🅂 Fox Prim Sch, W8 . . 80 C4
Fox Rd, E16 . . . . 72 A4

Foyle Rd, SE3 . . . . 156 A5
Frampton Pk Rd, E9 . . 22 A2
Frampton St, NW8 . . . 54 C2
Coll Frances King
　Sch of English,
　South Kensington,
　SW7 . . . . 110 B5
　Victoria, SW1 . . . . 113 F3
Frances St, SE18 . . . . 132 A5
Francis Chichester Way,
　SW11 . . . . 165 D4
Francis Cl, E14 . . . . . . 126 C5
Sch Francis Holland Sch,
　Marylebone, NW1 . . 56 A1
　Belgravia, SW1 . . . 141 D1
Francis St, SW1 . . . . . 114 A5
Francis Wk, N1 . . . . . . 16 A5
Sch Frank Barnes Sch,
　NW3 . . . . 11 D4
Frank Burton Cl,
　SE7 . . . . 157 F3
Frankham St, SE8 . . 176 C2
Frankland Cl, SE16 . . 121 F4
Frankland Rd, SW7 . . 110 C4
Franklin Cl, SE13 . . . . 177 E4
Franklin Pl, SE13 . . . . 177 E4
Franklin Sq, W14 . . . . 136 B3
Franklin's Row,
　SW3 . . . . 140 B2
Franklin St, E3 . . . . 47 F4
Frank St, E13 . . . . 73 D2
Fraser Cl, E6 . . . . 75 E5
Frazier St, SE1 . . . . . . 116 C2
Frean St, SE16 . . . . . . 120 C3
Freda Corbett Cl,
　SE15 . . . . 172 C1
Frederica St, N7 . . . . . 16 A3
Frederick Cl, W2 . . . . . 83 F2
Frederick Cres, SW9 . 169 E2
Frederick Rd, SE17 . . 145 F4
Frederick's Pl, EC2 . . . 90 C1
Frederick Sq, SE16 . . . . 95 E3
Frederick's Row, EC1 . 39 E4
Frederick St, WC1 . . . . 38 A5
Frederick Ter, E8 . . . . . 20 A4
Frederic Ms, SW1 . . . 112 B2
Fred White Wk, N7 . . . 15 F1
Freedom St, SW11 . . 164 B5
Freeling St, N1 . . . . 16 A4
Freemantle St, SE17 . 147 E2
★ Freemason's Hall
　(United Grand Lodge
　of England), WC2 . . 59 F5
Freemasons Rd, E16 . . 73 E4
Free Trade Wf, E1 . . . . 94 C2
★ Freightliners City Fm,
　N7 . . . . 16 B1
Fremont St, E9 . . . . 22 A5
French Ordinary Ct,
　EC3 . . . . 91 F2
French Pl, E1 . . . . 63 F1
Frensham St, SE15 . . 149 D5
Frere St, SW11 . . . . . 163 F5
Freshfield Av, E8 . . . . . 20 A4

Freston Rd, W10 . . . . . 78 C2
　W11 . . . . 79 D3
★ Freud Mus, NW3 . . . 10 C1
Friars Cl, SE1 . . . . 89 E5
Friars Mead, E14 . . . . 126 A4
Sch Friars Prim Sch,
　SE1 . . . . 117 F1
Friar St, EC4 . . . . 89 F1
Friary Ct, SW1 . . . . 86 B5
Friary Est, SE15 . . . . . 149 D5
Friary Rd, SE15 . . . . . 149 D5
Friday St, EC4 . . . . 90 A1
Friendly Pl, SE13 . . . . 177 F4
Friendly St, SE8 . . . . . 176 C4
Friendship Way, E15 . . 26 B5
Friend St, EC1 . . . . 39 E4
Frigate Ms, SE8 . . . . . 152 C4
Frimley Way, E1 . . . . . . 66 C2
Frinstead Ho, W10 . . . 78 C2
Frith St, W1 . . . . 86 C1
Frithville Gdns, W12 . . 78 A4
Frobisher Pas, E14 . . . . 97 D4
Frobisher Rd, E6 . . . . . 76 B4
Frobisher St, SE10 . . . 155 F4
Frognal, NW3 . . . . 10 A1
Frognal Ct, NW3 . . . . . 10 B1
Frognal Par, NW3 . . . . 10 A1
Frome St, N1 . . . . 40 A2
Frostic Wk, E1 . . . . 64 B4
Frying Pan All, E1 . . . . 64 A4
Fulbourne St, E1 . . . . . 65 E3
Fulford St, SE16 . . . . . 121 F2
⊖ Fulham Broadway . . . .
　161 . . . . D1
Fulham Bdy, SW6 . . . 161 D1
Fulham Ct, SW6 . . . . 160 C3
Sch Fulham Cross Sec Sch,
　SW6 . . . . 159 E1
★ Fulham FC, SW6 . . 158 C4
Fulham Palace Rd,
　SW6 . . . . 159 D1
　W6 . . . . 134 B2
Fulham Pk Rd,
　SW6 . . . . 160 A5
Sch Fulham Prep Sch,
　Upr Sch, W14 . . . . 135 F4
Sch Fulham Prim Sch,
　SW6 . . . . 136 C5
Fulham Rd, SW3 . . . . 138 C3
　SW6 . . . . 161 F1
　SW10 . . . . 138 C3
Fuller Cl, E2 . . . . 64 C1
Fullwoods Ms, N1 . . . . 41 D4
Fulmead St, SW6 . . . . 161 F4
Fulmer Rd, E16 . . . . . . 74 C4
Fulthorp Rd, SE3 . . . . 180 B5
Fulton Ms, W2 . . . . 82 A2
Fulwood Pl, WC1 . . . . . 60 B4
Furley Rd, SE15 . . . . . 173 D2
Furlong Rd, N7 . . . . 17 D1
Furness Rd, SW6 . . . . 161 F5
Furnival St, EC4 . . . . . . 60 C5
Furzefield Rd, SE3 . . . 181 E1
Furze St, E3 . . . . 69 D3

Fynes St, SW1 . . . . . . 114 C5

G

Gables Cl, SE5 . . . . . . 171 E3
Gabrielle Ct, NW3 . . . . 11 D2
Gabriel's Wf, SE1 . . . . 88 C4
Gadwall Cl, E16 . . . . . . 73 E5
Gage Rd, E16 . . . . 71 F3
Gage St, WC1 . . . . 59 F3
Gainford St, N1 . . . . . . 16 C5
Gainsborough Ct,
　W12 . . . . 106 A1
Gainsborough Ho,
　E14 . . . . 125 D2
Sch Gainsborough JMI Sch,
　E9 . . . . 24 C1
Sch Gainsborough Prim Sch,
　E15 . . . . 49 F5
Gainsborough Rd,
　E15 . . . . 49 E5
Gainsborough St, E9 . 24 B2
Gainsborough Studios,
　N1 . . . . 40 C1
Gainsford St, SE1 . . . . 120 A1
Gairloch Rd, SE5 . . . . 171 F5
Gaisford St, NW5 . . . . . 14 A1
Gaitskell Ct, SW11 . . 163 E5
Galbraith St, E14 . . . . 126 A3
Galen Pl, WC1 . . . . 59 F4
Gales Gdns, E2 . . . . 43 F5
Gale St, E3 . . . . 69 D3
Galleon Cl, SE16 . . . . 122 B1
Sch Galleywall Prim Sch,
　SE16 . . . . 149 F1
Galleywall Rd, SE16 . 149 E1
Sch Gallions Prim Sch,
　E6 . . . . 77 E5
DLR Gallions Reach . . . 105 F1
Gallions Rd, SE7 . . . . 157 F1
Gallions Rbt, E16 . . . . 105 E2
Galsworthy Av, E14 . . 67 F4
Galton St, W10 . . . . . . 51 E1
Galway Cl, SE16 . . . . . 149 F3
Galway Ho, EC1 . . . . . . 40 B5
Galway St, EC1 . . . . . . 40 B5
Gambia St, SE1 . . . . . . 89 F5
Gambier Ho, EC1 . . . . . 40 B4
Gandolfi St, SE15 . . . . 147 E5
Ganton St, W1 . . . . 86 A2
Garbutt Pl, W1 . . . . 57 D3
Garden Cl, EC4 . . . . 88 C2
Sch Garden Ho Prep Sch,
　SW1 . . . . 112 B4
Garden Ms, W2 . . . . . . 81 D3
Garden Pl, E8 . . . . 20 A5
Garden Rd, NW8 . . . . . 32 B4
Garden Row, SE1 . . . . 117 E4

Garden St, E1 . . . . 67 D4
Garden Ter, SW1 . . . . . 142 C2
Garden Wk, EC2 . . . . 41 E5
Gardner Rd, E13 . . . . . 73 E1
Gardners La, EC4 . . . . . 90 A2
Gard St, EC1 . . . . 39 F4
Garfield Rd, E13 . . . . . . 72 B2
Garford St, E14 . . . . . . 96 C3
Garlick Hill, EC4 . . . . . . 90 B2
Garlinge Rd, NW2 . . . . 8 A2
Garnault Ms, EC1 . . . . . 39 D5
Garnault Pl, EC1 . . . . . 39 D5
Garner St, E2 . . . . 43 D3
Garnet St, E1 . . . . 94 A3
Garnet Wk, E6 . . . . 75 F3
Garnies Cl, SE15 . . . . . 172 A1
Garrett St, EC1 . . . . . . 62 B1
Garrick St, WC2 . . . . . . 87 E2
Garter Way, SE16 . . . 122 C2
Garvary Rd, E16 . . . . . 73 F5
Garway Rd, W2 . . . . . . 81 E1
Gascoigne Pl, E2 . . . . . 42 A5
Gascony Av, NW6 . . . . . 8 C4
Gascoyne Rd, E9 . . . . 23 D3
Gaselee St, E14 . . . . . . 98 B3
Gaskell St, SW4 . . . . . 167 E5
Gaskin St, N1 . . . . 17 E5
Gaspar Cl, SW5 . . . . . 109 F5
Gaspar Ms, SW5 . . . . . 109 F5
Gastein Rd, W6 . . . . . 135 D4
Gataker St, SE16 . . . . 121 F3
Gatcombe Rd, E16 . . . 101 D4
Gateforth St, NW8 . . . 55 E2
Sch Gatehouse Sch, The,
    E2 . . . . 44 C2
Gate Ms, SW7 . . . . . . 111 F2
Gatesborough St, EC2 . 63 E1
Gate St, WC2 . . . . 60 A5
Gateway, SE17 . . . . . 146 B4
Sch Gateway Prim Sch,
    NW8 . . . . 55 D1
Gateway Retail Pk,
    E6 . . . . 77 F2
Gateways, The,
    SW3 . . . . 139 F1
Gathorne St, E2 . . . . . 45 D3
Gatliff Rd, SW1 . . . . . 141 D3
Gatonby St, SE15 . . . 172 B3
Gaunt St, SE1 . . . . . . 117 F3
Gautrey Rd, SE15 . . . 174 B5
Gautrey Sq, E6 . . . . . 104 B1
Gavel St, SE17 . . . . . 119 D5
Gaverick Ms, E14 . . . 124 C5
Gawber St, E2 . . . . 44 B4
Gaydon Ho, W2 . . . . . 53 F3
Gayfere St, SW1 . . . . . 115 E4
Gayhurst, SE17 . . . . . 147 D4
Sch Gayhurst JMI Sch,
    E8 . . . . 21 D3
Gayhurst Rd, E8 . . . . . . 20 C3

Gay Rd, E15 . . . . 48 C2
Gayton Ho, E3 . . . . 69 D2
Gaywood Est, SE1 . . . 117 F4
Gaywood St, SE1 . . . . 117 F4
Gaza St, SE17 . . . . . . 145 E3
Gazelle Ho, E15 . . . . . . 27 E1
Gedling Pl, SE1 . . . . . . 120 B3
Gees Ct, W1 . . . . 85 D1
Gee St, EC1 . . . . 62 A1
Geffrye Ct, N1 . . . . 41 F3
★ Geffrye Mus, E2 . . . 41 F3
Geffrye St, E2 . . . . 42 A2
Geldart Rd, SE15 . . . . 173 E2
Gellatly Rd, SE14 . . . . 174 B5
General Gordon Pl,
    SE18 . . . . 133 E5
General Wolfe Rd,
    SE10 . . . . 179 D3
Gentian Row, SE13 . . 178 A4
Gentry Gdns, E13 . . . . 73 D1
Sch Geoffrey Chaucer
    Tech Coll, SE1 . . . . 118 C4
George Beard Rd,
    SE8 . . . . 152 A1
George Ct, WC2 . . . . . . 87 F3
Sch George Eliot Inf Sch,
    NW8 . . . . 10 C5
Sch George Eliot Jun Sch,
    NW8 . . . . 10 C5
Sch George Green's Sec Sch,
    E14 . . . . 154 B2
★ George Inn, SE1 . . . . 90 C5
George Inn Yd, SE1 . . . 90 C5
George Loveless Ho,
    E2 . . . . 42 B4
George Lowe Ct, W2 . . 53 E3
George Mathers Rd,
    SE11 . . . . 117 E5
George Ms, NW1 . . . . 36 A5
George Row, SE16 . . . 120 C2
Georges Sq, SW6 . . . . 136 B4
George St, E16 . . . . . . 100 A1
    W1 . . . . 56 B5
Georgette Pl, SE10 . . 178 B2
George Yd, EC3 . . . . . . 91 D1
    W1 . . . . 85 D2
Georgiana St, NW1 . . . 14 A5
Georgina Gdns, E2 . . . 42 B4
Geraldine St, SE11 . . 117 E4
Gerald Ms, SW1 . . . . . 113 D5
Gerald Rd, E16 . . . . . . 72 A1
    SW1 . . . . 113 D5
Gerard Pl, E9 . . . . 22 C3
Gerards Cl, SE16 . . . . 150 A3
Germander Way, E15 . 49 F5
Gernon Rd, E3 . . . . 45 E3
Gerrard Pl, W1 . . . . 87 D2
Gerrard Rd, N1 . . . . . . 39 F2
Gerrard St, W1 . . . . . . 86 C2
Gerridge St, SE1 . . . . 117 D2
Gerry Raffles Sq, E15 . 27 D2
Gertrude St, SW10 . . 138 B5
Gervase St, SE15 . . . . 173 F1
Ghent Way, E8 . . . . . . 20 B1

Gibbins Rd, E15 . . . . . 26 B4
Gibbs St, W14 . . . . . 136 B2
Sch Gibbs Grn Sch,
    W14 . . . . 136 B2
Gibraltar Wk, E2 . . . . 42 B5
Gibson Cl, E1 . . . . 66 B1
Gibson Rd, SE11 . . . . 144 B1
Gibson Sq, N1 . . . . 17 D5
Gibson St, SE10 . . . . . 155 E3
Giffin St, SE8 . . . . 176 C1
Gifford St, N1 . . . . 15 F4
Gilbert Ho, SE8 . . . . . 153 D4
Gilbert Pl, WC1 . . . . . . 59 E4
Gilbert Rd, SE11 . . . . 145 D1
Gilbert St, W1 . . . . 85 D1
Gilbeys Yd, NW1 . . . . 13 D4
Gildea St, W1 . . . . 57 F4
Gill Av, E16 . . . . 101 D1
Gillender St, E3 . . . . . 70 A1
    E14 . . . . 70 A1
Gillfoot, NW1 . . . . 36 A3
Gilling Ct, NW3 . . . . . . 11 F1
Gillingham Ms, SW1 . 114 A5
Gillingham Row,
    SW1 . . . . 114 A5
Gillingham St, SW1 . . 113 F5
Gillison Wk, SE16 . . . 121 D3
Gill St, E14 . . . . 96 B2
Gilpin Cl, W2 . . . . 54 C3
Gilstead Rd, SW6 . . . 161 F5
Gilston Rd, SW10 . . . 138 B3
Giltspur St, EC1 . . . . . 61 F5
Giralda Cl, E16 . . . . . . 74 C4
Giraud St, E14 . . . . . . 69 E5
Girdlers Rd, W14 . . . . 107 D5
Gironde Rd, SW6 . . . . 160 B2
Girton Vil, W10 . . . . . . 51 D5
Gissing Wk, N1 . . . . . . 17 D4
Gladstone Ms, NW6 . . 8 A3
Gladstone Pl, E3 . . . . 46 B2
Gladstone St, SE1 . . . 117 E3
Gladys Rd, NW6 . . . . . 9 D3
Glaisher St, SE8 . . . . . 153 D4
Glamis Pl, E1 . . . . 94 B2
Glamis Rd, E1 . . . . 94 B2
Glasgow Ho, W9 . . . . . 31 F3
Glasgow Ter, SW1 . . . 142 A3
Glasshill St, SE1 . . . . 117 F1
Glasshouse Flds, E1 . . 94 C2
Glasshouse St, W1 . . . 86 B3
Glasshouse Wk,
    SE11 . . . . 143 F2
Glasshouse Yd, EC1 . . 62 A2
Glass St, E2 . . . . 65 F1
Glass Yd, SE18 . . . . . . 133 D3
Glastonbury Ho,
    SW1 . . . . 141 E2
Glastonbury Pl, E1 . . . 94 A1
Glaucus St, E3 . . . . . . 69 E3
Glazbury Rd, W14 . . . 135 F1
Glebe Pl, SW3 . . . . . . 139 E4
Glebe Rd, E8 . . . . 20 A4
Gledhow Gdns, SW5 . 138 A1
Gledstanes Rd, W14 . 135 F3

Glenaffric Av, E14 . . . 154 C1
Glenalvon Way,
　SE18 . . . . 131 E5
Glenavon Rd, E15 . . . . 27 F3
Glencairne Cl, E16 . . . . 74 C3
Glendower Pl, SW7 . . 110 C5
🏫 Glendower Sch,
　SW7 . . . . 110 C5
Gleneagles Cl, SE16 . . 149 E3
Glenfinlas Way, SE5 . 169 F1
Glenforth St, SE10 . . 156 B2
Glengall Causeway,
　E14 . . . . 124 C3
Glengall Gro, E14 . . 126 A3
Glengall Rd, NW6 . . . . 30 B1
　SE15 . . . . 148 B4
Glengall Ter, SE15 . . 148 B4
Glengarnock Av,
　E14 . . . . 154 B1
Glenilla Rd, NW3 . . . . . 11 E1
Glenister Rd, SE10 . . 156 A2
Glenister St, E16 . . . 105 D5
Glenkerry Ho, E14 . . . . 70 A5
Glenloch Rd, NW3 . . . . 11 E1
Glenluce Rd, SE3 . . . 156 C5
Glenmore Rd, NW3 . . . 11 E1
Glen Rd, E13 . . . . 74 A1
Glenrosa St, SW6 . . . 162 A5
Glenroy St, W12 . . . . . 50 A5
Glen Ter, E14 . . . . 126 B1
Glenthorne Rd, W6 . . 106 A5
Glentworth St, NW1 . . 56 B2
Glenville Gro, SE8 . . 176 B2
Glenworth Av, E14 . . 154 C1
Gliddon Rd, W14 . . . . 135 C1
Global App, E3 . . . . 47 F3
Globe Pond Rd, SE16 . . 95 E5
🏫 Globe Prim Sch, E2 . 44 B4
Globe Rd, E1 . . . . 44 B4
　E2 . . . . 44 A3
Globe Rope Wk, E14 . 154 A1
Globe St, SE1 . . . . 118 B3
Globe Ter, E2 . . . . 44 A4
Globe Wf, SE16 . . . . . . 95 D3
Globe Yd, W1 . . . . 85 E1
Gloucester Arc, SW7 . 110 A5
Gloucester Av, NW1 . . 13 D5
Gloucester Circ,
　SE10 . . . . 178 B1
Gloucester Cres, NW1 . 13 E5
Gloucester Gdns, W2 . 53 F5
Gloucester Gate,
　NW1 . . . . 35 E2
Gloucester Gate Ms,
　NW1 . . . . 35 E2
Gloucester Ho, NW6 . . 31 D3
Gloucester Ms, W2 . . . 82 B1
Gloucester Ms W, W2 . 82 A1
Gloucester Pk, SW7 . . 110 A5
Gloucester Pl, NW1 . . . 56 A1
　W1 . . . . 56 B3
Gloucester Pl Ms, W1 . 56 B4
🏫 Gloucester Prim Sch,
　SE15 . . . . 172 A1

🚇 Gloucester Road . . 110 B5
Gloucester Rd, SW7 . 110 A3
Gloucester Sq, E2 . . . . 42 C1
　W2 . . . . 83 D1
Gloucester St, SW1 . . 142 A3
Gloucester Ter, W2 . . . 54 A5
Gloucester Wk, W8 . . 109 D1
Gloucester Way, EC1 . . 39 D5
Glynde Ms, SW3 . . . . 111 F4
Glyn St, SE11 . . . . 144 A3
Goaters All, SW6 . . . . 160 A2
Godalming Rd, E14 . . . 69 E4
Godbold Rd, E15 . . . . . 49 F5
Godfrey Ho, EC1 . . . . . 40 C5
Godfrey St, E15 . . . . . . 48 B2
　SW3 . . . . 139 F2
Goding St, SE11 . . . . . 143 F3
Godley Cl, SE14 . . . . . 174 B4
Godliman St, EC4 . . . . 90 A1
Godson St, N1 . . . . 38 C2
Godwin Cl, N1 . . . . 40 B2
Godwin Ct, NW1 . . . . . 36 B2
🏛 Goethe Institut,
　SW7 . . . . 111 D3
Goffers Rd, SE3 . . . . . 179 E5
Golborne Gdns, W10 . . 51 F2
Golborne Ms, W10 . . . 51 E4
Golborne Rd, W10 . . . 51 F4
Goldcrest Cl, E16 . . . . 74 C3
Golden Cross Ms,
　W11 . . . . 52 A5
★ Golden Hinde,
　SE1 . . . . 90 C4
Golden Jubilee Br,
　SE1 . . . . 88 A5
　WC2 . . . . 88 A4
Golden La, EC1 . . . . . . 62 A2
Golden La Est, EC1 . . . 62 A2
Golden Plover Cl, E16 . 73 E5
Golden Sq, W1 . . . . . . 86 B2
🚇 Goldhawk Road . . 106 A2
Goldhurst Ter, NW6 . . 10 A4
Golding St, E1 . . . . 93 D1
Goldington Cres, NW1 36 C2
Goldington St, NW1 . . 36 C2
Goldman Cl, E2 . . . . . . 64 C1
Goldney Rd, W9 . . . . . 52 C2
Goldsboro Rd, SW8 . . 167 D3
Goldsmith Rd, SE15 . 172 C3
🎓 Goldsmiths Coll,
　SE14 . . . . 175 F3
★ Goldsmiths' Hall,
　EC2 . . . . 62 B5
Goldsmith's Row, E2 . 42 C3
Goldsmith's Sq, E2 . . . 43 D2
Goldsmith St, EC2 . . . 62 B5
Goldsworthy Gdns,
　SE16 . . . . 150 B1
Goldwin Cl, SE14 . . . . 174 B3
Goldwing Cl, E16 . . . . 101 D1
Gomm Rd, SE16 . . . . 122 A4
Gonson St, SE8 . . . . . 153 E5
Goodge Pl, W1 . . . . . . 58 B4
🚇 Goodge Street 58 B3

Goodge St, W1 . . . . 58 B4
Goodhart Pl, E14 . . . . . 95 F2
Goodinge Cl, N7 . . . . . . 15 E1
Goodmans Ct, E1 . . . . . 92 A2
Goodman's Stile, E1 . . 92 C1
Goodmans Yd, E1 . . . . 92 A2
Goods Way, NW1 . . . . . 37 E2
Goodway Gdns, E14 . . 70 C5
Goodwin Cl, SE16 . . . 120 B4
Goodwins Ct, WC2 . . . 87 C2
Goodwood Rd, SE14 . 175 E2
Goose Sq, E6 . . . . 104 A1
Gophir La, EC4 . . . . 90 C2
Gopsall St, N1 . . . . 41 D1
🏥 Gordon Hosp,
　SW1 . . . . 142 C1
Gordon Ho, E1 . . . . 94 A2
Gordon Pl, W8 . . . . . . 109 D1
Gordon Rd, SE15 . . . . 173 E4
Gordon Sq, WC1 . . . . . 59 D2
Gordon St, WC1 . . . . . 58 C1
Gorefield Pl, NW6 . . . . 30 C2
Gore Rd, E9 . . . . 44 B1
Gore St, SW7 . . . . 110 B3
Gorham Pl, W11 . . . . . 79 E3
Goring St, EC3 . . . . 63 F5
Gorleston St, W14 . . . 107 F5
Gorman Rd, SE18 . . . 132 B5
Gorse Cl, E16 . . . . 100 C1
Gorsuch Pl, E2 . . . . 42 A4
Gorsuch St, E2 . . . . 42 A4
Gosfield St, W1 . . . . . . 58 A3
Goslett Yd, WC2 . . . . . 87 D1
Gosling Way, SW9 . . . 169 D4
Gosset St, E2 . . . . 42 B4
Gosterwood St, SE8 . 151 F4
Goswell Rd, EC1 . . . . . 62 A2
Gough Sq, EC4 . . . . 61 D5
Gough St, WC1 . . . . . . 60 B1
Gough Wk, E14 . . . . . . 96 C1
Goulden Ho App,
　SW11 . . . . 163 E5
Goulston St, E1 . . . . . . 64 A5
Govan St, E2 . . . . 43 D1
Govier Cl, E15 . . . . 27 F4
Gowan Av, SW6 . . . . . 159 E4
Gower Ct, WC1 . . . . . . 58 C1
Gower Ms, WC1 . . . . . 58 C4
Gower Pl, WC1 . . . . . . 58 B1
Gower St, WC1 . . . . . . 58 B1
Gower's Wk, E1 . . . . . . 64 C5
Gracechurch St, EC3 . . 91 D2
Grace Jones Cl, E8 . . . 20 C2
Grace Pl, E3 . . . . 47 F5
Grace's All, E1 . . . . 92 C2
Graces Ms, SE5 . . . . . 171 D5
Graces Rd, SE5 . . . . . 171 E5
Grace St, E3 . . . . 47 F5
Grafton Cres, NW1 . . . 13 E2
Grafton Ho, E3 . . . . 46 C5

Grafton Ms, W1 . . . . . . 58 A2
Grafton Pl, NW1 . . . . . 36 C5
Grafton Rd, NW5 . . . . 13 E1
Grafton St, W1 . . . . 85 F3
Grafton Way, W1 . . . . 58 A2
   WC1 . . . . 58 A2
Grafton Yd, NW5 . . . . 13 F2
Graham Rd, E8 . . . . 20 C1
   E13 . . . . 72 C1
Graham St, N1 . . . . 39 F3
Graham Ter, SW1 . . . 140 C1
Granary Rd, E1 . . . . 65 E2
Granary Sq, N1 . . . . 17 D2
Granary St, NW1 . . . . . 36 C1
Granby Pl, SE1 . . . . . . 116 C2
Granby St, E2 . . . . 64 B1
Granby Ter, NW1 . . . . 36 A3
Grand Av, EC1 . . . . 61 F3
Grand Junct Wf, N1 . . . 40 A3
Grand Union Cl, W9 . . 52 B3
Grand Union Cres,
   E8 . . . . 21 D4
Grand Union Wk,
   NW1 . . . . 13 F4
Grand Wk, E1 . . . . 67 F1
Granfield St, SW11 . . 163 D4
Grange, The, SE1 . . . . 120 A3
Grange Ct, WC2 . . . . . . 88 B1
Grange Gro, N1 . . . . . . 17 F1
Grange Pl, NW6 . . . . 8 C4
Sch Grange Prim Sch,
   SE1 . . . . 119 E4
Grange Rd, SE1 . . . . . 119 F3
Grange St, N1 . . . . 41 D1
Grange Wk, SE1 . . . . . 119 F3
Grangeway, NW6 . . . . . . 8 C4
Grange Yd, SE1 . . . . . 120 A4
Gransden Av, E8 . . . . . 21 F4
Grantbridge St, N1 . . . 39 F2
Grantham Pl, W1 . . . . . 85 E5
Grantley St, E1 . . . . 44 C5
Grant's Quay Wf,
   EC3 . . . . 91 D3
Grant St, N1 . . . . 38 C2
Grantully Rd, W9 . . . . . 31 E5
Granville Ct, N1 . . . . . . 19 D5
Granville Pl, SW6 . . . . 161 E2
   W1 . . . . 84 C1
Granville Rd, NW6 . . . . 30 C3
Granville Sq, SE15 . . . 171 F1
   WC1 . . . . 38 B5
Granville St, WC1 . . . . 38 B5
Grape St, WC2 . . . . 59 E5
Graphite Sq, SE11 . . . 144 A2
Grasmere Pt, SE15 . . . 174 A1
Gratton Rd, W14 . . . . 107 E4
Gravel La, E1 . . . . 64 A5
Grayling Cl, E16 . . . . . . 71 F1
Grayling Sq, E2 . . . . 43 D4
★ Gray's Inn, WC1 . . . 60 B3

Gray's Inn Pl, WC1 . . . . 60 B4
Gray's Inn Rd, WC1 . . . 38 A5
Gray's Inn Sq, WC1 . . . 60 C3
Grayson Ho, EC1 . . . . . 40 B5
Gray St, SE1 . . . . 117 D2
Gray's Yd, W1 . . . . 85 D1
Great Arthur Ho, EC1 . 62 B4
Great Bell All, EC2 . . . . 62 C5
Great Castle St, W1 . . . 57 F5
Great Cen St, NW1 . . . . 56 A3
Great Chapel St, W1 . . 58 C5
Great Ch La, W6 . . . . 135 D2
Great Coll St, SW1 . . . 115 E3
Great Cross Av,
   SE10 . . . . 179 E2
Great Cumberland Ms,
   W1 . . . . 84 A1
Great Cumberland Pl,
   W1 . . . . 56 A5
Great Dover St,
   SE1 . . . . 118 B2
Great Eastern Enterprise
   Cen, E14 . . . . 125 E2
Great Eastern Rd,
   E15 . . . . 26 C3
Great Eastern St,
   EC2 . . . . 41 E5
Great Eastern Wk,
   EC2 . . . . 63 F4
Greatfield Av, E6 . . . . . 76 A1
Great George St,
   SW1 . . . . 115 D2
Great Guildford St,
   SE1 . . . . 90 A4
Great James St, WC1 . . 60 A2
Great Marlborough St,
   W1 . . . . 86 A1
Great Maze Pond,
   SE1 . . . . 119 D1
Great New St, EC4 . . . . 61 D5
Greatorex St, E1 . . . . . . 64 C3
Great Ormond St,
   WC1 . . . . 59 F3
H Great Ormond St Hosp
   for Children, The,
   WC1 . . . . 59 F2
Great Percy St, WC1 . . 38 B4
Great Peter St, SW1 . . 114 C4
⊖ Great Portland
   Street 57 F2
Great Portland St,
   W1 . . . . 57 F3
Great Pulteney St,
   W1 . . . . 86 B2
Great Queen St,
   WC2 . . . . 87 F1
Great Russell St,
   WC1 . . . . 59 D5
Great St. Helens,
   EC3 . . . . 63 E5
Great St. Thomas Apostle,
   EC4 . . . . 90 B2
Great Scotland Yd,
   SW1 . . . . 87 E5

Great Smith St, SW1 . 115 D3
Great Suffolk St, SE1 . . 89 F5
Great Sutton St, EC1 . . 61 F2
Great Swan All, EC2 . . 62 C5
Great Titchfield St,
   W1 . . . . 58 A5
Great Twr St, EC3 . . . . . 91 E2
Great Trinity La, EC4 . . 90 B2
Great Turnstile, WC1 . . 60 B4
Great Western Rd,
   W2 . . . . 52 C4
   W9 . . . . 52 B2
   W11 . . . . 52 C4
Great Winchester St,
   EC2 . . . . 63 D5
Great Windmill St,
   W1 . . . . 86 C2
Great Yd, SE1 . . . . 119 F1
Greaves Twr, SW10 . . 162 B1
Greek Ct, W1 . . . . 87 D1
★ Greek Orthodox Cath of
   the Divine Wisdom
   (St. Sophia), W2 . . . 81 E2
Greek St, W1 . . . . 87 D1
Greek Yd, WC2 . . . . 87 E2
Green, The, E15 . . . . . . 27 F2
Greenacre Sq, SE16 . . 123 D1
Green Arbour Ct, EC1 . 61 E5
Green Bk, E1 . . . . 93 E5
Greenberry St, NW8 . . 33 E3
Greencoat Pl, SW1 . . 114 B5
Greencoat Row,
   SW1 . . . . 114 B4
Greencroft Cl, E6 . . . . . 75 E4
Greencroft Gdns, NW6 . 9 E4
Green Dragon Ct, SE1 . 90 C4
Green Dragon Yd, E1 . . 64 C4
Greenfell Mans, SE8 . 153 E4
Greenfield Rd, E1 . . . . . 65 D4
Greenham Cl, SE1 . . . 116 C2
Greenhill's Rents, EC1 . 61 F3
Greenhills Ter, N1 . . . . 19 D2
Green Hundred Rd,
   SE15 . . . . 149 D5
Greenland Ms, SE8 . . 151 D3
Riv Greenland Pier . . . 124 A4
Greenland Pl, NW1 . . . 13 F5
Greenland Quay,
   SE16 . . . . 123 D5
Greenland Rd, NW1 . . 13 F5
Greenland St, NW1 . . . 13 F5
Greenlaw St, SE18 . . . 132 C4
Greenman St, N1 . . . . . 18 A4
★ Green Park, The,
   SW1 . . . . 113 F1
⊖ Green Park 86 A5
Green Pl, SE10 . . . . . . 127 E1
Green Pt, E15 . . . . 27 F2
Greenroof Way,
   SE10 . . . . 128 B4
Green's Ct, W1 . . . . 86 C2
Green's End, SE18 . . . 133 F1
Greenshields Ind Est,
   E16 . . . . 101 E5

★ Place of interest   ⇌ Railway station   **H** Hospital   ⊖ London Underground station

Green St, W1 . . . . 84 B2
Green Ter, EC1 . . . . 39 D5
Green Wk, SE1 . . . . 119 E4
Greenwell St, W1 . . . . . 57 F2
GREENWICH, SE10 . . 178 C1
≷ Greenwich 177 F1
DLR Greenwich 177 F1
Greenwich Ch St,
  SE10 . . . . 154 B4
Greenwich Cres, E6 . . . 75 E4
Greenwich Foot Tunnel,
  E14 . . . . 154 B3
  SE10 . . . . 154 B3
Greenwich High Rd,
  SE10 . . . . 177 E3
Greenwich Ind Est,
  SE7 . . . . 157 E1
Greenwich Mkt,
  SE10 . . . . 154 B5
★ Greenwich Park,
  SE10 . . . . 179 E1
Greenwich Pk St,
  SE10 . . . . 155 D3
★ Greenwich Pier,
  SE10 . . . . 154 A4
Greenwich Quay,
  SE8 . . . . 153 E5
Coll Greenwich Sch of
  Management,
  SE10 . . . . 178 A1
Greenwich Shop Pk,
  SE7 . . . . 157 D1
Greenwich S St,
  SE10 . . . . 177 F3
Greenwich Vw Pl,
  E14 . . . . 125 E4
Greenwood Ct, SW1 . 142 A2
Greenwood Rd, E8 . . . . 21 D2
Greet St, SE1 . . . . 89 D5
Gregor Ms, SE3 . . . . . . 181 D2
Gregory Pl, W8 . . . . . . 109 E1
Greig Ter, SE17 . . . . . 145 F4
Grenade St, E14 . . . . . . 96 B2
Grenadier St, E16 . . . . 104 C5
Grenard Cl, SE15 . . . . 172 C2
Grendon St, NW8 . . . . . 55 E1
Grenfell Rd, W11 . . . . . 79 D2
Grenfell Twr, W11 . . . . 79 D2
Grenfell Wk, W11 . . . . 79 D2
Grenville Ms, SW7 . . . 110 B5
Grenville Pl, SW7 . . . . 110 A4
Grenville St, WC1 . . . . 59 F2
Gresham Rd, E16 . . . . 101 F1
Gresham St, EC2 . . . . . 62 A5
Gresse St, W1 . . . . 58 C4
Greswell St, SW6 . . . . 158 C4
Greville Hall, NW6 . . . . 31 E2
Greville Ms, NW6 . . . . . 31 E1
Greville Pl, NW6 . . . . . 31 F2
Greville Rd, NW6 . . . . . 31 E2
Greville St, EC1 . . . . . . 61 D4
Sch Grey Coat Hosp Sch,
  SW1 . . . . 142 C1
  Upr Sch, SW1 . . . . 114 C4

Greycoat Pl, SW1 . . . . 114 C4
Greycoat St, SW1 . . . . 114 C4
Grey Eagle St, E1 . . . . . 64 A3
Greyfriars Pas, EC1 . . . 61 F5
Greyhound Rd, W6 . . 135 D4
  W14 . . . . 135 D4
Greystoke Pl, EC4 . . . . 60 C5
Griggs Pl, SE1 . . . . . . 119 F4
Grimsby Gro, E16 . . . 133 F1
Grimsby St, E2 . . . . 64 B2
Grimsel Path, SE5 . . . 169 F1
Grindal St, SE1 . . . . . . 116 C2
Sch Grinling Gibbons
  Prim Sch, SE8 . . . 152 B5
Grinling Pl, SE8 . . . . . 152 C5
Grinstead Rd, SE8 . . . 151 E3
Grittleton Rd, W9 . . . . 52 C1
Grocer's Hall Ct, EC2 . . 90 C1
Groombridge Rd, E9 . . 22 C4
Groom Pl, SW1 . . . . . . 113 D3
Grosvenor Cotts,
  SW1 . . . . 112 C5
Grosvenor Ct, NW6 . . . . 7 D5
Grosvenor Cres,
  SW1 . . . . 113 D2
Grosvenor Cres Ms,
  SW1 . . . . 112 C2
Grosvenor Est, SW1 . 115 D5
Grosvenor Gdns,
  SW1 . . . . 113 E3
Grosvenor Gdns Ms E,
  SW1 . . . . 113 F3
Grosvenor Gdns Ms N,
  SW1 . . . . 113 E4
Grosvenor Gdns Ms S,
  SW1 . . . . 113 F4
Grosvenor Gate, W1 . . 84 B3
Grosvenor Hill, W1 . . . 85 E2
Grosvenor Pk, SE5 . . . 146 A5
Grosvenor Pl, SW1 . . . 113 D2
Grosvenor Rd, SW1 . . 141 E4
Grosvenor Sq, W1 . . . . 85 D2
Grosvenor St, W1 . . . . 85 E2
Grosvenor Ter, SE5 . . . 169 F1
Grosvenor Wf Rd,
  E14 . . . . 154 C1
Grotto Pas, W1 . . . . . . 57 D3
Grove, The, E15 . . . . . . 27 E1
Grove Cotts, SW3 . . . 139 F4
Grove Ct, SE3 . . . . 181 D3
Grove Cres Rd, E15 . . . 27 D2
Grove End Rd, NW8 . . . 32 C3
Grove Gdns, NW8 . . . . 33 F5
Grove Hall Ct, NW8 . . . 32 B4
Groveland Ct, EC4 . . . . 90 B1
Grove La, SE5 . . . . 170 C4
Grove Ms, W6 . . . . . . 106 A3
  W11 . . . . 80 A1
Grove Pas, E2 . . . . 43 E2
Grove Rd, E3 . . . . 45 D2
  NW2 . . . . 6 A1
Grove St, SE8 . . . . 124 A5
Grove Vil, E14 . . . . 97 F2
Groveway, SW9 . . . . . 168 B4

Grummant Rd,
  SE15 . . . . 172 A3
Grundy St, E14 . . . . 97 E1
Sch Guardian Angels RC
  Prim Sch, E3 . . . . . . 67 F1
★ Guards Mus,
  SW1 . . . . 114 B2
Guerin Sq, E3 . . . . 46 A4
Guildford Gro,
  SE10 . . . . 177 F3
Guildford Rd, E6 . . . . 104 A1
  SW8 . . . . 167 F3
★ Guildhall, The, EC2 . 62 C5
★ Guildhall Art Gall,
Guildhall Lib, EC2 . . . . 62 B5
Guildhall Bldgs, EC2 . . 62 C5
Coll Guildhall Sch of Music &
  Drama, EC2 . . . . 62 B3
  Hall of Res, EC1 . . . . 62 C3
Guildhall Yd, EC2 . . . . 62 B5
Guildhouse St, SW1 . 114 A5
Guilford Pl, WC1 . . . . . 60 A2
Guilford St, WC1 . . . . . 59 F2
Guinness Cl, E9 . . . . . . 23 E4
Guinness Ct, E1 . . . . . . 92 B1
Guinness Sq, SE1 . . . . 119 E5
Guinness Trust Bldgs,
  SE11 . . . . 145 F2
  SW3 . . . . 140 A1
Guion Rd, SW6 . . . . . 160 B5
Gulliver St, SE16 . . . . 124 A3
Gulston Wk, SW3 . . . 140 B1
Gunmakers La, E3 . . . . 45 F1
Gunpowder Sq, EC4 . . 61 D5
Gun St, E1 . . . . 64 A4
Gunter Gro, SW10 . . . 138 A5
Gunterstone Rd,
  W14 . . . . 135 E1
Gunthorpe St, E1 . . . . 64 B4
Gunwhale Cl, SE16 . . . 95 D5
Gurdon Rd, SE7 . . . . . 157 D3
Guthrie St, SW3 . . . . . 139 E2
Gutter La, EC2 . . . . 62 B5
H Guy's Hosp, SE1 . . 119 D1
Guy St, SE1 . . . . 119 D1
Gwendwr Rd, W14 . . 135 F2
Gwyn Cl, SW6 . . . . . . 162 A2
Gwynne Pl, WC1 . . . . . 38 B5
Gwynne Rd, SW11 . . 162 C5

H

Haarlem Rd, W14 . . . 106 C4
Haberdasher Pl, N1 . . . 41 D4
Sch Haberdashers' Aske's
  Hatcham Coll, Girls,
  SE14 . . . . 175 E3
Haberdasher St, N1 . . . 41 D4

Hackford Rd, SW9 . . . 168 C2
Hackford Wk, SW9 . . 168 B4
HACKNEY, E8 . . . . 21 E2
⇌ Hackney Central . . . 21 E1
★ Hackney City Fm,
E2 . . . . 42 C3
⇌ Hackney Downs . . . 21 E1
Sch Hackney Free & Parochial
C of E Sec Sch (Lwr),
E9 . . . . 22 A2
★ Hackney Mus, E8 . . 21 F2
Hackney Rd, E2 . . . . . . 42 A5
⇌ Hackney Wick 24 C2
Hackworth Pt, E3 . . . . 47 E5
Hacon Sq, E8 . . . . 21 F3
Haddonfield, SE8 . . . . 151 D1
Haddo St, SE10 . . . . 154 A5
Hadleigh Cl, E1 . . . . . . 66 B1
Hadleigh St, E2 . . . . . . 44 B5
Hadleigh Wk, E6 . . . . . 75 F5
Hadley St, NW1 . . . . . 13 E2
Hadrian Est, E2 . . . . . . 43 D3
Hadrian Ms, N7 . . . . . 16 B3
Hadrian St, SE10 . . . . 155 E3
HAGGERSTON, E2 . . . 42 B2
Haggerston Rd, E8 . . . 20 A4
Sch Haggerston Sch,
E2 . . . . 42 B2
Sch Hague Prim Sch,
E2 . . . . 65 F1
Hague St, E2 . . . . 43 D5
Hainton Cl, E1 . . . . . . 93 F1
Halcomb St, N1 . . . . . 41 E1
Halcrow St, E1 . . . . . . 65 F4
Haldane Rd, SW6 . . . . 160 B1
Hale Rd, E6 . . . . 75 F2
Hales St, SE8 . . . . 176 C2
Hale St, E14 . . . . 97 E2
Half Moon Ct, EC1 . . . 62 A4
Half Moon Cres, N1 . . 38 B2
Half Moon Pas, E1 . . . . 92 B1
Half Moon St, W1 . . . . 85 F4
Halford Rd, SW6 . . . . 137 D5
Haliday Wk, N1 . . . . . 19 D1
Halkin Arc, SW1 . . . . 112 C3
Halkin Ms, SW1 . . . . . 112 C3
Halkin Pl, SW1 . . . . . . 112 C3
Halkin St, SW1 . . . . . . 113 D2
Hallam Ms, W1 . . . . . . 57 F3
Hallam St, W1 . . . . 57 F2
Sch Halley Prim Sch,
E14 . . . . 67 F4
Halley St, E14 . . . . 67 E4
Hallfield Est, W2 . . . . 82 A1
Sch Hallfield Inf Sch,
W2 . . . . 81 F1
Sch Hallfield Jun Sch,
W2 . . . . 81 F1
Hall Gate, NW8 . . . . . 32 B4
Halliford St, N1 . . . . . 18 B3

Hallings Wf Studios,
E15 . . . . 26 C5
Hall Oak Wk, NW6 . . . . . 8 B1
Hall Pl, W2 . . . . 54 C2
Hall Rd, NW8 . . . . 32 B5
Sch Hall Sch, The,
NW3 . . . . 11 D2
Hall St, EC1 . . . . 39 F4
Sch Hallsville Prim Sch,
E16 . . . . 100 C1
Hallsville Rd, E16 . . . 100 A1
Hall Twr, W2 . . . . 55 D3
Hallywell Cres, E6 . . . . 76 B4
Halpin Pl, SE17 . . . . . 147 D1
Halsey Ms, SW3 . . . . 112 A5
Halsey St, SW3 . . . . . 112 A5
Halsmere Rd, SE5 . . . 169 F3
Halstead Ct, N1 . . . . . . 41 D3
Sch Halstow Prim Sch,
SE10 . . . . 156 C3
Halstow Rd, NW10 . . . 28 C5
SE10 . . . . 156 C2
Halton Cross St, N1 . . . 17 F5
Halton Pl, N1 . . . . 18 A5
Halton Rd, N1 . . . . 17 F3
Hamelin St, E14 . . . . . . 98 A1
Hameway, E6 . . . . 76 C1
Hamilton Cl, NW8 . . . . 32 C5
SE16 . . . . 123 F2
Hamilton Ct, W9 . . . . . 32 A4
Hamilton Gdns, NW8 . 32 B4
Hamilton Ms, W1 . . . 113 E1
Hamilton Pl, W1 . . . . . 85 D5
Hamilton Rd, E15 . . . . 49 F5
Coll Hamilton Rd Cen,
E15 . . . . 49 F5
Hamilton Sq, SE1 . . . 119 D1
Hamilton Rd, SE8 . . . . 176 C1
Hamilton Ter, NW8 . . . 32 B4
Hamlets Way, E3 . . . . . 68 A1
Hamlet Way, SE1 . . . . 119 D1
★ Hamleys, W1 . . . . . . 86 A2
Hammelton Grn,
SW9 . . . . 169 E3
HAMMERSMITH,
W6 . . . . 134 B2
⊖ Hammersmith 134 B1
Coll Hammersmith &
W London Coll,
W14 . . . . 135 E2
Hammersmith Br Rd,
W6 . . . . 134 A3
Hammersmith Bdy,
W6 . . . . 134 B1
Hammersmith Flyover,
W6 . . . . 134 B2
Hammersmith Gro,
W6 . . . . 134 B1
Hammersmith Rd,
W6 . . . . 134 C1
W14 . . . . 134 C1
Hammett St, EC3 . . . . . 92 A2
Hammond St, NW5 . . . 14 A1
Hamond Sq, N1 . . . . . . 41 E2

Hampden Cl, NW1 . . . . 37 D3
Sch Hampden Gurney C of E
Prim Sch, W1 . . . . . . 55 F5
Hampden Gurney St,
W1 . . . . 84 A1
Sch Hampshire Sch, The,
Knightsbridge Upr Sch,
SW7 . . . . 111 E2
Bayswater, W2 . . . . 82 A2
Hampshire St, NW5 . . 14 C1
Hampson Way, SW8 . 168 A3
Hampstead Rd, NW1 . 36 A2
Hampton Cl, NW6 . . . . 30 C5
Hampton Ct, N1 . . . . . . 17 E2
Hampton St, SE1 . . . . 145 F1
SE17 . . . . 145 F1
Ham Yd, W1 . . . . 86 C2
Hanameel St, E16 . . . 101 D4
Hanbury Ms, N1 . . . . . . 40 B1
Hanbury St, E1 . . . . 64 A3
Hancock Rd, E3 . . . . . . 48 A5
Handa Wk, N1 . . . . 18 B1
Hand Ct, WC1 . . . . 60 B4
Handel St, WC1 . . . . . . 59 E1
Handforth Rd, SW9 . . 168 C1
Handley Rd, E9 . . . . . . 22 B5
Hands Wk, E16 . . . . . . 73 D5
Hanging Sword All,
EC4 . . . . 89 D1
Hankey Pl, SE1 . . . . . . 119 D2
Hannah Mary Way,
SE1 . . . . 149 D1
Hannell Rd, SW6 . . . . 159 E1
Hannibal Rd, E1 . . . . . . 66 B3
Hanover Av, E16 . . . . 100 C4
Hanover Gdns, SE11 . 144 C5
Hanover Gate, NW1 . . 33 F5
Hanover Gate Mans,
NW1 . . . . 55 F1
Hanover Pk, SE15 . . . 172 C4
Hanover Pl, E3 . . . . 46 A5
WC2 . . . . 87 F1
Sch Hanover Prim Sch,
N1 . . . . 39 F2
Hanover Rd, NW10 . . . . 6 B5
Hanover Sq, W1 . . . . . . 85 F1
Hanover St, W1 . . . . . . 85 F1
Hanover Ter, NW1 . . . . 33 F5
Hanover Ter Ms, NW1 . 33 F5
Hanover Yd, N1 . . . . . . 39 F2
Hansard Ms, W14 . . . 107 D1
Hans Cres, SW1 . . . . . 112 A3
Hanson St, W1 . . . . 58 A3
Hans Pl, SW1 . . . . 112 B3
Hans Rd, SW3 . . . . . . 112 A3
Hans St, SW1 . . . . 112 B4
Hanway Pl, W1 . . . . . . 58 C5
Hanway St, W1 . . . . . . 58 C5
Harads Pl, E1 . . . . 93 D3
Harben Rd, NW6 . . . . . 10 B3
Harbet Rd, W2 . . . . 55 D4
Sch Harbinger Prim Sch,
E14 . . . . 153 E1
Harbinger Rd, E14 . . . 153 E1

Harbledown Rd,
  SW6 .... 160 C3
Harbord Cl, SE5 ..... 170 C5
Harbord St, SW6 .... 158 C3
Harbour Av, SW10 .. 162 B3
Harbour Ex Sq, E14.. 125 F2
Harbour Yd, SW10 .. 162 B4
Harcourt St, W1 ..... 55 F4
Harcourt Ter, SW10 .137 F3
Hardens Manorway,
  SE7 .... 130 C4
Harders Rd, SE15 ... 173 E5
Harding Cl, SE17 .... 146 A4
Hardinge St, E1 ...... 94 B1
Hardman Rd, SE7 ... 157 E2
Hardwicke Ms, WC1 .. 38 B5
Hardwick St, EC1..... 39 D5
Hardwidge St, SE1.. 119 E1
Hardy Av, E16 ...... 101 D4
Hardy Cl, SE16...... 123 D2
Hardy Rd, SE3 ...... 156 B5
Hare & Billet Rd,
  SE3 .... 179 D4
Harebell Dr, E6....... 77 D4
Hare Ct, EC4 .... 88 C1
Harecourt Rd, N1 .... 18 A1
Hare Marsh, E2 ...... 64 C1
Hare Pl, EC4 .... 89 D1
Hare Row, E2 .... 43 F2
Hare St, SE18....... 133 D4
Hare Wk, N1.......... 41 F3
Harewood Av, NW1... 55 F2
Harewood Pl, W1..... 85 F1
Harewood Row, NW1. 55 F3
Harford St, E1 .... 67 E2
Harleyford Rd, SE11. 144 A4
Harleyford St, SE11.. 144 C5
Harley Gdns, SW10.. 138 B3
Harley Gro, E3 .... 46 B4
Harley Pl, W1........ 57 E4
Harley Rd, NW3...... 11 D4
Harley St, W1........ 57 E4
H Harley St Clinic, The,
  W1 .... 57 E3
Harling Ct, SW11.... 164 A5
Harlinger St, SE18... 131 E3
Harmony Pl, SE1 .... 148 B2
Harmood Gro, NW1 .. 13 E3
Harmood Pl, NW1 ... 13 E3
Harmood St, NW1.... 13 E2
Harmsworth Ms,
  SE11 .... 117 E4
Harmsworth St,
  SE17 .... 145 E3
Harold Est, SE1 ..... 119 F4
Harold Laski Ho,
  EC1 .... 39 E5
Harold Pl, SE11 .... 144 C3
Harp All, EC4 .... 61 E5
Harper Rd, E6 ...... 104 A1
  SE1 .... 118 A3
Harp La, EC3........ 91 E3
Sch Harpley Sch, E1.... 66 C1
Harpley Sq, E1 ...... 44 B5

Harpsden St, SW11.. 164 C4
Harpur Ms, WC1 ..... 60 A3
Harpur St, WC1 ...... 60 A3
Harrap St, E14 ...... 98 B2
Harrier Way, E6 ...... 76 B4
Harriet Cl, E8 .... 20 C5
Harriet St, SW1 ..... 112 B2
Harriet Wk, SW1 .... 112 B2
Harrington Gdns,
  SW7 .... 137 F1
Harrington Ho, NW1. 36 A4
Harrington Rd, SW7. 110 C5
Harrington Sq, NW1. 36 A3
Harrington St, NW1 . 36 A4
Harrington Way,
  SE18............. 131 D3
Harriott Cl, SE10.... 156 A1
Harrison St, WC1..... 37 F5
Harris St, SE5....... 171 D2
★ Harrods, SW1 .... 112 A3
Harrowby St, W1..... 55 F5
Harrowgate Rd, E9 .. 23 E2
Harrow La, E14 ...... 98 A3
Harrow Pl, E1....... 63 F5
Harrow Rd, NW10.... 28 C5
  W2 .... 53 E4
  W9 .... 52 C2
  W10 .... 51 F1
Sch Harry Gosling
  Prim Sch, E1 ..... 93 D1
Hartfield Ter, E3 ..... 47 D3
Hartington Rd, E16 .101 E1
  SW8 .... 167 E2
Hartismere Rd,
  SW6 .... 160 B1
Hartlake Rd, E9 ..... 23 D2
Hartland Rd, NW1.... 13 E3
  NW6 .... 30 A2
Hartlepool Ct, E16 .. 105 F5
Hartley St, E2........ 44 B4
Hartmann Rd, E16 .. 103 D4
Harton St, SE8...... 176 C3
Hartshorn All, EC3 .. 91 F1
Hartshorn Gdns, E6.. 76 C1
Harts La, SE14...... 175 E3
Hart St, EC3 .... 91 F2
Hartwell St, E8....... 20 A1
Harvey Pt, E16....... 73 D4
Harvey Rd, SE5 ..... 170 C3
Harvey St, N1........ 41 D1
Harvington Wk, E8 .. 21 D3
Harvist Rd, NW6 ..... 29 D4
Harwood Rd, SW6... 161 D2
Harwood Ter, SW6 .. 161 E3
Hascombe Ter, SE5.. 170 C5
Hasker St, SW3 ..... 111 F5
Haslam Cl, N1 .... 17 D3
Haslam St, SE15 ... 172 B2
Hassard St, E2 ...... 42 B3
Hassendean Rd, SE3.181 E1
Hassett Rd, E9 ...... 23 D1
Hastings Cl, SE15 .. 172 C2
Hastings St, WC1..... 37 E5
Hat & Mitre Ct, EC1... 61 F2

Hatcham Ms Business
  Cen, SE14 .... 175 D3
Hatcham Pk Ms,
  SE14............. 175 D3
Hatcham Pk Rd,
  SE14............. 175 D3
Hatcham Rd, SE15 .. 150 A5
Hatchers Ms, SE1 ... 119 F2
Hatcliffe St, SE10 ... 156 A2
Hatfield Cl, SE14 .... 174 C2
Hatfields, SE1........ 89 D4
Hatherley Gdns, E6 .. 75 D1
Hatherley Gro, W2 ... 53 E5
Hatherley St, SW1... 114 B5
Hathorne Cl, SE15... 173 F5
Hatteraick St, SE16.. 122 B1
Hatton Gdn, EC1 ..... 61 D3
Hatton Ho, E1 .... 93 D1
Hatton Pl, EC1 ...... 61 D2
Hatton Row, NW8.... 55 D2
Hatton St, NW8...... 55 D2
Hatton Wall, EC1..... 60 C3
Haul Rd, NW1 .... 37 E2
Haunch of Venison Yd,
  W1 .... 85 E1
Havannah St, E14... 125 D2
Havelock St, N1...... 15 F5
Havelock Ter, SW8 .. 165 F2
Haven Ms, E3 .... 68 A4
  N1................ 17 D4
Haven St, NW1 ...... 13 E4
Haverfield Rd, E3..... 45 E4
Havering St, E1 ...... 94 C1
Sch Haverstock Sch,
  NW1.............. 12 C2
Haverstock St, N1.... 39 F3
Havil St, SE5........ 171 E2
Hawes St, N1 .... 17 F4
Hawgood St, E3 ...... 69 D4
Hawke Pl, SE16 ..... 123 D1
Hawke Twr, SE14 ... 151 E3
Hawkshead, NW1 ... 36 A4
Hawks Ms, SE10 .... 178 B2
Hawksmoor Cl, E6... 75 E5
Hawksmoor Ms, E1... 93 E2
Hawksmoor St, W6.. 135 D5
Hawkstone Est,
  SE16............. 150 B1
Hawkstone Rd,
  SE16............. 150 B1
Hawkwell Wk, N1.... 18 B5
Hawley Cres, NW1... 13 F4
Sch Hawley Inf Sch,
  NW1.............. 13 F4
Hawley Ms, NW1..... 13 E3
Hawley Rd, NW1.... 13 F3
Hawley St, NW1..... 13 E4
Hawthorn Av, E3..... 24 A5
Hawthorne Cl, N1 ... 19 E1
Hawthorn Wk, W10.. 51 E1

Hawtrey Rd, NW3 . . . . 11 E4
Hay Cl, E15 . . . . 27 F3
Hay Currie St, E14 . . . 69 D5
Hayday Rd, E16 . . . . . . 72 C3
Haydens Pl, W11 . . . . . 52 A5
Haydon St, EC3 . . . . . . 92 A2
Haydon Wk, E1 . . . . . . 92 B2
Hayes Pl, NW1 . . . . 55 F2
Hayfield Pas, E1 . . . . . . 66 B2
Hayfield Yd, E1 . . . . 66 B2
Hay Hill, W1 . . . . 85 F3
Hayles St, SE11 . . . . . 117 E5
Hayman St, N1 . . . . 17 F4
Haymarket, SW1 . . . . . . 86 C3
Haymarket Arc, SW1 . 86 C3
Haymerle Rd, SE15 . . 148 C5
Sch Haymerle Spec Sch,
   SE15 . . . . 148 C5
Hayne St, EC1 . . . . 61 F3
★ Hay's Galleria,
   SE1 . . . . 91 E4
Hay's La, SE1 . . . . 91 E5
Hay's Ms, W1 . . . . 85 E3
Hay St, E2 . . . . 43 D1
Hayton Cl, E8 . . . . 20 B2
★ Hayward Gall, SE1 . 88 B4
Hayward's Pl, EC1 . . . . 61 E2
Hazelmere Rd, NW6 . . . 8 B5
Hazel Rd, NW10 . . . . . . 28 A4
Hazel Way, SE1 . . . . . 120 A5
Hazlebury Rd, SW6 . . 161 E5
Hazlewood Cres,
   W10 . . . . 51 F2
Hazlitt Ms, W14 . . . . 107 E4
Hazlitt Rd, W14 . . . . . 107 E4
Headfort Pl, SW1 . . . . 113 D2
Headlam St, E1 . . . . . . 65 F2
Head's Ms, W11 . . . . . . 80 C1
Head St, E1 . . . . 94 C1
Heald St, SE14 . . . . . . 176 C3
Healey St, NW1 . . . . . . 13 E2
Hearn's Bldgs, SE17 . 147 D1
Hearn St, EC2 . . . . 63 F2
H Heart Hosp, The,
   W1 . . . . 57 D4
Heathcote Pt, E9 . . . . . 22 C2
Heathcote St, WC1 . . . 60 A1
Heather Cl, E6 . . . . . . 105 E1
Coll Heatherley Sch of Fine
   Art, SW10 . . . . 162 B2
Heather Wk, W10 . . . . 51 F1
Heathfield Cl, E16 . . . . 74 C3
Heathfield Pk, NW2 . . . 6 A2
Heathfield St, W11 . . . 79 E3
Heathmans Rd,
   SW6 . . . . 160 B4
Heathway, SE3 . . . . . 180 C2
Hebden Ct, E2 . . . . 42 A1
Hebron Rd, W6 . . . . . 106 A4
Heckfield Pl, SW6 . . . 160 C2

Heckford St, E1 . . . . . . 95 D2
Heddon St, W1 . . . . 86 A2
Hedgers Gro, E9 . . . . . . 23 E2
Hedger St, SE11 . . . . . 117 E5
Hedingham Cl, N1 . . . . 18 A4
★ Heinz Gall, R.I.B.A.,
   W1 . . . . 56 C5
Heiron St, SE17 . . . . . 145 F5
Helena Pl, E9 . . . . 43 F1
Helena Sq, SE16 . . . . . . 95 E3
Helen's Pl, E2 . . . . 44 A4
Helen St, SE18 . . . . . . 133 F5
Hellings St, E1 . . . . 93 D5
Helmet Row, EC1 . . . . . 62 B1
Helmsley Pl, E8 . . . . . . 21 E4
Helsinki Sq, SE16 . . . 123 F3
Hemans St, SW8 . . . . . 167 D1
Hemingford Rd, N1 . . . 38 B1
Hemming St, E1 . . . . . . 65 D2
Hemp Wk, SE17 . . . . . 119 D5
Hemstal Rd, NW6 . . . . . 8 C3
Hemsworth Ct, N1 . . . . 41 E1
Hemsworth St, N1 . . . 41 E2
Hemus Pl, SW3 . . . . . 139 F3
Henderson Dr, NW8 . . 54 C1
Hendre Rd, SE1 . . . . . 147 F1
Heneage La, EC3 . . . . . 91 F1
Heneage St, E1 . . . . 64 B3
Henley Dr, SE1 . . . . . 120 B5
Henley Rd, E16 . . . . . 132 B1
   NW10 . . . . 6 B5
Henley St, SW11 . . . . 165 D5
Henniker Ms, SW3 . . 138 C4
Henning St, SW11 . . . 163 E4
Henrietta Cl, SE8 . . . . 153 D4
Henrietta Ms, WC1 . . . 59 F1
Henrietta Pl, W1 . . . . . 85 E1
Henrietta St, WC2 . . . . 87 F2
Henriques St, E1 . . . . . 65 D5
Henry Addlington Cl,
   E6 . . . . 77 E4
Sch Henry Compton
   Sec Sch, SW6 . . . . . 159 E3
Henry Dickens Ct,
   W11 . . . . 79 D4
Sch Henry Fawcett
   Prim Sch, SE11 . . . 144 C4
Henshall Pt, E3 . . . . . . 47 F4
Henshall St, N1 . . . . . . 19 D2
Henshaw St, SE17 . . . 118 C5
Hensley Pt, E9 . . . . 23 D2
Henstridge Pl,
   NW8 . . . . 33 E2
Henty Cl, SW11 . . . . . 163 F2
Hepscott Rd, E9 . . . . . . 24 C2
Hepworth Ct, SW1 . . 141 D3
Herald's Pl, SE11 . . . . 117 E5
Herald St, E2 . . . . 65 F1
Herbal Hill, EC1 . . . . . . 61 D2
Herbert Cres, SW1 . . 112 B3
Herbert Morrison Ho,
   SW6 . . . . 136 A5
Sch Herbert Morrison
   Prim Sch, SW8 . . . 167 E2

Herbert St, NW5 . . . . . 12 C1
Herbrand St, WC1 . . . . 59 E1
Hercules Rd, SE1 . . . . 116 B4
Hereford Ho, NW6 . . . . 31 D3
Hereford Ms, W2 . . . . . 81 D1
Hereford Pl, SE14 . . . 176 A1
Hereford Retreat,
   SE15 . . . . 148 C5
Hereford Rd, W2 . . . . . 53 D5
Hereford Sq, SW7 . . . 138 B1
Hereford St, E2 . . . . . . 64 C1
Sch Hereward Ho Sch,
   NW3 . . . . 11 E3
Hermes Cl, W9 . . . . 52 C2
Hermes St, N1 . . . . 38 C3
Sch Hermitage Prim Sch,
   E1 . . . . 93 D5
Hermitage St, W2 . . . . 54 C4
Hermitage Wall, E1 . . . 93 D5
Hermitage Waterside,
   E1 . . . . 92 C4
Hermit Pl, NW6 . . . . . . 31 E1
Hermit Rd, E16 . . . . . . 72 A3
Hermit St, EC1 . . . . 39 E4
Heron Pl, SE16 . . . . 95 F4
Heron Quay, E14 . . . . . 96 C5
DLR Heron Quays 97 D5
Herrick St, SW1 . . . . . 115 D5
Herries St, W10 . . . . . . 29 F3
Herringham Rd, SE7 . 130 B4
Hertford Pl, W1 . . . . . . 58 A2
Hertford Rd, N1 . . . . . . 19 F5
Hertford St, W1 . . . . . . 85 E4
Hertsmere Rd, E14 . . . 96 C3
Hervey Rd, SE3 . . . . . 181 F3
Hesketh Pl, W11 . . . . . 79 E3
Hesper Ms, SW5 . . . . 137 E2
Hesperus Cres, E14 . . 153 E1
Hessel St, E1 . . . . 93 E1
Hestercombe Av,
   SW6 . . . . 159 F5
Hester Rd, SW11 . . . . 163 E2
Heston St, SE14 . . . . . 176 C3
Hevelius Cl, SE10 . . . . 156 A2
Hewer St, W10 . . . . 51 D3
Hewett St, EC2 . . . . 63 F2
Hewison St, E3 . . . . 46 B2
Hewlett Rd, E3 . . . . 45 F2
Heyford Av, SW8 . . . . 167 F1
Heygate St, SE17 . . . . 146 A1
Heylyn Sq, E3 . . . . 46 B4
Uni Heythrop Coll,
   W8 . . . . 109 E3
Hickin St, E14 . . . . . . 126 A3
Hickman Cl, E16 . . . . . 74 C4
Hicks St, SE8 . . . . 151 E2
Hide, E6 . . . . 77 D5
Hide Pl, SW1 . . . . 142 C1
Hides St, N7 . . . . 16 B1
Hide Twr, SW1 . . . . . . 142 C1
High Br, SE10 . . . . 155 D3
High Br Wf, SE10 . . . . 154 C3
⇌ Highbury &
   Islington 17 D2

Highbury &
  Islington 17 D2
Highbury Cor, N5 ....17 E1
Highbury Gro, N5 ....17 F1
Highbury Ms, N7 ....17 D1
Highbury New Pk,
  N5................17 F1
Highbury Pl, N5 .....17 E1
Highbury Sta Rd, N1..17 D2
Highcombe, SE7 ....157 F4
Highfield Ms, NW6 ....9 E3
High Holborn, WC1 ...59 F5
Highlever Rd, W10 ...50 B4
High Meads Rd, E16 ..74 C5
Highmore Rd, SE3...179 F1
Highshore Rd, SE15 .172 B5
Highshore Spec Sch,
  SE15............172 B4
High St, E15 ....48 A2
High Street
  Kensington 109 E2
High Timber St, EC4 ..90 A2
Highway, The, E1.....93 D3
  E14..............93 D3
Hilary Cl, SW6 ......161 E1
Hilda Rd, E16........71 F2
Hilda Ter, SW9.......169 D5
Hildyard Rd, SW6 ...137 D4
Hiley Rd, NW10......28 A3
Hilgate Pl, W8.......80 C4
Hilgate St, W8.......80 C4
Hilliards Ct, E1.......93 F4
Hillingdon St, SE17..145 F5
Hillman Dr, W10 .....50 B2
Hillman St, E8 ....21 F2
Hill Rd, NW8........32 B3
Hillside Cl, NW8......31 F2
Hillsleigh Rd, W8....80 B4
Hills Pl, W1..........86 A1
Hill St, W1..........85 D4
Hilltop Rd, NW6.......9 D3
Hillyard St, SW9 ....168 B4
Hilton Docklands Nelson
  Dock Pier 96 A4
Hind Ct, EC4........89 D1
Hinde St, W1 ....57 D5
Hind Gro, E14........96 C1
Hindmarsh Cl, E1.....93 D2
Hindon Ct, SW1......114 A5
Hippodrome Ms, W11.79 E3
Hippodrome Pl, W11..79 F3
Hirst Ct, SW1 ....141 E3
Hitchin Sq, E3 ....45 F2
Hithe Gro, SE16.....122 B4
H.M.S. Belfast, SE1.91 F4
H.M.S. President,
  EC4...............89 D3
H.M. Treasury,
  SW1 ....115 E1

Hobart Pl, SW1 .....113 E3
Hobbs Pl Est, N1 ....41 E1
Hobday St, E14 ......69 E4
Hobsons Pl, E1.......64 C3
Hobury St, SW10....138 B5
Hocker St, E2 ....42 A5
Hockett Cl, SE8 ....123 F5
Hodister Cl, SE5....170 B2
Hodnet Gro, SE16 ..122 C5
Hofland Rd, W14....107 D3
Hogan Ms, W2 ......54 C3
Hogarth Cl, E16......74 C3
Hogarth Ct, EC3......91 F2
Hogarth Pl, SW5 ...137 E1
Hogarth Rd, SW5 ...137 E1
Hogshead Pas, E1 ....93 F3
Holbeck Row, SE15..173 D2
Holbein Ms, SW1....140 C2
Holbein Pl, SW1.....140 C1
HOLBORN, WC2 .....60 A5
Holborn 59 F4
Holborn, EC1 ....60 C4
Holborn Circ, EC1 ...61 D4
Holborn Coll, SE7 .131 D5
Holborn Pl, WC1 ....60 A4
Holborn Rd, E13 ....73 E2
Holborn Viaduct, EC1.61 D4
Holcroft Rd, E9 ......22 B3
Holden Pt, E15.......27 D1
Holegate St, SE7 ...130 C4
Holford Ms, WC1 ....38 C3
Holford Pl, WC1 ......38 B4
Holford St, WC1......38 C4
Holford Yd, WC1 ....38 B3
Holland Gdns, W14..107 F3
Holland Gro, SW9 ..169 D2
Holland Ho & Pk,
  W8 ....108 A2
Holland Park 80 A5
Holland Pk, W8 .....108 A1
  W11 ....79 F5
Holland Pk Av,
  W11 ....107 D1
Holland Pk Gdns,
  W14..............79 E5
Holland Pk Ms, W11 ..79 F5
Holland Pk Rd, W14 .108 A4
Holland Pk Rbt,
  W11............106 C1
Holland Pk Sch,
  W8 ....108 B1
Holland Pas, N1......18 A5
Holland Pl, W8......109 E1
Holland Rd, E15......49 F3
  W14 ....107 D1
Holland St, SE1 .....89 F4
  W8 ....109 D2
Holland Vil Rd, W14 .107 E1
Holland Wk, W8......80 B5
Hollen St, W1........58 C5
Holles St, W1........57 F5
Holloway Rd, N7....17 D1
Hollybush Gdns, E2..43 F4
Hollybush Pl, E2......43 F4

Hollydale Rd, SE15 ..174 A4
Hollydene, SE15 ....173 E3
Holly Gro, SE15....172 B5
Holly Ms, SW10....138 B3
Hollymount Cl,
  SE10.............178 A3
Holly St, E8..........20 B3
Hollywood Ms,
  SW10............138 A4
Hollywood Rd,
  SW10............138 A3
Holmead Rd, SW6...161 F2
Holmefield Ct, NW3 ..11 F1
Holmes Pl, SW10....138 B4
Holmes Rd, NW5.....13 E1
Holmes Ter, SE1....116 C1
Holms St, E2.........42 C2
Holmwood Vil, SE7..157 D2
Holsworthy Sq, WC1..60 B2
Holton St, E1........66 C1
Holt Rd, E16........103 F5
Holy Cross RC
  Prim Sch, SW6 ...160 C3
Holy Family RC
  Prim Sch, E14 ....97 E3
Holyhead Cl, E3 .....47 D5
  E6...............76 A3
Holyoake Ct, SE16...123 F1
Holyoak Rd, SE11...117 E5
Holyport Rd, SW6...158 B1
Holyrood Ms, E16 ...101 D4
Holyrood St, SE1 ....91 E5
Holy Trinity C of E
  JMI Sch, E8.......20 A2
Holy Trinity C of E
  Prim Sch, Jun,
  SW1............112 C5
  Inf, SW3.........112 B5
Holy Trinity Haverstock
  Hill C of E Prim Sch,
  NW1.............13 E3
Holy Trinity Prim Sch,
  NW3.............10 B2
Holywell Cl, SE3....157 D4
  SE16............149 F2
Holywell La, EC2 ....63 F1
Holywell Row, EC2 ..63 E1
Homefield St, N1.....41 E3
Home Office,
  SW1 ....114 C2
Homer Dr, E14......152 C1
Home Rd, SW11 ....163 E5
Homer Rd, E9.......23 F2
Homer Row, W1 .....55 F4
Homer St, W1 .....55 F4
Homerton 22 C1
Homerton Ter, E9 ...22 B1
Homestead Rd,
  SW6 ....160 A2
Honduras St, EC1 ...62 A1

College   Thames ferry landing stage   Docklands Light Railway station

Honey La, EC2 . . . . 90 B1
Honeyman Cl, NW6 . . . . . 6 C3
Honiton Rd, NW6 . . . . 30 A2
Hood St, EC4 . . . . 89 D1
Hooks Cl, SE15 . . . . . . 173 F4
Hooper Rd, E16 . . . . . 101 D1
Hooper's Ct, SW3 . . . 112 A2
Hooper St, E1 . . . . 92 C2
Hope Cl, N1 . . . . 18 B1
Hopedale Rd, SE7 . . . 157 E5
Hopefield Av, NW6 . . . 29 F2
Hopetown St, E1 . . . . 64 B4
Hopewell St, SE5 . . . . 171 D2
Hopewell Yd, SE5 . . . 171 D2
Hop Gdns, WC2 . . . . . . 87 E3
Hopgood St, W12 . . 106 B1
Hopkinsons Pl, NW1 . . 12 B5
Hopkins St, W1 . . . . . . 86 B1
Hopping La, N1 . . . . . . 17 F2
Hop St, SE10 . . . . . . 128 B5
Hopton Gdns, SE1 . . . . 89 D1
Hopton Rd, SE18 . . . . 133 F3
Hopton St, SE1 . . . . . . 89 F4
Hopwood Rd,
  SE17 . . . . 147 D4
Hopwood Wk, E8 . . . . 21 D3
Horatio Pl, E14 . . . . 126 B1
Horatio St, E2 . . . . . . 42 C3
Horbury Cres, W11 . . . 80 C3
Horbury Ms, W11 . . . 80 B3
Horder Rd, SW6 . . . . 159 F4
Hordle Prom E,
  SE15 . . . . 172 B1
Hordle Prom N,
  SE15 . . . . 172 A1
Hordle Prom S,
  SE15 . . . . 172 A1
Horizon Way, SE7 . . 157 F1
Horle Wk, SE5 . . . . . 169 E5
Hormead Rd, W9 . . . . 52 A2
Hornbeam Cl, SE11 . . 116 C5
Hornbeam Sq, E3 . . . . 24 A5
Hornblower Cl,
  SE16 . . . . 123 E5
Hornby Cl, NW3 . . . . . 11 D3
Horn La, SE10 . . . . . 156 C1
Horn Link Way,
  SE10 . . . . 128 C5
Hornshay St, SE15 . . 150 B5
Hornton Pl, W8 . . . . . 109 E2
Hornton St, W8 . . . . . 109 D1
Horse & Dolphin Yd,
  W1 . . . . 87 D2
Horseferry Pl, SE10 . . 154 A5
Horseferry Rd, E14 . . . 95 E2
  SW1 . . . . 114 C4
Horse Guards Av,
  SW1 . . . . 87 E5
★ Horse Guards Par,
  SW1 . . . . 87 D5

Horse Guards Rd,
  SW1 . . . . 87 D5
Horse Leaze, E6 . . . . . . 77 D5
Horselydown La,
  SE1 . . . . 120 A1
Horsemongers Ms,
  SE1 . . . . 118 B2
Horse Ride, SW1 . . . . 86 B5
Horseshoe Cl, E14 . . . 154 A2
Horse Yd, N1 . . . . 17 F5
Horsleydown Old Stairs,
  SE1 . . . . 92 A5
Horsley St, SE17 . . . 146 C4
Hortensia Rd,
  SW10 . . . . 138 A5
Horton Rd, E8 . . . . . . 21 E1
Hosier La, EC1 . . . . . . 61 C2
Hoskins Cl, E16 . . . . . . 74 B5
Hoskins St, SE10 . . . 155 D3
Ⓗ Hospital of St. John &
  St. Elizabeth, NW8 . 32 C3
Hotham St, E15 . . . . . 27 E5
Hothfield Pl, SE16 . . . 122 B4
Hotspur St, SE11 . . . . 144 C2
Houghton Cl, E8 . . . . . 20 B2
Houghton St, WC2 . . . 88 B1
Houndsditch, EC3 . . . . 63 F5
Houseman Way,
  SE5 . . . . 171 D2
★ Houses of Parliament,
  SW1 . . . . 115 F2
Howard Bldg, SW8 . . 141 E5
Howell Wk, SE1 . . . . . 145 F1
Howick Pl, SW1 . . . . 114 B4
Howie St, SW11 . . . . 163 E2
Howitt Cl, NW3 . . . . . 11 F1
Howitt Rd, NW3 . . . . . 11 E1
Howland Est, SE16 . . 122 B3
Howland Ms E, W1 . . 58 B3
Howland St, W1 . . . . . 58 A3
Howland Way, SE16 . 123 F2
Howley Pl, W2 . . . . . . 54 B3
Hows St, E2 . . . . 42 A2
HOXTON, N1 . . . . 41 E3
Hoxton Mkt, N1 . . . . . 41 E5
Hoxton Sq, N1 . . . . . . 41 E5
Hoxton St, N1 . . . . . . 41 F5
Hoyland Cl, SE15 . . . . 173 E1
Hoy St, E16 . . . . 100 A1
★ H.Q.S. Wellington,
  Master Mariners' Hall,
  WC2 . . . . 88 C2
Hubbard St, E15 . . . . 49 E1
Huddart St, E3 . . . . . . 68 B3
Huddleston Cl, E2 . . . . 44 A3
Hudson's Pl, SW1 . . . 113 F5
Huggin Ct, EC4 . . . . . . 90 B2
Huggin Hill, EC4 . . . . 90 B2
Hugh Dalton Av,
  SW6 . . . . 136 A5
Ⓢⓒⓗ Hughes Flds Prim Sch,
  SE8 . . . . 153 D4
Hugh Gaitskell Cl,
  SW6 . . . . 136 A5

Hugh Ms, SW1 . . . . . . 141 F1
Ⓢⓒⓗ Hugh Myddelton Jun &
  Inf Schs, EC1 . . . . . . 39 D5
Hugh St, SW1 . . . . 141 F1
Huguenot Pl, E1 . . . . . 64 B3
Hullbridge Ms, N1 . . . . 18 C5
Hull Cl, SE16 . . . . . . 123 D1
Hull St, EC1 . . . . 40 A5
Hulme Pl, SE1 . . . . . . 118 B2
Humber Dr, W10 . . . . 50 C2
Humber Rd, SE3 . . . . 156 A4
Humbolt Rd, W6 . . . . 135 E5
Hume Ter, E16 . . . . . . 74 A4
Humphrey St, SE1 . . . 148 A2
Hungerford Br, SE1 . . . 87 F4
  WC2 . . . . 87 F4
Hungerford La, WC2 . 87 E4
Ⓢⓒⓗ Hungerford Prim Sch,
  N7 . . . . 15 D1
Hungerford Rd, N7 . . . 15 D1
Hungerford St, E1 . . . 65 F5
Hunsdon Rd, SE14 . . 174 C1
Hunslett St, E2 . . . . . . 44 B3
Hunt Cl, W11 . . . . 79 D4
Hunter Cl, SE1 . . . . . 119 D4
Hunter St, WC1 . . . . . 59 F1
Huntingdon St,
  E16 . . . . 100 B1
  N1 . . . . 16 A4
Ⓗ Huntley Cen, WC1 . 58 C2
Huntley St, WC1 . . . . . 58 B2
Hunton St, E1 . . . . . . 64 C2
Hunt's Cl, SE3 . . . . . 181 D5
Hunt's Ct, WC2 . . . . . 87 D3
Hunts La, E15 . . . . . . 48 A3
Huntsman St, SE17 . . 147 D1
Huntsworth Ms,
  NW1 . . . . 56 A2
Hurley Cres, SE16 . . . 123 D1
Hurley Ho, SE11 . . . . 145 D1
Ⓤⓝⓘ Huron Uni USA
  in London, SW7 . . 111 D3
Hurry Cl, E15 . . . . . . 27 F4
Hurstway Wk, W11 . . 79 D2
Huson Cl, NW3 . . . . . 11 E3
Hutchings St, E14 . . . 124 C2
Hutchins Cl, E15 . . . . 26 B4
Hutton St, EC4 . . . . . . 89 D1
Huxley St, W10 . . . . . 29 E5
Hyde La, SW11 . . . . . 163 E3
★ Hyde Park, W2 . . . . 83 E4
Hyde Pk, SW7 . . . . 83 E4
  W1 . . . . 83 E4
⊖ Hyde Park Corner. 112 C1
Hyde Pk Cor, W1 . . . 113 D1
Hyde Pk Cres, W2 . . . 83 E1
Hyde Pk Gdns, W2 . . . 83 D2
Hyde Pk Gdns Ms, W2. 83 D2
Hyde Pk Gate, SW7 . . 110 B2
Hyde Pk Gate Ms,
  SW7 . . . . 110 B2
Hyde Pk Pl, W2 . . . . . 83 F2
Hyde Pk Sq, W2 . . . . . 83 E1
Hyde Pk Sq Ms, W2 . . 83 E1

Hyde Pk St, W2 ......83 E1
Hyderabad Way, E15 . 27 E3
Hyde Rd, N1..........41 D1
Hydes Pl, N1..........17 E3
Hyde St, SE8........152 C5
Hyde Vale, SE10 ....178 B2
Hyndman St, SE15 ..149 E5
Hyson Rd, SE16.....149 F2

I

🅂🅲🅷 Ian Mikardo High Sch,
  E3 ....47 F5
Ibbotson Av, E16 ....72 B5
Ibbott St, E1........66 B1
Ibex Ho, E15.........27 F1
★ Ice Ho, Holland Pk,
  W8 ....108 B2
Iceland Rd, E3 ......47 D1
Iceni Ct, E3 ....46 B1
Ice Wf, N1...........37 F2
Ida St, E14 ....98 A1
Idol La, EC3.........91 E3
Idonia St, SE8.......176 B1
Ifield Rd, SW10 ....137 F4
Ifor Evans Pl, E1......67 D2
Ilbert St, W10.......29 D5
Ilchester Gdns, W2 ..81 E2
Ilchester Pl, W14....108 A3
🅂🅲🅷 Ilderton Prim Sch,
  SE16............150 A3
Ilderton Rd, SE15 ...150 A4
  SE16............149 F2
Iliffe St, SE17......145 F2
Iliffe Yd, SE17.......145 F2
Ilkley Rd, E16 ....74 A4
Imber St, N1........40 C1
🅄🅽🅸 Imperial Coll of Science,
  Tech & Med,
  Charing Cross Campus,
  W6 ....134 C3
  St. Mary's Campus,
  W2 ....55 D5
  South Kensington
  Campus, SW7 ...110 C3
Imperial Coll Rd,
  SW7 ....110 C4
Imperial Ct, NW8......33 F2
Imperial Cres, SW6 .162 A5
Imperial Rd, SW6 ...161 F3
Imperial Sq, SW6....161 F3
Imperial St, E3 ......48 A5
★ Imperial War Mus,
  SE1............117 D4
Imperial Wf, SW6 ..162 B5
🅲🅾🅻 Inchbald Sch of Design,
  Garden Design Faculty,
  SW1 ....141 F1
  Interior Design Faculty,
  SW1 ....112 C5
Indescon Ct, E14....125 D2
India Pl, WC2 ....88 A2

India St, EC3.........92 A1
Indigo Ms, E14......98 B1
Ingal Rd, E13 ....72 C2
Ingate Pl, SW8......165 F4
Ingestre Pl, W1 ......86 B1
Inglebert St, EC1....38 C4
Ingleborough St,
  SW9 ....168 C5
Inglesham Wk, E9 ...24 B1
Ingleside Gro, SE3 ..156 B5
Inglethorpe St, SW6 .158 C3
Ingleton St, SW9 ....168 C5
Inglewood Cl, E14 ...125 D5
Inglis St, SE5 ....169 F4
Ingram Cl, SE11.....116 B5
Inigo Pl, WC2 ....87 E2
Inkerman Rd, NW5 ...13 E1
Inner Circle, NW1 ....34 C5
Inner Temple La, EC4 .88 C1
Innes St, SE15 ......171 F1
★ Institute of Contemporary
  Arts (I.C.A.), SW1 . 87 D4
🅄🅽🅸 Institute of Ed,
  WC1 ....59 D2
🅂🅲🅷 International Comm
  Sch, NW1.........57 D2
🅲🅾🅻 International Studies
  Cen, W1.........58 B5
Inver Ct, W2.........81 F1
Inverine Rd, SE7 ....157 F3
Inverness Gdns, W8 ..81 E5
Inverness Ms, W2 ....81 F2
Inverness Pl, W2 .....81 F2
Inverness St, NW1....13 E5
Inverness Ter, W2 ....81 F2
🅂🅲🅷 Invicta Inf Sch,
  SE3 ....157 D5
Invicta Plaza, SE1 ...89 E4
Invicta Rd, SE3 .....181 D1
Inville Rd, SE17.....147 D3
Inwen Ct, SE8 ......151 F3
Inworth St, SW11 ...163 F5
Inworth Wk, N1......18 A5
Ionian Bldg, E14 .....95 E2
Ion Sq, E2 ....42 C3
Ireland Cl, E6 ....76 A4
Ireland Yd, EC4......89 F1
Irene Rd, SW6 ......160 C4
Ireton St, E3 ....68 C1
Iris Cl, E6..........75 F3
Ironmonger La, EC2...90 C1
Ironmonger Pas, EC1 .62 B1
Ironmonger Row,
  EC1 ....40 B5
Ironmongers Pl, E14 .153 D1
Ironside Cl, SE16 ....122 C1
Irving Ms, E1........18 A2
Irving Rd, W14 ......107 D3
Irving St, WC2 ......87 D3
Isaac Way, SE1......118 B1
Isabella St, SE1 ......89 E5
Isabel St, SW9 ......168 B3
Isambard Ms, E14...126 B4
Isambard Pl, SE16 ...94 B5

🄳🄻🅁 Island Gardens ...154 A1
Island Rd, SE16....150 C1
Island Row, E14......96 A1
Islay Wk, N1.........18 B2
ISLINGTON, N1 ......38 C1
Islington Grn, N1.....39 D3
🅂🅲🅷 Islington Grn
  Sec Sch, N1 .....40 A1
Islington High St, N1. .39 D3
Islington Pk Ms, N1...17 E3
Islington Pk St, N1....17 D3
★ Ismaili Cen & Zamana
  Gall, SW7........111 D5
🅂🅲🅷 Italia Conti Acad of
  Thea Arts, EC1 ...62 A3
Ivatt Pl, W14 ....136 B3
Iveagh Cl, E9........23 D5
Iverna Ct, W8.......109 D3
Iverna Gdns, W8 ...109 D3
Iverson Rd, NW6 .....8 B2
Ives Rd, E16 ....71 E4
Ives St, SW3 ....111 F5
Ivimey St, E2 ....43 D4
Ivor Pl, NW1........56 A2
Ivor St, NW1........14 A4
Ivybridge La, WC2 ...87 F3
Ivychurch La, SE17 ..148 A2
Ivy Cotts, E14.......97 C2
Ivy Ct, SE16 ....149 D3
Ivy Rd, E16 ....72 C5
Ivy St, N1 ....41 E2
Ixworth Pl, SW3 ....139 E2

J

Jacaranda Gro, E8 ....20 B4
Jack Clow Rd, E15 ....49 F3
Jack Dash Way, E6....75 E2
Jackman St, E8......43 E1
Jackson Cl, E9.......22 B4
🅂🅲🅷 Jack Taylor Sch, The,
  NW8 ....10 A5
Jacob St, SE1 ....120 B1
Jacob's Well Ms, W1 ..57 D5
Jade Cl, E16 ....103 D1
Jago Wk, SE5 ....170 C2
🅂🅲🅷 Jamahiriya Sch,
  SW3 ....139 E4
Jamaica Rd, SE1.....120 B2
  SE16............121 E3
Jamaica St, E1 ......66 B5
James Clavell Sq,
  SE18............133 F3
James Collins Cl, W9 ..52 A2
James Ct, N1 ....18 B4
James Hammett Ho,
  E2 ....42 B3
Jameson Ct, E2.....44 A3

Jameson St, W8 ...... 81 D4
James Riley Pt, E15 ... 26 B5
James St, W1 .... 57 D5
　WC2 .... 87 F2
Jamestown Rd, NW1.. 13 E5
Jamestown Way, E14 . 99 D3
Sch James Wolfe Inf & Nurs
　Sch, SE10........ 178 A1
Sch James Wolfe Jun Sch,
　SE10............. 178 A1
Jamuna Cl, E14 ...... 67 F4
Jane St, E1 .... 65 E5
Janet St, E14 .... 125 D3
Janeway Pl, SE16.... 121 E2
Janeway St, SE16 ... 121 D2
Jardine Rd, E1....... 95 D2
Jarrow Rd, SE16..... 150 A1
Jasmine Sq, E3 .... 46 A1
Jasper Rd, E16 ...... 103 D1
Jasper Wk, N1 ...... 40 C4
Jay Ms, SW7 .... 110 B2
Jebb St, E3........... 47 D3
Jeffreys Pl, NW1...... 14 A3
Jeffreys Rd, SW4 .... 167 E5
Jeffreys St, NW1..... 13 F3
Jeffreys Wk, SW4.... 167 E5
Coll Jeff Wooller Coll,
　WC1 .... 59 F3
Jeger Av, E2 .... 42 A1
Jellicoe Rd, E13 ...... 73 D1
Jenkins Rd, E13 ...... 73 F2
Jenner Ho, SE3...... 155 F4
Jephson St, SE5 ..... 170 C4
Jerdan Pl, SW6 ..... 161 D1
Jeremiah St, E14 ..... 97 E1
Jermyn St, SW1 ...... 86 A4
Jerningham Rd,
　SE14............. 175 E3
Jerome Cres, NW8 .... 55 E1
Jerome St, E1 .... 64 A3
Jerrard St, N1 .... 41 F3
Jersey Rd, E16 .... 74 A5
Jersey St, E2 .... 43 F5
Jerusalem Pas, EC1 ... 61 E2
Jervis Ct, W1......... 85 F1
Jervis Rd, SW6 ...... 136 B5
Jessop Sq, E14 .... 96 C5
★ Jewel Twr, Houses of
　Parliament, SW1 . 115 E3
★ Jewish Mus, NW1 .. 35 E1
Jewry St, EC3 .... 92 A1
Joan St, SE1 .... 89 E5
Jocelyn St, SE15..... 172 C3
Jockey's Flds, WC1.... 60 B3
Jodane St, SE8 ...... 152 A1
Jodrell Rd, E3 .... 24 B5
Sch Johanna Prim Sch,
　SE1 .... 116 C2
Johanna St, SE1..... 116 C2
John Adam St, WC2... 87 F3

John Aird Ct, W2 ..... 54 B3
John Carpenter St,
　EC4 .... 89 E2
Sch John Donne
　Prim Sch, SE15 ... 173 E4
John Felton Rd,
　SE16............. 120 C2
John Fisher St, E1 .... 92 C2
Sch John F. Kennedy
　Spec Sch, E15 .... 27 D5
John Harrison Way,
　SE10............. 128 A4
John Horner Ms, N1 .. 40 A2
H John Howard Cen,
　E9 .... 23 E1
John Islip St, SW1 ... 143 E1
John Kennedy Ho,
　SE16............. 122 B5
John Maurice Cl,
　SE17............. 118 C5
John McKenna Wk,
　SE16............. 121 D3
John Penn St, SE13 .. 177 F4
John Princes St, W1... 57 F5
John Rennie Wk, E1... 93 F4
Sch John Roan Sec Sch, The,
　Lwr Sch, SE3..... 180 A1
　Upr Sch, SE3 ..... 179 F1
John Roll Way,
　SE16............. 121 D3
Sch John Ruskin
　Prim Sch, SE5 .... 146 A5
John Ruskin St, SE5.. 169 E1
Sch John Scurr Prim Sch,
　E1 .... 66 A2
John Silkin La, SE8... 151 D1
John's Ms, WC1 ...... 60 B2
John Smith Av, SW6 . 160 A1
John Smith Ms, E14... 98 C2
Johnson Cl, E8 ...... 20 C5
Johnson Ho, E2 ...... 43 D4
Johnson's Pl, SW1 ... 142 A3
Johnson St, E1 .... 94 B1
John Spencer Sq, N1 .. 17 F2
John's Pl, E1 .... 65 F5
Johnston Cl, SW9 .... 168 B4
John St, WC1 .... 60 B2
John Williams Cl,
　SE14............. 150 C5
John Wilson St,
　SE18............. 132 C4
Joiner's Arms Yd,
　SE5 .... 170 C4
Joiner St, SE1 .... 91 D5
Jonathan St, SE11... 144 A2
Jones Rd, E13........ 73 F2
Jones St, W1 .... 85 E3
Joseph Hardcastle Cl,
　SE14............. 175 D1
Sch Joseph Lancaster
　Prim Sch, SE1 ... 118 C4
Joseph St, E3 .... 68 B2
Joshua St, E14 .... 70 A5
Joubert St, SW11... 164 A5

Jowett St, SE15 ..... 172 B2
Jubilee Cres, E14 .... 126 B4
★ Jubilee Gdns, SE1 .. 88 A5
Jubilee Pl, SW3..... 139 F2
Jubilee St, E1 .... 66 A5
Judd St, WC1 .... 37 E5
Jude St, E16 .... 100 A1
Juer St, SW11....... 163 F2
Julia Garfield Ms,
　E16............. 101 F4
Julian Pl, E14 .... 153 F2
Julius Nyerere Cl, N1 . 38 A1
Junction Av, W10 ... 28 B5
Junction Ms, W2 ..... 55 E5
Junction Pl, W2 ...... 55 E5
Juniper Cres, NW1.... 13 D4
Juniper La, E6........ 75 F4
Juniper St, E1 .... 94 A2
Juno Way, SE14..... 151 D4
Jupiter Way, N7 ..... 16 B1
Jupp Rd, E15........ 26 C4
Jupp Rd W, E15...... 26 B5
Justice Wk, SW3 .... 139 E5
Jutland Rd, E13 ...... 73 D2
Juxon St, SE11 ...... 116 B5

K

Sch Kaizen Prim Sch,
　E13............... 73 E2
Karanjia Ct, NW2...... 6 B1
Kassala Rd, SW11... 164 B4
Katherine Cl, SE16 ... 94 C5
Katherine Sq, W11 ... 79 E4
Kay St, E2 .... 43 D2
Kay Way, SE10...... 177 F1
Kean St, WC2........ 88 A1
Keats Av, E16....... 101 E4
Keats Cl, SE1 .... 148 A1
Keats Pl, EC2 .... 62 C4
Kedleston Wk, E2 .... 43 F4
Keel Cl, SE16 .... 95 D5
Keeley St, WC2....... 88 A1
Sch Keen Students Sch,
　E1 .... 65 D3
Keens Yd, N1 .... 17 F2
Keetons Rd, SE16 ... 121 E3
Keir Hardie Ho, W6.. 134 B4
Sch Keir Hardie
　Prim Sch, E16 ..... 72 C4
Kelfield Gdns, W10 ... 50 B5
Kelfield Ms, W10..... 50 C5
Kelland Rd, E13...... 73 D1
Kell St, SE1......... 117 F3
Kelly Av, SE15 ...... 172 A2
Kelly Ms, W9 .... 52 B2
Kelly St, NW1....... 13 F2
Kelsall Cl, SE3 ...... 181 F5
Kelsey St, E2......... 65 D1
Kelson Ho, E14 ..... 126 B3
Kelso Pl, W8........ 109 F4
Kelvedon Ho, SW8 .. 167 F3

Kelvedon Rd, SW6...160 B2
Kember St, N1........16 A4
Kemble St, WC2......88 A1
Kempe Rd, NW6.....28 C3
Kemp's Ct, W1.......86 B1
Kemps Dr, E14.......97 D2
Kempsford Gdns,
    SW5.............137 D3
Kempsford Rd,
    SE11............145 D1
Kempson Rd, SW6..161 D3
Kempthorne Rd,
    SE8.............123 F5
Kempton Ct, E1......65 E3
Kemsing Rd, SE10...156 C2
Kenbury Gdns, SE5..170 A5
Kenbury St, SE5.....170 A5
Kenchester Cl, SW8.167 F2
Kendal Cl, SW9.....169 E1
Kendal Ho, N1.......38 B2
Kendall Pl, W1......56 C4
Kendal St, W2.......83 F1
Sch Kender Prim Sch,
    SE14............174 B3
Kender St, SE14.....174 B3
Kendrick Ms, SW7...110 C5
Kendrick Pl, SW7....138 C1
Kenilworth Rd, E3....45 E2
    NW6..............8 B5
Kenley Wk, W11.....79 E3
Kennacraig Cl, E16..101 D5
Kennard Rd, E15....26 C4
Kennard St, E16.....104 A5
    SW11...........164 C4
Kennet Ho, NW8....55 D3
Kennet Rd, W9.......52 B1
Kennet St, E1........93 D4
Kennet Wf La, EC4....90 B2
Kenning St, SE16....122 B1
Kennings Way, SE11.145 E2
Kenning Ter, N1......19 E5
KENNINGTON, SE11.144 C5
⊖ Kennington........145 E2
Kennington Grn,
    SE11............144 C3
Kennington La,
    SE11............145 D2
Kennington Oval,
    SE11............144 B4
Kennington Pk, SW9.169 D1
Kennington Pk Est,
    SE11............144 C5
Kennington Pk Gdns,
    SE11............145 E4
Kennington Pk Pl,
    SE11............145 D3
Kennington Pk Rd,
    SE11............145 D4
Kennington Rd,
    SE1.............116 C3
    SE11............116 C4
Kenrick Pl, W1.......56 C4
KENSAL GREEN,
    NW10............28 B4

≷ Kensal Green......28 B4
⊖ Kensal Green......28 B4
★ Kensal Green Cem,
    W10.............28 A5
KENSAL RISE, NW6...28 C3
≷ Kensal Rise.......28 B3
Sch Kensal Ri Prim Sch,
    NW6.............28 C3
Kensal Rd, W10......51 F1
KENSAL TOWN,
    W10.............51 D1
Kensal Wf, W10......51 D1
KENSINGTON, W8....80 B5
Coll Kensington & Chelsea
    Coll, Hortensia Cen,
    SW10............162 A1
    Marlborough Cen,
    SW3.............139 F1
    Wornington Cen,
    W10.............51 F3
Kensington Ch Ct,
    W8.............109 E2
Kensington Ch St,
    W8..............81 D4
Kensington Ch Wk,
    W8.............109 E2
Coll Kensington Coll of
    Business, WC2....60 A5
Kensington Ct, W8..109 F2
Kensington Ct Ms,
    W8.............109 E1
Kensington Ct Pl,
    W8.............109 F3
★ Kensington Gdns,
    W2..............82 B5
Kensington Gdns Sq,
    W2..............81 E1
Kensington Gate,
    W8.............110 A3
Kensington Gore,
    SW7............110 C2
Kensington Grn, W8.109 E4
Kensington Hall Gdns,
    W14............136 A2
Kensington High St,
    W8.............108 C3
    W14............108 A4
Kensington Mall,
    W8..............81 D4
≷ Kensington
    (Olympia).......107 E3
⊖ Kensington
    (Olympia).......107 E3
★ Kensington Palace,
    W8..............81 F5
Kensington Palace Gdns,
    W8..............81 E4
Kensington Pk Gdns,
    W11.............80 A3
Kensington Pk Ms,
    W11.............80 A1
Kensington Pk Rd,
    W11.............80 A2
Kensington Pl, W8....80 C5

Kensington Rd, SW7.111 D2
    W8.............109 F2
Kensington Sq, W8..109 E2
Kensington Village,
    W14............136 B1
Kentish Bldgs, SE1....90 C5
KENTISH TOWN,
    NW5.............14 A1
Kentish Town Rd,
    NW1.............13 F4
    NW5.............13 F4
≷ Kentish Town
    West............13 D2
Kenton Ct, W14.....108 A4
Kenton Rd, E9.......22 C2
Kenton St, WC1......59 E1
Kent Pas, NW1.......56 A1
Kent St, E2..........42 B2
Kent Ter, NW1.......33 F5
Kent Yd, SW7.......111 F2
Kenway Rd, SW5....137 E1
Kenwood Av, SE14..174 C3
Kenyon St, SW6.....158 C3
Keogh Rd, E15.......27 F1
Keppel Row, SE1.....90 A5
Keppel St, WC1......59 D3
Kerbela St, E2........64 C1
Kerbey St, E14.......69 E5
Kerfield Cres, SE5...170 C4
Kerfield Pl, SE5.....170 C4
Kerridge Ct, N1......19 F1
Kerrison Rd, E15.....26 C5
Kerry Cl, E16........101 E1
Kerry Path, SE14....152 A5
Kerry Rd, SE14......152 A5
Kersley Ms, SW11...164 A4
Kersley St, SW11....164 A5
Kerwick Cl, N7.......16 A3
Keslake Rd, NW6....28 C3
Kestrel Av, E6........75 E4
Kestrel Ho, EC1......40 A4
Kevan Ho, SE5......170 A2
Keybridge Ho, SW8..143 F5
Key Cl, E1...........65 F2
Keyse Rd, SE1......120 A4
Keystone Cres, N1....37 F3
Sch Keyworth
    Prim Sch, SE17...145 E3
Keyworth St, SE1...117 F3
Kezia St, SE8.......151 E3
Kibworth St, SW8...168 A2
Kidbrooke Gdns,
    SE3.............180 C5
Kidbrooke Gro, SE3..181 D3
Kidbrooke Pk Cl,
    SE3.............181 E4
Kidbrooke Pk Rd,
    SE3.............181 E3
Kiffen St, EC2........63 D1
KILBURN, NW6......30 C2

⊖ Kilburn 7 F2
Kilburn Br, NW6 . . . . . . 31 D1
Kilburn Gate, NW6 . . 31 E2
⇌ Kilburn High Road . 31 D1
Kilburn High Rd, NW6 . . 8 B3
Kilburn La, W9 . . . . 29 D5
W10 . . . . 29 D5
⊖ Kilburn Park 31 D2
Sch Kilburn Pk Jun Sch,
NW6 . . . . 30 B3
Kilburn Pk Rd, NW6 . . 30 C5
Kilburn Pl, NW6 . . . . . . 31 D1
Kilburn Priory, NW6 . . 31 E1
Kilburn Sq, NW6 . . . . . . 8 C5
Kilburn Vale, NW6 . . . . 31 E1
Kildare Gdns, W2 . . . . . 53 D5
Kildare Rd, E16 . . . . . . 73 D3
Kildare Ter, W2 . . . . . . 53 D5
Kildare Wk, E14 . . . . . . 96 C1
Killick St, N1 . . . . 38 A2
Killip Cl, E16 . . . . 72 B3
Killowen Rd, E9 . . . . . . 22 C2
Killyon Rd, SW8 . . . . . 166 B5
Kilmaine Rd, SW6 . . . 159 F2
Kilmarsh Rd, W6 . . . . 106 A5
Kilner St, E14 . . . . 68 C4
Kilravock St, W10 . . . . 29 E5
Kimbell Gdns, SW6 . . 159 E4
Kimberley Rd, E16 . . . . 72 A1
NW6 . . . . 7 F5
Kimbolton Row,
SW3 . . . . 139 E1
Kimpton Rd, SE5 . . . . 170 C3
Kinburn St, SE16 . . . . 122 C1
Kincaid Rd, SE15 . . . . 173 E2
Kincardine Gdns, W9 . 52 C2
Kinder St, E1 . . . . 93 E1
King & Queen St,
SE17 . . . . 146 B1
King & Queen Wf,
SE16 . . . . 94 C4
King Arthur Cl, SE15 . 174 A2
King Charles St,
SW1 . . . . 115 D1
King David La, E1 . . . . . 94 A2
Kingdon Rd, NW6 . . . . . 9 D4
🏥 King Edward VII's Hosp
for Officers, W1 . . . 57 D3
King Edwards Rd, E9 . . 21 F5
King Edward St, EC1 . . 62 A5
King Edward III Ms,
SE16 . . . . 121 F2
King Edward Wk,
SE1 . . . . 117 D3
Kingfield St, E14 . . . . 154 B1
Kingfisher Sq, SE8 . . . 152 B5
Kingfisher St, E6 . . . . 75 F3
King Frederik IX Twr,
SE16 . . . . 124 A3
King George Av, E16 . . 74 C5

DLA King George V 105 D5
King George St,
SE10 . . . . 178 B2
Kingham Cl, W11 . . . 107 E1
King Henry's Reach,
W6 . . . . 134 B4
King Henry's Rd,
NW3 . . . . 11 F4
King Henry's Wk, N1 . . 19 E1
King Henry Ter, E1 . . . 93 F3
Kinghorn St, EC1 . . . . . 62 A4
King James Ct, SE1 . . 117 F2
King James St, SE1 . . 117 F2
King John Ct, EC2 . . . . . 63 F1
King John St, E1 . . . . . . 67 D4
Kinglake Est, SE17 . . 147 F2
Kinglake St, SE17 . . . 147 E3
Kingly Ct, W1 . . . . 86 A2
Kingly St, W1 . . . . 86 A1
Kings Arms Ct, E1 . . . . 64 C4
Kings Arms Yd, EC2 . . 62 C5
Kings Bench St, SE1 . 117 F1
Kings Bench Wk, EC4 . 89 D1
Kingsbridge Rd, W10 . 50 B5
Kingsbury Rd, N1 . . . . 19 F1
Kingsbury Ter, N1 . . . . 19 F1
Uni King's Coll - Guy's
Campus, SE1 . . . . . 118 C3
Uni King's Coll - Maughan
Lib & Information
Services Cen, WC2 . 60 C5
Uni King's Coll - Strand
Campus, WC2 . . . . . 88 B2
Uni King's Coll - Waterloo
Campus, Franklin-Wilkins
Bldg, SE1 . . . . 88 C5
James Clerk Maxwell Bldg,
SE1 . . . . 88 C5
Stamford St Apartments,
SE1 . . . . 88 C5
Waterloo Br Wing,
SE1 . . . . 88 C5
Kings Coll Rd, NW3 . . 11 E3
Kingscote St, EC4 . . . . 89 E2
Kingscroft Rd, NW2 . . . 7 F1
KING'S CROSS, N1 . . . 15 D5
⇌ King's Cross 37 E3
King's Cross Br, N1 . . 37 F4
King's Cross Rd, WC1 . 38 B4
⊖ King's Cross
St. Pancras 37 E3
⇌ King's Cross
Thameslink 37 F3
Kingsdale Gdns, W11 . 79 D5
Kingsdown Cl, SE16 . 149 F3
W10 . . . . 79 D1
Sch Kingsford Comm Sch,
E6 . . . . 76 A5
Kingsford Way, E6 . . . 76 B4
Kings Gdns, NW6 . . . . . . 9 D4
Sch Kingsgate Inf & Jun Sch,
NW6 . . . . 8 C3
Kingsgate Pl, NW6 . . . . 8 C4
Kingsgate Rd, NW6 . . . . 8 C3

Kings Gro, SE15 . . . . . 173 F2
Kings Head Yd, SE1 . . . 90 C5
Kingshold Est, E9 . . . . . 22 A5
Kingshold Rd, E9 . . . . . 22 B4
Kingside Business Pk,
SE18 . . . . 131 F4
KINGSLAND, N1 . . . . . . 19 E2
Kingsland, NW8 . . . . . . 33 F1
Kingsland Grn, E8 . . . . 19 F1
Kingsland High St, E8 . 20 A1
Kingsland Pas, E8 . . . 19 F1
Kingsland Rd, E2 . . . . . 41 F4
E8 . . . . 19 F5
Kingsland Shop Cen,
E8 . . . . 20 A1
Kingsley Ms, E1 . . . . . . 93 F3
W8 . . . . 109 F4
Kingsley Rd, NW6 . . . . . 8 B5
Kings Mall, W6 . . . . . 134 A1
Kingsman Par, SE18 . 132 B4
Kingsman St, SE18 . . 132 B4
King's Ms, WC1 . . . . . . 60 B2
Kingsmill Ter, NW8 . . . 33 D2
Kings Pl, SE1 . . . . 118 A2
King Sq, EC1 . . . . 40 A5
King's Reach Twr,
SE1 . . . . 89 D4
King's Rd, SW1 . . . . . . 139 F2
SW3 . . . . 139 F2
SW6 . . . . 161 F2
SW10 . . . . 161 F2
King's Scholars' Pas,
SW1 . . . . 114 A4
King Stairs Cl, SE16 . . 121 F1
King's Ter, NW1 . . . . . . 36 A1
Kingstown St, NW1 . . . 12 C2
King St, E13 . . . . 72 C2
EC2 . . . . 90 B1
SW1 . . . . 86 B5
WC2 . . . . 87 E2
Kingsway, WC2 . . . . . . 60 A5
Kingsway Pl, EC1 . . . . . 61 D1
Kings Wf, E8 . . . . 19 F5
Kingswood Av, NW6 . . 29 E1
Kingswood Cl, SW8 . . 167 F2
King William La,
SE10 . . . . 155 E3
King William St, EC4 . . 91 D3
King William Wk,
SE10 . . . . 154 B4
Coll Kingwood City Learning
Cen, The, SW6 . . . . 159 E3
Kingwood Rd, SW6 . . 159 D3
Kinnerton Pl N, SW1 . 112 B2
Kinnerton Pl S, SW1 . 112 B2
Kinnerton St, SW1 . . 112 C2
Kinnerton Yd, SW1 . . 112 B2
Kinnoul Rd, W6 . . . . . 135 E4
Kintore Way, SE1 . . . . 120 A5
Kipling Est, SE1 . . . . . 119 D2
Kipling St, SE1 . . . . . . 119 D2
Kirby Est, SE16 . . . . . 121 E3
Kirby Gro, SE1 . . . . . . 119 E1
Kirby St, EC1 . . . . 61 D3

Kirkham Rd, E6 . . . . . . 75 F5
Kirkland Wk, E8 . . . . . . 20 A2
Kirkman Pl, W1 . . . . . . 58 C4
Kirkmichael Rd, E14 . . 70 B5
Kirkside Rd, SE3 . . . . 156 C4
Kirk St, WC1 . . . . 60 A2
Kirkwall Pl, E2 . . . . 44 B4
Kirkwood Rd, SE15 . . 173 F5
Kirtling St, SW8 . . . . . 166 A1
Kirton Gdns, E2 . . . . . . 42 B5
Kirwyn Way, SE5 . . . . 169 F1
Kitcat Ter, E3 . . . . 47 D4
Kite Pl, E2 . . . . 43 D4
Kite Yd, SW11 . . . . . . 164 A4
Kitson Rd, SE5 . . . . . . 170 B1
Knapp Rd, E3 . . . . 68 C2
Knaresborough Pl,
  SW5 . . . . 109 E5
Knatchbull Rd, SE5 . . 170 A4
Knighten St, E1 . . . . . . 93 D5
Knighthead Pt, E14 . . 124 C3
Knightrider St, EC4 . . . 90 A2
Knights Arc, SW1 . . . . 112 A2
✪ Knightsbridge 112 A2
Knightsbridge,
  SW1 . . . . 112 B2
  SW7 . . . . 111 F2
Knightsbridge Grn,
  SW1 . . . . 112 A2
Knights Rd, E16 . . . . . 129 D1
Knights Wk, SE11 . . . . 145 E1
Knivet Rd, SW6 . . . . . 136 C5
Knobs Hill Rd, E15 . . . . 25 E5
Knottisford St, E2 . . . . 44 C4
Knox St, W1 . . . . 56 A3
Knoyle St, SE14 . . . . . 151 E5
Sch Kobi Nazrul Prim Sch,
  E1 . . . . 65 D5
Kossuth St, SE10 . . . . 155 E2
Kotree Way, SE1 . . . . 149 D1
Kramer Ms, SW5 . . . . 137 D3
Kylemore Rd, NW6 . . . . 8 C3
Kynance Ms, SW7 . . . . 110 A4
Kynance Pl, SW7 . . . . 110 A4

L

Laburnum Cl, SE15 . . 174 A2
Laburnum Ct, E2 . . . . . 42 A1
Laburnum St, E2 . . . . . 42 A1
Lacey Wk, E3 . . . . 46 C3
Lackington St, EC2 . . . 63 D3
Ladbroke Cres, W11 . . 79 F1
Ladbroke Gdns, W11 . . 80 A2
✪ Ladbroke Grove 51 F5
Ladbroke Gro, W10 . . . 51 D1
  W11 . . . . 79 F1
Ladbroke Ms, W11 . . . 79 E5
Ladbroke Rd, W11 . . . . 79 F4
Ladbroke Sq, W11 . . . . 80 A3
Ladbroke Ter, W11 . . . 80 B3
Ladbroke Wk, W11 . . . 80 B4

Lady Dock Path,
  SE16 . . . . 123 E2
Sch Lady Eden's Sch,
  W8 . . . . 110 A3
Sch Lady Margaret Sec Sch,
  SW6 . . . . 160 C4
Lafone St, SE1 . . . . . . 120 A1
Lagado Ms, SE16 . . . . . 95 D5
Laird Ho, SE5 . . . . 170 A2
Lairs Cl, N7 . . . . 15 F1
Lakeside Rd, W14 . . . 106 C3
Lalor St, SW6 . . . . 159 E5
Lambert Rd, E16 . . . . . 73 E5
Lambert St, N1 . . . . . . 16 C4
LAMBETH, SE1 . . . . . . 116 A3
Lambeth Br, SE1 . . . . 115 F5
  SW1 . . . . 115 F5
Coll Lambeth Coll, Vauxhall
  Cen, SW8 . . . . 167 D3
Lambeth High St,
  SE1 . . . . 144 A1
Lambeth Hill, EC4 . . . . 90 A2
✪ Lambeth North 116 C2
★ Lambeth Palace,
  SE1 . . . . 116 A4
Lambeth Palace Rd,
  SE1 . . . . 116 A4
Lambeth Rd, SE1 . . . . 116 B4
  SE11 . . . . 116 B4
Lambeth Wk, SE11 . . . 116 B5
Lamb La, E8 . . . . 21 E4
Lambolle Pl, NW3 . . . . 11 F2
Lambolle Rd, NW3 . . . 11 E2
Lambourne Gro,
  SE16 . . . . 150 C1
Lambourne Pl, SE3 . . 181 E3
Lambrook Ter, SW6 . . 159 E3
Lamb's Bldgs, EC1 . . . . 62 C2
Lambs Conduit Pas,
  WC1 . . . . 60 A3
Lamb's Conduit St,
  WC1 . . . . 60 A2
Lambs Ms, N1 . . . . 39 E1
Lamb's Pas, EC1 . . . . . 62 C3
Lamb St, E1 . . . . 64 A3
Lambton Pl, W11 . . . . . 80 B2
Lamb Wk, SE1 . . . . . . 119 E2
Lamerton St, SE8 . . . . 152 C5
Lamlash St, SE11 . . . . 117 E5
Lammas Rd, E9 . . . . . . 23 D4
Lamont Rd, SW10 . . . 138 B5
Lampern Sq, E2 . . . . . . 43 D4
Lampeter Sq, W6 . . . . 135 E5
Lamplighter Cl, E1 . . . . 66 A2
Lamp Office Ct, WC1 . . 60 A2
Lamport Cl, SE18 . . . . 132 B5
Lanark Ms, W9 . . . . . . 32 A5
Lanark Pl, W9 . . . . 54 B1
Lanark Rd, W9 . . . . . . 32 A5
Lanark Sq, E14 . . . . . . 125 F3
Lancashire Ct, W1 . . . . 85 F2
Lancaster Cl, N1 . . . . . 19 F4
Lancaster Ct, SW6 . . . 160 C2
  W2 . . . . 82 B3

Lancaster Dr, E14 . . . . 98 B5
  NW3 . . . . 11 E2
✪ Lancaster Gate 82 C2
Lancaster Gate, W2 . . . 82 B3
Lancaster Gro, NW3 . . 11 D2
★ Lancaster Ho,
  SW1 . . . . 114 A1
Lancaster Ms, W2 . . . . 82 B2
Lancaster Pl, WC2 . . . . 88 A2
Lancaster Rd, W11 . . . 79 E1
Lancaster St, SE1 . . . 117 F2
Lancaster Ter, W2 . . . . 82 C2
Lancaster Wk, W2 . . . 110 C1
Lancefield St, W10 . . . 30 A4
Lancelot Pl, SW7 . . . . 112 A2
Lancer Sq, W8 . . . . . . 109 E1
Lancey Cl, SE7 . . . . . . 131 D5
Lanchester Way,
  SE14 . . . . 174 B3
Lancing St, NW1 . . . . . 36 C5
Lancresse Ct, N1 . . . . . 19 E5
Landmann Ho, SE16 . 149 F1
Landmann Way,
  SE14 . . . . 151 D4
Landon Pl, SW1 . . . . . 112 A3
Landons Cl, E14 . . . . . . 98 B4
Landon Wk, E14 . . . . . 97 F2
Landridge Rd, SW6 . . 159 F5
Lane, The, NW8 . . . . . . 32 A2
Lanesborough Pl,
  SW1 . . . . 113 D1
Lanfranc Rd, E3 . . . . . 45 E3
Lanfrey Pl, W14 . . . . . 136 A3
Langbourne Pl, E14 . . 153 E2
Langdale, NW1 . . . . . . 36 A4
Langdale Cl, SE17 . . . 146 A4
Langdale Rd, SE10 . . . 178 A2
Langdale St, E1 . . . . . . 93 E1
Sch Langdon Pk Sec Sch,
  E14 . . . . 69 F5
Langdon Way, SE1 . . 149 D1
Langford Cl, NW8 . . . . 32 B2
Langford Ct, NW8 . . . . 32 A3
Langford Pl, NW8 . . . . 32 B3
Sch Langford Prim Sch,
  SW6 . . . . 161 F5
Langford Rd, SW6 . . . 161 F5
Langham Pl, W1 . . . . . 57 F4
Langham St, W1 . . . . . 57 F4
Langler Rd, NW10 . . . . 28 B3
Langley Ct, WC2 . . . . . 87 E2
Langley La, SW8 . . . . 143 F4
Langley St, WC2 . . . . . 87 E1
Lang St, E1 . . . . 66 A1
Langthorn Ct, EC2 . . . . 62 C5
Langthorne St, SW6 . 158 C2
Langton Cl, WC1 . . . . . 38 B5
Langton Rd, SW9 . . . . 169 D2
Langton St, SW10 . . . 138 B5
Langton Way, SE3 . . . 180 B3

Langtry Pl, SW6.....137 D4
Langtry Rd, NW8.....31 E1
Langtry Wk, NW8 ....10 A5
Lanhill Rd, W9 ....52 C1
Lanrick Rd, E14 ......71 D5
Lansbury Est, E14 ...69 E5
Lansbury Gdns, E14 ..70 C5
Sch Lansbury Lawrence
   Prim Sch, E14 .....97 E1
Lanscombe Wk,
   SW8 ....167 E3
Coll Lansdowne Coll,
   W2 ....81 E3
Lansdowne Cres,
   W11 ....79 F3
Lansdowne Dr, E8 ....21 D2
Lansdowne Gdns,
   SW8 ....167 E3
Lansdowne Grn,
   SW8 ....167 E2
Lansdowne Ms, W11 .80 A4
Lansdowne Pl, SE1 ..119 D4
Lansdowne Ri, W11 ..79 F3
Lansdowne Rd, W11..79 F2
Lansdowne Row, W1 .85 F4
Lansdowne Ter, WC1 .59 F2
Lansdowne Wk, W11 .79 F4
Lansdowne Way,
   SW8 ....167 D3
Lanterns Ct, E14 ....125 D2
Lant St, SE1 ....118 A1
Lanvanor Rd, SE15 ..174 A5
Lapford Cl, W9 ....52 B1
Lapwing Twr, SE8 ...152 A4
Larch Cl, E13 ....74 A1
   SE8 ....152 B5
Larcom St, SE17 ....146 B1
Larissa St, SE17 ....147 D2
Lark Row, E2 ....44 A1
Larkspur Cl, E6.......75 E3
Sch Larmenier RC Inf Sch,
   W6 ....135 D1
Larnach Rd, W6 .....134 C5
Lassell St, SE10 .....155 D3
Lasseter Pl, SE3 .....155 F4
Latchmere Rd,
   SW11 ....164 A5
Latchmere St, SW11.164 A5
Latham Cl, E6........75 F5
Latham Ho, E1 ....67 D5
Latimer, SE17 ......147 E3
H Latimer Ho Day Hosp,
   W1 ....58 A3
Latimer Pl, W10......50 B5
⊖ Latimer Road 78 C2
Latimer Rd, W10.....50 A4
Latona Rd, SE15 ....148 C5
Latymer Ct, W6......135 D1
Lauderdale Rd, W9 ..31 E5
Lauderdale Twr, EC2 ..62 A3

Laud St, SE11.......144 A2
Launcelot St, SE1 ...116 C2
Launceston Pl, W8 ..110 A3
Launch St, E14......126 A3
Laundry La, N1 ....18 A4
Laundry Rd, W6 .....135 E5
Laurel Bk Gdns, SW6.160 B5
Laurel St, E8 ....20 B2
Laurence Pountney Hill,
   EC4 ....90 C2
Laurence Pountney La,
   EC4 ....90 C2
Laurie Gro, SE14 ....175 F3
Sch Lauriston JMI Sch,
   E9 ....22 C5
Lauriston Rd, E9 .....22 C5
Lausanne Rd, SE15 ..174 B4
Lavender Cl, SW3 ...139 D5
Lavender Gro, E8 .....20 B4
Lavender Rd, SE16 ...95 E4
Lavender St, E15 .....27 E1
Laverton Ms, SW5...137 F1
Laverton Pl, SW5...137 F1
Lavina Gro, N1 ....38 A2
Lavington Cl, E9......24 A1
Lavington St, SE1 ....89 F5
Sch Lawdale Jun Sch,
   E2 ....43 D4
Lawford Rd, N1 ......19 E4
   NW5 ....14 A2
Lawless St, E14 ......97 F2
Lawn Ho Cl, E14 ....126 A1
Lawn La, SW8 ......143 F5
Lawrence Cl, E3 ......46 C3
Lawrence La, EC2 ....90 B1
Lawrence Pl, N1......15 F5
Lawrence Rd, E16....72 B4
   SW3 ....139 E5
Lawson Cl, E16 ......74 B4
Lawson Est, SE1 ....118 C4
Law St, SE1.........119 D3
Lawton Rd, E3 ....45 F5
Laxley Cl, SE5......169 F1
Laxton Pl, NW1 ......57 F1
Layard Rd, SE16 ....121 F5
Layard Sq, SE16 ....121 F5
Sch Laycock Prim Sch,
   N1 ....17 E2
Laycock St, N1 ......17 D2
Laystall St, EC1 ......60 C2
Laytons Bldgs, SE1 .118 B1
Leabank Sq, E9.......24 C1
★ Leadenhall Mkt,
   EC3 ....91 E1
Leadenhall Pl, EC3....91 E1
Leadenhall St, EC3 ...91 E1
Leadenham Ct, E3....68 C2
Leake St, SE1 ......116 B1
Leamington Rd Vil,
   W11 ....52 B4
Leamouth Rd, E6.....75 E5
   E14 ....99 D1
Leander Ct, SE8.....176 C4
Learoyd Gdns, E6....104 C2

Lea Sq, E3 ....46 B1
Leatherdale St, E1....66 C5
Leather Gdns, E15....49 F1
Leather La, EC1 ......61 D4
★ Leather Mkt Bermondsey,
   SE1 ....119 E2
Leathermarket Ct,
   SE1 ....119 E2
Leathermarket St,
   SE1 ....119 E2
Leather Rd, SE16....150 C1
Leathwell Rd, SE8 ...177 F5
Lea Valley Wk, E3 ...48 A3
   E14 ....68 C5
   E15 ....25 D5
Lecky St, SW7 ......138 C2
Leda Rd, SE18 ......132 A4
Ledbury Est, SE15 ...173 E1
Ledbury Ms N, W11...80 C2
Ledbury Ms W, W11 ..80 C2
Ledbury Rd, W11.....52 B5
Ledbury St, SE15 ....173 D1
Leeke St, WC1 ....38 A4
Leerdam Dr, E14 ....126 B4
Leeside Ct, SE16 ....94 C4
Lees Pl, W1..........84 C2
Lee St, E8 ....20 A5
Leeway, SE8........152 A2
Lefevre Wk, E3.......46 C1
Leggatt Rd, E15......48 B2
Legion Cl, N1 ....17 D2
Leicester Ct, WC2 ....87 D2
Leicester Pl, WC2.....87 D2
⊖ Leicester Square...87 D2
Leicester Sq, WC2 ...87 D2
Leicester St, WC2 ...87 D2
Leigh Gdns, NW10....28 A3
Leigh Hunt St, SE1 ..118 A1
Leigh Pl, EC1.........60 C3
Leigh St, WC1.......59 E1
★ Leighton Ho Mus,
   W14 ....108 B3
Leinster Gdns, W2....82 A1
Leinster Ms, W2......82 A2
Leinster Pl, W2.......82 A1
Leinster Sq, W2 .....81 D2
Leinster Ter, W2 .....82 A2
Leith Yd, NW6 ....8 C5
Lelitia Cl, E8 ....20 C5
Leman St, E1 ....92 B1
Lemmon Rd, SE10...155 E4
Lena Gdns, W6......106 B4
Sch Lena Gdns Prim Sch,
   W6 ....106 B3
Lenanton Steps, E14 125 D1
Len Freeman Pl, SW6 136 A5
Lennox Gdns, SW1 ..112 A4
Lennox Gdns Ms,
   SW1 ....112 A4
Lenthall Rd, E8 ......20 B3
Lenthorp Rd, SE10 ..156 A2
Leonard St, E16.....103 F5
   EC2 ....63 D1
Leontine Cl, SE15 ...173 D2

Leopards Ct, EC1 . . . . . 60 C3
Leopold Ms, E9 . . . . 22 A5
Leopold St, E3 . . . . 68 B3
Leo St, SE15 . . . . 173 F1
Leo Yd, EC1 . . . . 61 F2
Leroy St, SE1 . . . . 119 E5
Lerry Cl, W14 . . . . 136 B4
Leslie Rd, E16 . . . . . . 101 F1
Lester Av, E15 . . . . 49 F5
Lethbridge Cl, SE13. . 178 A4
Letterstone Rd,
   SW6 . . . . 160 A2
Lettice St, SW6 . . . . . 160 A4
Lett Rd, E15 . . . . 26 C4
Lettsom St, SE5 . . . . . 171 E5
Levehurst Way,
   SW4 . . . . 167 F5
Leven Rd, E14 . . . . 70 B4
Leverett St, SW3 . . . . 111 F5
Lever St, EC1 . . . . 39 F5
Lewey Ho, E3 . . . . 68 B2
Sch Lewisham Coll,
   Deptford Campus,
   SE8 . . . . 177 D3
Lewisham Rd, SE13 . 177 F4
Lewisham St, SW1 . . 115 D2
Lewisham Way,
   SE4 . . . . 176 A3
   SE14 . . . . 176 A3
Lewis St, NW1 . . . . 13 F2
Lexham Gdns, W8 . . . 109 E5
Lexham Gdns Ms,
   W8 . . . . 109 F4
Lexham Ms, W8 . . . . . 109 D5
Lexham Wk, W8 . . . . 109 F4
Lexington, The, EC1 . . 62 C1
Lexington St, W1 . . . . . 86 B1
Leybourne Rd, NW1 . . 13 F4
Leybourne St, NW1 . . 13 E4
Leyden St, E1 . . . . 64 A4
Leydon Cl, SE16 . . . . . 95 D5
Leylang Rd, SE14 . . . . 175 D1
Leywick St, E15 . . . . . . 49 E2
Liardet St, SE14 . . . . . 151 F5
Liberia Rd, N5 . . . . 17 F1
★ Liberty, W1 . . . . 86 A1
Liberty St, SW9 . . . . . 168 B4
Libra Rd, E3 . . . . 46 B2
Library Pl, E1 . . . . 93 F2
Library St, SE1 . . . . . . 117 E2
Lichfield Rd, E3 . . . . . . 45 F4
Liddell Gdns, NW10. . . 28 A2
Liddell Rd, NW6 . . . . 8 C1
Lidgate Rd, SE15 . . . . 172 A2
Lidlington Pl, NW1 . . . 36 A3
Coll Lifelong Learning, The
   Shadwell Cen, E1 . . 94 C2
Lighter Cl, SE16 . . . . . 123 F5
Lighterman Ms, E1 . . . 67 D5
Lightermans Rd,
   E14 . . . . 125 D2
Ligonier St, E2 . . . . 64 A1
Lilac Pl, SE11 . . . . 144 A1
Lilestone Est, NW8 . . . 54 C2

Lilestone St, NW8 . . . . 55 E1
Lilford Rd, SE5 . . . . . . 169 E5
Sch Lilian Baylis Tech Sch,
   SE11 . . . . 144 B3
Lilley Cl, E1 . . . . 93 D5
Lillie Rd, SW6 . . . . 135 D5
Lillie Yd, SW6 . . . . 136 C4
Lillington Gdns Est,
   SW1 . . . . 142 B1
Lily Cl, W14 . . . . 135 E1
Lily Pl, EC1 . . . . 61 D3
Lilyville Rd, SW6 . . . . 160 A3
Limeburner La, EC4. . . 89 E1
Lime Cl, E1 . . . . 93 D4
Lime Gro, W12 . . . . . . 106 A1
Limeharbour, E14 . . . 125 F2
LIMEHOUSE, E14 . . . . . 95 F2
≷ Limehouse. 95 E1
DLR Limehouse. 95 E1
Limehouse Causeway,
   E14 . . . . 96 B2
Limehouse Flds Est,
   E14 . . . . 67 F4
Limehouse Link, E14. . 96 B3
Limekiln Dr, SE7 . . . . 157 F4
Limerston St, SW10 . 138 B4
Limes, The, W2 . . . . . . 81 D3
Lime St, EC3 . . . . 91 E2
Lime St Pas, EC3 . . . . . 91 E1
Lime Wk, E15 . . . . 27 F5
Linacre Ct, W6 . . . . . . 135 D2
Linberry Wk, SE8. . . . 152 A1
Lincoln Ms, NW6 . . . . . . 8 A5
Lincoln Rd, E13 . . . . . . 73 E2
★ Lincoln's Inn,
   WC2 . . . . 60 B5
Lincoln's Inn Flds,
   WC2 . . . . 60 A5
Lincoln St, SW3 . . . . . 140 A1
Linden Av, NW10. . . . . 28 C3
Linden Ct, W12 . . . . . . 78 A4
Linden Gdns, W2 . . . . . 81 D3
Linden Ms, W2 . . . . 81 D3
Lindfield Est, SE15 . . 172 C1
Lindfield St, E14 . . . . . 69 D5
Lindley Est, SE15 . . . 172 C1
Lindley St, E1 . . . . 66 A3
Lindrop St, SW6. . . . . 162 A5
Lindsay Sq, SW1 . . . . 143 D2
Lindsell St, SE10 . . . . 178 A3
Lindsey Ms, N1 . . . . . . 18 B3
Lindsey St, EC1 . . . . . . 61 F3
Lind St, SE8 . . . . 177 E5
Lindwood Cl, E6. . . . . . 75 F4
Linford St, SW8 . . . . . 166 A3
Lingham St, SW9. . . . 167 F5
Ling Rd, E16 . . . . 73 D3
Linhope St, NW1 . . . . . 56 A1
Link St, E9. . . . . 22 B1
Links Yd, E1 . . . . 64 C3
Linkwood Wk, NW1 . . 15 D3
★ Linley Sambourne Ho,
   W8 . . . . 109 D2
Linnell Rd, SE5 . . . . . 171 F5
Linsey St, SE16 . . . . . 120 C5

Linstead St, NW6 . . . . . . 8 C3
Lintaine Cl, W6 . . . . . 135 F5
Linton Gdns, E6 . . . . . . 75 E5
Linton St, N1 . . . . 40 B1
Linver Rd, SW6 . . . . . 160 B5
Lionel Ms, W10 . . . . . . 51 E3
Lion Rd, E6 . . . . 76 B4
Lipton Rd, E1 . . . . 94 C1
Lisford St, SE15 . . . . . 172 B3
Lisgar Ter, W14 . . . . . 108 A5
Liskeard Gdns, SE3 . . 181 D4
Lisle St, WC2 . . . . 87 D2
Lismore Wk, N1. . . . . . 18 B1
Lisson Grn Est, NW8 . . 33 E5
LISSON GROVE, NW8 . 55 D2
Lisson Gro, NW1 . . . . . 55 E1
   NW8 . . . . 33 D5
Lisson St, NW1. . . . . . . 55 E3
H Lister Hosp, The,
   SW1 . . . . 141 E3
Lister Ho, SE3 . . . . . . 155 F4
Listowel Cl, SW9 . . . . 169 D1
Litchfield Av, E15 . . . . 27 E2
Litchfield St, WC2 . . . . 87 D2
Lithos Rd, NW3 . . . . 9 F1
Little Albany St, NW1 . 57 F1
Little Argyll St, W1 . . . 86 A1
Little Boltons, The,
   SW5 . . . . 137 F2
   SW10 . . . . 137 F2
Little Britain, EC1 . . . . 62 A5
Little Chester St,
   SW1 . . . . 113 D3
Little Coll St, SW1 . . . 115 E3
Littlecombe, SE7 . . . . 157 F4
Little Dean's Yd,
   SW1 . . . . 115 E3
Little Dorrit Ct, SE1. . 118 B1
Little Edward St,
   NW1 . . . . 35 F4
Little Essex St, WC2 . . 88 C2
Little George St,
   SW1 . . . . 115 E2
Little Marlborough St,
   W1 . . . . 86 A1
Little Newport St,
   WC2 . . . . 87 D2
Little New St, EC4 . . . . 61 D5
Little Portland St,
   W1 . . . . 58 A5
Little Russell St, WC1 . 59 E4
Little St. James's St,
   SW1 . . . . 86 A5
Little Sanctuary,
   SW1 . . . . 115 D2
Little Smith St, SW1 . 115 D3
Little Somerset St, E1. 92 A1
Little Titchfield St,
   W1 . . . . 58 A4
Little Trinity La, EC4 . . 90 B2

Little Turnstile, WC1 . . 60 A5
★ Little Venice
(Waterbuses), W2 . 54 A3
Livermere Rd, E8 . . . . . 20 A5
Liverpool Gro, SE17 . 146 B3
Liverpool Rd, E16 . . . . 71 F3
N1 . . . . 17 D4
N7 . . . . 16 C1
⇌ Liverpool Street . . . 63 E4
⬤ Liverpool Street . . . 63 E4
Liverpool St, EC3 . . . . . 63 E4
★ Livesey Mus for Children,
SE15 . . . . 149 E5
Livesey Pl, SE15 . . . . . 149 E5
Livingstone Pl, E14 . . 154 A3
Livingstone Rd, E15 . . 48 B1
Livonia St, W1 . . . . 86 B1
Lizard St, EC1 . . . . 40 B5
Lizban St, SE3 . . . . . . 181 E1
Llewellyn St, SE16 . . . 121 D2
Lloyd Baker St, WC1 . . 38 B5
Lloyd's Av, EC3 . . . . 91 E1
★ Lloyds of London,
EC3 . . . . 91 E1
Lloyd Sq, WC1 . . . . 38 C4
Lloyd's Row, EC1 . . . . . 39 D5
Lloyd St, WC1 . . . . 38 C4
🏫 Lloyd Williamson Sch,
W10 . . . . 51 E3
Loanda Cl, E8 . . . . 20 A5
Lobelia Cl, E6 . . . . 75 E3
Lochaline St, W6 . . . . 134 B4
Lochnagar St, E14 . . . . 70 B4
Lock Bldg, The, E15 . . . 48 A2
Lockesfield Pl, E14 . . 153 F2
Lockhart Cl, N7 . . . . . . 16 A1
Lockhart St, E3 . . . . . . 68 B2
Lockington Rd, SW8 . 165 F3
Lock Ms, NW1 . . . . 14 C1
Locksley Est, E14 . . . . . 68 A5
Locksley St, E14 . . . . . . 68 A4
Lockton St, W10 . . . . . 78 C2
Lockwood St, SE16 . . . 121 E3
Lockyer Est, SE1 . . . . 119 D1
Lockyer St, SE1 . . . . 119 D2
Loddiges Rd, E9 . . . . . . 22 A3
Loder St, SE15 . . . . . . 174 A2
Lodge Rd, NW8 . . . . . . 33 D5
Lodore St, E14 . . . . 98 A1
Loftie St, SE16 . . . . . . 121 D2
Lofting Rd, N1 . . . . 16 C4
Logan Ms, W8 . . . . . . 108 C5
Logan Pl, W8 . . . . 108 C5
Lolesworth Cl, E1 . . . . 64 B4
Lollard St, SE11 . . . . . 116 B5
Loman St, SE1 . . . . . . 117 F1
Lomas Dr, E8 . . . . 20 B3
Lomas St, E1 . . . . 65 D3
Lombard Ct, EC3 . . . . . 91 D2
Lombard La, EC4 . . . . . 89 D1

Lombard St, EC3 . . . . . 91 D1
Lombard Wall, SE7 . . 129 E4
Lombardy Pl, W2 . . . . . 81 E3
Lomond Gro, SE5 . . . . 170 C1
Loncroft Rd, SE5 . . . . 147 F4
🎓 London Acad of Music &
Dramatic Art,
W14 . . . . 135 D2
★ London Aquarium,
SE1 . . . . 116 A1
★ London Brass Rubbing
Cen, St. Martin-in-the-
Fields Ch, WC2 . . . . 87 E3
⇌ London Bridge 91 E5
⬤ London Bridge 91 E5
London Br, EC4 . . . . . . 91 D4
SE1 . . . . 91 D4
🚢 London Bridge
City Pier 91 E4
🏥 London Br Hosp,
SE1 . . . . 91 D4
London Br St, SE1 . . . . 90 C5
London Br Wk, SE1 . . . 91 D4
🎓 London Business Sch,
NW1 . . . . 56 A1
★ London Canal Mus, The,
N1 (New Wf Rd) . . . 37 F2
★ London Cen Mosque,
NW8 . . . . 33 F5
🏥 London Chest Hosp,
E2 . . . . 44 B2
★ London City Airport,
E16 . . . . 103 E4
🚇 London City
Airport 103 F4
🎓 London City Coll,
SE1 . . . . 88 C5
🏥 London Clinic, The,
W1 . . . . 57 D2
🎓 London Coll of Beauty
Therapy, W1 . . . . . . 86 A1
🎓 London Coll of
Communication,
SE1 . . . . 117 F4
🎓 London Coll of Fashion,
Barrett St, W1 . . . . . 85 D1
Curtain Rd, EC2 . . . 63 F1
John Princes St,
W1 . . . . 57 F5
Lime Gro, W12 . . . 106 A1
Mare St, E8 . . . . 21 F3
★ London Commodity
Exchange, E1 . . . . . . 92 B3
★ London Dungeon,
SE1 . . . . 91 D5
🎓 London Electronics
Coll, SW5 . . . . 137 E2
★ London Eye, SE1 . . 116 A1
⇌ London Fields 21 E4
London Flds, E8 . . . . . 21 E3
London Flds E Side,
E8 . . . . 21 E4
🏫 London Flds JMI Sch,
E8 . . . . 21 E5

London Flds W Side,
E8 . . . . 21 D3
★ London Fire Brigade
Mus, SE1 . . . . 118 A1
🏥 London Foot Hosp &
Sch of Podiatric Med,
The, W1 . . . . 58 A2
🏥 London Indep Hosp,
E1 . . . . 66 C3
London La, E8 . . . . 21 F3
★ London Met Archives,
EC1 . . . . 61 D1
🎓 London Met Uni - London
City Campus, Calcutta Ho,
E1 . . . . 64 B5
Central Ho, E1 . . . . . 64 C5
Commercial Rd, E1 . 65 D5
Goulston St, E1 . . . . 64 A5
Jewry St, EC3 . . . . . . 92 A1
Moorgate, EC2 . . . . 63 D4
Students Union,
E1 . . . . 64 B5
Tower Hill, EC3 . . . . 92 A2
🎓 London Met Uni -
London N Campus,
James Leicester
Hall of Res, N7 . . . . . 15 F1
London Ms, W2 . . . . . . 83 D1
🎓 London Nautical Sch,
SE1 . . . . 89 D4
🎓 London Oratory Sec Sch,
The, SW6 . . . . 161 E1
★ London Palladium,
W1 . . . . 86 A1
London Pav, The,
W1 . . . . 86 C3
★ London Peace Pagoda,
SW11 . . . . 164 B1
★ London Regatta Cen,
E16 . . . . 103 D3
London Rd, SE1 . . . . . 117 E3
🎓 London Sch of Economics
& Political Science,
WC2 . . . . 88 B1
★ London Silver Vaults,
WC2 . . . . 60 C4
🎓 London S Bk Uni,
SE1 . . . . 117 F3
Caxton Ho, SE1 . . . 117 E3
★ London Stone, EC4 . 90 C2
London St, EC3 . . . . . . 91 F2
W2 . . . . 82 C1
🎓 London Studio Cen,
N1 . . . . 37 F2
★ London Transport Mus,
WC2 . . . . 87 F2
★ London Trocadero, The,
W1 . . . . 86 C3
London Wall, EC2 . . . . 62 B4
London Wall Bldgs,
EC2 . . . . 63 D4
★ London Wildlife Trust,
NW1 . . . . 37 D1
★ London Zoo, NW1 . . 34 C2

Long Acre, WC2 . . . . . . 87 E2
Longfellow Way,
  SE1 . . . . .148 B1
Longfield Est, SE1 . . 148 B1
Longford St, NW1 . . . . 57 F1
Longhedge St,
  SW11 . . . . .165 D5
Longhope Cl, SE15 . . 148 A5
Longlands Ct, W11 . . 80 B2
Long La, EC1 . . . . 61 F3
  SE1 . . . . .118 C2
Longley Ct, SW8 . . . .167 E3
Longley St, SE1 . . . . . 148 C1
Long Mark Rd, E16 . . 74 C4
Longmoore St, SW1 .142 A1
Longnor Rd, E1 . . . . . . 45 D5
Long Pond Rd, SE3 . .179 F4
Longridge Rd, SW5 . 136 C1
Long's Ct, WC2 . . . . 86 C2
Longshore, SE8 . . . . . 152 A1
Longstone Ct, SE1 . . .118 B2
Long St, E2 . . . . 42 A4
Longville Rd, SE11 . . 117 E5
Long Wk, SE1 . . . . . . .119 F3
Long Yd, WC1 . . . . 60 A2
Lonsdale Cl, E6 . . . . . . 75 E1
Lonsdale Pl, N1 . . . . . . 17 D4
Lonsdale Rd, NW6 . . . 30 A2
  W11 . . . . 80 B1
Lonsdale Sq, N1 . . . . . 17 D4
Lord Amory Way,
  E14 . . . . .126 A1
Lorden Wk, E2 . . . . 42 C5
Lord Hills Br, W2 . . . . . 53 F4
Lord Hills Rd, W2 . . . . . 53 F3
Lord Holland La,
  SW9 . . . . .169 D5
Lord N St, SW1 . . . . . .115 E4
Lord Roberts Ms,
  SW6 . . . . .161 E2
★ Lord's, Middlesex County
  Cricket Club & Mus,
  NW8 . . . . 33 D4
Lordship Pl, SW3 . . . .139 E5
Lord St, E16 . . . . 103 F5
Lord's Vw, NW8 . . . . . . 33 D5
Lord Warwick St,
  SE18 . . . . .132 A4
Lorenzo St, WC1 . . . . . 38 A4
Loring Rd, SE14 . . . . . 175 F3
Loris Rd, W6 . . . . 106 B4
Lorn Ct, SW9 . . . . 168 C5
Lorne Cl, NW8 . . . . 33 F5
Lorne Gdns, W11 . . . . 107 D1
Lorn Rd, SW9 . . . . 168 B5
Lorrimore Rd, SE17 . .145 F4
Lorrimore Sq, SE17 . .145 F4
Lothbury, EC2 . . . . 62 C5
Lothian Rd, SW9 . . . .169 F3
Lothrop St, W10 . . . . . 29 E4
Lots Rd, SW10 . . . . . . 162 A2
Loudoun Rd, NW8 . . . . 32 B2
Loughborough Rd,
  SW9 . . . . .168 C5

Loughborough St,
  SE11 . . . . .144 B2
Lough Rd, N7 . . . . 16 B1
Louisa Cl, E9 . . . . 23 D5
Louisa Gdns, E1 . . . . . . 66 C2
Louisa St, E1 . . . . 66 C2
Louise Rd, E15 . . . . 27 F1
Lovage App, E6 . . . . . . 75 F4
Lovat La, EC3 . . . . 91 E3
Lovegrove St, SE1 . . . 149 D3
Lovegrove Wk, E14 . . . 98 A5
Love La, EC2 . . . . 62 B5
Lovelinch Cl, SE15 . . .150 B5
Lovell Ho, E8 . . . . 20 C5
Lovell Pl, SE16 . . . . . . 123 F3
Loveridge Ms, NW6 . . . .8 B2
Loveridge Rd, NW6 . . . .8 B2
Lovers Wk, SE10 . . . . .179 E1
Lover's Wk, W1 . . . . . . 84 C4
Love Wk, SE5 . . . . 170 C5
Lowe Av, E16 . . . . 73 D4
Lowell St, E14 . . . . 95 F1
Lower Addison Gdns,
  W14 . . . . 107 D2
Lower Belgrave St,
  SW1 . . . . .113 E4
Lower Grosvenor Pl,
  SW1 . . . . .113 E3
Lower James St, W1 . . 86 B2
Lower John St, W1 . . . . 86 B2
Lower Lea Crossing,
  E14 . . . . 99 E2
  E16 . . . . 99 E2
Lower Marsh, SE1 . . . 116 C2
Lower Merton Ri,
  NW3 . . . . 11 F3
Lower Rd, SE8 . . . . . . 122 A3
  SE16 . . . . 122 C5
Lower Sloane St,
  SW1 . . . . .140 C1
Lower Thames St,
  EC3 . . . . 91 D3
Lowestoft Ms, E16 . . .133 F1
Lowfield Rd, NW6 . . . . .8 C3
Lowndes Cl, SW1 . . . .113 D4
Lowndes Ct, W1 . . . . . . 86 A1
Lowndes Pl, SW1 . . . .112 C4
Lowndes Sq, SW1 . . . 112 B2
Lowndes St, SW1 . . . 112 B3
Lowood St, E1 . . . . 93 F2
Lowther Gdns, SW7 . .111 D2
Lowth Rd, SE5 . . . . . . 170 A4
Loxham St, WC1 . . . . . 37 F5
ᴄᵒˡ L.S.O. St. Luke's,
  EC1 . . . . 62 B1
Lubbock St, SE14 . . . .174 B2
Lucan Pl, SW3 . . . . . . 139 E1
Lucas St, SE8 . . . . 176 C5
ˢᶜʰ Lucas Vale Prim Sch,
  SE8 . . . . 176 C4
Lucerne Ms, W8 . . . . . . 81 D4
Lucey Rd, SE16 . . . . . 120 C4
Lucey Way, SE16 . . . . 121 D4
Ludgate Bdy, EC4 . . . . 89 E1

Ludgate Circ, EC4 . . . . 89 E1
Ludgate Hill, EC4 . . . . . 89 E1
Ludgate Sq, EC4 . . . . . 89 F1
Ludlow St, EC1 . . . . 62 A1
Ludwick Ms, SE14 . . . 175 F1
Lugard Rd, SE15 . . . . 173 F5
Luke Ho, E1 . . . . 93 E1
Luke St, EC2 . . . . 63 E1
Lukin St, E1 . . . . 94 B1
Lulworth, SE17 . . . . . .146 C2
Lulworth Rd, SE15 . . .173 F5
Lumley Ct, WC2 . . . . . . 87 F3
Lumley St, W1 . . . . 85 D1
Lund Pt, E15 . . . . 26 A5
Lundy Wk, N1 . . . . 18 B2
Lupino Ct, SE11 . . . . . 144 B1
Lupus St, SW1 . . . . . . 142 B3
Luralda Gdns, E14 . . .154 B2
Lurgan Av, W6 . . . . . . 135 D4
Lurline Gdns, SW11 . 165 D3
Luscombe Way,
  SW8 . . . . .167 E1
Luton Pl, SE10 . . . . . . 178 B2
Luton St, NW8 . . . . 55 D2
Luxborough St, W1 . . . 56 C3
Luxemburg Gdns,
  W6 . . . . 106 C5
Luxford St, SE16 . . . . 150 C1
Luxmore St, SE4 . . . . 176 B4
Lyall Ms, SW1 . . . . . . .112 C4
Lyall Ms W, SW1 . . . . .112 C4
Lyall St, SW1 . . . . .112 C4
Lyal Rd, E3 . . . . 45 F3
Lycée, The, SE11 . . . . 145 D3
ˢᶜʰ Lycée Français
  Charles de Gaulle,
  SW7 . . . . .110 C5
Lydford Rd, NW2 . . . . . .6 B2
  W9 . . . . 52 B1
Lygon Pl, SW1 . . . . . . 113 E4
Lyme Gro, E9 . . . . 22 A3
Lyme St, NW1 . . . . 14 A4
Lyme Ter, NW1 . . . . 14 A4
Lymington Cl, E6 . . . . . 76 A3
Lymington Rd, NW6 . . .9 E1
Lympstone Gdns,
  SE15 . . . . .173 D1
Lynbrook Gro, SE15 . .171 F1
Lynch Wk, SE8 . . . . . . 152 B4
Lyndale Cl, SE3 . . . . . 156 A5
Lyndhurst Gro, SE15 . 171 F5
ˢᶜʰ Lyndhurst Prim Sch,
  SE5 . . . . 171 D5
Lyndhurst Sq, SE15 . .172 B4
Lyndhurst Way,
  SE15 . . . . .172 B3
Lyn Ms, E3 . . . . 46 A5
Lynton Est, SE1 . . . . . 148 C1
Lynton Rd, NW6 . . . . . 30 B1
  SE1 . . . . .148 B1

Lynx Way, E16 . . . . . . 102 C2
Lyons Pl, NW8 . . . . 54 C1
Lyon St, N1 . . . . 16 A4
Lyons Wk, W14 . . . . . 107 E5
★ Lyric Thea, W6 . . . 134 A1
Lysander Ho, E2 . . . . . . 43 E3
Lysia St, SW6 . . . . 158 C2
Lyte St, E2 . . . . 44 A2
Lytham St, SE17 . . . . 146 C3
Lyttelton Cl, NW3 . . . . 11 E4
Lyveden Rd, SE3 . . . . 181 E1

M

Mabledon Pl, WC1 . . . . 37 D5
Mablethorpe Rd,
SW6 . . . . 159 E2
Mabley St, E9 . . . . 23 E1
McAuley Cl, SE1 . . . . . 116 C3
Macauley Ms, SE13 . . 178 B4
Macbean St, SE18 . . . 133 D4
McCall Cl, SW4 . . . . . 167 E5
Macclesfield Br, NW1 . . 33 F2
Macclesfield Rd, EC1 . . 40 A4
Macclesfield St, W1 . . . 87 D2
McCoid Way, SE1 . . . . 118 A2
McCrone Ms, NW3 . . . 11 D1
McCullum Rd, E3 . . . . . 46 A2
McDowall Cl, E16 . . . . 72 B4
McDowall Rd, SE5 . . . 170 A4
Macduff Rd, SW11 . . . 165 D3
Mace Cl, E1 . . . . 93 E4
Mace St, E2 . . . . 44 C3
McEwen Way, E15 . . . . 27 D5
Macfarland Gro,
SE15 . . . . 171 F1
Macfarlane Rd, W12 . . 78 A4
Macfarren Pl, NW1 . . . 57 D2
Macgregor Rd, E16 . . . 74 B3
McGregor Rd, W11 . . . 52 B4
Mackennal Sts, NW8 . . 33 F3
Mackenzie Rd, N7 . . . . 16 A1
Mackenzie Wk, E14 . . . 97 D5
McKerrell Rd, SE15 . . 173 D4
Macklin St, WC2 . . . . . 59 F5
Mackrow Wk, E14 . . . . 98 A2
Macks Rd, SE16 . . . . . 121 D5
Mackworth St, NW1 . . 36 A4
McLeod's Ms, SW7 . . 109 F4
Macleod St, SE17 . . . 146 B3
Maclise Rd, W14 . . . . 107 E4
McMillan St, SE8 . . . . 153 D5
McMillan Student Village,
SE8 . . . . 153 D5
Maconochies Rd,
E14 . . . . 153 E2
Macquarie Way,
E14 . . . . 153 F1

Macroom Rd, W9 . . . . 30 B4
Mac's Pl, EC4 . . . . 60 C5
★ Madame Tussaud's,
NW1 . . . . 56 C2
[Sch] Madani Girls Sch,
E1 . . . . 65 E5
Maddams St, E3 . . . . . . 69 E2
Maddock Way, SE17 . 145 F5
Maddox St, W1 . . . . . . 85 F2
Madras Pl, N7 . . . . 16 C1
Madrigal La, SE5 . . . . 169 F2
Madron St, SE17 . . . . 147 F2
Mafeking Rd, E16 . . . . 72 A1
Magdalene Gdns, E6 . . 76 C1
Magdalen Pas, E1 . . . . 92 B2
Magdalen St, SE1 . . . . 91 E5
Magee St, SE11 . . . . . 144 C4
Magnin Cl, E8 . . . . 21 D5
Magpie All, EC4 . . . . . . 89 D1
Magri Wk, E1 . . . . 66 A4
Maguire St, SE1 . . . . . 120 B1
Mahogany Cl, SE16 . . . 95 F5
Maida Av, W2 . . . . 54 B3
MAIDA HILL, W9 . . . . . 52 C1
MAIDA VALE, W9 . . . . . 53 F1
⊖ Maida Vale 31 F4
Maida Vale, W9 . . . . . . 32 A5
Maiden La, NW1 . . . . . 15 D3
SE1 . . . . 90 B4
WC2 . . . . 87 F3
Maiden Rd, E15 . . . . . . 27 F3
Maidenstone Hill,
SE10 . . . . 178 A3
Maidstone Bldgs Ms,
SE1 . . . . 90 B5
Maidstone Ho, E14 . . . 69 F5
Maidstone St, E2 . . . . . 43 E2
Maisemore St, SE15 . 173 D1
Maitland Cl Est,
SE10 . . . . 177 F2
Maitland Pk Est, NW3 . 12 B1
Maitland Pk Rd, NW3 . 12 B2
Maitland Pk Vil, NW3 . 12 B1
Major Rd, SE16 . . . . . 121 D3
Makins St, SW3 . . . . . 139 F1
Malabar St, E14 . . . . . 124 C2
Malam Gdns, E14 . . . . 97 E2
Malcolm Pl, E2 . . . . 66 A1
Malcolm Rd, E1 . . . . . . 66 A1
Malden Cres, NW1 . . . 13 D2
Maldon Cl, N1 . . . . 18 A5
Malet Pl, WC1 . . . . 58 C2
Malet St, WC1 . . . . 58 C2
Mall, The, SW1 . . . . . . 114 B1
Mallard Cl, E9 . . . . 24 B1
NW6 . . . . 31 D1
Mallard Pt, E3 . . . . 47 E5
★ Mall Galleries,
SW1 . . . . 87 D4
Mallord St, SW3 . . . . 139 D4
Mallory St, NW8 . . . . . 55 F1
Mallow St, EC1 . . . . . . 62 C1
[Sch] Malmesbury Inf Sch,
E3 . . . . 46 B4

[Sch] Malmesbury Jun Sch,
E3 . . . . 46 B4
Malmesbury Rd, E3 . . . 46 A4
E16 . . . . 71 F3
Malmesbury Ter,
E16 . . . . 72 A3
[Sch] Malorees Inf & Jun Sch,
NW6 . . . . 7 D4
Malpas Rd, E8 . . . . 21 E1
Malta St, EC1 . . . . 61 F1
Maltby St, SE1 . . . . . . 120 A2
Malting Ho, E14 . . . . . . 96 A2
Maltings Pl, SW6 . . . . 161 F4
Malton Rd, W10 . . . . . . 51 E5
Maltravers St, WC2 . . . 88 C2
Malt St, SE1 . . . . 148 C4
Malvern Cl, W10 . . . . . 52 A4
Malvern Ct, SE14 . . . . 174 B1
SW7 . . . . 139 D1
Malvern Gdns, NW6 . . 30 B3
Malvern Ms, NW6 . . . . 30 C5
Malvern Pl, NW6 . . . . . 30 B4
Malvern Rd, E8 . . . . . . 20 C4
NW6 . . . . 30 C4
Malvern Ter, N1 . . . . . . 16 C5
Managers St, E14 . . . . 98 B5
Manbey Gro, E15 . . . . 27 E1
Manbey Pk Rd, E15 . . . 27 E1
Manbey Rd, E15 . . . . . 27 E1
Manbey St, E15 . . . . . . 27 E2
Manbre Rd, W6 . . . . . 134 B4
Manchester Ct, E16 . 101 F1
Manchester Dr, W10 . . 51 E2
Manchester Gro, E14 154 A2
Manchester Ms, W1 . . 56 C4
Manchester Rd, E14 . 154 A2
Manchester Sq, W1 . . . 56 C5
Manchester St, W1 . . . 56 C4
Manciple St, SE1 . . . . 118 C2
Mandarin St, E14 . . . . 96 C2
Mandela Rd, E16 . . . . 101 D1
Mandela St, NW1 . . . . 14 B5
SW9 . . . . 168 C2
Mandela Way, SE1 . . 119 F5
[Coll] Mander Portman
Woodward 6th Form
Tutorial Coll,
SW7 . . . . 138 C1
Mandeville Cl, SE3 . . 180 B2
Mandeville Pl, W1 . . . . 57 D5
Mandrake Way, E15 . . 27 E3
Manette St, W1 . . . . . . 87 D1
Manger Rd, N7 . . . . 15 F1
Manhattan Wf,
E16 . . . . 128 C1
Manilla St, E14 . . . . . . 124 C1
Manitoba Ct, SE16 . . 122 B2
Manley St, NW1 . . . . . . 12 C5
Manningford Cl, EC1 . . 39 E4
Manningtree St, E1 . . . 64 C5
Manor Ct, SW6 . . . . . 161 F4
[Sch] Manor Day Sch,
NW10 . . . . 28 B1
Manor Est, SE16 . . . . 149 E1

Sch Manorfield Prim Sch,
  E14 . . . . 69 F3
Manor Gro, SE15 . . . . 150 A5
Manor Ho Dr, NW6 . . . . 7 D4
Manor Ms, NW6 . . . . . 31 D2
  SE4 . . . . 176 B5
Manor Pl, SE17 . . . . . 145 F3
Sch Manor Prim Sch,
  E15 . . . . 49 E2
Manor Rd, E15 . . . . 49 E3
  E16 . . . . 71 E1
Manresa Rd, SW3 . . . 139 E3
Mansell St, E1 . . . . 92 B3
Mansfield Ms, W1 . . . . 57 E4
Mansfield St, W1 . . . . . 57 E4
Mansford St, E2 . . . . . . 43 D3
Mansion Cl, SW9 . . . . 169 D3
★ Mansion Ho, EC4 . . 90 C1
✪ Mansion House 90 B2
Mansion Ho Pl, EC4 . . . 90 C1
Mansion Ho St, EC4 . . . 90 C1
Manson Ms, SW7 . . . 138 B1
Manson Pl, SW7 . . . . 138 C1
Mantle Way, E15 . . . . . 27 E3
Mantus Cl, E1 . . . . 66 B1
Mantus Rd, E1 . . . . 66 A1
Manwood St, E16 . . . 104 B5
Mapesbury Rd, NW2 . . . 7 E2
Mapeshill Pl, NW2 . . . . 6 B2
Mape St, E2 . . . . 65 E1
Maplecroft Cl, E6 . . . . 75 E5
Mapledene Rd, E8 . . . . 20 B3
Maple Leaf Sq, SE16 . 123 D1
Maple Ms, NW6 . . . . . 31 E2
Maple Pl, W1 . . . . 58 B2
Maples Pl, E1 . . . . 65 F3
Maple St, E2 . . . . 43 D3
  W1 . . . . 58 A3
Maple Wk, W10 . . . . . . 29 D5
Maplin Rd, E16 . . . . . . 73 E5
Maplin St, E3 . . . . 46 A5
Marban Rd, W9 . . . . . . 30 A4
★ Marble Arch, W1 . . 84 B2
✪ Marble Arch 84 B2
Marble Quay, E1 . . . . . 92 C4
Marchant St, SE14 . . 151 E5
Marchbank Rd, W14 . 136 B4
Marchmont St, WC1 . . 59 E1
Marchwood Cl, SE5 . . 171 F2
Marcia Rd, SE1 . . . . . 147 F1
Marcus Ct, E15 . . . . . . 27 F5
Marcus St, E15 . . . . . . 27 F5
Marden Sq, SE16 . . . . 121 E4
Mare St, E8 . . . . 43 F1
Margaret Ct, W1 . . . . . 58 A5
Margaret Ingram Cl,
  SW6 . . . . 136 A5
Margaret St, W1 . . . . . 57 F5
Margaretta Ter,
  SW3 . . . . 139 E4
Margery St, WC1 . . . . . 38 C5
Margravine Gdns,
  W6 . . . . 135 D2
Margravine Rd, W6 . . 135 D3

Maria Cl, SE1 . . . . 121 E5
Sch Maria Fidelis Conv Sch,
  Lwr Sch, NW1 . . . . . 36 B5
  Upr Sch, NW1 . . . . . 36 C4
Marian Pl, E2 . . . . 43 E2
Marian Sq, E2 . . . . 43 D2
Marian St, E2 . . . . 43 E2
Maria Ter, E1 . . . . 66 C2
Marie Lloyd Wk, E8 . . 20 B2
Marigold All, SE1 . . . . . 89 E3
Marigold St, SE16 . . . 121 E2
Marinefield Rd, SW6 . 161 F5
Mariners Ms, E14 . . . 126 C5
Marine St, SE16 . . . . . 120 C3
Marine Twr, SE8 . . . . 152 A4
Sch Marion Richardson
  Prim Sch, E1 . . . . . . 94 C1
Maritime Ho, SE18 . . 133 E5
Maritime Quay,
  E14 . . . . 153 D2
Maritime St, E3 . . . . . . 68 B2
Marjorie Ms, E1 . . . . . . 94 C1
Market Ct, W1 . . . . 58 A5
Market Est, N7 . . . . 15 E1
Market Hill, SE18 . . . 133 D4
Market Ms, W1 . . . . . . 85 E5
Market Pl, SE16 . . . . . 121 D5
  W1 . . . . 58 A5
Market Rd, N7 . . . . 15 E2
Market Sq, E14 . . . . . . 97 F1
Market St, SE18 . . . . . 133 D5
Market Way, E14 . . . . . 97 F1
Market Yd Ms, SE1 . . 119 F3
Markham Pl, SW3 . . . 140 A2
Markham Sq, SW3 . . . 140 A2
Markham St, SW3 . . . 139 F2
Markland Ho, W10 . . . 78 C2
Mark La, EC3 . . . . 91 F3
Mark Sq, EC2 . . . . 63 E1
Mark St, E15 . . . . 27 E4
  EC2 . . . . 63 E1
Marlborough, SW3 . . 111 F5
Marlborough Av, E8 . . 42 C1
Marlborough Cl,
  SE17 . . . . 145 F1
Marlborough Ct, W1 . . 86 A1
  W8 . . . . 108 C5
Marlborough Gate Ho,
  W2 . . . . 82 C2
Marlborough Gro,
  SE1 . . . . 148 C3
Marlborough Hill,
  NW8 . . . . 32 B1
★ Marlborough Ho,
  SW1 . . . . 86 B5
Marlborough Pl,
  NW8 . . . . 32 A3
Sch Marlborough Prim Sch,
  SW3 . . . . 139 F1
Marlborough Rd,
  SE18 . . . . 133 F3
  SW1 . . . . 86 B5
Marlborough St,
  SW3 . . . . 139 E1

Marloes Rd, W8 . . . . . 109 E4
Marlow Ct, NW6 . . . . . . 7 D3
Marlowes, The, NW8 . 32 C1
Marlow Way, SE16 . . 122 C1
Marlton St, SE10 . . . . 156 B2
Marmont Rd, SE15 . . 173 D3
Sch Marner Prim Sch,
  E3 . . . . 69 F1
Marne St, W10 . . . . . . 29 E4
Maroon St, E14 . . . . . . 67 E4
Marquess Rd, N1 . . . . 18 C2
Marquis Rd, NW1 . . . . 15 D2
Marriott Rd, E15 . . . . . 27 E5
Marryat Sq, SW6 . . . . 159 E3
Marsden St, NW5 . . . . 12 C2
Marshall's Gro,
  SE18 . . . . 131 F5
Marshalls Pl, SE16 . . . 120 B4
Marshall St, W1 . . . . . . 86 B1
Marshalsea Rd, SE1 . 118 B1
Marsham St, SW1 . . . 115 D4
Marshfield St, E14 . . . 126 A3
Marshgate La, E15 . . . 25 E4
Marshgate Sidings,
  E15 . . . . 47 E1
Marsh St, E14 . . . . . . 153 E1
Marsh Wall, E14 . . . . . 96 C5
Marsland Cl, SE17 . . . 145 F3
Marston Cl, NW6 . . . . . 10 B3
Martara Ms, SE17 . . . 146 A3
Martello St, E8 . . . . . . 21 E3
Martello Ter, E8 . . . . . . 21 E3
Martel Pl, E8 . . . . 20 B1
Martha Ct, E2 . . . . 43 F2
Martha Rd, E15 . . . . . . 27 F1
Martha's Bldgs, EC1 . . 62 C1
Martha St, E1 . . . . 93 F1
Martindale Av, E16 . . . 101 D2
Martineau St, E1 . . . . . 94 A1
Martin La, EC4 . . . . 91 D2
Martlett Ct, WC2 . . . . . 87 F1
Marville Rd, SW6 . . . 160 A2
Marvin St, E8 . . . . 21 F1
Mary Ann Gdns,
  SE8 . . . . 152 C5
Marybank, SE18 . . . . 132 A5
Mary Datchelor Cl,
  SE5 . . . . 171 D3
Mary Grn, NW8 . . . . . . 31 F1
⇌ Maryland 27 E1
Marylands Rd, W9 . . . . 53 D2
Maryland Wk, N1 . . . . 18 A5
Mary Lawrenson Pl,
  SE3 . . . . 180 C2
MARYLEBONE, NW1 . . 56 A5
⇌ Marylebone 56 A2
✪ Marylebone 56 A2
Marylebone Flyover,
  NW1 . . . . 55 D4
  W2 . . . . 55 D4

Marylebone High St,
W1 . . . . 57 D3
Marylebone La, W1 . . 85 E1
Marylebone Ms, W1 . . 57 E4
Marylebone Pas, W1 . . 58 B5
Marylebone Rd, NW1 . 55 F3
Marylebone St, W1 . . . 57 D4
Marylee Way, SE11 . . 144 B2
Mary Macarthur Ho,
W6 . . . . 135 E4
Maryon Rd, SE7 . . . . . 131 E5
SE18 . . . . 131 E5
Mary Pl, W11 . . . . 79 E3
Mary Rose Mall, E6 . . . 76 B4
Mary Seacole Cl, E8 . . . 20 A5
Mary St, E16 . . . . 72 A4
N1 . . . . 40 B1
Mary Ter, NW1 . . . . 36 A1
Coll Mary Ward Adult Ed Cen,
The, WC1 . . . . 59 F3
Masbro Rd, W14 . . . . . 107 D4
Masefield Gdns, E6 . . . 76 C1
Maskelyne Cl, SW11 . 163 F3
Mason Cl, E16 . . . . . . 100 C2
SE16 . . . . 149 D2
Masons Arms Ms, W1 . 85 F1
Masons Av, EC2 . . . . . . 62 C5
Mason's Pl, EC1 . . . . . . 39 F4
Mason St, SE17 . . . . . 147 D1
Mason's Yd, SW1 . . . . . 86 B4
Massie Rd, E8 . . . . 20 C2
Massinger St, SE17 . . 147 E1
Massingham St, E1 . . . 66 C1
Masterman Ho, SE5 . 170 C1
Masters Dr, SE16 . . . . 149 E3
Masters St, E1 . . . . 67 D3
Riv Masthouse
Terrace 153 D2
Masthouse Ter, E14 . 153 D1
Mast Leisure Pk,
SE16 . . . . 123 D4
Mastmaker Rd, E14 . 125 D2
Matheson Rd, W14 . . 136 A1
Matilda St, N1 . . . . 38 B3
Matlock St, E14 . . . . . . 67 E5
Matson Ho, SE16 . . . . 121 F3
Matthew Cl, W10 . . . . 50 C2
Matthew Parker St,
SW1 . . . . 115 D2
Matthews St, SW11 . 164 A5
Matthews Yd, WC2 . . . 87 E1
Mattingley Way,
SE15 . . . . 172 A1
Maud Cashmore Way,
SE18 . . . . 132 B4
Maude Rd, SE5 . . . . . 171 E4
Maudlin's Grn, E1 . . . . 92 C4
H Maudsley Hosp, The,
SE5 . . . . 171 D5
Maud St, E16 . . . . 72 A4

Maunsel St, SW1 . . . . 114 C5
Mauritius Rd, SE10 . . 155 F1
Maverton Rd, E3 . . . . . 46 C1
Mavis Wk, E6 . . . . 75 E4
Mawbey Est, SE1 . . . . 148 C3
Mawbey Pl, SE1 . . . . . 148 B3
Mawbey Rd, SE1 . . . . 148 B3
Mawbey St, SW8 . . . . 167 E2
Maxilla Gdns, W10 . . . 51 D5
Maxilla Wk, W10 . . . . . 79 D1
Maxwell Rd, SW6 . . . 161 E2
Maya Cl, SE15 . . . . . . 173 E5
Maybury Rd, E13 . . . . . 74 A2
Maydew Ho, SE16 . . . 122 A5
MAYFAIR, W1 . . . . 85 E3
Mayfair Ms, NW1 . . . . 12 B4
Mayfair Pl, W1 . . . . 85 F4
Mayfield Cl, E8 . . . . 20 A2
Mayfield Rd, E8 . . . . . . 20 A4
E13 . . . . 72 B2
Mayflower Cl, SE16 . . 123 D5
Sch Mayflower Prim Sch,
E14 . . . . 97 E1
Mayflower St, SE16 . . 122 A2
Maygood St, N1 . . . . . . 38 B2
Maygrove Rd, NW6 . . . . 8 A2
Mayhill Rd, SE7 . . . . . 157 E5
Maynard Cl, SW6 . . . . 161 F2
Maynards Quay, E1 . . . 94 A3
May's Bldgs Ms,
SE10 . . . . 178 B2
Mays Ct, WC2 . . . . 87 E3
May St, W14 . . . . 136 B3
⇄ Maze Hill 155 E4
Maze Hill, SE3 . . . . . . 180 B3
SE10 . . . . 155 E4
Mazenod Av, NW6 . . . . 9 D4
Meadcroft Rd, SE11 . 145 E5
Meadowbank, NW3 . . 12 A4
Meadowbank Cl,
SW6 . . . . 158 B2
Meadow Ms, SW8 . . . 144 A5
Meadow Pl, SW8 . . . . 167 F1
Meadow Rd, SW8 . . . 168 A1
Meadow Row, SE1 . . . 118 A4
Meadowsweet Cl,
E16 . . . . 74 C4
Mead Pl, E9 . . . . 22 B2
Mead Row, SE1 . . . . . 116 C3
Meakin Est, SE1 . . . . . 119 E3
Meard St, W1 . . . . 86 C1
Meath St, SW11 . . . . . 165 E3
Mecklenburgh Pl,
WC1 . . . . 60 A1
Mecklenburgh Sq,
WC1 . . . . 60 A1
Mecklenburgh St,
WC1 . . . . 60 A1
Medburn St, NW1 . . . 36 C2
Medhurst Cl, E3 . . . . . . 45 F3
★ Medici Galleries,
W1 . . . . 85 F3
Medland Ho, E14 . . . . 95 E2
Medlar St, SE5 . . . . . . 170 B3

Medley Rd, NW6 . . . . . . 9 D2
Medway Bldgs, E3 . . . . 45 F3
Medway Ms, E3 . . . . . . 45 F3
Medway Rd, E3 . . . . . . 45 F3
Medway St, SW1 . . . . 115 D4
Meeting Fld Path, E9 . . 22 B1
Meeting Ho All, E1 . . . 93 F4
Meeting Ho La,
SE15 . . . . 173 E3
Mehetabel Rd, E9 . . . . 22 A1
Melba Way, SE13 . . . . 177 F4
Melbourne Ms, SW9 . 168 C4
Melbourne Pl, WC2 . . . 88 B2
Melbourne Sq, SW9 . 168 C4
Melbury Ct, W8 . . . . . 108 B3
Melbury Dr, SE5 . . . . 171 E2
Melbury Rd, W14 . . . 108 A3
Melcombe Pl, NW1 . . . 56 A3
Sch Melcombe Prim Sch,
W6 . . . . 134 C4
Melcombe St, NW1 . . . 56 B2
Meldon Cl, SW6 . . . . . 161 F4
Melford Rd, E6 . . . . 76 A1
Melina Pl, NW8 . . . . . . 32 C5
Melior Pl, SE1 . . . . . . 119 E1
Melior St, SE1 . . . . . . 119 D1
Mellish Ind Est,
SE18 . . . . 131 D3
Mellish St, E14 . . . . . . 124 C3
Mell St, SE10 . . . . 155 E3
Melon Pl, W8 . . . . 109 E1
Melon Rd, SE15 . . . . . 172 C3
Melrose Gdns, W6 . . . 106 B3
Melrose Ter, W6 . . . . . 106 B2
Melton Ct, SW7 . . . . . 139 D1
Melton St, NW1 . . . . . . 36 B5
Melville Pl, N1 . . . . 18 A4
Memel Ct, EC1 . . . . 62 A2
Memel St, EC1 . . . . 62 A2
Memorial Av, E15 . . . . 49 E4
Mendora Rd, SW6 . . . 159 F1
Menotti St, E2 . . . . 65 D1
Mentmore Ter, E8 . . . . 21 F4
Mepham St, SE1 . . . . . 88 B5
Mercator Pl, E14 . . . . 153 D2
Merceron St, E1 . . . . . . 65 E2
Mercers Cl, SE10 . . . . 156 A1
Mercers Pl, W6 . . . . . . 106 B5
Mercer St, WC2 . . . . . . 87 E1
Merchant St, E3 . . . . . . 46 B5
Mercury Way, SE14 . . 150 C4
Meredith St, EC1 . . . . . 39 E5
Meridian Gate, E14 . . 126 A1
Meridian Pl, E14 . . . . 126 A1
Sch Meridian Prim Sch,
SE10 . . . . 155 D3
Meridian Sq, E15 . . . . 26 C3
Meridian Trd Est,
SE7 . . . . 129 F5
Merlin St, WC1 . . . . 38 C5
Mermaid Ct, SE1 . . . . 118 C1
SE16 . . . . 96 A5
Mermaid Twr, SE8 . . . 152 A5
Merriam Av, E9 . . . . . . 24 B1

Merrick Sq, SE1 . . . . . 118 B3
Merrington Rd, SW6. 137 D4
Merrow St, SE17 . . . . 146 C4
Merrow Wk, SE17 . . . 147 D2
Merton Ri, NW3 . . . . . 11 F4
Messina Av, NW6. . . . . 8 C4
Methley St, SE11 . . . 145 D3
★ Methodist Cen Hall,
    SW1 . . . . 115 D2
Methwold Rd, W10. . . 50 C3
Metro Cen Hts, SE1. . 118 A4
Metropolitan Cl, E14. . 69 D4
Mews, The, N1 . . . . . . 18 B5
Mews Deck, E1. . . . . . 93 F3
Mews St, E1 . . . . 92 C4
Meymott St, SE1 . . . . . 89 E5
Meynell Cres, E9 . . . . 22 C3
Meynell Gdns, E9. . . . 22 C3
Meynell Rd, E9. . . . . . 22 C3
Micawber St, N1 . . . . . 40 B4
Michael Cliffe Ho,
    EC1 . . . . 39 D5
Michael Faraday Ho,
    SE17 . . . . 147 D3
Sch Michael Faraday
    Prim Sch, SE17 . . . 147 D4
Sch Michael Tippett Sch,
    SE11 . . . . 117 D5
Michigan Bldg, E14 . . . 98 B3
Micklethwaite Rd,
    SW6 . . . . 137 D5
Middle Fld, NW8 . . . . 10 C5
Middle Row, W10 . . . . 51 E2
Sch Middle Row Prim Sch,
    W10 . . . . 51 E1
★ Middlesex Guildhall,
    SW1 . . . . 115 E2
Middlesex Pas, EC1 . . 61 F4
Middlesex St, E1 . . . . . 63 F4
Middle St, EC1 . . . . . . 62 A3
Middle Temple, EC4. . . 88 C2
Middle Temple La,
    EC4 . . . . 88 C1
Middleton Dr, SE16. . 123 D2
Middleton Pl, W1. . . . . 58 A4
Middleton Rd, E8. . . . . 20 B4
Middleton St, E2 . . . . . 43 E4
Middle Yd, SE1 . . . . . . 91 D4
Midford Pl, W1. . . . . . 58 B2
Midhope St, WC1. . . . . 37 F5
Midland Cres, NW3 . . 10 A1
Midland Pl, E14 . . . . . 154 A2
Midland Rd, NW1 . . . . 37 D3
Midlothian Rd, E3 . . . . 68 A2
Midship Cl, SE16 . . . . . 95 D5
Midship Pt, E14. . . . . 124 C2
Milborne Gro, SW10. 138 B3
Milborne St, E9 . . . . . 22 B2
Milcote St, SE1 . . . . . 117 E2
Mildmay Av, N1. . . . . . 19 D1
Mildmay St, N1 . . . . . . 19 D1
MILE END, E1 . . . . 45 E5
⊖ Mile End. 68 A1

Mile End Pl, E1 . . . . . . 66 C1
Mile End Rd, E1 . . . . . 65 F3
    E3 . . . . 65 F3
Sch Miles Coverdale
    Prim Sch, W12 . . . 106 A1
Miles Pl, NW1. . . . . . . 55 D3
Miles St, SW8. . . . . . 143 E5
Milford La, WC2 . . . . . . 88 B2
Milk St, E16 . . . . 105 E5
    EC2. . . . . 90 B1
Milkwell Yd, SE5 . . . . 170 B4
Milk Yd, E1 . . . . 94 A3
Millbank, SW1 . . . . . 115 E4
Riv Millbank Millennium
    Pier. 143 F1
Sch Millbank Prim Sch,
    SW1 . . . . 143 D1
Millbank Twr, SW1 . . 143 E1
Millender Wk, SE16 . 150 B1
Millennium Br, EC4 . . . 90 A2
    SE1 . . . . 90 A2
Millennium Cl, E16 . . . 73 D5
Millennium Dr, E14. . 126 C5
Millennium Harbour,
    E14 . . . . 124 B1
Millennium Pl, E2 . . . . 43 F3
Millennium Sq, SE1. . 120 A1
Sch Millennium Village
    Sch, SE10 . . . . 128 A4
Millennium Way,
    SE10 . . . . 127 E1
Miller St, NW1 . . . . . . 36 A2
Millers Way, W6 . . . . 106 B2
Miller Wk, SE1 . . . . . . 89 D5
Millgrove St, SW11 . . 164 C5
Millharbour, E14. . . . 125 E3
Milligan St, E14 . . . . . 96 B3
Millman Ms, WC1 . . . . 60 A2
Millman St, WC1 . . . . . 60 A2
Mill Pl, E14 . . . . 95 F1
Mill Pond Cl, SW8 . . . 167 D2
Millpond Est, SE16 . . 121 E2
Mill Rd, E16 . . . . 101 F4
Mill Row, N1 . . . . 41 F1
Mills Ct, EC2 . . . . 41 F5
Mills Gro, E14. . . . . . . 70 A4
Mill Shot Cl, SW6. . . . 158 B3
Millstream Rd, SE1 . . 120 A2
Mill St, SE1 . . . . 120 B2
    W1 . . . . 85 F2
MILLWALL, E14 . . . . . 125 E5
Millwall Dock Rd,
    E14 . . . . 124 C3
★ Millwall FC, SE16. . 150 B3
Millwood St, W10 . . . . 51 E4
Mill Yd, E1. . . . . 92 C2
Milman Rd, NW6. . . . . 29 D2
Milman's St, SW10 . . 138 C5
Milner Pl, N1 . . . . 17 D5
Milner Rd, E15. . . . . . . 49 E5
Milner Sq, N1 . . . . 17 E4
Milner St, SW3 . . . . . 112 A5
Milroy Wk, SE1. . . . . . . 89 E4
Milson Rd, W14. . . . . 107 D3

Milton Cl, SE1 . . . . . . 148 A1
Milton Ct, EC2. . . . . . . 62 C3
Milton Ct Rd, SE14 . . 151 F5
Milton St, EC2 . . . . . . 62 C3
Milverton Rd, NW6 . . . . 6 B4
Milverton St, SE11 . . 145 D3
Milward St, E1. . . . . . . 65 F4
Mimosa St, SW6 . . . . 160 A4
Mina Rd, SE17 . . . . . . 147 F3
Mincing La, EC3 . . . . . 91 E2
Minera Ms, SW1 . . . . 113 D5
Minerva Cl, SW9 . . . . 169 D2
Minerva St, E2 . . . . . . 43 E3
Minet Rd, SW9. . . . . . 169 E5
Minford Gdns, W14. . 106 C2
Ming St, E14. . . . . 97 D2
★ Ministry of Defence,
    SW1 . . . . 87 E5
Minnow Wk, SE17. . . 147 F1
Minories, EC3 . . . . 92 A2
Minshull St, SW8. . . . 166 C4
Minson Rd, E9 . . . . . . 23 D5
Mint Business Pk, E16 73 D4
Mintern St, N1 . . . . . . 41 D2
Minton Ms, NW6 . . . . . 9 F1
Mint St, SE1 . . . . 118 A1
Mirabel Rd, SW6 . . . . 160 B1
Miranda Cl, E1 . . . . . . 66 A4
Mirfield St, SE7 . . . . . 130 C5
Mission Pl, SE15 . . . . 173 D3
Mitali Pas, E1 . . . . 92 C1
Mitchell St, EC1 . . . . . 62 A1
Mitchell Wk, E6 . . . . . 75 E4
Mitchison Rd, N1 . . . . 18 C2
Mitre, The, E14 . . . . . . 96 A2
Mitre Ct, EC2 . . . . 62 B5
    EC4 . . . . 89 D1
Mitre Rd, E15. . . . . 49 E2
    SE1 . . . . 117 D1
Mitre Sq, EC3 . . . . 91 F1
Mitre St, EC3 . . . . 91 F1
Modbury Gdns, NW5 . 12 B2
Modling Ho, E2 . . . . . . 44 C3
Molesford Rd, SW6 . . 161 D4
Molyneux St, W1. . . . . 55 F4
Monarch Dr, E16 . . . . . 74 C4
Mona Rd, SE15 . . . . . 174 B5
Mona St, E16 . . . . 72 B3
Monck St, SW1 . . . . . 115 D4
Moncorvo Cl, SW7 . . 111 E2
Moncrieff Cl, E6. . . . . 75 E5
Moncrieff Pl, SE15. . . 172 C5
Moncrieff St, SE15 . . 173 D5
Monier Rd, E3 . . . . . . 24 C4
Monk Dr, E16. . . . . . . 100 C1
Monk Pas, E16. . . . . . 100 C1
Monk St, SE18 . . . . . . 133 D5
Monkton St, SE11 . . . 117 D5
Monkwell Sq, EC2 . . . 62 B4
Monmouth Pl, W2. . . . 81 D1

Monmouth Rd, W2 . . . 81 D1
Monmouth St, WC2 . . 87 E1
Monnow Rd, SE1 . . . . 148 C2
Sch Monson Prim Sch,
    SE14 . . . . 174 C1
Monson Rd, SE14 . . . 174 C2
Montague Cl, SE1 . . . . 90 C4
Montague Pl, WC1 . . . . 59 D3
Montague Sq, SE15 . . 174 B2
Montague St, EC1 . . . . 62 A4
    WC1 . . . . 59 E3
Montagu Mans, W1 . . 56 B3
Montagu Ms N, W1 . . 56 B4
Montagu Ms S, W1 . . 56 B5
Montagu Ms W, W1 . . 56 B5
Montagu Pl, W1 . . . . . . 56 A4
Montagu Row, W1 . . . 56 B4
Montagu Sq, W1 . . . . . 56 B4
Montagu St, W1 . . . . . 56 B5
Montaigne Cl, SW1 . . 143 D1
Montclare St, E2 . . . . . 42 A5
Montevetro, SW11 . . 162 C3
Montford Pl, SE11 . . . 144 C3
Montgomery St, E14 . . 97 F5
Monthope Rd, E1 . . . . 64 C4
Montpelier Ms, SW7 . 111 F3
Montpelier Pl, E1 . . . . . 94 A1
    SW7 . . . . 111 F3
Montpelier Rd, SE15 . 173 F3
Montpelier Sq, SW7 . 111 F2
Montpelier St, SW7 . . 111 F2
Montpelier Ter, SW7 . 111 F2
Montpelier Wk, SW7 . 111 F3
Montreal Pl, WC2 . . . . 88 A2
Montrose Av, NW6 . . . 29 F2
Montrose Ct, SW7 . . . 111 D2
Montrose Pl, SW1 . . . 113 D2
★ Monument, The,
    EC3 . . . . 91 D3
⊖ Monument 91 D2
Monument St, EC3 . . . 91 D2
Monza St, E1 . . . . 94 A3
Moodkee St, SE16 . . . 122 A3
Moody Rd, SE15 . . . . 172 A2
Moody St, E1 . . . . 45 D5
Moon St, N1 . . . . 17 E5
Moore Ho, E14 . . . . . 125 D2
Moore Pk Rd, SW6 . . 161 E2
Moore St, SW3 . . . . . 112 A5
Moorfields, EC2 . . . . . 62 C4
🄷 Moorfields Eye Hosp,
    EC1 . . . . 40 C5
Sch Moorfields Prim Sch,
    EC1 . . . . 62 C1
⇌ Moorgate 62 C4
⊖ Moorgate 62 C4
Moorgate, EC2 . . . . . . 62 C5
Moorgate Pl, EC2 . . . . 62 C5
Moorhouse Rd, W2 . . 52 C5
Moor La, EC2 . . . . 62 C4

Moor Pl, EC2 . . . . 62 C4
Moor St, W1 . . . . 87 D1
Morant St, E14 . . . . . . 97 D2
Mora St, EC1 . . . . 40 B5
Morat St, SW9 . . . . . . 168 B3
Moravian Pl, SW10 . . 139 D5
Moravian St, E2 . . . . . . 44 A3
Morden Hill, SE13 . . . 178 A5
Morden La, SE13 . . . . 178 B4
Sch Morden Mt Prim Sch,
    SE13 . . . . 177 F5
Morden Rd, SE3 . . . . 180 C5
Morden St, SE13 . . . . 177 F4
Morden Wf Rd, SE10 . 127 E4
Morecambe Cl, E1 . . . 66 C3
Morecambe St,
    SE17 . . . . 146 B1
More Cl, E16 . . . . 72 B5
    W14 . . . . 135 D1
Sch More Ho Sch,
    SW1 . . . . 112 B4
Sch Moreland Prim Sch,
    EC1 . . . . 39 F4
Moreland St, EC1 . . . . 39 F4
More London Pl, SE1 . . 91 E5
More London Riverside,
    SE1 . . . . 91 F5
Moreton Cl, SW1 . . . . 142 B2
Moreton Ho, SE16 . . . 121 F3
Moreton Pl, SW1 . . . . 142 B2
Moreton St, SW1 . . . . 142 B2
Moreton Ter, SW1 . . . 142 B2
Moreton Ter Ms N,
    SW1 . . . . 142 B2
Moreton Ter Ms S,
    SW1 . . . . 142 B2
Morgan Rd, W10 . . . . 52 A3
Morgans La, SE1 . . . . . 91 E5
Morgan St, E3 . . . . 45 F5
    E16 . . . . 72 B3
Morland Ms, N1 . . . . . 17 D4
Coll Morley Coll, SE1 . . 117 D3
Morley St, SE1 . . . . . . 117 D3
Morna Rd, SE5 . . . . . . 170 B5
Morning La, E9 . . . . . . 22 A1
Sch Morningside
    JMI Sch, E9 . . . . 22 B1
Mornington Av,
    W14 . . . . 136 A1
⊖ Mornington
    Crescent 36 A2
Mornington Cres,
    NW1 . . . . 36 A2
Mornington Gro, E3 . . 46 C5
Mornington Ms, SE5 . 170 A3
Mornington Pl, NW1 . . 35 F2
Mornington Rd, SE8 . 176 B2
Mornington St, NW1 . . 35 F2
Mornington Ter, NW1 . 35 F1
Morocco St, SE1 . . . . 119 E2
Morpeth Gro, E9 . . . . . 22 C5
Morpeth Rd, E9 . . . . . . 44 B1
Sch Morpeth Sch, E2 . . 44 B5
    Annexe, E2 . . . . 44 A5

Morpeth St, E2 . . . . . . 44 C4
Morpeth Ter, SW1 . . . 114 A4
Morris Rd, E14 . . . . . . 69 E3
Morris St, E1 . . . . 93 F1
Morshead Rd, W9 . . . 31 D5
Mortham St, E15 . . . . . 49 E1
Mortimer Cres, NW6 . . 31 E1
Mortimer Est, NW6 . . . 31 E1
Mortimer Pl, NW6 . . . 31 E1
Mortimer Rd, N1 . . . . . 19 F4
    NW10 . . . . 28 A4
Mortimer Sq, W11 . . . 79 D3
Mortimer St, W1 . . . . . 58 A5
Mortlake Rd, E16 . . . . 73 F1
Mortlock Cl, SE15 . . . 173 E4
Morton Cl, E1 . . . . 94 A1
Morton Ms, SW5 . . . . 137 E1
Morton Pl, SE1 . . . . . . 116 C4
Morton Rd, N1 . . . . 18 B4
Morville St, E3 . . . . 46 C2
Morwell St, WC1 . . . . . 59 D4
Moscow Pl, W2 . . . . . . 81 E2
Moscow Rd, W2 . . . . . 81 E2
Moseley Row, SE10 . 128 B5
Moss Cl, E1 . . . . 65 D3
Mossford St, E3 . . . . . 68 A1
Mossington Gdns,
    SE16 . . . . 150 A1
Mossop St, SW3 . . . . 111 F5
Mostyn Gdns, NW10 . . 28 C4
Mostyn Gro, E3 . . . . . . 46 B3
Mostyn Rd, SW9 . . . . 168 C4
Motcomb St, SW1 . . . 112 B3
Motley Av, EC2 . . . . . . 63 E1
Motley St, SW8 . . . . . 166 A5
Moulins Rd, E9 . . . . . . 22 B4
Mountague Pl, E14 . . . 98 A2
Mountain Ho, SE11 . . 144 A2
Mountfort Cres, N1 . . . 16 C3
Mountfort Ter, N1 . . . . 16 C4
Mount Mills, EC1 . . . . . 39 F5
Mount Pleasant, WC1 . 60 B2
Mount Pleasant Rd,
    NW10 . . . . 6 B4
Mount Row, W1 . . . . . 85 E3
Mounts Pond Rd,
    SE3 . . . . 178 C5
Mount St, W1 . . . . 85 D3
Mount Ter, E1 . . . . 65 E4
Mowbray Rd, NW6 . . . . 7 E3
Sch Mowlem Prim Sch,
    E2 . . . . 44 A2
Mowlem St, E2 . . . . . . 43 F2
Mowll St, SW9 . . . . . . 168 C2
Moxon St, W1 . . . . 56 C4
Moye Cl, E2 . . . . 43 D2
Moylan Rd, W6 . . . . . 135 F5
Mozart St, W10 . . . . . 30 A5
Mozart Ter, SW1 . . . . 141 D1
DLR Mudchute 125 F5
Muirfield Cl, SE16 . . . 149 F3
Muirfield Cres, E14 . . 125 E3
Muir St, E16 . . . . 104 A5

Mulberry Business Cen,
  SE16.............123 D2
Mulberry Ms, SE14...176 A3
Mulberry Rd, E8......20 A3
Sch Mulberry Sch for Girls,
  E1.............93 E1
Coll Mulberry Sch for Girls -
  St. George's, E1...93 E2
Mulberry St, E1.....64 C5
Mulberry Wk, SW3..139 D4
Mulgrave Rd, SW6..136 A4
Sch Mulgrave Sch,
  SE18.............133 E4
Mullet Gdns, E2.....43 D4
Mull Wk, N1.........18 B2
Mulready St, NW8....55 E2
Mulvaney Way, SE1.119 D2
Mumford Ct, EC2.....62 B5
Mumford Mills,
  SE10.............177 E3
Munday Rd, E16....100 C1
Munden St, W14....107 E5
Mund St, W14......136 B3
Mundy St, N1........41 E4
Munro Ms, W10.....51 F3
Munro Ter, SW10...138 C5
Munster Ms, SW6...159 E1
Munster Rd, SW6...159 E1
Munster Sq, NW1....35 F5
Munton Rd, SE17...118 B5
Murdock Cl, E16.....72 B5
Murdock St, SE15...149 E5
Muriel St, N1........38 B2
Murphy St, SE1.....116 C2
Murray Gro, N1......40 B3
Murray Ms, NW1.....14 C3
Murray Sq, E16.....101 D1
Murray Yd, NW1.....14 B3
Murrays Yd, SE18...133 E5
Mursell Est, SW8...168 A3
Musard Rd, W6.....135 F4
  W14.............135 F4
Musbury St, E1.....66 A5
Muscal, W6........135 E4
Muscatel Pl, SE5...171 F2
Muscovy St, EC3....91 F3
★ Museum in Docklands,
  E14.............97 D3
★ Museum Interpretative
  Cen & Nature Reserve,
  E6 (Norman Rd)...76 B1
Museum La, SW7...110 C4
★ Museum of Childhood at
  Bethnal Green, E2.43 F4
★ Museum of Gdn History,
  SE1.............116 A4
★ Museum of Instruments,
  Royal Coll of Music,
  SW7.............110 C3
★ Museum of London,
  EC2.............62 A4
Museum Pas, E2.....44 A4
Museum St, WC1.....59 E4
Musgrave Cres, SW6.161 D2

Musgrove Rd, SE14..175 D4
Mustow Pl, SW6.....160 B5
Mutrix Rd, NW6......9 D5
Mutton Pl, NW1......13 D2
Sch Myatt Gdn Prim Sch,
  SE4.............176 B5
Myatt Rd, SW9.....169 E3
Mycenae Rd, SE3....180 C1
Myddelton Pas, EC1..39 D4
Myddelton Sq, EC1..39 D4
Myddelton St, EC1...39 D5
Myers La, SE14....150 C4
Mylius Cl, SE14....174 B3
Mylne St, EC1.......38 C3
Myrdle St, E1........65 D4
Myrtleberry Cl, E8....20 A2
Myrtle Wk, N1.......41 E3

N

N1 Shop Cen, N1.....39 D2
Nag's Head Ct, EC1..62 A2
Nairn St, E14........70 B4
Nankin St, E14.......97 D1
Nantes Pas, E1......64 A3
Nant St, E2..........43 F4
Naoroji St, WC1......38 C5
Napier Av, E14......153 D2
Napier Cl, SE8......176 B1
  W14.............108 A3
Napier Gro, N1......40 B3
Napier Pl, W14.....108 A4
Napier Rd, E15.......49 F3
  W14.............108 A4
Napier Ter, N1.......17 E4
Narrow St, E14.......95 E2
Nascot St, W12......50 A5
Naseby Cl, NW6......10 B3
Nash Ct, E14.........97 E5
Nash Ho, SW1......141 F3
Nash St, NW1........35 F5
Nassau St, W1.......58 A4
Nathaniel Cl, E1......64 B4
★ National Army Mus,
  SW3.............140 B4
★ National Gall,
  WC2.............87 D3
H National Hosp for
  Neurology &
  Neurosurgery, The,
  WC1.............59 F2
★ National Maritime Mus,
  SE10.............154 C5
★ National Portrait Gall,
  WC2.............87 D3
★ Natural History Mus,
  SW7.............110 C4
Naval Row, E14......98 B2
Navarino Gro, E8....21 D1
Navarino Rd, E8.....21 D1
Navarre St, E2.......64 A1
Navenby Wk, E3.....69 D1

Naxos Bldg, E14.....124 C2
Naylor Rd, SE15.....173 E1
Nazareth Gdns,
  SE15.............173 E5
Nazrul St, E2........42 A4
Neal St, WC2........87 E1
Neal's Yd, WC2......87 E1
Neate St, SE5......147 F4
Neathouse Pl, SW1..114 A5
Neatscourt Rd, E6...75 D4
Nebraska St, SE1....118 C2
Neckinger, SE16....120 B3
Neckinger Est, SE16.120 B3
Neckinger St, SE1...120 B2
Nectarine Way,
  SE13.............177 F5
Needham Rd, W11...80 C1
Needleman St,
  SE16.............122 C2
Nella Rd, W6.......134 C5
Nelldale Rd, SE16...122 A5
Nelson Cl, NW6......30 C4
Nelson Gdns, E2.....43 D4
Nelson Pas, EC1.....40 B5
Nelson Pl, N1........39 F3
Nelson Rd, SE10....154 B5
★ Nelson's Column,
  WC2.............87 E4
Nelson Sq, SE1.....117 E1
Nelson St, E1........65 E5
  E16.............100 A2
Nelsons Yd, NW1.....36 A2
Nelson Ter, N1.......39 F3
Nelson Wk, SE16....95 F5
Neptune St, SE16...122 A3
Nesham St, E1.......92 C4
Ness St, SE16.......120 C3
Netherhall Gdns,
  NW3.............10 B1
Netherton Gro,
  SW10.............138 B5
Netherwood Pl,
  W14.............106 C3
Netherwood Rd,
  W14.............106 C3
Netherwood St,
  NW6.............8 B3
Sch Netley Prim Sch,
  NW1.............36 A5
Netley St, NW1......36 A5
Nettleton Rd, SE14..175 D3
Nevada St, SE10....178 B1
Nevern Pl, SW5.....137 D1
Nevern Rd, SW5....136 C1
Nevern Sq, SW5.....137 D1
Neville Cl, NW1......37 D3
  NW6.............30 B3
  SE15.............172 C2
Neville Rd, NW6.....30 B3
Neville St, SW7.....138 C2

Neville Ter, SW7 .... 138 C2
Newark Knok, E6..... 76 C5
Newark St, E1 .... 65 E4
New Atlas Wf, E14 .. 124 B4
New Barn St, E13 .... 73 D1
New Bond St, W1 .... 85 E1
New Br St, EC4....... 89 E1
New Broad St, EC2 .. 63 E4
Newburgh St, W1 .... 86 A1
New Burlington Ms,
  W1 .... 86 A2
New Burlington Pl,
  W1 .... 86 A2
New Burlington St,
  W1 .... 86 A2
Newburn St, SE11... 144 B3
Newbury Ms, NW5 ... 13 D2
Newbury St, EC1 ..... 62 A4
New Butt La, SE8 ... 177 D2
New Butt La N, SE8.. 177 D2
Newby Pl, E14 .... 98 A2
New Caledonian Wf,
  SE16............... 124 A3
Newcastle Cl, EC4 .... 61 E5
Newcastle Pl, W2 .... 55 D4
Newcastle Row, EC1.. 61 D1
New Cavendish St,
  W1 .... 57 F3
New Change, EC4 .... 90 A1
New Charles St, EC1 .. 39 F4
NEW CHARLTON,
  SE7............... 130 A5
New Ch Rd, SE5..... 170 B1
New Coll Ms, N1 ..... 17 D3
Newcombe St, W8.... 81 D4
Newcomen St, SE1 .. 118 C1
New Compton St,
  WC2 .... 87 D1
New Concordia Wf,
  SE1............... 120 C1
New Ct, EC4 .... 88 C2
Newcourt St, NW8 ... 33 E3
★ New Covent Garden
  Flower Mkt, SW8 . 143 E5
★ New Covent Garden
  Mkt, SW8........ 166 C2
New Crane Pl, E1..... 94 A4
NEW CROSS, SE14 .. 175 E3
⇌ New Cross....... 176 B2
● New Cross....... 176 B2
NEW CROSS GATE,
  SE14............... 174 C3
⇌ New Cross Gate .. 175 E2
● New Cross Gate .. 175 E2
New Cross Rd, SE14 . 174 B2
Newell St, E14 .... 96 A1
Newent Cl, SE15 .... 171 E1
New Ferry App,
  SE18............... 132 C3
New Fetter La, EC4 ... 61 D5

Newgate St, EC1 ..... 61 F5
New Globe Wk, SE1... 90 A4
New Goulston St, E1.. 64 A5
🄷 Newham Cen for
  Mental Health,
  E13............... 74 C2
🄲🄾🄻🄻 Newham Coll of
  Further Ed, Stratford
  Campus, E15 ...... 27 F4
🄲🄾🄻🄻 Newham Comm Ed
  Eastlea Learning Zone,
  E16............... 71 F1
🄷 Newham Gen Hosp,
  E13............... 74 B1
🄲🄾🄻🄻 Newham 6th Form Coll,
  Main Site, E13..... 73 F1
  Stratford Site, E15 . 27 D4
Newhams Row, SE1 . 119 F2
Newham Way, E16 ... 72 C4
Newhaven La, E16 ... 72 B2
NEWINGTON, SE1 .. 118 A5
Newington Butts,
  SE1............... 145 F1
  SE11............... 145 F1
Newington Causeway,
  SE1............... 117 F4
New Inn Bdy, EC2 .... 63 F1
New Inn Pas, WC2.... 88 B1
New Inn Sq, EC2 ..... 63 F1
New Inn St, EC2...... 63 F1
New Inn Yd, EC2 ..... 63 F1
New Kent Rd, SE1 ... 118 A4
🄲🄷 New King's Prim Sch,
  SW6 .... 160 B5
New King St, SE8.... 152 C4
Newlands Quay, E1... 94 A3
Newland St, E16 .... 103 F5
Newling Cl, E6 .... 76 B5
New London St, EC3 .. 91 F2
New Lydenburg St,
  SE7............... 130 B4
Newman Pas, W1 .... 58 B4
Newman's Ct, EC3.... 91 D1
Newman's Row,
  WC2 .... 60 B4
Newman St, W1...... 58 B4
Newman Yd, W1..... 58 B5
New Mt St, E15 ...... 27 D5
Newnham Ter, SE1 .. 116 C3
🄲🄷 New North Comm Sch,
  N1............... 18 C3
New N Pl, EC2 .... 63 E2
New N Rd, N1 .... 41 D3
New N St, WC1....... 60 A3
New Oxford St, WC1 .. 59 D5
New Pl Sq, SE16..... 121 E3
New Plaistow Rd,
  E15............... 27 F5
Newport Av, E13..... 73 F2
  E14 .... 99 D3
Newport Ct, WC2 .... 87 D2
Newport Pl, WC2..... 87 D2
Newport St, SE11 ... 144 A4
New Priory Ct, NW6 ... 9 D4

New Providence Wf,
  E14............... 98 C4
New Quebec St, W1 .. 84 B1
New Ride, SW7 ..... 112 A1
New River Head, EC1 . 39 D4
New River Wk, N1..... 18 A2
New Rd, E1........... 65 E4
New Row, WC2 ...... 87 E2
★ New Scotland Yd,
  SW1 .... 114 C3
New Spring Gdns Wk,
  SE11............... 143 F3
New Sq, WC2 .... 60 B5
New St, EC2 .... 63 F4
New St Sq, EC4....... 61 D5
Newton Pl, E14 ..... 124 C5
🄲🄷 Newton Prep Sch,
  SW8 .... 165 F3
Newton Rd, W2...... 81 D1
Newton St, WC2 ..... 59 F5
Newtown St, SW11.. 165 E3
New Turnstile, WC1 .. 60 A4
New Union Cl, E14 .. 126 B3
New Union St, EC2 ... 62 C4
New Wf Rd, N1 .... 37 F2
Nicholas La, EC4 ..... 91 D2
Nicholas Pas, EC4 .... 91 D2
Nicholas Rd, E1 ...... 66 B1
Nicholl St, E2 .... 42 C1
Nichols Ct, E2......... 42 A3
Nicholson St, SE1 .... 89 E5
Nightingale Ms, E3 ... 45 E2
  SE11............... 117 D5
Nightingale Pl,
  SW10 .... 138 B4
Nightingale Rd, N1... 18 B2
Nightingale Way, E6 .. 75 F3
Nile St, N1 .... 40 B4
Nile Ter, SE15....... 148 A3
Nimrod Pas, N1 ...... 19 F2
Nina Mackay Cl, E15.. 27 E5
NINE ELMS, SW8.... 166 B1
Nine Elms La, SW8 .. 142 B5
Niton St, SW6 ...... 158 C1
Noble St, EC2 .... 62 A5
Noel Rd, E6.......... 75 E2
  N1................ 39 E2
Noel St, W1 .... 86 B1
Norbiton Rd, E14..... 68 A5
Norburn St, W10..... 51 E4
Norfolk Cres, W2..... 55 F5
Norfolk Ho, SE3..... 155 F5
Norfolk Ms, W10..... 51 F4
Norfolk Pl, W2 ...... 55 D5
Norfolk Rd, NW8 .... 33 D1
Norfolk Row, SE1 ... 116 A5
Norfolk Sq, W2....... 83 D1
Norfolk Sq Ms, W2 ... 83 D1
Norfolk Ter, W6..... 135 E3
Norland Ho, W11..... 79 D5
Norland Pl, W11 ..... 79 F5
🄲🄷 Norland Pl Sch,
  W11............... 79 E5
Norland Rd, W11..... 79 D5

Norland Sq, W11 . . . . 79 F5
Normand Ms, W14 . . 135 F4
Sch Normand Pk Prim Sch,
  SW6 . . . . 136 B4
Normand Rd, W14 . . 136 A4
Normandy Rd, SW9 . 168 C4
Normandy Ter, E16 . . 101 E1
Norman Gro, E3 . . . . . . 45 F3
Norman Rd, E6 . . . . . . 76 B1
  SE10 . . . . 177 F1
Norman St, EC1 . . . . . . 40 A5
Norris St, SW1 . . . . . . 86 C3
Northampton Pk, N1 . 18 B1
Northampton Rd,
  EC1 . . . . 61 D1
Northampton Row,
  EC1 . . . . 39 D5
Northampton Sq,
  EC1 . . . . 39 E5
Northampton St, N1 . . 18 A3
North Audley St, W1 . . 84 C1
North Bk, NW8 . . . . . . 33 D5
NORTH BECKTON, E6 . 75 F2
Sch North Beckton
  Prim Sch, E6 . . . . . . 76 B3
North Branch Av,
  W10 . . . . 28 B5
Sch North Br Ho Jun Sch,
  NW1 . . . . 35 E1
Sch North Br Ho Sen Sch,
  NW1 . . . . 35 E1
Northburgh St, EC1 . . . 61 F1
North Carriage Dr,
  W2 . . . . 83 E2
Northchurch, SE17 . . 147 D2
Northchurch Rd, N1 . . 18 C3
Northchurch Ter, N1 . . 19 E4
North Colonnade,
  E14 . . . . 97 D4
North Cres, E16 . . . . . . 71 D1
  WC1 . . . . 58 C3
Northdown St, N1 . . . . 37 F2
North End Cres,
  W14 . . . . 136 A1
North End Ho, W14 . 135 F1
North End Par, W14 . 135 F1
North End Rd, SW6 . . 136 B4
  W14 . . . . 136 A2
Northey St, E14 . . . . . . 95 F2
North Flockton St,
  SE16 . . . . 120 C1
North Gate, NW8 . . . . 33 E3
North Gower St,
  NW1 . . . . 36 B5
✦ North Greenwich . 127 E1
Northiam St, E9 . . . . . . 43 F1
Northington St, WC1 . 60 A2
NORTH KENSINGTON,
  W10 . . . . 51 D4
North Ms, WC1 . . . . . . 60 B2
Northpoint Sq, NW1 . . 14 C1
North Pole Rd, W10 . . 50 A4
Northport St, N1 . . . . . 41 D1
North Ride, W2 . . . . . . 83 E3

North Rd, N7 . . . . 15 D1
North Row, W1 . . . . . . 84 B2
North Tenter St, E1 . . . 92 B1
North Ter, SW3 . . . . . 111 E4
Northumberland All,
  EC3 . . . . 91 F1
Northumberland Av,
  WC2 . . . . 87 E4
Northumberland Pl,
  W2 . . . . 52 C5
Northumberland Rd,
  E6 . . . . 75 F5
Northumberland St,
  WC2 . . . . 87 E4
Northumbria St,
  E14 . . . . 69 D5
North Vil, NW1 . . . . . . 14 C2
North Wk, W2 . . . . 82 A3
Sch North W London Jewish
  Prim Sch, NW6 . . . . . 7 E3
Sch North Westminster
  Comm Sch, W2 . . . . 55 D4
Sch North Westminster
  Comm Sch (Lwr),
  Marylebone Lwr Ho,
  NW1 . . . . 55 E3
  Paddington Lwr Ho,
  W9 . . . . 53 D1
Northwest Pl, N1 . . . . . 39 D2
North Wf Rd, W2 . . . . . 54 C4
Northwick Cl, NW8 . . . 54 C1
Northwick Ter, NW8 . . 54 C1
NORTH WOOLWICH,
  E16 . . . . 131 F1
⇌ North Woolwich . . 132 C1
★ North Woolwich
  Old Sta Mus, E16 . 133 D1
North Woolwich Rd,
  E16 . . . . 100 B4
North Woolwich Rbt,
  E16 . . . . 102 C5
Norton Folgate, E1 . . . 63 F3
Norway Gate, SE16 . . 123 F3
Norway Pl, E14 . . . . . . 96 A1
Norway St, SE10 . . . . 153 F4
Norwich Ho, E14 . . . . . 69 F5
Norwich St, EC4 . . . . . 60 C1
Notley St, SE5 . . . . . . 170 C1
Sch Notre Dame Sch,
  SE1 . . . . 117 E3
Notting Barn Rd,
  W10 . . . . 50 C2
Nottingdale Sq, W11 . 79 E3
Nottingham Av, E16 . . 74 A4
Nottingham Ct, WC2 . 87 E1
Nottingham Pl, W1 . . . 56 C2
Nottingham St, W1 . . . 56 C3
Nottingham Ter,
  NW1 . . . . 56 C2
NOTTING HILL, W11 . . 79 F2
✦ Notting Hill Gate . . 80 C3
Notting Hill Gate,
  W11 . . . . 80 C4
Nova, E14 . . . . 124 C5

Novello St, SW6 . . . . . 160 C4
Nugent Ter, NW8 . . . . . 32 B3
Nun Ct, EC2 . . . . 62 C5
Nursery La, E2 . . . . 42 A1
  W10 . . . . 50 A4
Nursery Rd, E9 . . . . . . 22 A1
Nursery Row, SE17 . . 146 C1
Nutbourne St, W10 . . . 29 E4
Nutcroft Rd, SE15 . . . 173 E2
Nutford Pl, W1 . . . . 55 F5
Nutley Ter, NW3 . . . . . 10 B1
Nutmeg Cl, E16 . . . . . . 71 F1
Nutmeg La, E14 . . . . . . 98 C1
Nuttall St, N1 . . . . 41 F2
Nutt St, SE15 . . . . 172 B1
Nynehead St, SE14 . . 175 E1

O

O2 Shop Cen, NW3 . . . 10 A1
Oak Cres, E16 . . . . 71 F4
Oakdene, SE15 . . . . . 173 E3
Oakden St, SE11 . . . . 117 D5
Oakes Cl, E6 . . . . 104 B1
Oakey La, SE1 . . . . . . 116 C3
Oakfield St, SW10 . . . 138 A4
Oakington Rd, W9 . . . . 53 D1
Sch Oaklands
  Sec Sch, E2 . . . . . . 43 E4
Oak La, E14 . . . . 96 A2
Oakley Cl, E6 . . . . 75 F5
Oakley Cres, EC1 . . . . . 39 F3
Oakley Gdns, SW3 . . . 139 F4
Oakley Pl, SE1 . . . . . . 148 A3
Oakley Rd, N1 . . . . 18 C3
Oakley Sq, NW1 . . . . . . 36 B3
Oakley St, SW3 . . . . . 139 E4
Oakley Wk, W6 . . . . . 135 D4
Oakley Yd, E2 . . . . 64 B1
Oak Tree Rd, NW8 . . . 33 D5
Oakwood Ct, W14 . . 108 A3
Oakwood La, W14 . . 108 A3
Oakworth Rd, W10 . . . 50 B3
Oat La, EC2 . . . . 62 A5
Oban Cl, E13 . . . . 74 A2
Oban St, E14 . . . . 71 D5
Observatory Gdns,
  W8 . . . . 109 D1
Observatory Ms,
  E14 . . . . 126 C5
Occupation Rd,
  SE17 . . . . 146 A2
Ocean Est, E1 . . . . 67 D2
Ocean St, E1 . . . . 67 D3
Ocean Wf, E14 . . . . . . 124 C2
Ockendon Ms, N1 . . . . 18 C2
Ockendon Rd, N1 . . . . 18 C2
Octagon Arc, EC2 . . . . 63 E4

Octavia Ms, W9 . . . . . . 52 A1
Octavia St, SW11 . . . . 163 E4
Octavius St, SE8 . . . . 176 C1
Odessa St, SE16. . . . . 124 A2
Odger St, SW11 . . . . . 164 B5
Odhams Wk, WC2 . . . . 87 F1
Offenbach Ho, E2 . . . . 44 C3
Offley Rd, SW9 . . . . . 168 C1
Offord Rd, N1 . . . . 16 A3
Offord St, N1 . . . . 16 B3
Ogle St, W1 . . . . 58 A3
Ohio Rd, E13 . . . . 72 B2
Okehampton Rd,
    NW10 . . . . 28 B1
Olaf St, W11 . . . . 79 D3
★ Old Admiralty Bldgs
    (M.o.D.), SW1 . . . . 87 D5
Old Bailey, EC4 . . . . . 89 F1
Old Barrack Yd, SW1. 112 C1
Old Barrowfield, E15. . 49 F1
Old Bellgate Pl, E14 . 124 C4
Old Bethnal Grn Rd,
    E2 . . . . 42 C4
Old Bond St, W1 . . . . 86 A3
Old Brewers Yd, WC2 . 87 E1
Old Broad St, EC2 . . . 91 D1
Old Brompton Rd,
    SW5 . . . . 137 D3
    SW7 . . . . 137 D3
Old Bldgs, WC2 . . . . . 60 C5
Old Burlington St,
    W1 . . . . 86 A2
Oldbury Pl, W1. . . . . . 57 D3
Old Canal Ms, SE15. . 148 B3
Old Castle St, E1 . . . . 64 A4
Old Cavendish St, W1 . 57 E5
Old Chelsea Ms,
    SW3 . . . . 139 D5
Old Ch Rd, E1 . . . . . . 66 C5
Old Ch St, SW3 . . . . 139 D3
Old Compton St, W1. . 86 C2
Old Ct Pl, W8 . . . . . . 109 E1
★ Old Curiosity Shop,
    WC2 . . . . 60 A5
Old Dover Rd, SE3. . . 181 D1
Oldfield Gro, SE16. . . 150 C1
Old Fish St Hill, EC4 . . 90 C4
Old Fleet La, EC4 . . . . 61 E5
OLD FORD, E3 . . . . . . 24 A4
Sch Old Ford Prim Sch,
    E3 . . . . 46 A2
Old Ford Rd, E2 . . . . . 43 F4
    E3 . . . . 45 D2
Old Gloucester St,
    WC1 . . . . 59 F3
Old Jamaica Rd,
    SE16 . . . . 120 C3
Old Jewry, EC2 . . . . . 90 C1
Old Kent Rd, SE1. . . . 119 D4
    SE15 . . . . 149 D4

Old Manor Yd, SW5. . 137 D2
Old Mkt Sq, E2 . . . . . 42 A4
Old Marylebone Rd,
    NW1 . . . . 55 F4
Old Montague St, E1. . 64 C4
Old Nichol St, E2 . . . . 64 A1
Old N St, WC1 . . . . . . 60 A3
★ Old Operating Thea
    Mus & Herb Garret,
    SE1 . . . . 91 D5
Sch Old Palace Prim Sch,
    E3 . . . . 47 F4
Old Palace Yd, SW1. . 115 E3
Old Paradise St,
    SE11 . . . . 116 A5
Old Pk La, W1. . . . . . 85 D5
Old Pye St, SW1. . . . 114 C3
Old Quebec St, W1 . . 84 B1
Old Queen St, SW1 . . 115 D2
Old River Lea Towpath,
    E15 . . . . 25 D5
Old Royal Free Sq,
    N1 . . . . 39 D1
Old Sch Cl, SE10 . . . . 127 F4
Old Sch Sq, E14 . . . . . 96 C1
Old Seacoal La, EC4. . . 61 E5
Old S Lambeth Rd,
    SW8 . . . . 167 F1
★ Old Spitalfields Mkt,
    E1 . . . . 64 A3
Old Sq, WC2 . . . . 60 B5
⇌ Old Street 40 C5
⊖ Old Street 40 C5
Old St, EC1 . . . . 62 A1
Old Woolwich Rd,
    SE10 . . . . 155 D4
O'Leary Sq, E1 . . . . . . 66 A3
Sch Olga Prim Sch, E3. . 45 F3
Olga St, E3 . . . . 45 F3
Oliphant St, W10 . . . . 29 D4
Oliver Gdns, E6 . . . . . . 75 F5
Oliver-Goldsmith Est,
    SE15 . . . . 173 D3
Sch Oliver Goldsmith Prim
    Sch, SE5 . . . . 172 A3
Oliver Ms, SE15 . . . . 172 C5
Olivers Yd, EC1. . . . . . 63 D1
Ollerton Grn, E3 . . . . . 24 B5
Olliffe St, E14. . . . . . 126 B4
Olmar St, SE1. . . . . . 148 C4
Olney Rd, SE17 . . . . . 146 A4
★ Olympia, W14 . . . 107 F4
Olympia Ms, W2 . . . . . 81 F3
Olympia Way, W14 . . 107 F4
O'Meara St, SE1. . . . . 90 B5
Omega Cl, E14. . . . . . 125 E3
Omega Pl, N1. . . . . . . 37 F3
Omega St, SE14. . . . . 176 B3
Ommaney Rd, SE14 . . 175 E4
Onega Gate, SE16. . . 123 E3
Ongar Rd, SW6 . . . . . 136 C4
Onslow Cl, W10. . . . . . 30 A4
Onslow Cres, SW7. . . 139 D1
Onslow Gdns, SW7 . . 138 C1

Onslow Ms E, SW7 . . 138 C1
Onslow Ms W, SW7. . 138 C1
Onslow Sq, SW7 . . . . 111 D5
Onslow St, EC1 . . . . . . 61 D2
Ontario St, SE1 . . . . . 117 F4
Ontario Way, E14 . . . . 96 C3
Opal Cl, E16. . . . . 103 D1
Opal Ms, NW6 . . . . 8 B5
Opal St, SE11 . . . . . . 145 E1
Uni Open Uni in London, The,
    NW1 . . . . 13 F3
Ophir Ter, SE15 . . . . . 172 C4
Oppenheim Rd,
    SE13. . . . . 178 A5
Oppidans Ms, NW3 . . . 12 A4
Oppidans Rd, NW3 . . . 12 A4
Orange Ct, E1. . . . . . . 93 D5
Orange Pl, SE16. . . . . 122 B4
Orange Sq, SW1. . . . . 141 D1
Orange St, WC2 . . . . . 86 C3
Orange Yd, W1. . . . . . 87 D1
Oransay Rd, N1 . . . . . 18 B2
Oratory La, SW3 . . . . 139 D2
Sch Oratory RC Prim Sch,
    SW3 . . . . 139 E2
Orbain Rd, SW6 . . . . . 159 F2
Orbel St, SW11 . . . . . 163 E4
Orb St, SE17. . . . . . . 146 C1
Orchard, The, SE3 . . . 179 D5
Orchard Cl, N1. . . . . . 18 B4
    W10 . . . . 51 F3
Orchard Dr, SE3. . . . . 179 D5
Orchard Hill, SE13. . . 177 F5
Sch Orchard JMI Sch,
    E9 . . . . 22 B4
Orchard Ms, N1 . . . . . 19 D4
Orchard Pl, E14 . . . . . 99 E2
Orchard Rd, SE3 . . . . 179 E5
Orchardson St, NW8. . 54 C2
Orchard Sq, W14. . . . 136 A3
Orchard St, W1 . . . . . 84 C1
Orchid Cl, E6 . . . . 75 E3
Orde Hall St, WC1 . . . 60 A2
Ordell Rd, E3 . . . . 46 B3
Ordnance Cres,
    SE10. . . . . 127 D1
Ordnance Hill, NW8 . . 33 D1
Ordnance Ms, NW8. . . 33 D2
Ordnance Rd, E16 . . . . 72 A3
Oregano Dr, E14 . . . . . 99 D1
Oriel Rd, E9 . . . . 23 D1
Oriental Rd, E16 . . . . 103 D4
Oriental St, E14. . . . . 97 D2
Orient St, SE11 . . . . . 117 E5
Orion Ho, E1. . . . . 65 F2
Orion Pt, E14. . . . . . . 124 C5
Orkney St, SW11. . . . 164 C5
Orleston Ms, N7 . . . . . 17 D2
Orleston Rd, N7. . . . . 17 D1
Orlop St, SE10 . . . . . 155 E3
Orme Ct, W2 . . . . 81 E3
Orme Ct Ms, W2 . . . . 81 F3
Orme La, W2 . . . . 81 E3
Orme Sq, W2 . . . . 81 E3

★ Place of interest   ⇌ Railway station   🄷 Hospital   ⊖ London Underground station

Ormiston Rd, SE10 . . 156 C3
Ormond Cl, WC1 . . . . . 59 F3
Ormonde Gate, SW3 . 140 B3
Ormonde Pl, SW1 . . . . 140 C1
Ormonde Ter, NW8 . . . 34 A1
Ormond Ms, WC1 . . . . 59 F2
Ormond Yd, SW1 . . . . . 86 B4
Ormsby St, E2 . . . . 42 A2
Ormside St, SE15 . . . . 150 A5
Orpheus St, SE5 . . . . . 170 C4
Orsett St, SE11 . . . . . 144 B2
Orsett Ter, W2 . . . . 53 F5
Orsman Rd, N1 . . . . . . 41 E1
Orton St, E1 . . . . 92 C5
Orville Rd, SW11 . . . . 163 D5
Osbert St, SW1 . . . . . 142 C1
Osborn Cl, E8 . . . . 20 C5
Osborne Rd, E9 . . . . . . 24 B1
Osborn St, E1 . . . . 64 B4
Oscar Faber Pl, N1 . . . . 19 F4
Oscar St, SE8 . . . . . . 176 C5
Oseney Cres, NW5 . . . . 14 B1
Osier La, SE10 . . . . . . 128 B4
Osier St, E1 . . . . 66 B2
Oslo Ct, NW8 . . . . 33 E3
Oslo Sq, SE16 . . . . 123 F3
Sch Osmani Prim Sch,
  E1 . . . . 65 D3
Osman Rd, W6 . . . . . 106 B3
Osnaburgh St, NW1 . . 57 F2
  NW1 (north section) . . 35 F5
Osnaburgh Ter, NW1 . 57 F1
Osprey Cl, E6 . . . . 75 E4
Osram Ct, W6 . . . . . . 106 B4
Osric Path, N1 . . . . . . 41 E3
Ossington Bldgs, W1 . . 56 C3
Ossington Cl, W2 . . . . . 81 D3
Ossington St, W2 . . . . 81 D3
Ossory Rd, SE1 . . . . . 148 C3
Ossulston St, NW1 . . . 36 C3
Osten Ms, SW7 . . . . . 109 F4
Osterley Ho, E14 . . . . . 69 E5
Oswald Bldg, SW8 . . . 141 E5
Oswell Ho, E1 . . . . 93 F4
Oswin St, SE11 . . . . . 117 F5
Oswyth Rd, SE5 . . . . . 171 F5
Othello Cl, SE11 . . . . 145 E2
Otis St, E3 . . . . 48 A4
Otley Rd, E16 . . . . 74 A5
Otterburn Ho, SE5 . . 170 A1
Otter Cl, E15 . . . . 48 A1
Otto St, SE17 . . . . 145 E5
Sch Our Lady & St. Joseph
  JMI Sch, N1 . . . . 19 E2
Sch Our Lady of Dolours RC
  Prim Sch, W2 . . . . . . 53 E3
Sch Our Lady of Grace RC
  JMI Sch, SE7 . . . . . . 157 F5
Sch Our Lady of Victories RC
  Prim Sch, SW7 . . . 138 B1
Sch Our Lady Prim Sch,
  E14 . . . . 96 B1
Sch Our Lady's RC Prim Sch,
  NW1 . . . . 14 A5

Outer Circle, NW1 . . . . 56 C2
Outram Pl, N1 . . . . 15 F5
Outwich St, EC3 . . . . . 63 F5
★ Oval, The, Surrey County
  Cricket Club,
  SE11 . . . . 144 B4
● Oval 144 C5
Oval, The, E2 . . . . 43 E2
Oval Pl, SW8 . . . . 168 A1
Oval Rd, NW1 . . . . 13 E4
Oval Way, SE11 . . . . . 144 B3
Oversley Ho, W2 . . . . . 53 D3
Overstone Rd, W6 . . . 106 A4
Ovex Cl, E14 . . . . 126 B2
Ovington Gdns,
  SW3 . . . . 111 F4
Ovington Ms, SW3 . . 111 F4
Ovington Sq, SW3 . . . 111 F4
Ovington St, SW3 . . . 111 F4
Owen's Row, EC1 . . . . . 39 E4
Owen St, EC1 . . . . 39 E3
Owgan Cl, SE5 . . . . . . 171 D2
Oxberry Av, SW6 . . . . 159 F5
Oxendon St, SW1 . . . . 86 C3
Oxenholme, NW1 . . . . 36 B3
Oxestalls Rd, SE8 . . . 151 F2
★ Oxford Circ, W1 . . . 58 A5
● Oxford Circus 58 A5
Oxford Circ Av, W1 . . . 86 A1
Oxford Ct, EC4 . . . . . . 90 C2
Oxford Dr, SE1 . . . . . . 91 E5
Oxford Gdns, W10 . . . . 50 C5
Sch Oxford Gdns Prim Sch,
  W10 . . . . 50 C5
Oxford Gate, W6 . . . . 107 D5
Oxford Rd, E15 . . . . . . 27 D2
  NW6 . . . . 31 D3
Oxford Sq, W2 . . . . . . 83 F1
Oxford St, W1 . . . . 58 B5
Oxleas, E6 . . . . 77 E5
Oxley Cl, SE1 . . . . 148 B2
Oxo Twr Wf, SE1 . . . . . 89 D3
Oyster Catchers Cl,
  E16 . . . . 73 E5
Oyster Row, E1 . . . . . . 94 B1
Oyster Wf, SW11 . . . . 162 C5
Ozolins Way, E16 . . . . 72 C5

P

Pace Pl, E1 . . . . 93 F1
Pacific Rd, E16 . . . . . . 72 C5
Packington Sq, N1 . . . 40 A1
Packington St, N1 . . . . 17 F5
Padbury, SE17 . . . . . . 147 E3
Padbury Ct, E2 . . . . . . 42 B5
PADDINGTON, W2 . . . 54 A4
⇌ Paddington 54 C5
● Paddington 54 C5
Paddington Grn, W2 . . 55 D3
Sch Paddington Grn
  Prim Sch, W2 . . . . . . 54 C2

Paddington St, W1 . . . 56 C3
Pagden St, SW8 . . . . . 165 F3
Pageant Cres, SE16 . . . 95 F4
Pageantmaster Ct,
  EC4 . . . . 89 E1
Page St, SW1 . . . . 115 D5
Pages Wk, SE1 . . . . . . 119 E5
Paget St, EC1 . . . . 39 E4
Pagnell St, SE14 . . . . 176 A1
Pakenham St, WC1 . . . 38 B5
Palace Av, W8 . . . . 81 F5
Palace Ct, W2 . . . . 81 E2
Palace Gdns Ms, W8 . . 81 D4
Palace Gdns Ter, W8 . . 81 D4
Palace Gate, W8 . . . . 110 A2
Palace Grn, W8 . . . . . 109 F1
Palace Ms, SW1 . . . . . 141 D1
  SW6 . . . . 160 B2
Palace Pl, SW1 . . . . . . 114 A3
Palace St, SW1 . . . . . . 114 A3
Palfrey Pl, SW8 . . . . . 168 B1
Palgrave Gdns, NW1 . . 55 F1
Palissy St, E2 . . . . 42 A5
Palliser Rd, W14 . . . . . 135 E2
Pall Mall, SW1 . . . . . . 86 B5
Pall Mall E, SW1 . . . . . 87 D4
Palmer Rd, E13 . . . . . . 73 F2
Palmers Rd, E2 . . . . . . 45 D3
Palmerston Rd, NW6 . . 8 C3
Palmerston Way,
  SW8 . . . . 165 F2
Palmer St, SW1 . . . . . 114 C2
Pamela Wk, E8 . . . . . . 20 C5
Pancras La, EC4 . . . . . 90 B1
Pancras Rd, NW1 . . . . 36 C2
Pandian Way, NW1 . . . 14 C1
Pandora Rd, NW6 . . . . . 8 C1
Pangbourne Av,
  W10 . . . . 50 B3
Pankhurst Av, E16 . . 101 F4
Pankhurst Cl, SE14 . . 174 C2
Panton St, SW1 . . . . . . 86 C3
Panyer All, EC4 . . . . . . 90 A1
Parade, The, SW11 . . 164 B1
Paradise Rd, SW4 . . . 167 E5
Paradise Row, E2 . . . . . 43 F4
Paradise St, SE16 . . . 121 E2
Paradise Wk, SW3 . . . 140 A4
Paragon, The, SE3 . . . 180 B5
Paragon Cl, E16 . . . . . 72 C5
Paragon Ms, SE1 . . . . 119 D5
Paragon Pl, SE3 . . . . . 180 B5
Paragon Rd, E9 . . . . . . 21 F2
Pardoner St, SE1 . . . . 119 D3
Pardon St, EC1 . . . . . . 61 F1
Parfett St, E1 . . . . 65 D4
Parfrey St, W6 . . . . . . 134 B4
Paris Gdn, SE1 . . . . . . 89 E4
Parish Wf, SE18 . . . . . 131 F5
Park Av, E15 . . . . 27 E2

Park Cl, E9 .... 22 B5
  SW1 .... 112 A2
  W14 .... 108 B3
Park Cres, W1 .... 57 E2
Park Cres Ms E, W1 ... 57 F2
Park Cres Ms W, W1 .. 57 E2
Parker Cl, E16 ...... 103 E5
Parker Ms, WC2 ...... 59 F5
Parkers Row, SE1 ... 120 B2
Parker St, E16 ...... 103 E5
  WC2 .... 59 F5
Parkfield Rd, SE14... 176 A3
Parkfield St, N1 ..... 39 D2
Parkgate Rd, SW11.. 163 E2
Parkham St, SW11 .. 163 D4
Parkhill Rd, NW3..... 12 B1
Parkholme Rd, E8 ... 20 B1
Parkhouse St, SE5... 171 D1
Park La, E15 .... 26 C5
  W1 .... 85 D5
Park Pl, E14 .... 96 C4
  N1 .... 19 D5
  SW1 .... 86 A5
Park Pl Vil, W2 ...... 54 B3
Park Rd, NW1........ 33 E4
  NW8 .... 33 E4
Park Row, SE10..... 154 C4
Parkside, SE3 .... 180 A1
Parkside Business Est,
  SE8 .... 151 F4
Parkside Est, E9 ..... 22 C5
Parkside Rd, SW11 .. 164 C4
Parkside Wk, SE10 .. 127 E4
Park S, SW11 .... 164 C4
Park Sq E, NW1 ..... 57 E1
Park Sq Ms, NW1.... 57 E2
Park Sq W, NW1..... 57 E1
Park St, SE1 .... 90 A4
  W1 .... 84 C2
Park Vw Est, E2 ..... 44 C2
Park Vw Ms, SW9 ... 168 B5
Park Village E, NW1 .. 35 E1
Park Village W, NW1.. 35 E2
Parkville Rd, SW6 .. 160 A2
Park Vista, SE10 .... 155 D5
Park Wk, SE10 ..... 178 C2
  SW10 .... 138 B4
Sch Park Wk Prim Sch,
  SW10 .... 138 C5
Parkway, NW1....... 35 E1
Park W, W2.......... 83 F1
Park W Pl, W2 .... 55 F5
Parliament Sq, SW1 . 115 E2
Parliament St, SW1.. 115 E2
Parliament Vw Apartments,
  SE1 .... 116 A5
Parmiter St, E2 ...... 43 F2
Parmoor Ct, EC1 .... 62 A1
Parnell Rd, E3........ 46 B1
Parnham St, E14 .... 67 F5

Parr Ct, N1 .... 40 C2
Parr St, N1 .... 40 C2
Parry Av, E6 .... 104 A1
Parry Pl, SE18 ...... 133 F5
Parry Rd, W10 ...... 29 F4
Parry St, SW8....... 143 E4
Parsonage St, E14... 154 B1
PARSONS GREEN,
  SW6 .... 160 C3
  ⊖ Parsons Green .. 160 B4
Parsons Grn, SW6.. 160 C4
Parsons Grn La,
  SW6 .... 160 C3
Parson's Ho, W2 .... 54 C2
Parthenia Rd, SW6.. 161 D4
Partridge Cl, E16 .... 74 C4
Partridge Sq, E6..... 75 F3
Parvin St, SW8...... 166 C3
Pascal St, SW8...... 167 D1
Pasley Cl, SE17 ..... 146 A3
Passfield Dr, E14..... 69 F3
Passing All, EC1 ..... 61 F2
Passmore St, SW1... 140 C1
★ Passport Office,
  SW1 .... 113 F5
Pastor St, SE11 ..... 117 F5
Patcham Ter, SW8... 165 F3
Paternoster Row,
  EC4 .... 90 A1
Paternoster Sq, EC4 .. 89 F1
Pater St, W8........ 108 C4
Patmore Est, SW8... 166 B3
Patmore St, SW8.... 166 B3
Patmos Rd, SW9 .... 169 E2
Paton Cl, E3 .... 47 D4
Paton St, EC1 .... 40 A5
Patrick Connolly Gdns,
  E3 .... 47 F5
Patriot Sq, E2........ 43 F3
Patshull Ho, NW5 ... 14 A2
Patshull Rd, NW5 ... 13 F1
Patterdale Rd,
  SE15 .... 174 A1
Pattina Wk, SE16.... 95 F5
Pattison Pt, E16...... 73 D4
Paul Cl, E15 .... 27 E4
Paulet Rd, SE5...... 169 F5
Paul Julius Cl, E14 ... 98 C3
Paul St, E15 .... 27 E5
  EC2 .... 63 D2
Paul's Wk, EC4 ...... 89 F2
Paultons Sq, SW3... 139 D4
Paultons St, SW3.... 139 D5
Paveley Dr, SW11 ... 163 E2
Paveley St, NW8 .... 55 F1
Pavilion Rd, SW1.... 112 B4
Pavilion St, SW1 .... 112 B4
Paxton Ter, SW1 .... 141 F4
Payne Rd, E3........ 47 E3
Payne St, SE8....... 152 B5
Paynes Wk, W6 ..... 135 E5
Peabody Av, SW1 ... 141 E2
Peabody Cl, SE10... 177 F3
  SW1 .... 141 F3

Peabody Dws, WC1 ... 59 E1
Peabody Est, EC1.... 62 B2
  N1 (Islington) 18 A4
  SE1 .... 89 D5
  SW1 .... 114 A5
  SW3 .... 139 F4
  SW6 .... 136 C4
  W6 .... 134 B3
  W10 .... 50 B3
Peabody Sq, SE1 .... 117 E2
Peabody Trust, SE1 ... 90 A5
Peabody Yd, N1 ..... 18 A5
Peach Rd, W10 ...... 29 D4
Peachum Rd, SE3 ... 156 B4
Peachwalk Ms, E3... 45 D2
Peacock St, SE17... 145 F1
Peacock Wk, E16.... 73 F5
Peacock Yd, SE17 ... 145 F1
Pear Cl, SE14 .... 175 E1
Pearl Cl, E6 .... 76 C5
Pearl St, E1 .... 93 F4
Pearman St, SE1 .... 117 D3
Pear Pl, SE1 .... 116 C1
Pearscroft Ct, SW6 .. 161 F4
Pearscroft Rd, SW6.. 161 E5
Pearse St, SE15 .... 147 F5
Pearson Cl, SE5 ..... 170 B3
Pearsons Av, SE14... 176 C3
Pearson St, E2 ...... 41 F2
Pear Tree Cl, E2 ..... 42 A1
Pear Tree Ct, EC1 .... 61 D2
Peartree La, E1 ..... 94 B3
Pear Tree St, EC1 ... 61 F1
Peartree Way, SE10 . 128 C5
Peary Pl, E2 .... 44 B4
PECKHAM, SE15 .... 172 A5
Peckham Gro, SE15.. 171 F1
Peckham High St,
  SE15 .... 172 C4
Peckham Hill St,
  SE15 .... 172 C1
Peckham Pk Rd,
  SE15 .... 172 C1
Sch Peckham Pk Sch,
  SE15 .... 173 D2
Peckham Rd, SE5 ... 171 D4
  SE15 .... 171 D4
↼ Peckham Rye 172 C5
Pecks Yd, E1 .... 64 A3
Pedlars Wk, N7 ..... 15 F1
Pedley St, E1 .... 64 B2
Pedworth Gdns,
  SE16 .... 150 A1
Peel Gro, E2 .... 44 A3
Peel Pas, W8........ 80 C5
Peel Prec, NW6 ..... 30 C3
Peel Rd, NW6........ 30 B4
Peel St, W8 .... 80 C5
Peerless St, EC1..... 40 C5
Pegasus Pl, SE11 .... 144 C4
Pekin Cl, E14 .... 97 D1
Pekin St, E14 .... 97 D1
Peldon Wk, N1....... 17 F5
Pelham Cres, SW7... 139 E1

Pelham Ho, W14 . . . . 136 A1
Pelham Pl, SW7 . . . . . 139 E1
Pelham St, SW7 . . . . . 111 D5
Pelican Est, SE15 . . . . 172 A4
Pelican Pas, E1 . . . . 66 A1
Pelier St, SE17 . . . . . . 146 B4
Pellant Rd, SW6 . . . . . 135 F5
Pelling St, E14 . . . . 68 C5
Pelter St, E2 . . . . 42 A4
Pelton Rd, SE10 . . . . . 155 E2
Pember Rd, NW10 . . . . 28 C5
Pemberton Pl, E8 . . . . 21 F4
Pemberton Row, EC4 . 61 D5
Pembridge Cres, W11 . 80 C2
Pembridge Gdns, W2 . 80 C3
Coll Pembridge Hall,
  W2 . . . . 81 D3
Sch Pembridge Hall Sch,
  W2 . . . . 81 D3
Pembridge Ms, W11 . . 80 C2
Pembridge Pl, W2 . . . . 81 D2
Pembridge Rd, W11 . . 80 C3
Pembridge Sq, W2 . . . 80 C3
Pembridge Vil, W2 . . . 80 C2
  W11 . . . . 80 C2
Pembroke Av, N1 . . . . 15 F5
Pembroke Cl, SW1 . . . 113 D2
Pembroke Gdns,
  W8 . . . . 108 B5
Pembroke Gdns Cl,
  W8 . . . . 108 B4
Pembroke Ms, E3 . . . . . 45 C4
  W8 . . . . 108 C4
Pembroke Pl, W8 . . . . 108 C4
Pembroke Rd, E6 . . . . . 76 A3
  W8 . . . . 108 C5
Pembroke Sq, W8 . . . 108 C4
Pembroke St, N1 . . . . . 15 F4
Pembroke Studios,
  W8 . . . . 108 B4
Pembroke Vil, W8 . . . 108 C5
Pembroke Wk, W8 . . 108 C5
Pembry Cl, SW9 . . . . . 168 C4
Pemell Cl, E1 . . . . 66 B1
Penally Pl, N1 . . . . 19 D5
Penang St, E1 . . . . 93 F4
Penarth St, SE15 . . . . 150 A4
Pencombe Ms, W11 . . 80 B2
Pencraig Way, SE15 . 149 E5
Penfold Pl, NW1 . . . . . 55 D3
Penfold St, NW1 . . . . . 55 D2
  NW8 . . . . 55 D2
Penford St, SE5 . . . . . 169 E5
Penhall Rd, SE7 . . . . . 130 C5
Penhurst Pl, SE1 . . . . 116 B4
Peninsula Hts, SE1 . . 143 F2
Peninsular Pk Rd,
  SE7 . . . . 157 D1
Pennack Rd, SE15 . . . 148 B5
Pennant Ms, W8 . . . . 109 E5
Pennard Rd, W12 . . . 106 A1
Pennethorne Cl, E9 . . 44 A1
Pennethorne Rd,
  SE15 . . . . 173 E2

Pennington St, E1 . . . . 93 D3
Penn St, N1 . . . . 41 D1
Pennyfields, E14 . . . . . 97 D2
Pennymoor Wk,
  W9 . . . . 52 B1
Pennyroyal Av, E6 . . . 104 C1
Penpoll Rd, E8 . . . . . . 21 E1
Penrose Gro, SE17 . . . 146 A3
Penrose Ho, SE17 . . . 146 A3
Penrose St, SE17 . . . . 146 A3
Penryn St, NW1 . . . . . 36 C2
Penry St, SE1 . . . . 147 F1
Pensbury Pl, SW8 . . . 166 B5
Pensbury St, SW8 . . . 166 B5
Penshurst Rd, E9 . . . . . 22 C4
Pentland Rd, NW6 . . . . 30 C4
Penton Gro, N1 . . . . . . 38 C3
Penton Pl, SE17 . . . . . 145 F2
Penton Ri, WC1 . . . . . . 38 B4
Penton St, N1 . . . . 38 C2
PENTONVILLE, N1 . . . 38 C3
Pentonville Rd, N1 . . . 38 A3
Pentridge St, SE15 . . . 172 A1
Penywern Rd, SW5 . . 137 D2
Penzance Pl, W11 . . . . 79 E4
Penzance St, W11 . . . . 79 E4
Pepler Ms, SE5 . . . . . . 148 A4
Peploe Rd, NW6 . . . . . 29 D2
Pepper Cl, E6 . . . . 76 B3
Pepper St, E14 . . . . . . 125 E3
  SE1 . . . . 118 A1
Pepys Cres, E16 . . . . . 101 D4
Pepys Rd, SE14 . . . . . 175 D4
Pepys St, EC3 . . . . 91 F2
★ Percival David Foundation
  of Chinese Art,
  WC1 (Gordon Sq) . . . 59 D2
Percival St, EC1 . . . . . . 61 E1
Percy Circ, WC1 . . . . . . 38 B4
Percy Ms, W1 . . . . 58 C4
Percy Pas, W1 . . . . 58 B4
Percy Rd, E16 . . . . 71 F3
Percy St, W1 . . . . 58 C4
Percy Yd, WC1 . . . . 38 B4
Peregrine Ho, EC1 . . . . 39 F4
Perham Rd, W14 . . . . 135 F3
Peridot St, E6 . . . . 75 F3
Perkin's Rents, SW1 . 114 C3
Perkins Sq, SE1 . . . . . . 90 B4
Perren St, NW5 . . . . . . 13 E1
Perrymead St, SW6 . . 161 D4
Perryn Rd, SE16 . . . . . 121 E3
Perrys Pl, W1 . . . . 58 C5
Perseverance Pl,
  SW9 . . . . 169 D2
Peterboat Cl, SE10 . . 127 F5
Peterborough Ms,
  SW6 . . . . 160 C5
Peterborough Rd,
  SW6 . . . . 160 C5
Peterborough Vil,
  SW6 . . . . 161 D5
Peterchurch Ho,
  SE15 . . . . 173 E1

Sch Peter Hills with St. Mary's
  & St. Paul's C of E
  Prim Sch, SE16 . . . . 95 D4
Peterhouse Gdns,
  SW6 . . . . 161 F4
Peterley Business Cen,
  E2 . . . . 43 E3
★ Peter Pan Statue,
  W2 . . . . 82 C4
Petersham La,
  SW7 . . . . 110 A3
Petersham Ms,
  SW7 . . . . 110 A4
Petersham Pl,
  SW7 . . . . 110 A3
Peters Hill, EC4 . . . . . . 90 A2
Peter's La, EC1 . . . . . . 61 F3
Peter St, W1 . . . . 86 B2
Petley Rd, W6 . . . . . . 134 B5
Peto Pl, NW1 . . . . 57 F1
Peto St N, E16 . . . . . . 100 A2
Petrie Cl, NW2 . . . . 7 F1
★ Petrie Mus of Egyptian
  Archaeology,
  WC1 (Malet Pl) 58 C2
★ Petticoat Lane Mkt,
  E1 . . . . 63 F4
Petticoat Sq, E1 . . . . . 64 A5
Pett St, SE18 . . . . 131 E5
Petty France, SW1 . . 114 B3
Petty Wales, EC3 . . . . 91 F3
Petworth St, SW11 . . 163 F3
Petyt Pl, SW3 . . . . 139 E5
Petyward, SW3 . . . . . 139 F1
Peverel, E6 . . . . 76 C5
Peyton Pl, SE10 . . . . . 178 A1
Pheasant Cl, E16 . . . . . 73 D5
Phelp St, SE17 . . . . . . 146 C4
Phene St, SW3 . . . . . . 139 F4
Philbeach Gdns,
  SW5 . . . . 136 B2
Philchurch Pl, E1 . . . . . 93 D1
Philip St, E13 . . . . 72 C1
Phillimore Gdns,
  NW10 . . . . 6 A5
  W8 . . . . 108 C2
Phillimore Gdns Cl,
  W8 . . . . 108 C3
Phillimore Pl, W8 . . . 108 C2
Phillimore Wk, W8 . . 108 C3
Phillipp St, N1 . . . . 41 E1
Philpot La, EC3 . . . . . . 91 E2
Philpot St, E1 . . . . 65 F5
Phipp's Ms, SW1 . . . . 113 F4
Phipp St, EC2 . . . . 63 E1
Phoenix Cl, E8 . . . . . . 20 A5
Phoenix Pl, WC1 . . . . . 60 B1
Phoenix Rd, NW1 . . . . 36 C4
Sch Phoenix Sch, E3 . . . 46 B4
  NW3 . . . . 10 B2

Phoenix St, WC2 . . . . . 87 D1
Phoenix Wf, SE10 . . . . 128 A1
Phoenix Wf Rd, SE1 . 120 B2
Phoenix Yd, WC1 . . . . . 38 B5
★ Photographers' Gall,
 WC2 . . . . 87 D2
★ Physical Energy Statue,
 W2 . . . . 82 B5
Physic Pl, SW3 . . . . . . 140 A4
Piccadilly, W1 . . . . 85 F5
Piccadilly Arc, SW1 . . 86 A4
🚇 Piccadilly Circus . . . 86 B3
Piccadilly Circ, W1 . . . 86 C3
Piccadilly Ct, N7 . . . . . 16 A1
Piccadilly Pl, W1 . . . . . 86 B3
Pickard St, EC1 . . . . . . 39 F4
Pickering Cl, E9 . . . . . . 22 C3
Pickering Ms, W2 . . . . 53 F5
Pickering Pl, SW1 . . . . 86 B5
Pickering St, N1 . . . . . 17 F5
Pickfords Wf, N1 . . . . . 40 A3
Pickwick St, SE1 . . . . 118 A2
Pickworth Cl, SW8 . . 167 F2
Picton Pl, W1 . . . . 85 D1
Picton St, SE5 . . . . . . 170 C2
Pier Head, E1 . . . . 93 E5
Pierrepoint Row,
 N1 . . . . 39 E2
Pier Rd, E16 . . . . 132 B1
Pier St, E14 . . . . 126 B5
Pigott St, E14 . . . . 96 C1
Pilgrimage St, SE1 . . 118 C2
Pilgrims Ct, SE3 . . . . . 181 D3
Pilgrims Ms, E14 . . . . . 99 D2
Pilgrim St, EC4 . . . . . . 89 E1
🏫 Pilgrims' Way
 Prim Sch, SE15 . . . 150 A5
Pilot Cl, SE8 . . . . 152 A4
Pilton Pl, SE17 . . . . . . 146 B2
PIMLICO, SW1 . . . . . . 142 A2
🚇 Pimlico. 142 C2
Pimlico Rd, SW1 . . . . 140 C2
🏫 Pimlico Sch,
 SW1 . . . . 142 B3
Pimlico Wk, N1 . . . . . . 41 E4
Pinchin St, E1 . . . . 93 D2
Pindar St, EC2 . . . . 63 E3
Pindock Ms, W9 . . . . . . 53 F2
Pineapple Ct, SW1 . . 114 A3
Pinedene, SE15 . . . . . 173 E3
Pinefield Cl, E14 . . . . . 96 C1
Pinelands Cl, SE3 . . . . 180 B2
Pine Ms, NW10 . . . . . . 28 C2
Pine St, EC1 . . . . 60 C1
Pintail Cl, E6 . . . . 75 E4
Pioneer St, SE15 . . . . 172 C3
Piper Cl, N7 . . . . 16 A1
Pirie St, E16 . . . . 101 F5
Pitchford St, E15 . . . . . 27 D4

Pitfield Est, N1 . . . . 41 D4
Pitfield St, N1 . . . . 41 E5
Pitman St, SE5 . . . . . . 170 A1
Pitmaston Ho,
 SE13 . . . . 178 A5
Pitmaston Rd,
 SE13 . . . . 178 A5
Pitsea Pl, E1 . . . . 95 D1
Pitsea St, E1 . . . . 95 D1
Pitt's Head Ms, W1 . . . 85 D5
Pitt St, W8 . . . . 109 D1
Pixley St, E14 . . . . 68 B5
★ Planetarium,
 NW1 . . . . 56 B2
Plantain Pl, SE1 . . . . . 118 C1
Platina St, EC2 . . . . 63 D1
Platt St, NW1 . . . . 36 C2
Playfair St, W6 . . . . . . 134 B3
Playhouse Yd, EC4 . . . . 89 E1
Plaza Shop Cen, The,
 W1 . . . . 58 B5
Pleasant Pl, N1 . . . . . . 17 F4
Pleasant Row, NW1 . . 35 F1
Plender St, NW1 . . . . . 36 A1
Plevna St, E14 . . . . . . 126 A3
Pleydell Ct, EC4 . . . . . . 89 D1
Pleydell St, EC4 . . . . . . 89 D1
Plimsoll Cl, E14 . . . . . . 97 E1
Plough Ct, EC3 . . . . 91 D2
Ploughmans Cl,
 NW1 . . . . 14 C5
Plough Pl, EC4 . . . . 61 D5
Plough St, E1 . . . . 64 C5
Plough Way, SE16 . . . 123 D5
Plough Yd, EC2 . . . . 63 F2
Plover Way, SE16 . . . . 123 E3
Plumbers Row, E1 . . . . 64 C4
Plumbridge St,
 SE10 . . . . 178 A3
Plumstead Rd,
 SE18 . . . . 133 F5
Plumtree Ct, EC4 . . . . . 61 D5
Plymouth Rd, E16 . . . . 72 C4
Plymouth Wf, E14 . . . 126 C5
Plympton Av, NW6 . . . . 8 A4
Plympton Pl, NW8 . . . . 55 E2
Plympton Rd, NW6 . . . . 8 A4
Plympton St, NW8 . . . 55 E2
Pocock St, SE1 . . . . . . 117 E1
Podium, The, E2 . . . . . 44 B4
Point Cl, SE10 . . . . 178 B3
🏫 Pointer Sch, The,
 SE3 . . . . 180 C2
Pointers Cl, E14 . . . . . 153 E2
Point Hill, SE10 . . . . . 178 B2
Point of Thomas Path,
 E1 . . . . 94 B3
Point W, SW7 . . . . 109 F5
Poland Ho, E15 . . . . . . 26 C5
Poland St, W1 . . . . 86 B1
Polesworth Ho, W2 . . . 53 D3
★ Polish Inst & Sikorski Mus,
 SW7 (Princes Gate) . 111 D2
Pollard Cl, E16 . . . . . . 100 C2

Pollard Row, E2 . . . . . . 43 D4
Pollard St, E2 . . . . 43 D4
Pollen St, W1 . . . . 85 F1
Pollitt Dr, NW8 . . . . . . 54 C1
★ Pollock's Toy Mus,
 W1 . . . . 58 B3
Polperro Ms, SE11 . . . 117 D5
Polygon Rd, NW1 . . . . 36 C3
Polytechnic St,
 SE18 . . . . 133 D5
Pomeroy St, SE14 . . . 174 B2
Pond Pl, SW3 . . . . 139 E1
Pond Rd, E15 . . . . 49 E2
 SE3 . . . . 180 B5
Ponler St, E1 . . . . 93 E1
Ponsford St, E9 . . . . . . 22 B1
Ponsonby Pl, SW1 . . . 143 D2
Ponsonby Ter, SW1 . . 143 D2
Ponton Rd, SW8 . . . . . 143 D5
🚈 Pontoon Dock 102 A5
Pont St, SW1 . . . . 112 A4
Pont St Ms, SW1 . . . . . 112 A4
Pontypool Pl, SE1 . . . 117 E1
Poole Rd, E9 . . . . 22 C2
Pooles Bldgs, EC1 . . . . 60 C2
Pooles La, SW10 . . . . . 162 A2
Poole St, N1 . . . . 40 C1
Poolmans St,
 SE16 . . . . 122 C1
Poonah St, E1 . . . . 94 B1
Pope Ho, SE16 . . . . . . 149 E1
Pope St, SE1 . . . . 119 F2
Popham Rd, N1 . . . . . . 40 A1
Popham St, N1 . . . . 17 F5
POPLAR, E14 . . . . 97 E4
🚈 Poplar. 97 E3
Poplar Bath St, E14 . . 97 F2
Poplar Business Pk,
 E14 . . . . 98 A3
Poplar Gro, W6 . . . . . . 106 C2
Poplar High St, E14 . . 97 E2
Poplar Pl, W2 . . . . 81 E2
Poplars Av, NW10 . . . . . 6 A2
Poppins Ct, EC4 . . . . . . 89 E1
Porchester Gdns,
 W2 . . . . 81 E2
Porchester Gdns Ms,
 W2 . . . . 81 F1
Porchester Ms, W2 . . . 53 F5
Porchester Pl, W2 . . . . 83 F1
Porchester Rd, W2 . . . 53 E5
Porchester Sq, W2 . . . 53 F5
Porchester Ter, W2 . . . 82 A1
Porchester Ter N,
 W2 . . . . 53 F5
Porlock St, SE1 . . . . . . 118 C1
Portbury Cl, SE15 . . . 173 D4
Port Cres, E13 . . . . 73 E2
★ Portcullis Ho,
 SW1 . . . . 115 E1
Portelet Ct, N1 . . . . 19 D5
Portelet Rd, E1 . . . . . . 44 C5
Porten Rd, W14 . . . . . 107 E4
Porter Rd, E6 . . . . 76 B5

Porter St, SE1	90	B4
W1	56	B3
Porters Wk, E1	93	F3
Porteus Rd, W2	54	B4
Portgate Cl, W9	52	B1
Portia Way, E3	68	A2
Portland Gro, SW8	168	A3
H Portland Hosp for Women & Children, The,		
W1	57	F2
Portland Ms, W1	86	B1
Portland Pl, W1	57	F4
Portland Rd, W11	79	F4
Portland Sq, E1	93	E4
Portland St, SE17	146	C2
Portland Wk, SE17	147	D4
Portman Cl, W1	56	B5
Portman Gate, NW1	55	F2
Portman Ms S, W1	84	C1
Portman Pl, E2	44	B5
Portman Sq, W1	56	B5
Portman St, W1	84	C1
Portnall Rd, W9	52	A1
Portobello Ct, W11	80	B1
Portobello Ms, W11	80	C3
Portobello Rd, W10	52	A5
W11	80	B2
Portpool La, EC1	60	C3
Portree St, E14	71	D5
Portsea Ms, W2	83	F1
Portsea Pl, W2	83	F1
Portslade Rd, SW8	166	A5
Portsmouth Ms,		
E16	101	F4
Portsmouth St,		
WC2	88	A1
Portsoken St, E1	92	A2
Portugal St, WC2	88	A1
Post Office Ct, EC3	91	D1
Post Office Way,		
SW8	166	C1
Potier St, SE1	119	D4
Potters Cl, SE15	171	F1
Potters Flds, SE1	91	F5
Pottery La, W11	79	E3
Pottery St, SE16	121	E2
Pott St, E2	43	F5
Poulton Cl, E8	21	E1
Poultry, EC2	90	C1
Powis Gdns, W11	52	B5
Powis Ms, W11	52	B5
Powis Pl, WC1	59	F2
Powis Rd, E3	47	F5
Powis Sq, W11	52	B5
Powis St, SE18	132	C4
Powis Ter, W11	52	B5
Powlett Pl, NW1	13	D3
Pownall Rd, E8	42	B1
Poynter Ho, W11	79	D4
Poyser St, E2	43	F3
Praed Ms, W2	55	D5
Praed St, W2	55	E4
Pratt Ms, NW1	36	A1
Pratt St, NW1	36	A1

Pratt Wk, SE11	116	B5
Prebend St, N1	40	A1
Premier Cor, W9	30	A3
Premiere Pl, E14	96	C3
Prescot St, E1	92	B2
Prescott Ho, SE17	145	F5
President Dr, E1	93	E4
President St, EC1	40	A4
Prestage Way, E14	98	B2
Preston Cl, SE1	119	E5
Prestons Rd, E14	126	B1
Prestwood St, N1	40	B3
Pretoria Rd, E16	72	A1
Prices Ms, N1	16	B5
Price's St, SE1	89	F5
Prideaux Pl, WC1	38	B4
Priest Ct, EC2	62	A5
Priestman Pt, E3	47	E5
Prima Rd, SW9	168	C1
Primrose Cl, E3	46	C3
Primrose Gdns,		
NW3	11	F1
PRIMROSE HILL,		
NW8	12	A5
Primrose Hill, EC4	89	D1
Primrose Hill Ct, NW3	12	A4
Sch Primrose Hill Prim Sch,		
NW1	13	D5
Primrose Hill Rd,		
NW3	12	A3
Primrose Hill Studios,		
NW1	12	C5
Primrose Ms, NW1	12	B4
SE3	181	E2
Primrose Sq, E9	22	B4
Primrose St, EC2	63	E3
Primrose Wk, SE14	175	F1
Prince Albert Rd,		
NW1	33	F3
NW8	33	F3
Prince Charles Rd,		
SE3	180	A3
Prince Consort Rd,		
SW7	110	B3
Princedale Rd, W11	79	F4
Prince Edwards Rd,		
E9	24	B2
★ Prince Henry's Room,		
EC4	88	C1
Princelet St, E1	64	B3
Prince of Orange La,		
SE10	178	A1
Prince of Wales Dr,		
SW8	165	F2
SW11	164	A4
Prince of Wales Gate,		
SW7	111	E1
Prince of Wales Pas,		
NW1	36	A5
Prince of Wales Rd,		
NW5	13	D2
SE3	180	B4
Prince of Wales Ter,		
W8	109	F2

DLR Prince Regent	102	A2
Prince Regent La,		
E13	74	A4
E16	74	A4
Prince Regent Ms,		
NW1	36	A5
Prince's Arc, SW1	86	B4
Princes Ct, SE16	124	A4
Princes Ct Business Cen,		
E1	93	F3
Coll Prince's Foundation, The,		
EC2	63	E1
Princes Gdns, SW7	111	D3
Princes Gate, SW7	111	E2
Princes Gate Ct,		
SW7	111	D2
Princes Gate Ms,		
SW7	111	D3
Princes Ms, W2	81	E2
Princes Pl, SW1	86	B4
W11	79	E4
Princes Ri, SE13	178	B5
Princes Riverside Rd,		
SE16	94	C4
Sch Princess Frederica C of E Prim Sch, NW10	28	A3
H Princess Grace Hosp, The,		
W1	56	C2
Princess Louise Cl,		
W2	55	D3
H Princess Louise Hosp,		
W10	50	C4
Princess Ms, NW3	11	D1
Princess Sq, W2	81	E2
Princess Rd, NW1	12	C5
NW6	30	C3
Princess St, SE1	117	F4
Princes St, EC2	62	C5
W1	85	F1
Prince St, SE8	152	B4
Princes Yd, W11	79	F5
Princethorpe Ho,		
W2	53	E3
Princeton St, WC1	60	A3
Printers Inn Ct, EC4	60	C5
Printers Ms, E3	45	F1
Printer St, EC4	61	D5
Printing Ho Yd, E2	45	F4
Prior Bolton St, N1	17	F2
Prioress St, SE1	119	D4
Prior St, SE10	178	A2
Sch Prior Weston Prim Sch,		
EC1	62	B2
Priory Ct, SW8	167	D4
Priory Grn Est, N1	38	A2
Priory Gro, SW8	167	E5
Priory Hts, N1	38	A2
Priory Ms, SW8	167	E4
Priory Pk Rd, NW6	8	B5
Priory Rd, NW6	9	E5

Priory St, E3 . . . . 47 F4
Priory Ter, NW6 . . . . 9 E5
Priory Wk, SW10 . . . . 138 B3
Pritchard's Rd, E2 . . . . 43 D1
Priter Rd, SE16 . . . . . 121 D4
Procter Ho, SE1 . . . . . 148 C2
Procter St, WC1 . . . . . . 60 A4
Prospect Pl, E1 . . . . 94 A4
Prospect St, SE16 . . . 121 F3
Prospect Vale,
  SE18 . . . . 131 E5
Protea Cl, E16 . . . . 72 A1
Prothero Rd, SW6 . . . 159 F1
Providence Cl, E9 . . . . . 23 D5
Providence Ct, W1 . . . . 85 D2
Providence Pl, N1 . . . . 17 E5
Providence Yd, E2 . . . . 42 C4
Provost Est, N1 . . . . . . 40 C4
Provost Rd, NW3 . . . . . 12 B3
Provost St, N1 . . . . 40 C5
Prowse Pl, NW1 . . . . . . 14 A3
Prudent Pas, EC2 . . . . . 62 B5
Prusom St, E1 . . . . 93 F5
★ P.S. Tattershall Castle,
  SW1 . . . . 87 F5
Pudding La, EC3 . . . . . . 91 D3
🚈 Pudding Mill Lane . . 47 E1
Pudding Mill La, E15 . . 25 E5
Puddle Dock, EC4 . . . . 89 F2
Pulteney Cl, E3 . . . . 46 A1
Pulteney Ter, N1 . . . . . 38 B1
Pulton Pl, SW6 . . . . . . 160 C2
Puma Ct, E1 . . . . 64 A3
Pump Ct, EC4 . . . . 88 C1
Pump Ho Cl, SE16 . . . 122 B2
Pump Ho Ms, E1 . . . . . 92 C2
Pump La, SE14 . . . . . . 174 B1
Pundersons Gdns,
  E2 . . . . 43 F4
Purbrook Est, SE1 . . . 119 F2
Purbrook St, SE1 . . . . 119 F3
Purcell Cres, SW6 . . . 159 E1
Purcell St, N1 . . . . 41 E2
Purchese St, NW1 . . . . 37 D2
Purdy St, E3 . . . . 69 E1
Purley Pl, N1 . . . . 17 E3
Purser's Cross Rd,
  SW6 . . . . 160 B3
Purves Rd, NW10 . . . . 28 A3
Puteaux Ho, E2 . . . . . . 44 C3
Pynfolds, SE16 . . . . . . 121 F2

Q

Quadrangle, The,
  W2 . . . . 55 E5
Quadrangle Cl, SE1 . . 119 E5
Quadrangle Ho, E15 . . 27 F2

Quadrant Arc, W1 . . . . 86 B3
Quaker Ct, E1 . . . . 64 A2
Quaker St, E1 . . . . 64 A2
Quality Ct, WC2 . . . . . . 60 C5
Quarrendon St,
  SW6 . . . . 161 D4
Quarterdeck, The,
  E14 . . . . 124 C2
Quebec Ms, W1 . . . . . . 84 B1
Quebec Way, SE16 . . . 123 D2
Queen Anne Ms, W1 . . 57 F4
Queen Anne Rd, E9 . . . 22 C2
Queen Anne's Gate,
  SW1 . . . . 114 C2
Queen Anne St, W1 . . . 57 E5
Queen Caroline Est,
  W6 . . . . 134 B3
Queen Caroline St,
  W6 . . . . 134 B1
★ Queen Elizabeth Hall &
  Purcell Room,
  SE1 . . . . 88 A4
★ Queen Elizabeth II
  Conf Cen, SW1 . . . 115 D2
🏫 Queen Elizabeth II
  Jubilee Sch, W9 . . . 52 B1
Queen Elizabeth St,
  SE1 . . . . 119 F1
Queenhithe, EC4 . . . . . 90 B2
🎓 Queen Mary, E1 . . . 67 E1
🎓 Queen Mary - Barts &
  The London Sch of Med
  & Dentistry,
  Royal London Hosp,
  E1 . . . . 65 E4
  EC1 . . . . 61 F2
★ Queen Mary's Gdns,
  NW1 . . . . 34 C5
Queen of Denmark Ct,
  SE16 . . . . 124 A3
Queensberry Ms W,
  SW7 . . . . 110 C5
Queensberry Pl,
  SW7 . . . . 110 C5
Queensberry Way,
  SW7 . . . . 110 C5
Queensborough Ms,
  W2 . . . . 82 A2
Queensborough Pas,
  W2 . . . . 82 A2
Queensborough Studios,
  W2 . . . . 82 A2
Queensborough Ter,
  W2 . . . . 81 F2
🏫 Queensbridge Inf Sch,
  E8 . . . . 20 B4
Queensbridge Rd,
  E2 . . . . 20 B5
  E8 . . . . 20 B2
Queensbury St, N1 . . . 18 B4
Queen's Circ, SW8 . . . 165 E2
  SW11 . . . . 165 E2
★ Queens Club (Tennis Cen),
  W14 . . . . 135 E3

Queens Club Gdns,
  W14 . . . . 135 F4
🏫 Queen's Coll, W1 . . 57 E4
Queen's Cres, NW5 . . . 12 C2
Queensdale Cres,
  W11 . . . . 79 D4
Queensdale Pl,
  W11 . . . . 79 E4
Queensdale Rd,
  W11 . . . . 79 D5
Queensdale Wk,
  W11 . . . . 79 E5
Queen's Elm Sq,
  SW3 . . . . 139 D3
★ Queen's Gall, The,
  SW1 . . . . 113 F2
Queens Gdns, W2 . . . . 82 A2
Queen's Gate, SW7 . . 110 B2
Queen's Gate Gdns,
  SW7 . . . . 110 B4
Queen's Gate Ms,
  SW7 . . . . 110 B2
Queensgate Pl, NW6 . . 8 C4
Queen's Gate Pl,
  SW7 . . . . 110 B4
Queen's Gate Pl Ms,
  SW7 . . . . 110 B4
🏫 Queen's Gate Sch,
  SW7 . . . . 110 C5
Queen's Gate Ter,
  SW7 . . . . 110 A3
Queen's Gro, NW8 . . . . 32 C1
Queen's Gro Ms,
  NW8 . . . . 32 C1
Queen's Head Pas,
  EC4 . . . . 62 A5
Queen's Head St, N1 . . 39 F1
Queens Head Yd,
  SE1 . . . . 90 C5
★ Queen's Ice Rink,
  W2 . . . . 81 F3
🏫 Queen's Manor Prim Sch,
  SW6 . . . . 158 C2
Queensmead, NW8 . . . 11 D5
Queens Ms, W2 . . . . . . 81 F2
Queensmill Rd,
  SW6 . . . . 158 C2
🚉 Queen's Park 29 F3
⊖ Queen's Park 29 F3
🏫 Queens Pk Comm Sch,
  NW6 . . . . 6 C5
Queens Pk Ct, W10 . . . 29 D5
🏫 Queen's Pk Prim Sch,
  W10 . . . . 51 F1
Queen Sq, WC1 . . . . . . 59 F2
Queen Sq Pl, WC1 . . . . 59 F2
Queens Rd, SE14 . . . . 173 E3
  SE15 . . . . 173 E3
🚉 Queens Road
  Peckham 173 F3
Queen's Row, SE17 . . 146 C4
Queen's Ter, NW8 . . . . 32 C2
★ Queen's Twr,
  SW7 . . . . 110 C3

Queenstown Ms,
  SW8 . . . . 165 E4
Queenstown Rd,
  SW8 . . . . 141 E5
⇌ Queenstown Road
  (Battersea) 165 F2
Queen St, EC4 . . . . 90 B2
  W1 . . . . 85 E4
Queen St Pl, EC4 . . . . . 90 B3
Queen's Wk, SE1 . . . . . 88 A5
  SW1 . . . . 86 A5
⊖ Queensway 81 F3
Queensway, W2 . . . . 81 F1
Queens Yd, WC1 . . . . 58 B2
★ Queen Victoria Mem,
  SW1 . . . . 114 A1
Queen Victoria St,
  EC4 . . . . 89 F2
Quex Ms, NW6 . . . . 9 D5
Quex Rd, NW6 . . . . 9 D5
Quick St, N1 . . . . 39 F3
Quick St Ms, N1 . . . . . 39 E3
Quickswood, NW3 . . . 11 F3
Quilp St, SE1 . . . . 118 A1
Quilter St, E2 . . . . 42 C4
Quince Rd, SE13 . . . . 177 F5
Sch Quintin Kynaston Sch,
  NW8 . . . . 32 C1
Quixley St, E14 . . . . . . 98 C2

R

Rabbit Row, W8 . . . . . 81 D4
Raby St, E14 . . . . 67 E5
Racton Rd, SW6 . . . . 136 C5
Radcliffe Rd, SE1 . . . . 119 F3
Radcot St, SE11 . . . . . 145 D3
Raddington Rd,
  W10 . . . . 51 F4
Radipole Rd, SW6 . . . 160 A3
Radland Rd, E16 . . . . 100 B1
Radlett Pl, NW8 . . . . . 11 E5
Radley Ct, SE16 . . . . . 123 D1
Radley Ms, W8 . . . . . . 109 D4
Radnor Ms, W2 . . . . . . 83 D1
Radnor Pl, W2 . . . . . . 83 E1
Radnor Rd, NW6 . . . . . 29 E1
  SE15 . . . . 172 C1
Radnor St, EC1 . . . . . . 40 B5
Radnor Ter, W14 . . . . 108 A5
Radnor Wk, E14 . . . . 125 D5
  SW3 . . . . 139 F3
Radstock St,
  SW11 . . . . 163 E2
★ Ragged Sch Mus,
  E3 . . . . 67 F3
Raglan St, NW5 . . . . . 13 F1
Rahere Ho, EC1 . . . . . 40 A4
Railway App, SE1 . . . . 91 D4
Railway Av, SE16 . . . . 122 B1
Railway Ms, E3 . . . . . . 46 C5
  W10 . . . . 51 F5

Railway St, N1 . . . . 37 F3
Rainbow Av, E14 . . . . 153 E2
Rainbow Quay,
  SE16 . . . . 123 F4
Rainbow St, SE5 . . . . 171 E2
Sch Raine's Foundation Sch,
  E2 . . . . 44 B3
  Lwr Sch, E2 . . . . 43 F4
Raine St, E1 . . . . 93 F4
Rainham Rd, NW10 . . 28 B5
Rainhill Way, E3 . . . . . 47 D4
Rainsborough Av,
  SE8 . . . . 151 E1
Rainsford St, W2 . . . . 55 E5
Rainton Rd, SE7 . . . . 157 D2
Rainville Rd, W6 . . . . 134 B5
Raleana Rd, E14 . . . . . 98 B4
Raleigh St, N1 . . . . 39 F1
Ralph Ct, W2 . . . . 53 F5
Ralston St, SW3 . . . . 140 A3
Ramac Way, SE7 . . . . 157 E1
Ramillies Pl, W1 . . . . . 86 A1
Ramillies St, W1 . . . . . 86 A1
Rampart St, E1 . . . . . . 93 E1
Rampayne St, SW1 . . 142 C2
Ram Pl, E9 . . . . 22 B1
Ramsay Ms, SW3 . . . . 139 E4
Ramsey St, E2 . . . . 65 D1
Ramsey Wk, N1 . . . . . . 18 C2
Ramsgate Cl, E16 . . . . 101 E5
Ramsgate St, E8 . . . . . 20 B1
Sch Randal Cremer
  JMI Sch, E2 . . . . 42 A2
Randall Cl, SW11 . . . . 163 E3
Randall Pl, SE10 . . . . 178 A1
Randall Rd, SE11 . . . . 144 A2
Randall Row, SE11 . . 144 A1
Randell's Rd, N1 . . . . . 15 F5
Randolph App, E16 . . 102 B1
Randolph Av, W9 . . . . 54 B1
Randolph Cres, W9 . . . 54 A2
Randolph Gdns,
  NW6 . . . . 31 E3
Randolph Ms, W9 . . . . 54 B2
Randolph Rd, W9 . . . . 54 A1
Randolph St, NW1 . . . . 14 B4
★ Ranelagh Gdns,
  SW3 . . . . 140 C3
Ranelagh Gro, SW1 . . 141 D2
Sch Ranelagh Prim Sch,
  E15 . . . . 49 F2
Ranelagh Rd, E15 . . . . 49 F1
  SW1 . . . . 142 B3
Rangers Sq, SE10 . . . 178 C3
Rangoon St, EC3 . . . . . 92 A1
Rannoch Rd, W6 . . . . 134 B4
Ransome's Dock Business
  Cen, SW11 . . . . 163 F2
Ranston St, NW1 . . . . 55 E3
Ranwell Cl, E3 . . . . 46 A1
Ranwell St, E3 . . . . 46 A1
Raphael St, SW7 . . . . 112 A2
Ratcliffe Cross St,
  E1 . . . . 95 D1

Ratcliffe La, E14 . . . . . 95 E1
Ratcliffe Orchard, E1 . 95 D2
Rathbone Mkt, E16 . . 72 A4
Rathbone Pl, W1 . . . . . 58 C5
Rathbone St, E16 . . . . 72 A4
  W1 . . . . 58 B4
Rathmore Rd, SE7 . . . 157 F2
Raul Rd, SE15 . . . . . . 173 D5
Ravenet St, SW11 . . . 165 E4
Raven Row, E1 . . . . . . 65 F3
Ravensbourne Pl,
  SE13 . . . . 177 F5
Ravenscroft Cl, E16 . . 72 C3
Ravenscroft Pt, E9 . . . 22 C2
Sch Ravenscroft
  Prim Sch, E16 . . . . . 73 D2
Ravenscroft Rd, E16 . . 73 D3
Ravenscroft St, E2 . . . 42 B3
Ravensdon St,
  SE11 . . . . 145 D3
Ravenstone, SE17 . . . 147 F3
Ravey St, EC2 . . . . 63 E1
Rawlings St, SW3 . . . . 112 A5
Rawreth Wk, N1 . . . . . 18 B5
Rawson St, SW11 . . . 165 E4
Rawsthorne Cl,
  E16 . . . . 104 A5
Rawstorne Pl, EC1 . . . 39 E4
Rawstorne St, EC1 . . . 39 E4
Rayleigh Rd, E16 . . . . 101 F4
Raymond Bldgs,
  WC1 . . . . 60 B3
Raymouth Rd,
  SE16 . . . . 121 F5
Raynor Pl, N1 . . . . 18 B4
Ray St, EC1 . . . . 61 D2
Ray St Br, EC1 . . . . 61 D2
Reachview Cl, NW1 . . 14 B4
Reading La, E8 . . . . . . 21 E2
Reapers Cl, NW1 . . . . 14 C5
Reardon Path, E1 . . . . 93 F5
Reardon St, E1 . . . . . . 93 E4
Reaston St, SE14 . . . . 174 B1
Sch Reay Prim Sch,
  SW9 . . . . 168 B2
Record St, SE15 . . . . . 150 A4
Rector St, N1 . . . . 40 A1
Rectory Pl, SE18 . . . . 132 C4
Rectory Sq, E1 . . . . . . 67 D3
Reculver Rd, SE16 . . . 150 C2
Red Anchor Cl,
  SW3 . . . . 139 E5
Redan Pl, W2 . . . . 81 E1
Redan St, W14 . . . . . . 107 D3
Redan Ter, SE5 . . . . . . 169 F5
Redbridge Gdns,
  SE5 . . . . 171 F2
Redburn St, SW3 . . . . 140 A4
Redcar St, SE5 . . . . . . 170 A2
Redcastle Cl, E1 . . . . . 94 A2

Redchurch St, E2 . . . . . 64 A1
Redcliffe Gdns,
 SW5 . . . . 137 F3
 SW10 . . . . 137 F3
Redcliffe Ms, SW10 . . 137 F3
Redcliffe Pl, SW10 . . . 138 A5
Redcliffe Rd, SW10 . . 138 A3
Sch Redcliffe Sch,
 SW10 . . . . 138 A4
Redcliffe Sq, SW10 . . 137 F3
Redcliffe St, SW10 . . 137 F4
Redcross Way, SE1 . . 118 B1
Reddington Ho, N1 . . . 38 B2
Reddins Rd, SE15 . . . 148 C5
Rede Pl, W2 . . . . 81 D1
Redesdale St, SW3 . . 139 F4
Redfield La, SW5 . . . . 109 D5
Redfield Ms, SW5 . . . 109 D5
Redford Wk, N1 . . . . . . 17 F5
Redhill St, NW1 . . . . . . 35 F4
Red Ho Sq, N1 . . . . 18 B2
Sch Redlands Prim Sch,
 E1 . . . . 66 B3
Red Lion Ct, SE17 . . . 146 B4
Red Lion Ct, EC4 . . . . . 61 D5
Red Lion Row,
 SE17 . . . . 146 B4
Red Lion Sq, WC1 . . . . 60 A4
Red Lion St, WC1 . . . . . 60 A3
Red Lion Yd, W1 . . . . . 85 D4
Redman's Rd, E1 . . . . . 66 A3
Redmead La, E1 . . . . . . 92 C5
Red Path, E9 . . . . 23 F1
Red Pl, W1 . . . . 84 C2
Redriff Est, SE16 . . . . 124 A3
Sch Redriff Prim Sch,
 SE16 . . . . 123 F1
Redriff Rd, SE16 . . . . 123 D4
Redruth Rd, E9 . . . . . . 22 B5
Redstart Cl, E6 . . . . 75 E3
 SE16 . . . . 175 E1
Redvers St, N1 . . . . 41 F4
Redwood Cl, E3 . . . . . . 46 C2
 SE16 . . . . 95 F5
Redwood Ct, NW6 . . . . . 7 F4
Reece Ms, SW7 . . . . . 110 C5
Reed Cl, E16 . . . . 72 C4
Reeds Pl, NW1 . . . . 14 A3
Reedworth St,
 SE11 . . . . 145 D1
Rees St, N1 . . . . 40 B1
Reeves Ms, W1 . . . . . . 84 C3
Reeves Rd, E3 . . . . 69 E1
Reflection, The,
 E16 . . . . 133 E1
Reform St, SW11 . . . . 164 A5
Regal Cl, E1 . . . . 65 D3
Regal La, NW1 . . . . 35 D1
Regal Pl, E3 . . . . 46 B5
 SW6 . . . . 161 F2

Regal Row, SE15 . . . . 174 A3
Regan Way, N1 . . . . 41 E3
Regency Ms, SW9 . . . 169 F2
Regency Pl, SW1 . . . . 115 D5
Regency St, SW1 . . . . 114 C5
Regeneration Rd,
 SE16 . . . . 150 C1
Regent Pl, W1 . . . . 86 B2
Regents Br Gdns,
 SW8 . . . . 167 F1
Coll Regent's Coll,
 NW1 . . . . 56 C1
Regents Ms, NW8 . . . . 32 B2
REGENT'S PARK,
 NW1 . . . . 35 D3
★ Regent's Park, The,
 NW1 . . . . 34 B3
⊖ Regent's Park 57 E2
Regent's Pk Est,
 NW1 . . . . 35 F5
Regents Pk Rd, NW1 . . 12 B5
Regents Pk Ter,
 NW1 . . . . 13 E5
Regent's Pl, SE3 . . . . 180 C5
Regent Sq, E3 . . . . 47 E5
 WC1 . . . . 37 F5
Regents Row, E8 . . . . . 42 C1
Regent St, NW10 . . . . . 29 D5
 SW1 . . . . 86 C3
 W1 . . . . 57 F5
Regents Wf, N1 . . . . . . 38 A2
Reginald Rd, SE8 . . . . 176 C2
Reginald Sq, SE8 . . . . 176 C2
Regina Pt, SE16 . . . . . 122 B3
Regnart Bldgs, NW1 . . 58 B1
Relay Rd, W12 . . . . 78 B3
Reliance Sq, EC2 . . . . . 63 F1
Relton Ms, SW7 . . . . . 111 F3
Rembrandt Cl, E14 . . 126 C4
 SW1 . . . . 140 C1
Remington Rd, E6 . . . . 75 E5
Remington St, N1 . . . . 39 F3
Remnant St, WC2 . . . . 60 A5
Remus Rd, E3 . . . . 24 C4
Renaissance Wk,
 SE10 . . . . 128 B3
Renforth St, SE16 . . . 122 B2
Renfrew Cl, E6 . . . . . . 104 C1
Renfrew Rd, SE11 . . . 117 E5
Rennie Est, SE16 . . . . 149 F1
Rennie St, SE1 . . . . 89 E4
Renovation, The,
 E16 . . . . 133 E1
Rephidim St, SE1 . . . . 119 E4
Reporton Rd, SW6 . . . 159 F2
Repton St, E14 . . . . 67 F5
Resolution Wk,
 SE18 . . . . 132 A3
Resolution Way,
 SE8 . . . . 176 C1
Restell Cl, SE3 . . . . . . 155 F4
Reston Pl, SW7 . . . . . 110 A2
Retford St, N1 . . . . 41 F3
Retreat Pl, E9 . . . . 22 B2

Reunion Row, E1 . . . . . 93 F3
Reveley Sq, SE16 . . . . 123 F2
Reverdy Rd, SE1 . . . . 148 C1
Rewell St, SW6 . . . . . 162 A2
Rex Pl, W1 . . . . 85 D3
Reynolah Gdns,
 SE7 . . . . 157 F2
Reynolds Pl, SE3 . . . . 181 F1
Rheidol Ms, N1 . . . . . . 40 A2
Rheidol Ter, N1 . . . . . . 39 F2
Rhoda St, E2 . . . . 64 B1
Rhodeswell Rd, E14 . . 67 F3
Rhondda Gro, E3 . . . . . 45 F5
Sch Rhyl Prim Sch,
 NW5 . . . . 13 D1
Rhyl St, NW5 . . . . 13 D1
Ribbon Dance Ms,
 SE5 . . . . 171 D4
Ricardo St, E14 . . . . . . 97 E1
Sch Richard Cloudesley Sch,
 EC1 . . . . 62 A2
Sch Richard Cobden Prim Sch,
 NW1 . . . . 36 B2
Richard Ho Dr, E16 . . 103 D1
Richardson Cl, E8 . . . . 20 A5
Richardson Rd, E15 . . . 49 E2
Richardson's Ms,
 W1 . . . . 58 A2
Richards Pl, SW3 . . . . 111 F5
Richard St, E1 . . . . 93 E1
Richbell Pl, WC1 . . . . . 60 A3
Richborne Ter,
 SW8 . . . . 168 B1
Richford St, W6 . . . . . 106 A2
Rich Ind Est, SE1 . . . . 119 F4
Rich La, SW5 . . . . 137 E3
Richmond Av, N1 . . . . 16 A5
 NW10 . . . . 6 A2
Richmond Bldgs,
 W1 . . . . 86 C1
Richmond Cres, N1 . . . 16 B5
Richmond Gro, N1 . . . . 17 E4
Richmond Ms, W1 . . . . 86 C1
Richmond Rd, E8 . . . . . 20 A3
Richmond Ter,
 SW1 . . . . 115 E1
Uni Richmond Uni -
 The American Int Uni
 In London,
 Kensington Campus,
 W8 . . . . 109 F3
Richmond Way,
 W12 . . . . 107 D2
 W14 . . . . 107 D3
Rich St, E14 . . . . 96 B2
Rickett St, SW6 . . . . . 137 D4
Rickman St, E1 . . . . 66 B1
Rick Roberts Way,
 E15 . . . . 48 B1
Ridgdale St, E3 . . . . 47 D3
Ridgewell Cl, N1 . . . . . 18 B5
Ridgmount Gdns,
 WC1 . . . . 58 C2
Ridgmount Pl, WC1 . . . 58 C3

Ridgmount St, WC1 . . 58 C3
Ridgwell Rd, E16 . . . . . 74 B3
Riding Ho St, W1 . . . . . 58 A4
Rifle Ct, SE11 . . . . 145 D4
Rifle St, E14 . . . . 69 F4
Rigden St, E14 . . . . 97 E1
Riley Rd, SE1 . . . . 119 F3
Riley St, SW10 . . . . . . 162 C1
Ring, The, W2 . . . . 83 E2
Ringlet Cl, E16 . . . . . . 73 E4
Ringmer Av, SW6 . . . 159 F4
Ring Rd, W12 . . . . 78 A3
Ringwood Gdns,
 E14 . . . . 125 D5
Ripley Rd, E16 . . . . 74 A5
Ripplevale Gro, N1 . . . 16 B4
Risborough St, SE1 . . 117 F1
Risdon St, SE16 . . . . . 122 B2
Risinghill St, N1 . . . . . . 38 C2
Rising Sun Ct, EC1 . . . . 61 F4
Rita Rd, SW8 . . . . 143 F5
Ritchie St, N1 . . . . 39 D2
Ritson Rd, E8 . . . . 20 B1
Rivaz Pl, E9 . . . . 22 B1
River Barge Cl,
 E14 . . . . 126 B2
Rivermill, SW1 . . . . . . 143 D3
River Pl, N1 . . . . 18 A4
Riverside, SE7 . . . . . . 129 E4
Riverside Ct, SW8 . . . 143 D4
Riverside Mans, E1 . . . 94 A3
Sch Riverside Prim Sch,
 SE16 . . . . 121 D2
Riverside Rd, E15 . . . . 48 B3
Riverside Twr,
 SW6 . . . . 162 B5
River St, EC1 . . . . 38 C4
River Ter, W6 . . . . 134 A3
Riverton Cl, W9 . . . . . . 30 B5
River Vw Hts, SE16 . . 120 C1
Rivington Pl, EC2 . . . . . 41 F5
Rivington St, EC2 . . . . 41 E5
Rivington Wk, E8 . . . . . 21 D5
Roach Rd, E3 . . . . 24 C3
Roan St, SE10 . . . . . . 154 A5
Robert Adam St,
 W1 . . . . 56 C5
Roberta St, E2 . . . . 42 C4
Sch Robert Blair Prim Sch,
 N7 . . . . 15 F2
Sch Robert Browning
 Prim Sch, SE17 . . 146 C2
Robert Cl, W9 . . . . 54 B2
Robert Dashwood Way,
 SE17 . . . . 146 A1
Robert Keen Cl,
 SE15 . . . . 173 D4
Robert Lowe Cl,
 SE14 . . . . 175 D1
Robert Owen Ho,
 SW6 . . . . 159 D3
Roberts Cl, SE16 . . . . 123 D2
Roberts Ms, SW1 . . . . 112 C4
Robertson Rd, E15 . . . 26 B5

Robert's Pl, EC1 . . . . . . 61 D1
Robert St, E16 . . . . . . 105 E5
 NW1 . . . . 35 F5
 WC2 . . . . 87 F3
Robeson St, E3 . . . . 68 B3
Robin Ct, SE16 . . . . . . 120 C5
Robin Cres, E6 . . . . 75 D3
Robin Hood Gdns,
 E14 . . . . 98 B2
Robin Hood La, E14 . . 98 B2
Robinscroft Ms,
 SE10 . . . . 177 F4
Sch Robinsfield Inf Sch,
 NW8 . . . . 33 E2
Robinson Rd, E2 . . . . 44 A3
Robinson St, SW3 . . . 140 A4
Robsart St, SW9 . . . . 168 B5
Robson Cl, E6 . . . . 75 E5
Rochdale Way,
 SE8 . . . . 176 C1
Rochelle St, E2 . . . . 42 A5
Rochemont Wk, E8 . . . 42 B1
Rochester Ms, NW1 . . 14 A3
Rochester Pl, NW1 . . . 14 B3
Rochester Rd, NW1 . . 14 A2
Rochester Row,
 SW1 . . . . 114 B5
Rochester Sq, NW1 . . 14 B3
Rochester St, SW1 . . 114 C4
Rochester Ter, NW1 . . 14 A2
Rochester Wk, SE1 . . 90 C4
Rochester Way, SE3 . 181 E3
Rochester Way Relief Rd,
 SE3 . . . . 181 F4
Rochford Wk, E8 . . . . . 21 D3
★ Rock Circ, W1 . . . . . 86 C3
Rock Gro Way,
 SE16 . . . . 121 D5
Rockingham Est,
 SE1 . . . . 118 A4
Rockingham St,
 SE1 . . . . 118 A4
Rockley Rd, W14 . . . . 106 C2
Rockwood Pl, W12 . . 106 B1
Rocliffe St, N1 . . . . 39 F3
Roding Ms, E1 . . . . 93 D4
Roding Rd, E6 . . . . 77 E3
Rodmarton St, W1 . . . 56 B4
Rodmere St, SE10 . . . 155 F3
Rodney Ct, W9 . . . . 54 B1
Rodney Pl, SE17 . . . . 118 B5
Rodney Rd, SE17 . . . . 118 B5
Rodney St, N1 . . . . 38 B2
Roebourne Way,
 E16 . . . . 132 C1
Roffey St, E14 . . . . . . 126 A2
Rogers Rd, E16 . . . . . 100 B1
Roger St, WC1 . . . . 60 B2
Rokeby Rd, SE4 . . . . . 176 A5
Sch Rokeby Sec Sch,
 E15 . . . . 27 D4
Rokeby St, E15 . . . . . . 27 D5
Roland Gdns, SW7 . . 138 B2
Roland Ms, E1 . . . . 66 C3

Roland Way, SE17 . . . 147 D3
 SW7 . . . . 138 B2
Rollins St, SE15 . . . . . 150 B4
Rolls Bldgs, EC4 . . . . . . 60 C5
Rolls Pas, EC4 . . . . 60 C5
Rolls Rd, SE1 . . . . 148 B2
Rolt St, SE8 . . . . 151 E4
★ Roman Bath,
 WC2 (Strand La) . . . 88 B2
Roman Rd, E2 . . . . 44 A5
 E3 . . . . 45 E3
 E6 . . . . 75 D2
Sch Roman Rd
 Prim Sch, E6 . . . . . . 75 D1
Roman Way, N7 . . . . . . 16 B2
 SE15 . . . . 174 A2
Roman Way Ind Est,
 N1 . . . . 16 A3
Romford Rd, E15 . . . . . 27 E3
Romford St, E1 . . . . 65 D4
Romilly St, W1 . . . . 86 C2
Romney Cl, SE14 . . . . 174 B2
Romney Ms, W1 . . . . . 56 C3
Romney Rd, SE10 . . . 154 B5
Romney St, SW1 . . . . 115 D4
Ronald Av, E15 . . . . . . 49 F5
Ronald St, E1 . . . . 94 B1
Rona Wk, N1 . . . . 18 C2
Rood La, EC3 . . . . 91 E2
Rooke Way, SE10 . . . 156 A2
Rook Wk, E6 . . . . 75 E5
★ Roosevelt Mem,
 W1 . . . . 85 D2
Rootes Dr, W10 . . . . . . 50 C3
Ropemaker Rd,
 SE16 . . . . 123 E2
Ropemakers Flds,
 E14 . . . . 96 A3
Ropemaker St, EC2 . . 62 C3
Roper La, SE1 . . . . 119 F2
Ropers Orchard,
 SW3 . . . . 139 D5
Ropery St, E3 . . . . 68 A2
Rope St, SE16 . . . . . . 123 F4
Rope Wk Gdns, E1 . . . 93 D1
Ropewalk Ms, E8 . . . . 20 C4
Rope Yd Rails,
 SE18 . . . . 133 E4
Ropley St, E2 . . . . 42 C3
Rosaline Rd, SW6 . . . 159 F2
Rosary Gdns, SW7 . . 138 B1
Rosaville Rd, SW6 . . . 160 A2
Roscoe St, EC1 . . . . . . 62 B2
Rose All, SE1 . . . . 90 B4
Rose & Crown Ct,
 EC2 . . . . 62 A5
Rose & Crown Yd,
 SW1 . . . . 86 B4
Rosebank Gdns, E3 . . 45 F3
Rosebank Wk, NW1 . . 15 D3

Roseberry Pl, E8 .....20 A2
Roseberry St, SE16 ..149 E1
Rosebery Av, EC1 ....60 C2
Rosebery Sq, EC1.....60 C2
Rose Ct, E1 ....64 A4
Rosedene, NW6 ....7 D5
Rosedew Rd, W6....134 C5
Rosefield Gdns,
    E14 ....96 C2
Roseford Ct, W12 ...106 C2
Rosehart Ms, W11 ...80 C1
Rosemary Dr, E14.....98 C1
Rosemary Rd, SE15 .172 B1
Rosemary St, N1 .....18 C5
Rosemont Rd,
    NW3 ....10 A1
Rosemoor St,
    SW3 ....140 A1
Rosenau Cres,
    SW11 ....163 F4
Rosenau Rd,
    SW11 ....163 F3
Roserton St, E14....126 A2
Rose Sq, SW3.......139 D2
Rose St, EC4 ....61 F5
    WC2 ....87 E2
Rosetta Cl, SW8 ....167 F2
Sch Rosetta Prim Sch,
    E16 ....73 F4
Rosher Cl, E15 ....26 C4
Rosmead Rd, W11....79 F2
Rosoman Pl, EC1 .....61 D1
Rosoman St, EC1.....39 D5
Rosse Ms, SE3 ......181 E3
Rossendale Way,
    NW1 ....14 B4
Rossetti Rd, SE16 ...149 E2
Rossmore Ct, NW1 ...56 A1
Rossmore Rd, NW1...55 F2
Rostrevor Ms, SW6 .160 A4
Rostrevor Rd, SW6 .160 A3
Rotary St, SE1 ......117 E3
Rothbury Rd, E9 ....24 B3
Sch Rotherfield Jun &
    Inf Sch, N1........18 B5
Rotherfield St, N1 ....18 B4
Rotherham Wk, SE1 ..89 E5
ROTHERHITHE,
    SE16..............122 C3
⊖ Rotherhithe 122 B1
★ Rotherhithe Heritage
    Mus, SE16 ....95 F4
Rotherhithe New Rd,
    SE16..............149 D3
Rotherhithe Old Rd,
    SE16..............122 C4
Sch Rotherhithe
    Prim Sch, SE16 ...122 C5
Rotherhithe St,
    SE16..............122 B1

Rotherhithe Tunnel,
    E1 ....94 C4
Rotherhithe Tunnel App,
    E14 ....95 E2
    SE16..............122 A2
Rothery St, N1.......17 E5
Rothery Ter, SW9 ...169 E2
Rothsay St, SE1.....119 E3
Rothsay Wk, E14....125 D5
Rothwell St, NW1 ...12 B5
Rotten Row, SW1 ...112 C1
    SW7 ....111 E1
Rotterdam Dr, E14 ..126 B4
Rouel Rd, SE16 .....120 C4
Rounton Rd, E3......69 D1
Roupell St, SE1 .....89 D5
Rousden St, NW1 ....14 B4
Routh St, E6.........76 B4
Rowallan Rd, SW6 ..159 E2
Rowan Rd, W6......134 C1
Rowan Ter, W6 .....134 C1
Rowan Wk, W10 .....51 E1
Rowberry Cl, SW6...158 B2
Rowcross St, SE1....148 A2
Rowditch La,
    SW11 ....164 C5
Rowington Cl, W2 ....53 E3
Rowland Ct, E16 .....72 A1
Rowley Way, NW8.....9 F5
Rowntree Clifford Cl,
    E13 ....73 E1
Rowse Cl, E15 ....26 B5
Roxby Pl, SW6 ......137 D4
★ Royal Acad of Arts,
    W1 ....86 A3
Coll Royal Acad of Dance,
    SW11 ....163 D4
★ Royal Acad of Dramatic
    Art (R.A.D.A.),
    WC1 ....58 C3
Uni Royal Acad of Music,
    NW1 ....57 D2
DLR Royal Albert 103 E2
Royal Albert Dock,
    E16..............104 B3
★ Royal Albert Hall,
    SW7 ....110 C2
Royal Albert Rbt,
    E16..............103 E2
Royal Albert Way,
    E16..............102 B2
Royal Arc, W1 ....86 A3
Royal Av, SW3 ......140 A2
Coll Royal Ballet Sch, The,
    Upr Sch, WC2 .....87 F1
H Royal Brompton Hosp,
    SW3 ....139 E2
    Annexe, SW3.....139 D2
Royal Cl, SE8 ....152 A4
Coll Royal Coll of
    Anaesthetists, The,
    WC1 ....59 E3
Uni Royal Coll of Art,
    SW7 ....110 B2

Coll Royal Coll of Defence
    Studies, SW1.....113 D3
Coll Royal Coll of Music,
    SW7 ....110 C3
Coll Royal Coll of Nursing,
    W1 ....57 E5
Coll Royal Coll of Obstetricians
    & Gynaecologists,
    NW1 ....56 A1
Coll Royal Coll of Physicians,
    NW1 ....57 F1
★ Royal College of Surgeons
    of England, WC2 ...60 B5
Royal Coll St, NW1 ...14 A3
Royal Ct, SE16 ......124 A3
★ Royal Courts of Justice,
    WC2 ....88 B1
Royal Cres, W11 .....79 D5
Royal Cres Ms,
    W11 ....79 D5
Sch Royal Docks Comm Sch,
    The, E16..........102 B1
Royal Docks Rd,
    E6 ....105 F2
★ Royal Exchange,
    EC3 ....91 D1
Royal Ex Av, EC3 .....91 D1
Royal Ex Bldgs, EC3...91 D1
★ Royal Festival Hall,
    SE1 ....88 A4
★ Royal Geographical
    Society, SW7.....110 C2
Royal Hill, SE10....178 A2
★ Royal Horticultural
    Society (Lawrence Hall),
    SW1 ....114 C4
★ Royal Horticultural
    Society (Lindley Hall),
    SW1 ....114 C5
★ Royal Hosp Chelsea &
    Mus, SW3 ....140 C3
Royal Hosp Rd,
    SW3 ....140 A4
H Royal London
    Homoeopathic Hosp,
    WC1 ....59 F3
H Royal London Hosp, The,
    Mile End, E1.......67 D1
    St. Clements, E3 ...46 B5
    Whitechapel, E1 ...65 E4
H Royal London Hosp
    (Whitechapel)
    Dentistry Cen, E1 ..65 E4
H Royal Marsden Hosp
    (Fulham), The,
    SW3 ....139 D2
★ Royal Mews, The,
    SW1 ....113 F3
Royal Mint Ct, EC3 ...92 B3
Royal Mint Pl, E1.....92 B2
Royal Mint St, E1.....92 B2
H Royal Nat Ear, Nose &
    Throat Hosp,
    WC1 ....38 A4

🏥 Royal Nat Orthopaedic Hosp, W1 . . . . . 57 F2
★ Royal Nat Thea, SE1 . . . . 88 B4
Royal Naval Pl, SE14 . . . . 176 A1
⊖ Royal Oak 53 F4
Royal Oak Rd, E8 . . . . . 21 E1
Royal Oak Yd, SE1 . . . 119 E2
Royal Opera Arc, SW1 . . . . 86 C4
★ Royal Opera Ho, WC2 . . . . 87 F1
Royal Pl, SE10 . . . . . . 178 B2
Royal Rd, E16 . . . . . . 102 C1
SE17 . . . . 145 E4
Royal St, SE1 . . . . 116 B3
Royalty Ms, W1 . . . . . . 86 C1
🎓 Royal Vet Coll - Camden Campus, Beaumont Animal's Hosp, NW1 . . . . 36 B1
Royal Coll St, NW1 . . . . 36 C1
🚈 Royal Victoria 100 C2
Royal Victoria Dock, E16 . . . . 101 E3
Royal Victoria Pl, E16 . . . . 101 F4
Royal Victoria Sq, E16 . . . . 101 E3
Royal Victor Pl, E3 . . . 45 D2
Roydon Cl, SW11 . . . . 164 B5
Roydon St, SW11 . . . 165 E3
Roy Sq, E14 . . . . 95 F2
Royston St, E2 . . . . . . 44 B3
Rozel Ct, N1 . . . . 19 E5
Ruby St, SE15 . . . . . . 149 E4
Ruby Triangle, SE15 . . . . 149 E4
Rudgwick Ter, NW8 . . . . 33 F1
Rudolf Pl, SW8 . . . . . 143 F5
Rudolph Rd, NW6 . . . . 31 D3
Rufford St, N1 . . . . . . 15 F5
Rufus St, N1 . . . . 41 E5
Rugby St, WC1 . . . . . . 60 A2
Rugg St, E14 . . . . 96 C2
Rumbold Rd, SW6 . . . 161 F2
Rum Cl, E1 . . . . 94 A3
Runcorn Pl, W11 . . . . . 79 E2
Rundell Twr, SW8 . . . 168 A3
Rupack St, SE16 . . . 122 A2
Rupert Ct, W1 . . . . 86 C2
Rupert Rd, NW6 . . . . . 30 B3
Rupert St, W1 . . . . 86 C2
Ruscoe Rd, E16 . . . . . . 72 A5
Rushmead, E2 . . . . 43 E5
Rushton St, N1 . . . . . . 41 D2
Rushworth St, SE1 . . . . 117 F1
Russell Ct, SW1 . . . . . . 86 B5
Russell Gdns, W14 . . . . 107 E3

Russell Gdns Ms, W14 . . . . 107 E2
Russell Gro, SW9 . . . 169 D2
Russell Pl, SE16 . . . . . 123 E4
Russell Rd, E16 . . . . . . 73 E5
W14 . . . . 107 E3
⊖ Russell Square . . . 59 E2
Russell Sq, WC1 . . . . . 59 E2
Russell St, WC2 . . . . . 87 F2
Russia Ct, EC2 . . . . . . 62 B5
Russia Dock Rd, SE16 . . . . 95 F5
Russia La, E2 . . . . 44 A2
Russia Row, EC2 . . . . . 90 B1
Russia Wk, SE16 . . . . 123 E2
Rustic Wk, E16 . . . . . . 73 E5
Ruston Ms, W11 . . . . . 79 E1
Ruston Rd, SE18 . . . . 131 E4
Ruston St, E3 . . . . 24 B5
Rust Sq, SE5 . . . . 170 C1
Rutherford St, SW1 . . . . 114 C5
Ruthin Rd, SE3 . . . . . 156 C4
Ruthven St, E9 . . . . . . 22 C5
Rutland Gdns, SW7 . . . . 111 F2
Rutland Gdns Ms, SW7 . . . . 111 F2
Rutland Gate, SW7 . . 111 F2
Rutland Gate Ms, SW7 . . . . 111 E2
Rutland Ms, NW8 . . . . 31 F1
Rutland Ms E, SW7 . . 111 E3
Rutland Ms S, SW7 . . 111 E3
Rutland Pk, NW2 . . . . . . 6 B2
Rutland Pl, EC1 . . . . . . 62 A2
Rutland Rd, E9 . . . . . . 22 B5
Rutland St, SW7 . . . . 111 F3
Rutley Cl, SE17 . . . . . 145 E4
Rutts Ter, SE14 . . . . . 174 C4
Ryculff Sq, SE3 . . . . . 180 B5
Ryder Ct, SW1 . . . . 86 B4
Ryder Dr, SE16 . . . . . 149 E3
Ryders Ter, NW8 . . . . . 32 A2
Ryder St, SW1 . . . . 86 B4
Ryder Yd, SW1 . . . . 86 B4
Rydon St, N1 . . . . 18 B5
Rydston Cl, N7 . . . . . . 16 A3
Ryecroft St, SW6 . . . . 161 E4
Ryegates, SE15 . . . . . 173 F5
Rye La, SE15 . . . . 172 C4
Ryland Rd, NW5 . . . . . 13 E1
Rylston Rd, SW6 . . . . 136 A5
Rymill St, E16 . . . . . . 104 C5
Rysbrack St, SW3 . . . 112 A3

S

Sabbarton St, E16 . . . 100 A1
Sabella Ct, E3 . . . . 46 B3
Sable St, N1 . . . . 17 F3
Sackville St, W1 . . . . . . 86 B3

🎓 Sacred Heart RC High Sch, W6 . . . . 135 D1
🎓 Sacred Heart RC Jun Sch, W6 . . . . . . 135 D1
🎓 Sacred Heart RC Sec Sch, SE5 . . . . . . 170 A3
Saddle Yd, W1 . . . . 85 E4
★ Sadler's Wells Thea, EC1 . . . . 39 E4
Saffron Av, E14 . . . . . . 98 C2
Saffron Hill, EC1 . . . . . 61 D2
Saffron St, EC1 . . . . . . 61 D3
Sage Cl, E6 . . . . 76 A4
Sage St, E1 . . . . 94 A2
Sage Way, WC1 . . . . . . 38 A5
Saigasso Cl, E16 . . . . 102 C1
Sail St, SE11 . . . . 116 B5
St. Agnes Cl, E9 . . . . . . 44 A1
St. Agnes Pl, SE11 . . . 145 E5
🎓 St. Agnes RC Prim Sch, E3 . . . . . . 47 E4
🎓 St. Alban's C of E Prim Sch, EC1 . . . . . 60 C3
St. Albans Ct, EC2 . . . . 62 B5
St. Albans Gro, W8 . . 109 F3
St. Alban's Pl, N1 . . . . . 39 E1
St. Albans St, SW1 . . . . 86 C3
St. Albans Ter, W6 . . . 135 E4
🎓 St. Alfege with St. Peters C of E Prim Sch, SE10 . . . . 154 A5
🎓 St. Aloysius RC Inf Sch, NW1 . . . . . . 36 C4
🎓 St. Aloysius RC Jun Sch, NW1 . . . . . 36 B3
St. Alphage Gdns, EC2 . . . . 62 B4
St. Alphage Highwalk, EC2 . . . . 62 C4
St. Andrews Cl, SE16 . . . . 149 F3
🎓 St. Andrew's C of E Prim Sch, N1 . . . . . . 16 B5
🎓 St. Andrew's Greek Sch, NW5 . . . . 14 A2
St. Andrew's Hill, EC4 . . . . 89 F2
🏥 St. Andrew's Hosp, E3 . . . . 69 F1
St. Andrews Ms, SE3 . . . . 180 C1
St. Andrews Pl, NW1 . . 57 F1
St. Andrews Rd, W14 . . . . 135 F4
St. Andrews Sq, W11 . . . . 79 E1
St. Andrew St, EC4 . . . 61 D4
St. Andrews Way, E3 . . . . 69 E2

St. Anne's Ct, W1.....86 C1
St. Annes Pas, E14....96 A1
Sch St. Anne's Prim Sch,
    E1 ....64 C2
Sch St. Anne's RC Prim Sch,
    SE11.............144 A4
St. Anne's Row,
    E14...............96 B1
St. Anne St, E14......96 B1
St. Ann's Gdns,
    NW5.............12 C1
St. Ann's La, SW1 ....115 D3
St. Anns Rd, W11 ....79 D3
St. Ann's St, SW1.....115 D3
St. Ann's Ter, NW8....33 D2
St. Anns Vil, W11.....79 D3
St. Anselm's Pl, W1...85 E1
St. Anthonys Cl, E1...92 C4
Sch St. Augustine RC
    Prim Sch, W6 ...135 F5
Sch St. Augustine's C of E
    Sec Sch, NW6 .....31 D3
Sch St. Augustine's Prim Sch,
    NW6.............31 E2
St. Augustines Rd,
    NW1.............14 C3
St. Austell Rd,
    SE13............178 B5
Sch St. Barnabas & St. Philip
    C of E Prim Sch,
    W8.............108 C4
Sch St. Barnabas C of E
    Prim Sch, SW1 ...141 D2
St. Barnabas St,
    SW1............141 D2
St. Barnabas Vil,
    SW8............167 F3
🏥 St. Bartholomew's Hosp,
    EC1..............61 F4
★ St. Bartholomew-the-
    Great Ch, EC1.....61 F4
St. Benet's Pl, EC3....91 D2
St. Botolph Row,
    EC3..............92 A1
St. Botolph St, EC3 ...92 A1
St. Brides Av, EC4 ....89 E1
★ St. Bride's Ch & Crypt
    Mus, EC4.........89 E1
St. Bride's Pas, EC4 ...89 E1
St. Bride St, EC4......61 E5
St. Catherine's Ms,
    SW3............112 A5
St. Chad's Pl, WC1....37 F4
St. Chad's St, WC1....37 F4
Coll St. Charles Catholic
    6th Form Coll,
    W10.............51 D4
🏥 St. Charles Hosp,
    W10.............51 D3
St. Charles Pl, W10...51 E4

Sch St. Charles RC
    Prim Sch, W10 ....51 D3
St. Charles Sq, W10...51 E3
Sch St. Christina's Sch,
    NW8.............33 F2
St. Christopher's Pl,
    W1..............57 D5
St. Clare St, EC3......92 A1
★ St. Clement Danes Ch,
    WC2.............88 B1
Sch St. Clement Danes C of E
    Prim Sch, WC2 ....88 A1
Sch St. Clements & St. James
    C of E Prim Sch,
    W11.............79 E4
St. Clements Ct, N7...16 C2
St. Clement's La,
    WC2.............88 B1
St. Clements St, N7...16 C2
St. Cross St, EC1 .....61 D3
St. Cuthberts Rd,
    NW2..............8 A1
Sch St. Cuthbert with
    St. Matthias C of E
    Prim Sch, SW5 ...137 E2
St. Davids Cl, SE16 ..149 F3
St. Davids Sq, E14...153 F2
St. Dionis Rd, SW6 ..160 B5
Sch St. Dominic's RC Sch,
    E9..............23 E1
St. Donatts Rd,
    SE14............176 A4
St. Dunstan's All,
    EC3..............91 E2
St. Dunstan's Hill,
    EC3..............91 E3
St. Dunstan's La,
    EC3..............91 E3
St. Dunstans Rd,
    W6.............134 C3
St. Edmunds Cl,
    NW8.............34 A1
Sch St. Edmund's RC
    Prim Sch, E14 ...125 D5
St. Edmunds Sq,
    SW13...........134 A5
St. Edmunds Ter,
    NW8.............33 F2
Sch St. Edward's RC
    Prim Sch, NW1 ...55 F2
Sch St. Elizabeth's
    Prim Sch, E1 .....44 B2
St. Elmos Rd, SE16 ..123 E1
St. Ermin's Hill,
    SW1............114 C3
St. Ervans Rd, W10...51 F3
Sch St. Eugene de Mazenod
    RC Prim Sch, NW6 ..9 D4
Sch St. Francis of Assisi RC
    Prim Sch, W11 ....79 D3
Sch St. Francis RC Prim Sch,
    SE15............173 D1
St. Frideswides Ms,
    E14..............98 A1

Sch St. Gabriel's C of E
    Prim Sch, SW1 ...142 A3
Sch St. George's Catholic
    School, Westminster,
    W9..............31 F3
St. Georges Circ,
    SE1............117 E3
St. George's Cl,
    SW8............166 B3
Sch St. George's C of E
    Prim Sch, SE5 ...171 E1
    SW8............166 B2
St. Georges Ct, E6 ...76 A1
    EC4..............61 E5
    SW7............110 A3
St. George's Dr,
    SW1............142 A2
St. Georges Flds,
    W2..............83 F1
Sch St. George's Hanover Sq
    Prim Sch, W1.....85 D3
St. Georges La, EC3...91 E2
St. Georges Ms,
    NW1.............12 B4
    SE1............117 D3
Sch St. George's Prim Sch,
    SE1............117 E3
St. Georges Rd,
    SE1............117 D3
St. Georges Sq,
    E14..............95 E2
    SE8............124 A5
St. George's Sq,
    SW1............142 C2
St. George's Sq Ms,
    SW1............142 C3
St. Georges Ter,
    NW1.............12 B4
St. George St, W1 ....85 F1
St. Georges Way,
    SE15............147 E5
Sch St. George the Martyr
    C of E Prim Sch,
    WC1..............60 A2
St. George Wf,
    SW8............143 E3
St. German's Pl,
    SE3............180 C4
Coll St. Giles Coll,
    London Cen, WC1 ..59 F3
St. Giles High St,
    WC2..............59 D5
St. Giles Pas, WC2 ....87 D1
St. Giles Rd, SE5 ....171 E2
St. Gilles Ho, E2 ......44 C3
St. Helena Rd,
    SE16............150 C1
St. Helena St, WC1 ...38 C5
St. Helens Gdns,
    W10.............50 C4
St. Helens Pl, EC3 ....63 E5
Sch St. Helen's RC
    Prim Sch, E13 ....72 C1
St. Hildas Cl, NW6 .....7 D4

Sch St. James' & St. Michael's
C of E Prim Sch,
W2 .... 82 B2
St. James Gate,
NW1 .... 15 D4
St. James Gro,
SW11 .... 164 B5
Sch St. James Indep Sch,
Jun & Sen Girls,
W14 .... 107 F5
St. James Ms, E14 ... 126 B4
ST. JAMES'S, SW1 ..... 86 B5
St. James's, SE14 ... 175 F3
Coll St. James's & Lucie
Clayton Coll,
SW5 .... 138 A1
St. James's Av, E2 ... 44 B3
Sch St. James's C of E
Prim Sch, SE16 ... 120 C3
St. James's Ct,
SW1 .... 114 B3
St. James's Gdns,
W11 .... 79 E4
Sch St. James's Hatcham
C of E Prim Sch,
SE14 .... 175 F3
St. James's Mkt,
SW1 .... 86 C3
★ St. James's Palace,
SW1 .... 114 B1
★ St. James's Park,
SW1 .... 114 C1
⊖ St. James's Park .. 114 C3
St. James's Pas, EC3 .. 91 F1
St. James's Pl, SW1 ... 86 A5
St. James's Rd, SE1 .. 149 D2
SE16 .... 121 D3
St. James's Sq, SW1 ... 86 B4
St. James's St, SW1 ... 86 A4
St. James's Ter, NW8 .. 34 A2
St. James's Ter Ms,
NW8 .... 34 A1
St. James St, W6 .... 134 A3
St. James's Wk, EC1 ... 61 E1
Sch St. James the Gt RC
Prim Sch, SE15 ... 172 B3
Sch St. Joachim's RC
Prim Sch, E16 .... 102 A1
Sch St. John Evangelist RC
Prim Sch, N1 ..... 39 E2
Sch St. John of Jerusalem
C of E JMI Sch, E9 .. 22 B4
ST. JOHN'S, SE8 ..... 176 C5
⇌ St. John's 177 D5
St. John's Cl, SW6 ... 160 C1
Sch St. John's C of E
Prim Sch, SW6 ... 159 F3
St. John's Est, N1 ..... 41 D3
SE1 .... 120 A1
St. John's Gdns,
W11 .... 80 A3
★ St. John's Gate &
Mus of the Order of
St. John, EC1 ...... 61 E2

St. John's La, EC1 ..... 61 E2
St. John's Ms, W11 ... 80 C1
St. John's Pk, SE3 .... 180 B2
St. John's Path, EC1 ... 61 E2
St. John's Pl, EC1 ..... 61 E2
Sch St. John's Prim Sch,
E2 .... 44 A3
Sch St. John's RC Prim Sch,
SE16 .... 123 E2
St. Johns Rd, E16 .... 72 C5
St. John's Sq, EC1 ..... 61 E2
St. Johns Ter, W10 .... 51 D1
St. John St, EC1 ..... 61 F2
St. Johns Vale, SE8 .. 177 D5
St. John's Vil, W8 .... 109 F4
Sch St. John's Walworth
C of E Prim Sch,
SE17 .... 146 B1
ST. JOHN'S WOOD,
NW8 .... 32 C4
⊖ St. John's Wood 32 C2
St. John's Wd Ct,
NW8 .... 33 D5
St. John's Wd High St,
NW8 .... 33 D3
St. John's Wd Pk,
NW8 .... 33 D1
St. John's Wd Rd,
NW8 .... 54 C1
St. John's Wd Ter,
NW8 .... 33 E2
Sch St. John the Baptist
Hoxton C of E
JMI Sch, N1 .... 41 E3
Sch St. John the Divine C of E
Prim Sch, SE5 ... 169 E1
St. Josephs Cl, W10 ... 51 F4
St. Joseph's Ct, SE7 .. 157 F5
Sch St. Joseph's Prim Sch,
SW3 .... 140 A1
Sch St. Joseph's RC Inf &
Jun Sch, SE5 .... 170 A1
Sch St. Joseph's RC Prim Sch,
The Borough,
SE1 .... 118 B1
SE8 .... 176 C1
SE10 .... 155 F2
Bermondsey,
SE16 .... 120 C2
Rotherhithe,
SE16 .... 122 B4
W9 .... 32 A5
WC2 .... 59 F5
St. Josephs St,
SW8 .... 165 F3
Sch St. Jude's &
St. Paul's C of E
Prim Sch, N1 ...... 19 E1
Sch St. Jude's C of E
Prim Sch, SE1 .... 117 E3
St. Jude's Rd, E2 ...... 43 F3
St. Julian's Rd, NW6 ... 8 B4
★ St. Katharine's Dock,
E1 .... 92 B3

Riv St. Katharine's
Pier 92 A4
St. Katharines Prec,
NW1 .... 35 E2
St. Katharine's Way,
E1 .... 92 B4
St. Katherine's Row,
EC3 .... 91 F1
St. Katherine's Wk,
W11 .... 79 D4
St. Laurence Cl,
NW6 .... 29 D1
★ St. Lawrence Jewry Ch,
EC2 .... 62 B5
St. Lawrence St,
E14 .... 98 B4
St. Lawrence Ter,
W10 .... 51 E3
St. Lawrence Way,
SW9 .... 169 D4
St. Leonards Ct, N1 ... 40 B4
St. Leonards Rd, E14 .. 69 F4
St. Leonards Sq,
NW5 .... 13 D2
St. Leonards St, E3 ... 47 F4
St. Leonard's Ter,
SW3 .... 140 A3
St. Loo Av, SW3 ..... 139 F4
ST. LUKE'S, EC1 ...... 62 B1
St. Luke's Cl, EC1 ..... 62 B1
Sch St. Luke's C of E
Prim Sch, EC1 ..... 40 B5
W9 .... 30 A4
Sch St. Luke's C of E (VA)
Prim Sch, E16 .... 72 B5
St. Luke's Est, EC1 .... 40 C5
H St. Luke's Hosp for
the Clergy, W1 .... 58 A2
St. Lukes Ms, W11 .... 52 B5
Sch St. Luke's Prim Sch,
E14 .... 154 C1
St. Lukes Rd, W11 .... 52 B4
St. Lukes Sq, E16 .... 100 B1
St. Luke's St, SW3 ... 139 E2
St. Luke's Yd, W9 ..... 30 A3
St. Margaret's Ct,
SE1 .... 90 B5
St. Margarets La,
W8 .... 109 E4
St. Margaret's Rd,
NW10 .... 28 A3
St. Margaret's St,
SW1 .... 115 E2
St. Marks Cl, SE10 ... 178 A2
SW6 .... 160 C4
W11 .... 79 E1
Sch St. Mark's C of E
Prim Sch, SE11 ... 144 B4
St. Marks Cres, NW1 .. 13 D5
St. Mark's Gate, E9 ... 24 B4

St. Mark's Gro,
  SW10 . . . . 161 F1
St. Marks Pl, W11 . . . . 79 F1
St. Marks Rd,
  W10 . . . . 51 D5
  W11 . . . . 79 E1
St. Marks Sq, NW1 . . . 12 C5
St. Mark St, E1 . . . . . . 92 B1
★ St. Martin-in-the-Fields
  Ch, WC2 . . . . 87 E3
St. Martins Cl,
  NW1 . . . . 14 A5
Coll St. Martin's Coll,
  Tower Hamlets
  Professional Dev
  Cen, E3 . . . . 68 A2
St. Martin's La,
  WC2 . . . . 87 E2
St. Martin's-le-Grand,
  EC1 . . . . 62 A5
St. Martin's Ms,
  WC2 . . . . 87 E3
St. Martin's Pl,
  WC2 . . . . 87 E3
St. Martin's Rd,
  SW9 . . . . 168 A5
St. Martin's St, WC2 . . 87 D3
Sch St. Mary Abbots C of E
  Prim Sch, W8 . . . . 109 E2
St. Mary Abbots Pl,
  W8 . . . . 108 B4
St. Mary Abbots Ter,
  W14 . . . . 108 B4
Sch St. Mary & St. Michael
  Prim Sch, E1 . . . . . . 94 A1
Sch St. Mary & St. Pancras
  C of E Prim Sch,
  NW1 . . . . 36 C3
St. Mary at Hill,
  EC3 . . . . 91 E3
★ St. Mary at Hill Ch,
  EC3 . . . . 91 E3
St. Mary Axe, EC3 . . . 91 E1
St. Marychurch St,
  SE16 . . . . 122 A2
Sch St. Marylebone
  C of E Sch, W1 . . . . . 57 D3
★ St. Mary-le-Bow Ch,
  EC2 . . . . 90 B1
Sch St. Mary Magdalene
  C of E Prim Sch,
  N7 . . . . 16 C1
Sch St. Mary Magdalene's
  C of E Prim Sch,
  W2 . . . . 53 E3
Sch St. Mary of the Angels
  RC Prim Sch, W2 . . . 52 C5
Sch St. Mary's Bryanston Sq
  C of E Prim Sch,
  W1 . . . . 56 A3

Sch St. Mary's C of E
  Prim Sch, N1 . . . . . . 17 F5
  SE18 . . . . 132 C5
St. Marys Ct, E6 . . . . 76 A1
St. Mary's Gdns,
  SE11 . . . . 117 D5
St. Mary's Gate,
  W8 . . . . 109 E4
St. Mary's Gro, N1 . . . 17 F2
H St. Mary's Hosp,
  W2 . . . . 55 D5
Sch St. Mary's Kilburn C of E
  Prim Sch, NW6 . . . . . 9 D4
St. Marys Mans, W2 . . 54 C3
St. Mary's Ms, NW6 . . . 9 E4
St. Marys Path, N1 . . . 17 F5
St. Mary's Pl, W8 . . . 109 E4
Sch St. Mary's RC Inf &
  Jun Sch, Annexe,
  NW6 . . . . 30 C3
Sch St. Mary's RC Inf Sch,
  NW6 . . . . 30 C2
Sch St. Mary's RC Jun Sch,
  NW6 . . . . 30 C2
Sch St. Mary's RC Prim Sch,
  SW8 . . . . 165 F3
  W10 . . . . 51 E2
  W14 . . . . 107 D4
St. Mary's Rd, SE15 . . 174 A4
St. Marys Sq, W2 . . . . 54 C3
St. Marys Ter, W2 . . . . 54 C3
St. Mary St, SE18 . . . 132 B5
St. Mary's Wk,
  SE11 . . . . 117 D5
Sch St. Matthew's C of E
  Prim Sch, SW1 . . . . 115 D3
St. Matthew's Row,
  E2 . . . . 42 C5
St. Matthew St,
  SW1 . . . . 114 C4
Sch St. Matthias C of E
  Prim Sch, E2 . . . . . . 64 B1
St. Maur Rd, SW6 . . . 160 B3
St. Michael's All,
  EC3 . . . . 91 D1
Sch St. Michael's Camden
  Town C of E Prim Sch,
  NW1 . . . . 14 A5
St. Michaels Cl,
  E16 . . . . 74 C4
St. Michaels Gdns,
  W10 . . . . 51 E4
Sch St. Michael's RC Sch,
  SE16 . . . . 120 C2
St. Michael's Rd,
  SW9 . . . . 168 A5
St. Michaels St, W2 . . 55 D5
Sch St. Monica's RC
  Prim Sch, N1 . . . . . . 41 E4
Sch St. Nicholas Prep Sch,
  SW7 . . . . 111 D2
St. Nicholas St,
  SE8 . . . . 176 B4
St. Olaf's Rd, SW6 . . . 159 F2

St. Olaves Ct, EC2 . . . . 90 C1
St. Olave's Est, SE1 . . 119 F1
St. Olaves Gdns,
  SE11 . . . . 116 C5
St. Olav's Sq, SE16 . . 122 A3
St. Oswald's Pl,
  SE11 . . . . 144 A3
St. Oswulf St, SW1 . . 143 D1
ST. PANCRAS, WC1 . . 37 E5
⇌ St. Pancras 37 E4
H St. Pancras Hosp,
  NW1 . . . . 36 C1
St. Pancras Way,
  NW1 . . . . 14 B5
Sch St. Patrick's RC
  Prim Sch, NW5 . . . . 13 F1
⊖ St. Paul's 62 A5
St. Paul's Av, SE16 . . . 95 D4
★ St. Paul's Cath,
  EC4 . . . . 90 A1
Sch St. Paul's Cath Choir
  Sch, EC4 . . . . 90 A1
St. Paul's Chyd, EC4 . . . 89 F1
Sch St. Paul's C of E
  Prim Sch, NW3 . . . . 12 A4
  SE17 . . . . 146 A3
  W6 . . . . 134 A2
St. Paul's Ct, W14 . . . 135 D1
St. Paul's Cres, NW1 . . 15 D3
Sch St. Paul's Girls Sch,
  W6 . . . . 106 C5
St. Paul's Ms, NW1 . . . 15 D3
St. Paul's Pl, N1 . . . . . 18 C1
Sch St. Paul's Prim Sch,
  E1 . . . . 93 D2
St. Paul's Rd, N1 . . . . . 17 E2
St. Paul's Shrubbery,
  N1 . . . . 18 C1
St. Paul's Ter, SE17 . . 145 F4
St. Paul St, N1 . . . . . . 40 A1
St. Pauls Way, E3 . . . . 68 A4
  E14 . . . . 68 A4
Sch St. Paul's Way
  Comm Sch, E3 . . . . . 68 C3
Sch St. Paul's with St. Luke's
  Prim Sch, E3 . . . . . . 68 B3
Sch St. Paul's with St.
  Michael's C of E
  Prim Sch, E8 . . . . . . 21 D5
St. Peter's All, EC3 . . . 91 D1
Sch St. Peter's & St. Paul's RC
  JMI Sch, EC1 . . . . . . 61 F1
St. Peter's Av, E2 . . . . . 43 D3
St. Petersburgh Ms,
  W2 . . . . 81 E2
St. Petersburgh Pl,
  W2 . . . . 81 E2
St. Peter's Cl, E2 . . . . . 43 D3
Sch St. Peter's C of E
  Prim Sch, SE17 . . . 146 C3
  W9 . . . . 52 C2
Sch St. Peter's Eaton Sq
  C of E Prim Sch,
  SW1 . . . . 113 F4

★ Place of interest   ⇌ Railway station   **H** Hospital   ⊖ London Underground station

St. Peter's Pl, W9 . . . . . 53 E2
Sch St. Peter's Prim Sch,
    E1 . . . . 94 A4
St. Peters Sq, E2 . . . . . 43 D3
St. Peters St, N1 . . . . . . 39 F1
St. Peter's Ter, SW6 . . 159 F2
St. Peter's Way, N1 . . . 19 F4
St. Philip Sq, SW8 . . 165 E5
St. Philip's Rd, E8. . . . . 20 C2
Sch St. Philip's Sch,
    SW7 . . . . 138 B1
St. Philip's Way, N1. . . 18 B5
St. Quintin Av, W10 . . 50 B4
St. Quintin Gdns,
    W10 . . . . 50 A4
St. Rule St, SW8 . . . . 166 A5
Sch St. Saviour's & St. Olave's
    C of E Sch, SE1 . . . 119 D4
Sch St. Saviour's C of E
    Prim Sch, W9 . . . . . 53 F2
St. Saviour's Est,
    SE1 . . . . 120 A3
Sch St. Saviour's Prim Sch,
    E14 . . . . 69 E4
St. Silas Pl, NW5 . . . . . 12 C2
St. Silas St Est,
    NW5 . . . . 12 C1
St. Stephens Cl,
    NW8 . . . . 33 F1
Sch St. Stephen's C of E
    Prim Sch, SE8 . . . . 177 D5
    SW8 . . . . 168 A1
    W2 . . . . 53 D4
    W12 . . . . 106 A1
St. Stephens Cres,
    W2 . . . . 53 D5
St. Stephens Gdn Est,
    W2 . . . . 52 C5
St. Stephens Gdns,
    W2 . . . . 53 D4
St. Stephens Ms,
    W2 . . . . 53 D4
St. Stephen's Rd,
    E3 . . . . 46 A2
St. Stephens Row,
    EC4 . . . . 90 C1
St. Stephens Ter,
    SW8 . . . . 168 A2
St. Stephen's Wk,
    SW7 . . . . 110 A5
St. Swithin's La,
    EC4 . . . . 90 C2
Sch St. Thomas C of E
    Prim Sch, W10 . . 51 F2
H St. Thomas' Hosp,
    SE1 . . . . 116 A3
Coll St. Thomas' Med Sch &
    the Nightingale Sch,
    SE1 . . . . 116 A4
Sch St. Thomas More
    Sec Sch, SW3 . . . . 140 A1
Sch St. Thomas RC Prim Sch,
    SW6 . . . . 160 A1
St. Thomas Rd, E16. . . 72 C5

St. Thomas's Gdns,
    NW5 . . . . 12 C1
St. Thomas's Pl, E9 . . . 22 A3
St. Thomas's Sq, E9 . . . 21 F3
St. Thomas St, SE1 . . . 90 C5
St. Thomas's Way,
    SW6 . . . . 160 A1
Sch St. Thomas the Apostle
    Sch, SE15 . . . . 174 A5
Sch St. Ursula's Conv
    Sec Sch, SE10 . . . . 178 C2
Sch St. Vincent de Paul RC
    Prim Sch, SW1 . . . 114 A4
Sch St. Vincent's RC
    Prim Sch, W1 . . . . . 57 D4
St. Vincent St, W1. . . . 57 D4
Salamanca Pl, SE1 . . 144 A1
Salamanca St, SE1 . . 143 F1
Salem Rd, W2. . . . . 81 F2
Sale Pl, W2 . . . . 55 E4
Sch Salesian Coll,
    SW11 . . . . 163 E4
Sale St, E2. . . . . 64 C1
Salisbury Cl, SE17 . . . 118 C5
Salisbury Ct, EC4 . . . . . 89 E1
Salisbury Ho, E14 . . . . 69 E5
Salisbury Ms, SW6 . . 160 A2
Salisbury Pl, SW9 . . . 169 F2
    W1 . . . . 56 A3
Salisbury Sq, EC4 . . . . . 89 D1
Salisbury St, NW8 . . . . 55 D2
Salmon La, E14 . . . . . . 67 E5
Salmon St, E14 . . . . . . 68 A5
Salomons Rd, E13 . . . . 74 A3
Salter Rd, SE16 . . . . . . 94 C5
Salters Hall Ct, EC4 . . . 90 C2
Salters Rd, W10 . . . . . . 50 C2
Salter St, E14 . . . . 96 C2
Saltley Cl, E6 . . . . 75 F5
Saltram Cres, W9 . . . . . 30 B4
Saltwell St, E14 . . . . . . 97 D2
Saltwood Gro,
    SE17 . . . . 146 C3
Sch Salusbury Prim Sch,
    NW6 . . . . 8 B5
Salusbury Rd, NW6 . . . 30 A3
Salutation Rd,
    SE10 . . . . 127 F5
Salway Pl, E15 . . . . 27 D2
Salway Rd, E15 . . . . . . 27 D2
Samford St, NW8 . . . . . 55 D2
Sampson St, E1 . . . . . . 93 D5
Samuel Cl, E8 . . . . 20 B5
    SE14 . . . . 150 C5
    SE18 . . . . 131 F5
Samuel Lewis Trust Dws,
    N1. . . . . 17 D2
    SW3 . . . . 139 E1
    SW6 . . . . 161 D1
Sch Samuel Rhodes Sch,
    N1. . . . . 16 C5
Samuel St, SE15 . . . . 172 A1
    SE18 . . . . 132 A5
Sancroft St, SE11 . . . 144 B2

Sanctuary, The, SW1 115 D2
Sanctuary St, SE1 . . . 118 B2
Sandall Rd, NW5 . . . . . 14 B2
Sandal St, E15 . . . . 27 E5
Sandalwood Cl, E1 . . . 67 E2
Sandbourne Rd,
    SE4 . . . . 175 E5
Sandell St, SE1 . . . . . . 116 C1
Sandford Cl, E6 . . . . . . 76 A1
Sandford St, SW6 . . . 161 F2
Sandgate St, SE15 . . . 149 E4
Sandilands Rd,
    SW6 . . . . 161 E4
Sandland St, WC1 . . . . 60 B4
Sandpiper Cl, SE16 . . 124 A1
Sandringham Ct,
    W9 . . . . 32 B5
SANDS END, SW6 . . . 162 A4
Sand's End La, SW6 . . 161 F3
Sandstone La, E16 . . 101 E2
Sandtoft Rd, SE7 . . . . 157 E4
Sandwell Cres, NW6 . . . 9 D1
Sandwich St, WC1 . . . . 37 E5
Sandy's Row, E1 . . . . . . 63 F4
Sanford St, SE14 . . . . 151 E5
Sanford Wk, SE14 . . . 151 E5
San Ho, E9 . . . . 23 D2
Sansom St, SE5 . . . . . 171 D2
Sans Wk, EC1 . . . . 61 D1
Saperton Wk, SE11 . . 116 B5
Sapperton Ct, EC1. . . . 62 A1
Sapphire Cl, E6. . . . . . . 76 B5
Sapphire Rd, SE8 . . . . 151 F1
Saracen's Head Yd,
    EC3 . . . . 91 F1
Saracen St, E14 . . . . . . 97 D1
Sch Sarah Bonnell
    Sec Sch, E15 . . . . . 27 F2
Sardinia St, WC2 . . . . . 88 A1
Sark Wk, E16 . . . . 73 F5
Sarnesfield Ho,
    SE15 . . . . 149 E5
Sch Sarum Hall Sch,
    NW3 . . . . 11 E3
Sarum Ter, E3. . . . . 68 A2
Satanita Cl, E15 . . . . . . 74 C5
Satchwell Rd, E2 . . . . . 42 C5
Saunders Cl, E14 . . . . . 96 B3
Saunders Ness Rd,
    E14 . . . . 154 B2
Saunders St, SE11 . . . 144 C1
Savage Gdns, E6 . . . . 104 B1
    EC3 . . . . 91 F2
Savannah Cl, SE15 . . 172 A2
Savile Row, W1 . . . . . . 86 A2
Saville Rd, E16. . . . . . . 103 F5
Savona Est, SW8 . . . . 166 A2
Savona St, SW8 . . . . . 166 A2
Savoy Bldgs, WC2 . . . . 88 A3
Savoy Cl, E15 . . . . 27 E5

Savoy Ct, WC2 . . . . 87　F3
Savoy Hill, WC2 . . . . . . 88　A3
Riv Savoy Pier . . . . 88　A3
Savoy Pl, WC2 . . . . 87　F3
Savoy Row, WC2 . . . . . . 88　A2
Savoy St, WC2 . . . . 88　A2
Savoy Way, WC2 . . . . . 88　A3
Sawmill Yd, E3 . . . . 45　F1
Sawyer St, SE1 . . . . . . 118　A1
Saxon Rd, E3 . . . . 46　A3
　E6 . . . . 76　A2
Sayes Ct, SE8 . . . . 152　B4
Sayes Ct St, SE8 . . . . . 152　B4
Scala St, W1 . . . . 58　B3
Scampston Ms,
　W10 . . . . 51　D5
Scandrett St, E1 . . . . . . 93　E5
Scarba Wk, N1 . . . . 18　C2
Scarborough St, E1 . . . 92　B1
Scarsdale Pl, W8 . . . . . 109　E3
Scarsdale Vil, W8 . . . . 109　D4
Scawen Rd, SE8 . . . . . 151　E3
Scawfell St, E2 . . . . 42　B3
Sceaux Est, SE5 . . . . . 171　F3
Sceptre Rd, E2 . . . . 44　B5
Uni Schiller Int Uni,
　SE1 . . . . 88　C5
Schofield Wk, SE3 . . . 181　E1
Schoolbank Rd,
　SE10 . . . . 128　A5
Schoolbell Ms, E3 . . . . 45　F3
Schoolhouse La, E1 . . . 94　C2
Coll School of Economic
　Science, W1 . . . . 57　D5
Uni School of Oriental &
　African Studies,
　Russell Sq Campus,
　WC1 . . . . 59　D2
　Vernon Sq Campus,
　WC1 . . . . 38　B4
Uni School of Pharmacy,
　WC1 . . . . 59　F1
Schooner Cl, E14 . . . . 126　C4
　SE16 . . . . 122　C4
★ Science Mus,
　SW7 . . . . 111　D4
Sclater St, E1 . . . . 64　A1
Scoresby St, SE1 . . . . . 89　E5
Scotland Pl, SW1 . . . . . 87　E4
Scotswood St, EC1 . . . 61　D1
Scott Ellis Gdns,
　NW8 . . . . 32　C5
Scott Lidgett Cres,
　SE16 . . . . 120　C2
Scott Russell Pl,
　E14 . . . . 153　E2
Scott St, E1 . . . . 65　E2
Sch Scott Wilkie
　Prim Sch, E16 . . . . 74　C5
Scoulding Rd, E16 . . . . 72　B5

Scouler St, E14 . . . . 98　C3
Scovell Cres, SE1 . . . . 118　A2
Scovell Rd, SE1 . . . . . 118　A2
Scriven St, E8 . . . . 20　B5
Scrutton St, EC2 . . . . . . 63　E2
Sch Seabright
　JMI Sch, E2 . . . . 43　D2
Seabright St, E2 . . . . . . 43　E5
Seacon Twr, E14 . . . . . 124　B2
Seaford St, WC1 . . . . . . 37　F5
Seagrave Rd, SW6 . . . 137　D4
Seagull La, E16 . . . . . 101　D2
Searles Cl, SW11 . . . . 163　F2
Searles Dr, E6 . . . . 77　E4
Searles Rd, SE1 . . . . . 119　D5
Sears St, SE5 . . . . 170　C1
Seaton Cl, E13 . . . . 73　D2
　SE11 . . . . 145　D2
Sebastian St, EC1 . . . . 39　F5
Sebbon St, N1 . . . . 17　F4
Sebright Pas, E2 . . . . . . 43　D3
Secker St, SE1 . . . . 88　C5
Second Av, W10 . . . . . . 51　F1
Sedan Way, SE17 . . . . 147　E2
Sedding St, SW1 . . . . . 112　C5
Seddon St, WC1 . . . . . . 38　B5
Sedgmoor Pl, SE5 . . . 171　F2
Sedlescombe Rd,
　SW6 . . . . 136　B5
Sedley Pl, W1 . . . . 85　E1
Seething La, EC3 . . . . . 91　F3
Sekforde St, EC1 . . . . . 61　E2
Selborne Rd, SE5 . . . . 170　C5
Selby Cl, E6 . . . . 75　E4
Selby Rd, E13 . . . . 73　F3
Selby Sq, W10 . . . . 29　F4
Selby St, E1 . . . . 65　D2
★ Selfridges, W1 . . . . . 85　D1
Selsdon Way, E14 . . . . 125　F4
Selsey St, E14 . . . . 68　C4
Selwood Pl, SW7 . . . . 138　C2
Selwood Ter, SW7 . . . 138　C2
Selworthy Ho,
　SW11 . . . . 163　D3
Selwyn Rd, E3 . . . . 46　A3
Semley Pl, SW1 . . . . . 141　D1
Senior St, W2 . . . . 53　E3
Senrab St, E1 . . . . 66　C5
Serjeants Inn, EC4 . . . . 89　D1
Serle St, WC2 . . . . 60　B5
Sermon La, EC4 . . . . . . 90　A1
★ Serpentine, The,
　W2 . . . . 83　E5
★ Serpentine Gall,
　W2 . . . . 83　D5
Serpentine Rd, W2 . . . 84　A5
Sch Servite RC
　Prim Sch, SW10 . . 138　A4
Setchell Rd, SE1 . . . . . 120　A5
Setchell Way, SE1 . . . 120　A5
Seth St, SE16 . . . . 122　B2
Settles St, E1 . . . . 65　D4
Sch Seven Mills
　Prim Sch, E14 . . . . 125　D2

Seven Stars Yd, E1 . . . . 64　B3
Severnake Cl, E14 . . . 125　D5
Severn Av, W10 . . . . . . 29　F4
Seville Ms, N1 . . . . 19　E4
Seville St, SW1 . . . . . . 112　B2
Sevington St, W9 . . . . . 53　E2
Sewardstone Rd, E2 . . 44　B2
Seward St, EC1 . . . . 61　F1
Sextant Av, E14 . . . . . 126　C5
Seymour Ms, W1 . . . . . 56　C5
Seymour Pl, W1 . . . . . . 56　A4
Seymour St, W1 . . . . . . 84　A1
　W2 . . . . 84　A1
Seymour Wk,
　SW10 . . . . 138　A4
Seyssel St, E14 . . . . . . 126　B5
Shacklewell St, E2 . . . . 64　B1
Shad Thames, SE1 . . . . 92　A5
SHADWELL, E1 . . . . 94　A3
● Shadwell . . . . 93　F2
DLR Shadwell . . . . 93　F2
Shadwell Gdns Est,
　E1 . . . . 94　A2
Shadwell Pierhead,
　E1 . . . . 94　B3
Shadwell Pl, E1 . . . . . . 94　A2
Shaftesbury Av, W1 . . 86　C2
　WC2 . . . . 86　C2
Shaftesbury Ms,
　W8 . . . . 109　D4
Shaftesbury Pl,
　W14 . . . . 136　B1
Shaftesbury St, N1 . . . 40　B3
Shafto Ms, SW1 . . . . . 112　A4
Shafton Rd, E9 . . . . 23　D5
★ Shakespeare's
　Globe Thea, SE1 . . 90　A3
Shakespeare Twr, EC2. 62　B3
Shalbourne Sq, E9 . . . 24　A1
Shalcomb St,
　SW10 . . . . 138　B5
Shalfleet Dr, W10 . . . . 78　C2
Shand St, SE1 . . . . 119　E1
Shandy St, E1 . . . . 67　D2
Shannon Pl, NW8 . . . . 33　F2
Sch Shapla Prim Sch,
　E1 . . . . 92　C2
Shardeloes Rd,
　SE14 . . . . 176　A5
Sharnbrook Ho,
　W14 . . . . 136　C4
Sharon Gdns, E9 . . . . . 22　A5
Sharpleshall St,
　NW1 . . . . 12　B4
Sharratt St, SE15 . . . . 150　B4
Sharsted St, SE17 . . . 145　E3
Shavers Pl, SW1 . . . . . . 86　C3
Shawfield St, SW3 . . . 139　F3
Shearling Way, N7 . . . 15　F1
Shearsmith Ho, E1 . . . 93　D2
Sheen Gro, N1 . . . . 16　C5
Sheep La, E8 . . . . 43　E1
Sheerness Ms, E16 . . 133　F1
Sheerwater Rd, E16 . . 74　C3

Sheffield Sq, E3 . . . . . . 46 B4
Sheffield St, WC2 . . . . . 88 A1
Sheffield Ter, W8 . . . . . 80 C5
Sheldon Pl, E2 . . . . 43 D3
Sheldon Sq, W2 . . . . . . 54 B4
Sheldrake Cl, E16 . . . 104 A5
Sheldrake Pl, W8 . . . . 108 C1
★ Shell Cen, SE1 . . . . . 88 B5
Shelley Cl, SE15 . . . . . 173 F5
Shelmerdine Cl, E3 . . . 68 C3
Shelton St, WC2 . . . . . . 87 E1
Shenfield St, N1 . . . . . . 41 F3
Shenley Rd, SE5 . . . . . 171 F4
Shepherdess Pl, N1 . . 40 B4
Shepherdess Wk, N1 . . 40 B2
Shepherd Mkt, W1 . . 85 E4
SHEPHERD'S BUSH,
    W12 . . . . 78 B4
⊖ Shepherd's Bush . . 78 A5
Shepherds Bush Grn,
    W12 . . . . 106 B1
Shepherds Bush Mkt,
    W12 . . . . 106 A2
Shepherds Bush Pl,
    W12 . . . . 106 C1
Shepherds Bush Rd,
    W6 . . . . 106 B4
Shepherds Ct, W12 . . 106 C1
Shepherd's Pl, W1 . . . 84 C2
Shepherd St, W1 . . . . . 85 E5
Sheppard Dr, SE16 . . 149 E2
Sheppard St, E16 . . . . . 72 B1
Shepperton Rd, N1 . . . 18 B5
Sheppey Wk, N1 . . . . . 18 B3
Sheraton St, W1 . . . . . 86 C1
Sherborne La, EC4 . . . 90 C2
Sherborne St, N1 . . . . . 18 C5
Sherbrooke Rd,
    SW6 . . . . 159 F2
Sheridan St, E1 . . . . . . 93 F1
Sheringham Rd, N7 . . . 16 B1
Sꞓʰ Sherington Jun Sch,
    SE7 . . . . 157 F5
Sherington Rd,
    SE7 . . . . 157 E5
★ Sherlock Holmes Mus,
    NW1 . . . . 56 B2
Sherlock Ms, W1 . . . . . 56 C3
Sherriff Rd, NW6 . . . . . . 9 D2
Sherwin Rd, SE14 . . . 174 C4
Sherwood Gdns,
    E14 . . . . 125 D5
    SE16 . . . . 149 D3
Sherwood St, W1 . . . . . 86 B2
Shetland Rd, E3 . . . . . . 46 A3
Shillibeer Pl, W1 . . . . . 55 F3
Shillingford St, N1 . . . 17 F4
Shinfield St, W12 . . . . 78 A1
Ship & Mermaid Row,
    SE1 . . . . 119 D1
Shipman Rd, E16 . . . . 101 F1
Ship St, SE8 . . . . 176 C3
Ship Tavern Pas, EC3 . . 91 E2
Shipton St, E2 . . . . 42 B4

Shipwright Rd,
    SE16 . . . . 123 E2
Shipwright Yd, SE1 . . . 91 E5
Ship Yd, E14 . . . . 153 E2
Shirbutt St, E14 . . . . . . 97 E2
Shirland Ms, W9 . . . . . 30 B5
Shirland Rd, W9 . . . . . . 30 C5
Shirley Rd, E15 . . . . . . 27 F3
Shirley St, E16 . . . . 72 A5
Shoe La, EC4 . . . . 61 D5
Shona Ho, E13 . . . . 74 A3
Shooters Hill Rd,
    SE3 . . . . 180 B3
    SE10 . . . . 178 B4
SHOREDITCH, E1 . . . . . 64 A2
⊖ Shoreditch 64 B2
Shoreditch High St,
    E1 . . . . 63 F2
Shoreditch Ho, N1 . . . . 41 D5
Shore Pl, E9 . . . . 22 A4
Shore Rd, E9 . . . . 22 A4
Shorncliffe Rd, SE1 . . 148 A2
Shorrolds Rd, SW6 . . 160 B1
Shorter St, E1 . . . . 92 A2
Shortlands, W6 . . . . . 134 C1
Shorts Gdns, WC2 . . . . 87 E1
Short St, SE1 . . . . 117 D1
Short Wall, E15 . . . . . . 48 B4
Shottendane Rd,
    SW6 . . . . 160 C3
Shoulder of Mutton All,
    E14 . . . . 95 F2
Shouldham St, W1 . . . 55 F4
Shrewsbury Ms, W2 . . 52 C4
Shrewsbury Rd, W2 . . 52 C5
Shrewsbury St, W10 . . 50 B2
Shropshire Pl, WC1 . . . 58 B3
Shroton St, NW1 . . . . . 55 E3
Shrubbery Cl, N1 . . . . . 40 B1
Shrubland Rd, E8 . . . . . 20 B5
Shurland Gdns,
    SE15 . . . . 172 B1
Shuters Sq, W14 . . . . 136 A3
Shuttle St, E1 . . . . 64 C2
Shuttleworth Rd,
    SW11 . . . . 163 D5
Sicilian Av, WC1 . . . . . 59 F4
Sidbury St, SW6 . . . . 159 E3
Siddons La, NW1 . . . . . 56 B2
Sidford Pl, SE1 . . . . . . 116 B4
Sidmouth Rd, NW2 . . . . 6 B3
Sidmouth St, WC1 . . . . 37 F3
Sidney Gro, EC1 . . . . . . 39 E3
Sidney Sq, E1 . . . . 66 A4
Sidney St, E1 . . . . 66 A5
Sidworth St, E8 . . . . . . 21 F4
Siebert Rd, SE3 . . . . . 157 D5
Siemens Rd, SE18 . . . 131 D4
Signmakers Yd,
    NW1 . . . . 35 F1
Silbury St, N1 . . . . 40 C4
Silchester Rd, W10 . . . 79 D1
Silesia Bldgs, E8 . . . . . 21 F3
Silex St, SE1 . . . . 117 F2

Silk Mills Pas, SE13 . . 177 F5
Silk Mills Sq, E9 . . . . . 24 B1
Silk St, EC2 . . . . 62 B3
Silver Birch Gdns, E6 . . 76 A2
Silverbirch Wk, NW3 . . 12 B2
Silver Cl, SE14 . . . . . . 175 E1
Silverland St, E16 . . . 104 B5
Silver Pl, W1 . . . . 86 B2
Silver Rd, W12 . . . . 78 C3
Silverthorne Rd,
    SW8 . . . . 165 E4
Silverton Rd, W6 . . . . 134 C5
SILVERTOWN, E16 . . . 130 A1
⇌ Silvertown & London City
    Airport 103 D5
Silvertown Way,
    E16 . . . . 71 F5
Silver Wk, SE16 . . . . . . 96 A5
Silvester St, SE1 . . . . . 118 B2
Silvocea Way, E14 . . . 99 D1
Silwood St, SE16 . . . . 150 B1
Simla Ho, SE1 . . . . . . 119 D2
Simms Rd, SE1 . . . . . . 148 C1
Simon Cl, W11 . . . . 80 B2
Simpsons Rd, E14 . . . . 97 F3
Simpson St, SW11 . . . 163 E5
Sinclair Gdns, W14 . . 107 D2
Sinclair Rd, W14 . . . . 107 D2
Singer St, EC2 . . . . 41 D5
Sꞓʰ Sion Manning RC Sch,
    The, W10 . . . . 51 E4
Sirdar Rd, W11 . . . . 79 D3
Sꞓʰ Sir Francis Drake
    Prim Sch, SE8 . . . . 151 E3
Sirinham Pt, SW8 . . . 144 B5
Sꞓʰ Sir James Barrie
    Prim Sch, SW8 . . . 166 B4
Sꞓʰ Sir John Cass's Foundation
    & Redcoat Sch,
    E1 . . . . 67 D4
Sꞓʰ Sir John Cass's Foundation
    C of E Prim Sch,
    EC3 . . . . 92 A1
Sir John Kirk Cl,
    SE5 . . . . 170 A1
Sꞓʰ Sir John Lillie Prim Sch,
    SW6 . . . . 135 F5
★ Sir John Soane's Mus, WC2
    (Lincoln's Inn Flds) . 60 A5
Sir Thomas More Est,
    SW3 . . . . 139 D5
Sꞓʰ Sir William Burrough
    Prim Sch, E14 . . . . . 67 F5
Sise La, EC4 . . . . 90 C1
Sister Mabel's Way,
    SE15 . . . . 172 C1
Sivill Ho, E2 . . . . 42 B4
Six Bridges Trd Est,
    SE1 . . . . 149 D3
Sixth Av, W10 . . . . 29 E5

Skelton Cl, E8 . . . . 20 B2
Skelwith Rd, W6 . . . . 134 B5
Skenfrith Ho,
  SE15 . . . . 149 E5
Sketchley Gdns,
  SE16 . . . . 150 C2
Skiers St, E15 . . . . 49 E1
Skinner Ct, E2 . . . . 43 F2
Skinner Pl, SW1 . . . . . 140 C1
★ Skinners' Hall, EC4
  (Dowgate Hill) 90 C2
Skinners La, EC4 . . . . . 90 B2
Skinner St, EC1 . . . . . . 39 D5
Skipworth Rd, E9 . . . . 22 B5
Skylines Village,
  E14 . . . . 126 A2
Slade Wk, SE17 . . . . . 145 F5
Slaidburn St,
  SW10 . . . . 138 B5
Sleaford Ho, E3 . . . . . . 69 D2
Sleaford St, SW8 . . . . 166 A1
Slingsby Pl, WC2 . . . . . 87 C2
Slippers Pl, SE16 . . . . 121 F3
Slippers Pl Est,
  SE16 . . . . 121 F4
Sloane Av, SW3 . . . . . 111 E5
Sloane Ct E, SW3 . . . . 140 C2
Sloane Ct W, SW3 . . . . 140 C2
Sloane Gdns, SW1 . . . 140 C1
➤ Sloane Square 140 C1
Sloane Sq, SW1 . . . . . 140 C1
Sloane St, SW1 . . . . . . 112 B3
Sloane Ter, SW1 . . . . . 112 B5
Sly St, E1 . . . . 93 E1
Smallbrook Ms, W2 . . . 82 C1
Smart's Pl, WC2 . . . . . 59 F5
Smart St, E2 . . . . 44 C4
Smeaton Ct, SE1 . . . . 118 A4
Smeaton St, E1 . . . . . . 93 E4
Smedley St, SW4 . . . . 167 D5
  SW8 . . . . 167 D5
Smeed Rd, E3 . . . . 24 C4
Smiles Pl, SE13 . . . . . 178 A5
Smith Cl, SE16 . . . . 94 C5
★ Smithfield Cen Mkt,
  EC1 . . . . 61 F4
Smithfield St, EC1 . . . . 61 E4
Smith's Ct, W1 . . . . 86 B2
Smith Sq, SW1 . . . . . . 115 E4
Smith St, SW3 . . . . . . 140 A2
Smith Ter, SW3 . . . . . 140 A3
Smithy St, E1 . . . . 66 A3
Sch Smithy St Prim Sch,
  E1 . . . . 66 B3
Smokehouse Yd,
  EC1 . . . . 61 F3
Smyrks Rd, SE17 . . . . 147 F3
Smyrna Rd, NW6 . . . . . 8 C4
Smythe St, E14 . . . . . . 97 F2
Snarsgate St, W10 . . . . 50 B4

Snowden St, EC2 . . . . . 63 E2
Snow Hill, EC1 . . . . 61 E4
Snow Hill Ct, EC1 . . . . . 61 F5
Snowman Ho, NW6 . . . . 9 F5
Snowsfields, SE1 . . . . 119 D1
Sch Snowsfields Prim Sch,
  SE1 . . . . 119 E1
SOHO, W1 . . . . 86 C2
Sch Soho Parish Sch,
  W1 . . . . 86 C2
Soho Sq, W1 . . . . 58 C5
Soho St, W1 . . . . 58 C5
Sojourner Truth Cl,
  E8 . . . . 21 F2
Solander Gdns, E1 . . . . 94 A2
Solebay St, E1 . . . . 67 E2
Soley Ms, WC1 . . . . 38 C4
Solway Cl, E8 . . . . 20 B2
Somerfield St,
  SE16 . . . . 150 C2
Somerford St, E1 . . . . . 65 E2
Somerford Way,
  SE16 . . . . 123 E2
Somers Cl, NW1 . . . . . . 36 C2
Somers Cres, W2 . . . . . 83 E1
Somerset Est,
  SW11 . . . . 163 D3
★ Somerset Ho,
  WC2 . . . . 88 A2
Somerset Sq,
  W14 . . . . 107 F2
Somers Ms, W2 . . . . . . 83 E1
SOMERS TOWN,
  NW1 . . . . 37 D4
Sondes St, SE17 . . . . . 146 C4
Sophia Cl, E14 . . . . 16 A1
Sophia Rd, E16 . . . . 73 E5
Sophia Sq, SE16 . . . . . . 95 E3
Sopwith Way, SW8 . . 165 E1
Sorrel Gdns, E6 . . . . . . 75 E3
Sorrel La, E14 . . . . 99 D1
Sorrell Cl, SE14 . . . . . 175 E1
Sotheran Cl, E8 . . . . . . 21 D5
Sotheron Rd, SW6 . . . 161 F2
Soudan Rd, SW11 . . . . 164 A4
Souldern Rd, W14 . . . 107 D4
Southall Pl, SE1 . . . . . 118 C2
Southampton Bldgs,
  WC2 . . . . 60 C5
Southampton Ms,
  E16 . . . . 101 E4
Southampton Pl,
  WC1 . . . . 59 F4
Southampton Row,
  WC1 . . . . 59 F3
Southampton St,
  WC2 . . . . 87 F2
Southampton Way,
  SE5 . . . . 171 D1
Southam St, W10 . . . . 51 F2
South Audley St,
  W1 . . . . 85 D3
Southbank Business Cen,
  SW8 . . . . 143 D5

Sch Southbank Int Sch,
  NW3 . . . . 10 B1
  W11 . . . . 80 C3
➤ South
  Bermondsey 150 A2
South Bolton Gdns,
  SW5 . . . . 137 F2
Southborough Rd,
  E9 . . . . 22 C5
Coll South Camden City
  Learning Cen,
  NW1 . . . . 36 C2
Sch South Camden
  Comm Sch, NW1 . . 36 C2
South Carriage Dr,
  SW1 . . . . 112 A1
  SW7 . . . . 111 D2
South Colonnade,
  E14 . . . . 97 D4
Southcombe St,
  W14 . . . . 107 E5
Southcott Ms, NW8 . . 33 E3
South Cres, E16 . . . . . . 70 C2
  WC1 . . . . 58 C4
South Eaton Pl,
  SW1 . . . . 113 D5
South Edwardes Sq,
  W8 . . . . 108 B4
South End, W8 . . . . . . 109 F3
South End Row, W8 . 109 F3
Southerngate Way,
  SE14 . . . . 175 E1
Southern Gro, E3 . . . . 68 A1
Southern Row, W10 . . 51 E2
Southern St, N1 . . . . . 38 A2
Southern Way,
  SE10 . . . . 128 B5
Southerton Rd, W6 . . 106 A4
Southey Ms, E16 . . . . 101 D4
Southey Rd, SW9 . . . . 168 C3
Southgate Gro, N1 . . . 19 D4
Southgate Rd, N1 . . . . 19 D5
SOUTH HACKNEY,
  E9 . . . . 21 F4
SOUTH HAMPSTEAD,
  NW6 . . . . 9 F3
➤ South Hampstead . 10 B4
Sch South Hampstead
  High Sch, NW3 . . . . 10 B2
Southill St, E14 . . . . . . 69 F5
South Island Pl,
  SW9 . . . . 168 B2
SOUTH KENSINGTON,
  SW7 . . . . 138 A1
➤ South
  Kensington 111 D5
SOUTH LAMBETH,
  SW8 . . . . 167 F3
South Lambeth Pl,
  SW8 . . . . 143 F4
South Lambeth Rd,
  SW8 . . . . 143 F5
★ South London Art Gall,
  SE5 . . . . 171 F3

★ Place of interest   ➤ Railway station   H Hospital   ➤ London Underground station

South Molton La,
W1 ....85 E1
South Molton Rd,
E16 ....73 D5
South Molton St,
W1 ....85 E1
Southmoor Way,
E9 ....24 B1
Southolm St, SW11..165 G4
South Par, SW3 .....139 D2
South Pl, EC2 ....63 D3
South Pl Ms, EC2 .....63 D4
DLR South Quay......125 E1
South Quay Plaza,
E14..............125 E1
South Row, SE3.....180 B5
South Sea St,
SE16.............124 A3
South Sq, WC1.......60 C4
South St, W1 ....85 D4
South Tenter St, E1...92 B2
South Ter, SW7 .....111 E5
South Vil, NW1 ......15 D2
Southville, SW8.....167 D3
SOUTHWARK, SE1... 89 F5
⊖ Southwark........89 E5
Southwark Br, EC4 ...90 B4
SE1 ....90 B4
Southwark Br Rd,
SE1 ....117 F3
★ Southwark Cath,
SE1 ....90 C4
Coll Southwark Coll,
Bermondsey Cen,
SE16.............121 E3
Camberwell Cen,
SE5 ....171 E2
Grange Cen, SE1 ...119 F4
Waterloo Cen,
SE1 ....117 E1
Southwark Pk Est,
SE16.............121 F5
Sch Southwark Pk
Prim Sch, SE16 ...121 F4
Southwark Pk Rd,
SE16.............120 B5
Southwark St, SE1...89 F4
Southwater Cl, E14...68 A5
Southwell Gdns,
SW7 ....110 A5
South Wf Rd, W2.....54 C5
Southwick Ms, W2 ...55 D5
Southwick Pl, W2 ....83 E1
Southwick St, W2 ....55 E5
Southwood Smith St,
N1................39 E1
Sovereign Cl, E1......93 F3
Sovereign Cres,
SE16.............95 E3
Sovereign Ms, E2.....42 A2
Spafield St, EC1 ......60 C1
Spa Grn Est, EC1 .....39 D4
Spanby Rd, E3 ....69 D2
Spanish Pl, W1.......57 D5

Sparkford Ho,
SW11 ....163 D3
Spa Rd, SE16 ....120 A4
Sparta St, SE10 .....177 F4
Sch Spa Spec Sch,
SE1 ....148 C1
★ Speaker's Cor,
W2 ....84 B2
Spear Ms, SW5.....137 D1
Speed Ho, EC2 ......62 C3
Speedwell St, SE8 ...176 C2
Speedy Pl, WC1 ......37 E5
Speke Ho, SE5 .....170 B2
Speldhurst Rd, E9 ...22 C4
Spellbrook Wk, N1...18 B5
Spelman St, E1......64 C3
Spence Cl, SE16.....124 A2
★ Spencer Ho,
SW1 ....86 A5
Spencer Ms, SW8....168 A4
W6 ....135 E4
Spencer Pas, E2 .....43 E2
Spencer Pl, N1 ....17 E3
Spencer St, EC1 .....39 E5
Spenser St, SW1 ....114 B3
Spert St, E14 ....95 E2
Spey St, E14 ....70 A4
Spice Quay Hts,
SE1 ....92 B5
Spicer Cl, SW9 ......169 F5
Spindle Cl, SE18.....131 F4
Spindrift Av, E14.....125 E5
Spire Ho, W2 ....82 B2
Spirit Quay, E1.......93 D4
★ Spitalfields City Fm,
E1 ....64 C2
Spital Sq, E1 ....63 F3
Spital St, E1 ....64 C3
Spital Yd, E1 ....63 F3
Spray St, SE18 ......133 F5
Sprimont Pl, SW3 ...140 A2
Springall St, SE15 ...173 F2
Springbank Wk,
NW1 ....15 D3
Springfield La, NW6 . .31 E1
Springfield Rd, E15 ...49 F4
NW8 ....32 A1
Springfield Wk,
NW6 ....31 E1
Spring Gdns, SW1 ....87 D4
Spring Ms, W1 ......56 B3
Spring St, W2........82 C1
Springtide Cl, SE15 ..173 D3
Springvale Est,
W14.............107 E4
Springvale Ter,
W14 ....107 D4
Spring Wk, E1........64 C3
Springwood Cl, E3....46 C3
Spurgeon St, SE1....118 C4
Spur Rd, SE1 ....116 C1
SW1 ....114 A2
Square, The, W6 ....134 B3
Squire Gdns, NW8 ....32 C5

Squirries St, E2 ......43 D4
Stables Way, SE11...144 C2
Stable Way, W10.....78 B1
Stable Yd, SW1 .....114 A1
Stable Yd Rd, SW1...86 A5
Stacey St, WC2.......87 D1
Stackhouse St,
SW3 ....112 A3
Stacy Path, SW5 ....171 E2
Stadium St, SW10...162 B2
Stafford Cl, NW6 .....30 C5
Stafford Ct, W8 .....108 C3
Stafford Pl, SW1 ....114 A3
Stafford Rd, E3.......46 A3
NW6...............30 C4
Staffordshire St,
SE15.............173 D3
Stafford St, W1 ......86 A4
Stafford Ter, W8 ....108 C3
Staff St, EC1 ....41 D5
Stag Pl, SW1.......114 A3
Stainer St, SE1......91 D5
Staining La, EC2......62 B5
Stainsbury St, E2.....44 B3
Stainsby Rd, E14.....68 C5
Stalbridge St, NW1 ...55 F3
Stalham St, SE16....121 F4
Stamford Cotts,
SW10 ....161 F1
Stamford Rd, N1 .....19 F3
Stamford St, SE1 ....88 C5
Stamp Pl, E2.........42 A4
Stanborough Pas,
E8 ....20 A1
Stanbury Rd, SE15 ..173 F4
Standard Ind Est,
E16..............132 B1
Standard Pl, EC2 .....41 F5
Stanfield Rd, E3......45 F3
Stanford Ct, SW6....161 F4
Stanford Pl, SE17....147 E1
Stanford Rd, W8 ....109 F3
Stanford St, SW1 ....142 C1
Stanhope Cl, SE16...123 F3
Stanhope Gdns,
SW7 ....110 B5
Stanhope Gate, W1...85 D4
Stanhope Ms E,
SW7 ....110 B5
Stanhope Ms S,
SW7 ....138 B1
Stanhope Ms W,
SW7 ....110 B5
Stanhope Pl, W2 .....84 A1
Stanhope Row, W1...85 E5
Stanhope St, NW1....36 A5
Stanhope Ter, W2 ....83 D2
Stanier Cl, W14 .....136 B3
Stanlake Ms, W12....78 A5
Stanlake Vil, W12 ....78 A5

Stanley Cl, SW8 . . . . . 144 A5
Stanley Cres, W11 . . . . 80 A2
Stanley Gdns, W11 . . . . 80 A2
Stanley Gdns Ms,
  W11 . . . . 80 B2
Stanley Rd, E15 . . . . . 48 C1
Stanley St, SE8 . . . . . 176 B2
Stanliff Ho, E14 . . . . . 125 D3
Stanmer St, SW11 . . . 163 F4
Stanmore St, N1 . . . . . 16 A5
Stannard Ms, E8 . . . . . 20 C1
Stannard Rd, E8 . . . . . 20 C1
Stannary Pl, SE11 . . . 145 D3
Stannary St, SE11 . . . 145 D4
Stansbury Sq, W10 . . . 29 F4
Stansfeld Rd, E6 . . . . . 75 D4
Stanswood Gdns,
  SE5 . . . . 171 F2
Stanton Ho, SE16 . . . 124 A1
Stanway Ct, N1 . . . . . . 41 F3
Stanway St, N1 . . . . . . 41 F2
Stanwick Rd, W14 . . . 136 A1
Stanworth St, SE1 . . . 120 A2
Staple Inn, WC1 . . . . . 60 C4
Staple Inn Bldgs,
  WC1 . . . . 60 C4
Staples Cl, SE16 . . . . . 95 E4
Staple St, SE1 . . . . . . 119 D2
Star All, EC3 . . . . 91 F2
Starboard Way,
  E14 . . . . 125 D3
Starcross St, NW1 . . . . 36 B5
Star La, E16 . . . . 71 E2
Star Pl, E1 . . . . 92 B3
Sch Star Prim Sch,
  E16 . . . . 71 F2
Star Rd, W14 . . . . 136 A4
Star St, E16 . . . . 72 B3
  W2 . . . . 55 D5
Star Yd, WC2 . . . . 60 C5
Station App, SE1 . . . . . 88 B5
Station Ct, SW6 . . . . . 162 A4
Station Cres, SE3 . . . . 156 C3
Station Par, NW2 . . . . . 6 B1
Station Pas, SE15 . . . 174 A3
Station Path, E8 . . . . . 21 F1
Station St, E15 . . . . . . 26 C3
  E16 . . . . 105 E5
Station Ter, NW10 . . . . 28 C3
  SE5 . . . . 170 B3
Staunton St, SE8 . . . . 152 B4
★ Stave Hill Ecological Pk,
  SE16 . . . . 123 E1
Staveley Cl, SE15 . . . 173 F3
Staverton Rd, NW2 . . . 6 A3
Stave Yd Rd, SE16 . . . . 95 E5
Stayner's Rd, E1 . . . . . 66 C1
Stead St, SE17 . . . . . . 146 C1
Stean St, E8 . . . . 20 A5
Stebbing Ho, W11 . . . . 79 D4

Stebondale St, E14 . . 154 B1
Sch Stebon Prim Sch,
  E14 . . . . 68 C4
Stedham Pl, WC1 . . . . . 59 E5
Steedman St, SE17 . . 146 A1
Steeles Ms N, NW3 . . . 12 B2
Steeles Ms S, NW3 . . . 12 B2
Steeles Rd, NW3 . . . . . 12 A2
Steel's La, E1 . . . . 94 B1
Steeple Wk, N1 . . . . . . 18 B5
Steers Way, SE16 . . . 123 F2
Stephan Cl, E8 . . . . . . 21 D5
Stephendale Rd,
  SW6 . . . . 161 F5
Sch Stephen Hawking Sch,
  E14 . . . . 95 F1
Stephen Ms, W1 . . . . . 58 C4
Stephenson St, E16 . . . 71 E2
Stephenson Way,
  NW1 . . . . 58 B1
Stephen's Rd, E15 . . . . 49 F1
Stephen St, W1 . . . . . . 58 C4
STEPNEY, E1 . . . . 66 C4
Stepney Causeway,
  E1 . . . . 95 D1
◆ Stepney Green 66 C2
Stepney Grn, E1 . . . . . 66 B3
Sch Stepney Greencoat C of E
  Prim Sch, E14 . . . . . 68 A5
Sch Stepney Grn Sch,
  E1 . . . . 67 D4
Stepney High St, E1 . . 67 D4
Stepney Way, E1 . . . . . 65 E4
Sterling Gdns, SE14 . 151 E5
Sterling St, SW7 . . . . 111 F3
Sterndale Rd, W14 . . 106 C4
Sterne St, W12 . . . . . 106 C1
Sterry St, SE1 . . . . . . 118 C2
Stevedore St, E1 . . . . . 93 E4
Stevenage Rd, SW6 . . 158 C2
Stevens Av, E9 . . . . . . 22 B1
Stevenson Cres,
  SE16 . . . . 149 D2
Stevens St, SE1 . . . . . 119 F3
Steward St, E1 . . . . . . 63 F4
Sch Stewart Headlam
  Prim Sch, E1 . . . . . . 65 E1
Stewart's Gro, SW3 . . 139 D2
Stewart's Rd, SW8 . . 166 A2
Stewart St, E14 . . . . . 126 B2
Stew La, EC4 . . . . 90 A2
Stillington St, SW1 . . 114 B5
★ Stock Exchange,
  EC4 . . . . 61 F5
Stockholm Ho, E1 . . . . 93 E2
Stockholm Rd,
  SE16 . . . . 150 B3
Stockholm Way, E1 . . . 92 C4
Stocks Pl, E14 . . . . . . 96 B2
◆ Stockwell 167 F5
Stockwell Gdns,
  SW9 . . . . 168 A4
Stockwell Gdns Est,
  SW9 . . . . 168 A5

Stockwell Pk Cres,
  SW9 . . . . 168 B5
Stockwell Pk Rd,
  SW9 . . . . 168 A4
Sch Stockwell Pk SM Sch,
  SW9 . . . . 168 A4
Stockwell Rd, SW9 . . 168 A5
Stockwell St, SE10 . . 154 B5
Stockwell Ter, SW9 . . 168 A4
Stokenchurch St,
  SW6 . . . . 161 E4
Stokes Rd, E6 . . . . 75 E2
Stonebridge Common,
  E8 . . . . 20 A4
Stone Bldgs, WC2 . . . . 60 B4
Stonechat Sq, E6 . . . . 75 F3
Stonecutter St, EC4 . . 61 E5
Stonefield St, N1 . . . . 17 D5
Stone Hall Gdns,
  W8 . . . . 109 E4
Stone Hall Pl, W8 . . . 109 E4
Stone Ho Ct, EC3 . . . . 63 E5
Stone Lake Retail Pk,
  SE7 . . . . 157 F1
Stoneleigh Ms, E3 . . . 45 F3
Stoneleigh Pl, W11 . . . 79 D3
Stoneleigh St, W11 . . . 79 D2
Stones End St, SE1 . . 118 A2
Stonewall, E6 . . . . 77 D4
Stoneyard La, E14 . . . 97 E3
Stoney La, E1 . . . . 63 F5
Stoney St, SE1 . . . . . . 90 C4
Stonor Rd, W14 . . . . . 136 A1
Stopes St, SE15 . . . . . 172 B2
Stopford Rd, SE17 . . . 145 F3
Store Rd, E16 . . . . 132 C1
Storers Quay, E14 . . . 154 C1
Store St, WC1 . . . . 58 C4
Sch Storey Prim Sch,
  E16 . . . . 105 E5
Storey's Gate, SW1 . . 115 D2
Storey St, E16 . . . . . . 105 D5
Storks Rd, SE16 . . . . . 121 D4
Story St, N1 . . . . 16 A4
Stothard St, E1 . . . . . . 66 A1
Stoughton Cl, SE11 . . 144 B1
Stourcliffe St, W1 . . . . 84 A1
Stour Rd, E3 . . . . 24 C4
Stowage, SE8 . . . . 153 D5
Strafford St, E14 . . . . 124 C1
Strahan Rd, E3 . . . . . . 45 F4
Straightsmouth,
  SE10 . . . . 178 A1
Strait Rd, E6 . . . . 104 B2
STRAND, WC2 . . . . 87 E3
Strand, WC2 . . . . 87 E3
Strand La, WC2 . . . . . . 88 B2
Strangways Ter,
  W14 . . . . 108 A4
Stranraer Way, N1 . . . 16 A4
Strasburg Rd,
  SW11 . . . . 165 D4
STRATFORD, E15 . . . . . 26 B2
⇌ Stratford 26 B2

➤ Stratford 26 B3
🚈 Stratford 26 B3
Stratford Av, W8 . . . . 109 D4
Stratford Cen, The,
   E15 . . . . 27 D3
⇌ Stratford
   International. 26 A2
Stratford Pl, W1 . . . . . . 85 E1
Stratford Rd, W8 . . . . 109 D5
Stratford Vil, NW1. . . . 14 B3
Strathearn Pl, W2 . . . . 83 D2
Stratheden Rd, SE3. . 180 C3
Strathmore Gdns,
   W8 . . . . 81 D4
Strathnairn St,
   SE1 . . . . 149 D1
Strathray Gdns,
   NW3 . . . . 11 E2
Strattondale St,
   E14 . . . . 126 A3
Stratton St, W1 . . . . . . 85 F4
Streatham St, WC1 . . . 59 D5
Streatley Rd, NW6 . . . . . 8 A4
Streimer Rd, E15 . . . . . 48 B2
Stretton Mans, SE8 . . 153 D3
Strickland St, SE8 . . . 177 D4
Strode Rd, SW6 . . . . . 159 D1
Stroudley Wk, E3. . . . 47 E4
Strouts Pl, E2 . . . . 42 A4
Strutton Grd, SW1 . . . 114 C3
Strype St, E1. . . . . 64 A4
Stuart Rd, NW6 . . . . . . 30 C5
Stuart Twr, W9 . . . . . . 32 B5
Stubbs Dr, SE16. . . . . 149 E2
Stubbs Pt, E13 . . . . 73 E2
Stucley Pl, NW1 . . . . . . 13 F4
Studd St, N1. . . . . 17 E5
Studholme St,
   SE15 . . . . 173 E2
Studio Pl, SW1 . . . . . . 112 B2
Studland, SE17 . . . . . 146 C2
Studley Est, SW4 . . . . 167 F4
Studley Rd, SW4 . . . . 167 E4
Stukeley St, WC2 . . . . 59 F5
Sturgeon Rd, SE17 . . 146 A3
Sturge St, SE1 . . . . . . 118 A1
Sturry St, E14. . . . . 97 F1
Sturt St, N1 . . . . 40 B3
Stutfield St, E1. . . . . . . 93 D1
Sudbury, E6 . . . . 77 D5
Sudeley St, N1 . . . . 39 F3
Sudrey St, SE1 . . . . . . 118 A2
Suffolk La, EC4 . . . . . . 90 C2
Suffolk Pl, SW1. . . . . . . 87 D4
Suffolk St, SW1 . . . . . . 87 D4
Sugar Ho La, E15 . . . . . 48 A2
Sugar Loaf Wk, E2 . . . . 44 A4
Sugar Quay Wk, EC3. . 91 F3
Sulgrave Gdns, W6 . . 106 B2
Sulgrave Rd, W6 . . . . 106 B2
Sullivan Av, E16. . . . . . 74 C3
Sullivan Rd, SE11 . . . 117 D5
Sultan St, SE5 . . . . . . 170 A1
Sumatra Rd, NW6 . . . . . 9 D1

Summercourt Rd,
   E1 . . . . 66 B5
Summerfield Av,
   NW6 . . . . 29 F2
Summer St, EC1 . . . . . . 60 C2
Summit Ct, NW2 . . . . . . 7 F1
Sumner Av, SE15 . . . . 172 B3
Sumner Pl, SW7 . . . . . 139 D1
Sumner Pl Ms,
   SW7 . . . . 139 D1
Sumner Rd, SE15 . . . 148 B5
Sumner St, SE1 . . . . . . 89 F4
Sumpter Cl, NW3 . . . . . 10 B2
Sunbeam Cres,
   W10 . . . . 50 B2
Sunbury La, SW11. . . 163 D3
Sunbury St, SE18. . . . 132 B4
Sun Ct, EC3. . . . . 91 D1
Sunderland Ter, W2. . . 53 E5
Sundra Wk, E1 . . . . 66 C2
Sunfields Pl, SE3 . . . . 181 E1
Sun La, SE3. . . . . 181 F2
Sunlight Sq, E2. . . . . . . 43 F5
Sunningdale Cl,
   SE16. . . . . 149 E3
Sunningdale Gdns,
   W8 . . . . 109 D4
Sun Pas, SE16 . . . . . . 120 C3
Sun Rd, W14 . . . . 136 A3
Sun St, EC2. . . . . 63 E4
Sun Wk, E1 . . . . 92 C3
Sunwell Cl, SE15 . . . . 173 E4
Surma Cl, E1. . . . . 65 D2
Surrendale Pl, W9 . . . . 53 D2
Surrey Canal Rd,
   SE14. . . . . 150 B4
   SE15. . . . . 150 B4
★ Surrey Docks City Fm,
   SE16. . . . . 124 A2
Surrey Gro, SE17 . . . . 147 E3
Surrey La, SW11 . . . . 163 E4
Surrey La Est,
   SW11 . . . . 163 E3
Surrey Lo, SE1 . . . . . . 116 C4
➤ Surrey Quays 122 C5
Surrey Quays Retail Cen,
   SE16. . . . . 122 C4
Surrey Quays Rd,
   SE16. . . . . 122 B3
Surrey Row, SE1 . . . . 117 E1
Surrey Sq, SE17 . . . . 147 E2
🏫 Surrey Sq Inf Sch,
   SE17. . . . . 147 E2
🏫 Surrey Sq Jun Sch,
   SE17. . . . . 147 E2
Surrey St, WC2. . . . . . . 88 B2
Surrey Ter, SE17 . . . . 147 F2
Surrey Water Rd,
   SE16. . . . . 95 D5
Susannah St, E14 . . . . 98 A1
Sussex Gdns, W2 . . . . . 82 C2
🏫 Sussex Ho Prep Sch,
   SW1 . . . . 112 A5
Sussex Ms E, W2 . . . . . 83 D1

Sussex Ms W, W2 . . . . 83 D2
Sussex Pl, NW1 . . . . . . 34 A5
   W2 . . . . 83 D1
   W6 . . . . 134 A2
Sussex Sq, W2 . . . . 83 D2
Sussex St, SW1 . . . . . 141 F3
Sutherland Av, W9 . . . 32 A5
Sutherland Pl, W2 . . . . 52 C5
Sutherland Row,
   SW1 . . . . 141 F2
Sutherland Sq,
   SE17. . . . . 146 A3
Sutherland St,
   SW1 . . . . 141 E2
Sutherland Wk,
   SE17. . . . . 146 B3
Sutterton St, N7 . . . . . 16 A2
Sutton Est, SW3 . . . . 139 F2
   W10 . . . . 50 A3
Sutton Est, The, N1 . . 17 E3
Sutton La, EC1 . . . . 61 F2
Sutton Rd, E13 . . . . . . 72 B2
Sutton Row, W1 . . . . . 59 D5
Sutton St, E1 . . . . 94 A2
Sutton's Way, EC1 . . . . 62 B2
Sutton Wk, SE1 . . . . . . 88 B5
Sutton Way, W10 . . . . 50 A2
Swain St, NW8. . . . . . . 55 E1
Swallow Cl, SE14 . . . . 174 B4
Swallowfield Rd,
   SE7 . . . . 157 F3
Swallow Pl, W1 . . . . . . 85 F1
Swallow St, E6 . . . . . . 75 F4
   W1 . . . . 86 B3
Swan App, E6. . . . . 75 E4
Swan Ct, SW3 . . . . . . 139 F3
Swanfield St, E2. . . . . . 42 A5
Swan La, EC4 . . . . 90 C3
🏫 Swanley Sec Sch,
   E1 . . . . 65 E2
Swan Mead, SE1 . . . . 119 E4
Swan Rd, SE16. . . . . . 122 B1
   SE18. . . . . 131 D4
Swanscombe Rd,
   W11 . . . . 79 D5
Swansea Ct, E16. . . . . 105 F5
Swan St, SE1 . . . . 118 B3
Swan Wk, SW3 . . . . . 140 A4
Swan Yd, N1. . . . . 17 E2
Swaton Rd, E3 . . . . 69 D2
Swedenborg Gdns,
   E1 . . . . 93 D2
Sweden Gate,
   SE16. . . . . 123 E4
Sweeney Cres, SE1 . . 120 B2
Swift St, SW6. . . . . . . 159 F3
Swinbrook Rd, W10 . . 51 F3
Swinton Pl, WC1 . . . . . 38 A4
Swinton St, WC1 . . . . . 38 A4
➤ Swiss Cottage 10 C3

🅂🅲🅷 Swiss Cottage Sch,
  NW8 . . . . 11 D4
Swiss Ct, W1 . . . . 87 D3
Swiss Ter, NW6 . . . . . . 10 C3
Switch Ho, E14 . . . . . . 99 D2
Sybil Phoenix Cl,
  SE8 . . . . 151 D2
Sycamore Av, E3 . . . . . 24 A5
Sycamore Cl, E16 . . . . . 71 E2
Sycamore St, EC1 . . . . 62 A2
Sycamore Wk, W10 . . 51 E1
Sydney Cl, SW3 . . . . 139 D1
Sydney Ms, SW3 . . . . 139 D1
Sydney Pl, SW7 . . . . 139 D1
Sydney St, SW3 . . . . 139 E2
Sylvan Gro, SE15 . . . . 173 F1
Sylvester Path, E8 . . . . 21 F1
Sylvester Rd, E8 . . . . . 21 F1
🅂🅲🅷 Sylvia Young Thea Sch,
  NW1 . . . . 55 F2
Symes Ms, NW1 . . . . . . 36 A2
Symister Ms, N1 . . . . 41 E5
Symons St, SW3 . . . . 140 B1
Symphony Ms, W10 . . 29 F4
🆄🅽🅸 Syracuse Uni,
  W11 . . . . 80 A3

T

Tabard Gdn Est,
  SE1 . . . . 119 D2
Tabard St, SE1 . . . . . . 118 C2
Tabernacle Av, E13 . . . 72 C2
Tabernacle St, EC2 . . . 63 D2
Tachbrook Est, SW1 . 143 D3
Tachbrook Ms, SW1 . . 114 A5
Tachbrook St, SW1 . . 142 B1
Tadema Ho, NW8 . . . . 55 D2
Tadema Rd, SW10 . . 162 B3
Tadmor St, W12 . . . . . . 78 C5
Taeping St, E14 . . . . . 125 E5
Taft Way, E3 . . . . 47 F4
Tailworth St, E1 . . . . . . 64 C4
Talacre Rd, NW5 . . . . . 13 D1
Talbot Ct, EC3 . . . . . . 91 D2
Talbot Ho, E14 . . . . 69 E5
Talbot Pl, SE3 . . . . 179 E5
Talbot Rd, W2 . . . . 53 D5
  W11 . . . . 52 B5
Talbot Sq, W2 . . . . 83 D1
Talbot Wk, W11 . . . . . . 79 E1
Talbot Yd, SE1 . . . . 90 C5
Talfourd Pl, SE15 . . . . 172 A4
Talfourd Rd, SE15 . . . 172 A4
Talgarth Rd, W6 . . . . 134 B2
  W14 . . . . 135 D2
Tallis Cl, E16 . . . . 101 E1
Tallis Gro, SE7 . . . . . . 157 F4

Tallis St, EC4 . . . . 89 D2
Talwin St, E3 . . . . 47 F5
Tamar Cl, E3 . . . . 46 B1
Tamar Yd, E1 . . . . 93 D4
Tamar St, SE7 . . . . . . 131 E5
Tamworth St,
  SW6 . . . . 136 C4
Tankerton St, WC1 . . . 37 F5
Tanners Hill, SE8 . . . . 176 B4
Tanners Ms, SE8 . . . . 176 B4
Tanner St, SE1 . . . . . . 119 F2
Tanswell Est, SE1 . . . 117 D2
Tanswell St, SE1 . . . . 116 C2
Tansy Cl, E6 . . . . 105 D1
Tant Av, E16 . . . . 72 A5
Taplow, NW3 . . . . 11 D4
  SE17 . . . . 147 E3
Taplow St, N1 . . . . 40 B3
Tapp St, E1 . . . . 65 E1
Taransay Wk, N1 . . . . . 18 C1
Tarbert Wk, E1 . . . . 94 A2
Tariff Cres, SE8 . . . . . 124 A5
Tarling Rd, E16 . . . . . 100 B1
Tarling St, E1 . . . . 94 A1
Tarling St Est, E1 . . . . . 94 A1
Tarn St, SE1 . . . . 118 A4
Tarragon Cl, SE14 . . . 175 E1
Tarrant Pl, W1 . . . . 56 A4
Tarver Rd, SE17 . . . . . 145 F3
Tarves Way, SE10 . . . 177 F1
Tasman Wk, E16 . . . . 102 C1
Tasso Rd, W6 . . . . 135 E4
Tate & Lyle Jetty,
  E16 . . . . 131 E2
★ Tate Britain,
  SW1 . . . . 143 E1
★ Tate Modern,
  SE1 . . . . 89 F4
Tate Rd, E16 . . . . 104 A5
Tatham Pl, NW8 . . . . . 33 D2
Tatum St, SE17 . . . . . 147 D1
Taunton Ms, NW1 . . . . 56 A2
Taunton Pl, NW1 . . . . . 56 A1
Taverners Cl, W11 . . . 79 E5
Tavern La, SW9 . . . . . 169 D5
Tavistock Cres, W11 . . 52 B4
Tavistock Pl, WC1 . . . . 59 D1
Tavistock Rd, W11 . . . 52 A5
Tavistock Sq, WC1 . . . 59 D1
Tavistock St, WC2 . . . . 87 F2
Tavistock Twr,
  SE16 . . . . 123 E4
Taviton St, WC1 . . . . . . 58 C1
Tavy Cl, SE11 . . . . 145 D2
Tawny Way, SE16 . . . . 123 D5
Tayburn Cl, E14 . . . . . . 70 A3
Taylor Cl, SE8 . . . . 152 A4
Taylors Bldgs, SE18 . . 133 F5
Tayport Cl, N1 . . . . 16 A4
Teak Cl, SE16 . . . . 95 F5
Teal Cl, E16 . . . . 74 C4
Teale St, E2 . . . . 43 D2
Teal St, SE10 . . . . 128 B3
Teasel Way, E15 . . . . . 49 E4

Tedworth Gdns,
  SW3 . . . . 140 A3
Tedworth Sq,
  SW3 . . . . 140 A3
Teesdale Cl, E2 . . . . 43 D3
Teesdale St, E2 . . . . 43 E3
Teesdale Yd, E2 . . . . . . 43 D2
★ Telecom Twr, W1 . . 58 A3
Telegraph Pl, E14 . . . 125 E5
Telegraph St, EC2 . . . 62 C5
Telephone Pl, SW6 . . 136 B4
Telford Rd, W10 . . . . . . 51 E3
Telfords Yd, E1 . . . . 93 D3
Telford Ter, SW1 . . . . 142 A4
Temeraire St, SE16 . . 122 B2
Templar Ho, NW2 . . . . . 8 A1
Templar St, SE5 . . . . . 169 F4
★ Temple, The, EC4 . . 88 C2
⊖ Temple 88 B2
Temple Av, EC4 . . . . . . 89 D2
★ Temple Bar, EC4 . . 88 C1
Templecombe Rd,
  E9 . . . . 22 A5
Temple La, EC4 . . . . . . 89 D1
★ Temple of Mithras, EC4
  (Queen Victoria St) . 90 C1
Temple Pl, WC2 . . . . . . 88 B2
Temple St, E2 . . . . 43 E3
Templeton Pl, SW5 . . 137 D1
Temple W Ms,
  SE11 . . . . 117 E4
Temple Yd, E2 . . . . 43 E3
Tench St, E1 . . . . 93 E5
Tenda Rd, SE16 . . . . . 149 E1
Tenison Ct, W1 . . . . . . 86 A2
Tenison Way, SE1 . . . . 88 C5
Tenniel Cl, W2 . . . . 82 A1
Tennis St, SE1 . . . . . . 118 C1
Tennyson Rd, E15 . . . . 27 E3
  NW6 . . . . 8 A5
Tenterden St, W1 . . . . 85 F1
Tenter Grd, E1 . . . . 64 A4
Tenter Pas, E1 . . . . 92 B1
Tent St, E1 . . . . 65 E1
Teredo St, SE16 . . . . . 123 D4
Terling Wk, N1 . . . . 18 A5
Terminus Pl, SW1 . . . 113 F4
Terrace, The, NW6 . . . . 8 C5
Terrace Rd, E9 . . . . 22 B3
Terretts Pl, N1 . . . . 17 E4
Testerton Wk, W11 . . . 79 D2
Tetbury Pl, N1 . . . . 39 E1
Tetcott Rd, SW10 . . . 162 A1
Teversham La,
  SW8 . . . . 167 F3
Teviot St, E14 . . . . 70 A3
Thackeray St, W8 . . . 109 F2
Thalia Cl, SE10 . . . . . 155 D4
Thame Rd, SE16 . . . . 123 D1
Thames Av, SW10 . . . 162 B3
Thames Circle, E14 . . 125 D5
★ Thames Flood Barrier &
  Visitors Cen,
  SE18 . . . . 130 B2

★ Thames Ho,
SW1 . . . . 115 E5
Thameside Ind Est,
E16 . . . . 131 E1
Thames Pt, SW6 . . . . 162 B4
Thames Quay,
SW10 . . . . 162 B4
Thames Rd, E16 . . . . 102 C5
Thames St, SE10 . . . . 153 F4
Thames Wf, E16 . . . . 100 A4
Thanet St, WC1 . . . . . . 37 E5
Thavies Inn, EC1 . . . . . 61 D5
Thaxted Ct, N1 . . . . . . 40 C3
Thaxton Rd, W14 . . 136 B4
Thayer St, W1 . . . . 57 D4
★ Theatre Mus,
WC2 (Russell St) . . . 87 F2
★ Theatre Royal,
WC2 . . . . 87 F1
Theatre Sq, E15 . . . . . . 27 D2
Theberton St, N1 . . . . . 17 D5
Theed St, SE1 . . . . 88 C5
Theobald's Rd, WC1 . . 60 A3
Theobald St, SE1 . . . . 118 C4
Thermopylae Gate,
E14 . . . . 153 F1
Theseus Wk, N1 . . . . . . 39 F3
Thessaly Rd, SW8 . . 166 A2
Third Av, W10 . . . . 51 F1
Thirleby Rd, SW1 . . . . 114 B4
Thistle Gro, SW10 . . . 138 B2
Sch Thomas Buxton Inf &
Jun Sch, E1 . . . . 65 D2
Thomas Cribb Ms,
E6 . . . . 76 B5
Thomas Darby Ct,
W11 . . . . 79 E1
Thomas Doyle St,
SE1 . . . . 117 E3
Sch Thomas Fairchild JMI
Sch, N1 . . . . 40 B2
Sch Thomas Jones
Prim Sch, W11 . . . . 79 E1
Thomas More St, E1 . . 92 C3
Thomas Pl, W8 . . . . . . 109 E4
Thomas Rd, E14 . . . . . . 68 B5
Sch Thomas's Prep Sch,
Battersea, SW11 . . 163 D4
Kensington, W8 . . 109 F3
Thomas St, SE18 . . . . 133 D5
Thompson's Av, SE5 . 170 A1
Thorburn Sq, SE1 . . . 148 C1
Thoresby St, N1 . . . . . . 40 B4
Thorncroft St, SW8 . . 167 E2
Thorndike Cl, SW10 . 162 A1
Thorndike Rd, N1 . . . . 18 B2
Thorndike St, SW1 . . 142 C1
Thorne Cl, E16 . . . . . . 72 C5
Thorne Rd, SW8 . . . . 167 E2
Thorne St, E16 . . . . . . 72 B5
Thorney Cres,
SW11 . . . . 163 D2
Thorney St, SW1 . . . . 115 E5
Thorngate Rd, W9 . . . 53 D1

Thornham St, SE10 . . 153 F5
Thornhaugh Ms,
WC1 . . . . 59 D2
Thornhaugh St,
WC1 . . . . 59 D3
Thornhill Br Wf, N1 . . . 38 A1
Thornhill Cres, N1 . . . . 16 A4
Thornhill Gro, N1 . . . . . 16 B4
Sch Thornhill Prim Sch,
N1 . . . . 16 C4
Thornhill Rd, N1 . . . . . 16 C3
Thornhill Sq, N1 . . . . . . 16 B4
Thornley Pl, SE10 . . . . 155 E3
Thornton Pl, W1 . . . . . . 56 B3
Thornton St, SW9 . . . 168 C5
Thornville St, SE8 . . . 176 C4
Thorparch Rd, SW8 . . 167 D3
Thorpe Cl, W10 . . . . . . 51 F5
Thoydon Rd, E3 . . . . . . 45 E3
Thrale St, SE1 . . . . 90 B5
Thrasher Cl, E8 . . . . 20 A5
Thrawl St, E1 . . . . 64 B4
Threadneedle St,
EC2 . . . . 91 D1
Three Barrels Wk,
EC4 . . . . 90 B2
Three Colts Cor, E2 . . . 64 C1
Three Colts La, E2 . . . . 65 E1
Three Colt St, E14 . . . . 96 B1
Three Cups Yd, WC1 . . 60 B4
Three Kings Yd, W1 . . . 85 E2
Three Mill La, E3 . . . . . 48 A4
Three Oak La, SE1 . . . 120 A1
Three Quays Wk,
EC3 . . . . 91 F3
Threshers Pl, W11 . . . . 79 E2
Throckmorten Rd,
E16 . . . . 101 F1
Throgmorton Av,
EC2 . . . . 63 D5
Throgmorton St,
EC2 . . . . 63 D5
Thrush St, SE17 . . . . . 146 A2
Thurland Rd, SE16 . . 120 C3
Thurloe Cl, SW7 . . . . . 111 E5
Thurloe Pl, SW7 . . . . . 111 D5
Thurloe Pl Ms, SW7 . . 111 D5
Thurloe Sq, SW7 . . . . 111 E5
Thurloe St, SW7 . . . . . 111 D5
Thurlow St, SE17 . . . . 147 D2
Thurtle Rd, E2 . . . . 42 B1
Tibbatts Rd, E3 . . . . . . 69 E1
Tibberton Sq, N1 . . . . . 18 A4
Tiber Gdns, N1 . . . . 37 F1
Tidal Basin Rd, E16 . . 100 B3
Sch Tidemill Prim Sch,
SE8 . . . . 177 D2
Tideway Ind Est,
SW8 . . . . 142 B5
Tidey St, E3 . . . . 69 D3
Tidworth Rd, E3 . . . . . . 68 C1
Tilbury Cl, SE15 . . . . . 172 B1
Tile Yd, E14 . . . . 96 B1
Tileyard Rd, N7 . . . . . . 15 E3

Tiller Rd, E14 . . . . 124 C3
Tillett Sq, SE16 . . . . . 123 F2
Tillett Way, E2 . . . . 42 C4
Tillman St, E1 . . . . 93 F1
Tilloch St, N1 . . . . 16 A4
Tilney Ct, EC1 . . . . 62 B1
Tilney Gdns, N1 . . . . . . 19 D2
Tilney St, W1 . . . . 85 D4
Tilson Cl, SE5 . . . . 171 E1
Tilton St, SW6 . . . . . . 136 A5
Timberland Cl,
SE15 . . . . 172 C2
Timberland Rd, E1 . . . . 93 F1
Timber Pond Rd,
SE16 . . . . 95 D5
Timber St, EC1 . . . . 62 A1
Timbrell Pl, SE16 . . . . . 96 A5
Timothy Rd, E3 . . . . . . 68 A4
Tindal St, SW9 . . . . . . 169 E3
Tinsley Rd, E1 . . . . 66 B3
Tinto Rd, E16 . . . . 73 D2
Tinworth St, SE11 . . . 143 F2
Tisdall Pl, SE17 . . . . . 147 D1
Titchborne Row, W2 . . 83 F1
Titchfield Rd, NW8 . . . 33 F1
Tite St, SW3 . . . . 140 A3
Tiverton Rd, NW10 . . . 28 C1
Tiverton St, SE1 . . . . . 118 A4
Tivoli Ct, SE16 . . . . . . 124 A1
Tivoli Gdns, SE18 . . . . 131 E5
Tobacco Dock, E1 . . . . 93 E3
Tobacco Quay, E1 . . . . 93 E3
Tobago St, E14 . . . . . . 124 C1
Tobin Cl, NW3 . . . . 11 F3
Toby La, E1 . . . . 67 E2
Tokenhouse Yd, EC2 . . 62 C5
Tolhurst Dr, W10 . . . . . 29 F4
Tollbridge Cl, W10 . . . 51 F1
Tollet St, E1 . . . . 66 C1
Tollgate Gdns, NW6 . . 31 E2
Sch Tollgate Prim Sch,
E13 . . . . 74 B1
Tollgate Rd, E6 . . . . 74 C4
E16 . . . . 74 A3
Tolmers Sq, NW1 . . . . . 58 B1
Tolpuddle St, N1 . . . . . 38 C2
Tom Jenkinson Rd,
E16 . . . . 101 D4
Tomlins Gro, E3 . . . . . . 47 D4
Tomlinson Cl, E2 . . . . . 42 B5
Tomlins Ter, E14 . . . . . 67 F5
Tom Nolan Cl, E15 . . . . 49 F3
Tompion St, EC1 . . . . . 39 E5
Tom Smith Cl, SE10 . 155 E4
Tonbridge St, WC1 . . . 37 E4
Tony Cannell Ms, E3 . . 46 A5
Took's Ct, EC4 . . . . 60 C5
Tooley St, SE1 . . . . 91 D4
Topham St, EC1 . . . . . . 60 C1
Topmast Pt, E14 . . . . 124 C2

Torbay Rd, NW6 . . . . 8 A4
Torbay St, NW1 . . . . . . 13 F4
Tor Gdns, W8 . . . . 108 C1
Torquay St, W2 . . . . . . 53 E4
Torrens Sq, E15 . . . . . . 27 F1
Torrens St, EC1 . . . . . . 39 D3
Torrey Dr, SW9 . . . . . . 169 D5
Sch Torriano Inf Sch,
    NW5 . . . . 14 C1
Torrington Pl, E1 . . . . 93 D4
    WC1 . . . . 58 B3
Torrington Sq, WC1 . . . 59 D2
Tothill St, SW1 . . . . . . 114 C2
Tottan Ter, E1 . . . . 67 D5
⊖ Tottenham Court
    Road 58 C5
Tottenham Ct Rd,
    W1 . . . . 58 B2
Tottenham Ms, W1 . . 58 B3
Tottenham Rd, N1 . . . . 19 E2
Tottenham St, W1 . . . 58 B4
Toulmin St, SE1 . . . . . 118 A2
Toulon St, SE5 . . . . . . 170 A1
Tournay Rd, SW6 . . . . 160 B1
Toussaint Wk,
    SE16 . . . . 121 D3
Tovy Ho, SE1 . . . . 148 C3
Towcester Rd, E3 . . . . 69 F2
Tower 42, EC2 . . . . 63 E5
Tower Br, E1 . . . . 92 A5
    SE1 . . . . 92 A5
Tower Br App, E1 . . . . 92 A4
★ Tower Br Exhib,
    SE1 . . . . 92 A5
Tower Br Piazza, SE1 . . 92 A5
Sch Tower Br Prim Sch,
    SE1 . . . . 120 A1
Tower Br Rd, SE1 . . . . 119 E4
Tower Br Wf, E1 . . . . . . 92 D5
Tower Ct, WC2 . . . . 87 E1
DLR Tower Gateway 92 B2
Coll Tower Hamlets Coll,
    Arbour Sq Cen, E1 . . 66 C5
    Bethnal Grn Cen,
    E2 . . . . 42 C5
    East India Dock Rd,
    E14 . . . . 97 F1
    Poplar Cen, E14 . . . 97 E3
⊖ Tower Hill 92 A2
Tower Hill, EC3 . . . . 92 A3
★ Tower Millennium
    Pier, EC3 . . . . 91 F4
Tower Mill Rd,
    SE15 . . . . 147 E5
★ Tower of London,
    EC3 . . . . 92 A3
Tower Pl, EC3 . . . . 91 F3
Tower Royal, EC4 . . . . . 90 B2
Tower St, WC2 . . . . 87 D1
Towing Path Wk, N1 . . 37 E2

Townley St, SE17 . . . . 146 C2
Sch Townsend Prim Sch,
    SE17 . . . . 119 E5
Townsend St, SE17 . . 147 D1
Townshend Est,
    NW8 . . . . 33 E2
Townshend Rd,
    NW8 . . . . 33 E1
★ Toynbee Hall,
    E1 . . . . 64 B4
Toynbee St, E1 . . . . 64 A4
Trader Rd, E6 . . . . 105 E1
Tradescant Rd,
    SW8 . . . . 167 F2
Trafalgar Av, SE15 . . 148 B3
Trafalgar Cl, SE16 . . . 123 E5
Trafalgar Ct, E1 . . . . . . 94 B3
Trafalgar Gdns, E1 . . . 67 D3
    W8 . . . . 109 F3
Trafalgar Gro, SE10 . . 155 D4
Trafalgar Ms, E9 . . . . . 24 A1
Trafalgar Rd, SE10 . . 155 D4
Trafalgar Sq, SW1 . . . . 87 D4
    WC2 . . . . 87 D4
Trafalgar St, SE17 . . . 146 C2
Trafalgar Way, E14 . . . 98 A4
Trahorn Cl, E1 . . . . 65 E2
Tralee Ct, SE16 . . . . . . 149 F2
Tramway Av, E15 . . . . . 27 E4
Transept St, NW1 . . . . 55 F4
Transom Cl, SE16 . . . 123 F5
Transom Sq, E14 . . . . 153 E1
Tranton Rd, SE16 . . . 121 D3
Treadgold St, W11 . . . . 79 D2
Treadway St, E2 . . . . . . 43 E3
Treaty St, N1 . . . . 38 A1
Trebeck St, W1 . . . . . . 85 E4
Trebovir Rd, SW5 . . . 137 D2
Treby St, E3 . . . . 68 A2
Tredegar Ms, E3 . . . . . . 46 A4
Tredegar Rd, E3 . . . . . . 46 A3
Tredegar Sq, E3 . . . . . . 46 A4
Tredegar Ter, E3 . . . . . . 46 A4
Trederwen Rd, E8 . . . . 21 D5
Tree Rd, E16 . . . . 74 A5
Trego Rd, E9 . . . . 24 C3
Tregunter Rd,
    SW10 . . . . 138 A4
Treherne Ct, SW9 . . . 169 D3
Trelawney Est, E9 . . . . 22 A2
Trellick Twr, W10 . . . . . 52 A2
Trellis Sq, E3 . . . . 46 B4
Trenchard St, SE10 . . 155 D3
Trenchold St, SW8 . . 143 E5
Tresham Cres, NW8 . . 55 E1
Tressell Cl, N1 . . . . 17 F4
Trevanion Rd, W14 . . 135 F2
Trevelyan Gdns,
    NW10 . . . . 28 A1
Treveris St, SE1 . . . . . . 89 E5
Treverton St, W10 . . . . 51 D2
Trevithick Ho,
    SE16 . . . . 149 F1
Trevithick St, SE8 . . . 152 C4

Trevor Pl, SW7 . . . . . . 111 F2
Trevor Sq, SW7 . . . . . 112 A2
Trevor St, SW7 . . . . . . 111 F2
Triangle, The, EC1 . . . . 61 F1
Triangle Ct, E16 . . . . . . 74 C3
Triangle Est, SE11 . . . 144 C3
Triangle Rd, E8 . . . . . . 21 E5
Trident St, SE16 . . . . . 123 D5
Trig La, EC4 . . . . 90 A2
Trigon Rd, SW8 . . . . . 168 B1
Trim St, SE14 . . . . 152 A5
Trinidad St, E14 . . . . . . 96 B2
Trinity Buoy Wf,
    E14 . . . . 100 A3
Trinity Ch Sq, SE1 . . . 118 B3
Trinity Cl, E8 . . . . 20 B1
Coll Trinity Coll of Music,
    SE10 . . . . 154 B4
Trinity Ct, N1 . . . . 19 E5
Trinity Gdns, E16 . . . . . 72 B3
Trinity Gro, SE10 . . . . 178 A3
★ Trinity Ho, EC3 . . . . . 91 F2
Trinity Ms, W10 . . . . . . 51 D5
Trinity Pl, EC3 . . . . 92 A3
Trinity Sq, EC3 . . . . 91 F3
Trinity St, E16 . . . . 72 C4
    SE1 . . . . 118 B2
Trinity Wk, NW3 . . . . . 10 B2
Trio Pl, SE1 . . . . 118 B2
Triton Sq, NW1 . . . . . . 58 A1
Triumph Rd, E6 . . . . . . 76 B5
Troon Cl, SE16 . . . . . . 149 F2
Troon St, E1 . . . . 67 E5
Trothy Rd, SE1 . . . . . . 121 D5
Trott St, SW11 . . . . . . 163 D4
Troughton Rd, SE7 . . . 157 E2
Troutbeck Rd, SE14 . . 175 E3
Trowbridge Est, E9 . . . 24 B1
Trowbridge Rd, E9 . . . . 24 B2
Truesdale Rd, E6 . . . . 104 B1
Trump St, EC2 . . . . 90 B1
Trundle St, SE1 . . . . . 118 A1
Trundleys Rd, SE8 . . . 151 D2
Trundleys Ter, SE8 . . . 151 D1
Truro St, NW5 . . . . 12 C2
Trussley Rd, W6 . . . . . 106 A4
Tryon Cres, E9 . . . . 22 A5
Tryon St, SW3 . . . . . . 140 A3
Tudor Gro, E9 . . . . 22 A4
Tudor Rd, E9 . . . . 21 F5
Tudor St, EC4 . . . . 89 D2
Tufton St, SW1 . . . . . . 115 D3
Tuilerie St, E2 . . . . 42 C2
Sch Tuke Sch, SE15 . . . 173 E4
Tulip Cl, E6 . . . . 76 A4
Tunnan Leys, E6 . . . . . 77 D5
Tunnel Av, SE10 . . . . . 127 D1
Tunnel Rd, SE16 . . . . . 122 A1
Turin St, E2 . . . . 42 C5
Turk's Head Yd, EC1 . . 61 E3
Turks Row, SW3 . . . . . 140 B2
Turley Cl, E15 . . . . 49 F1
Turnagain La, EC4 . . . . 61 E5
Turnberry Cl, SE16 . . . 149 F3

★ Place of interest   ⇌ Railway station   🅷 Hospital   ⊖ London Underground station

Upper Thames St,
  EC4 .... 89 F2
Upper Wimpole St,
  W1 .... 57 E3
Upper Woburn Pl,
  WC1 .... 37 D5
Upstall St, SE5 ...... 169 F4
Coll Urban Learning
  Foundation, E14... 96 C2
Coll Urdang Acad, The,
  WC2 .... 87 E1
Urlwin St, SE5 ...... 146 A5
Urlwin Wk, SW9 .... 169 D4
Ursula St, SW11 ..... 163 E4
Usborne Ms, SW8 ... 168 A1
Usher Rd, E3 .... 46 B2
Usk St, E2 .... 44 C4
Utopia Village, NW1 .. 12 C5
Uverdale Rd, SW10 . 162 B3
Uxbridge Rd, W12... 106 B1
Uxbridge St, W8...... 80 C4

V

Vale, The, SW3...... 138 C4
Vale Cl, W9.......... 32 A5
Vale Ct, W9.......... 32 A5
Valentine Pl, SE1 ... 117 E1
Valentine Rd, E9 ..... 22 C2
Valentine Row,
  SE1.............. 117 E2
Valerian Way, E15.... 49 F5
Vale Royal, N7 .... 15 E4
Sch Vale Sch, The,
  SW7 .... 110 A4
Valette St, E9 .... 21 F1
Valiant Way, E6 ...... 76 A4
Vallance Rd, E1 ...... 43 D5
  E2 .... 43 D5
Valmar Rd, SE5 ..... 170 B4
Vanbrugh Cl, E16..... 74 C4
Vanbrugh Flds, SE3 .. 156 A5
Vanbrugh Hill, SE3 .. 156 A4
  SE10 .... 155 F3
Vanbrugh Pk, SE3 ... 180 A2
Vanbrugh Pk Rd,
  SE3 .... 180 B1
Vanbrugh Pk Rd W,
  SE3 .... 180 A1
Vanbrugh Ter, SE3... 180 B3
Vandome Cl, E16.... 101 E1
Vandon Pas, SW1 ... 114 B3
Vandon St, SW1..... 114 B3
Vandy St, EC2....... 63 E2
Vane St, SW1 .... 114 B5
Vanguard Cl, E16..... 73 D4
Vanguard Ho, E8 ..... 21 F3
Vanguard St, SE8.... 176 C3

Vanner Pt, E9 .... 22 C2
Vansittart St, SE14 .. 175 F1
Vanston Pl, SW6 ..... 160 C1
Vantage Ms, E14 ..... 98 B5
Vantage Pl, W8 ..... 109 D4
Varcoe Rd, SE16 .... 149 F3
Varden St, E1 .... 65 E5
Varley Rd, E16 .... 73 F5
Varna Rd, SW6...... 159 F1
Varndell St, NW1...... 36 A4
Vassall Rd, SW9...... 168 C2
Vauban Est, SE16 ... 120 B4
Vauban St, SE16 ... 120 B4
Vaughan St, SE16 ... 124 A2
Vaughan Way, E1 ... 92 C3
Vaughan Williams Cl,
  SE8 .... 176 C2
VAUXHALL, SE11 ... 143 F3
⇌ Vauxhall 143 F4
⊖ Vauxhall 143 F4
Vauxhall Br, SE1 ... 143 E3
  SW1 .... 143 E3
Vauxhall Br Rd,
  SW1 .... 114 B5
Vauxhall Gdns Est,
  SE11 .... 144 A3
Vauxhall Gro, SW8 .. 144 A4
Sch Vauxhall Prim Sch,
  SE11 .... 144 B2
Vauxhall St, SE11 ... 144 B2
Vauxhall Wk, SE11 .. 144 A2
Vawdrey Cl, E1....... 66 A2
Velletri Ho, E2 .... 45 D3
Venables St, NW8 .... 55 D3
Ventnor Rd, SE14 ... 175 D2
Venue St, E14....... 70 A3
Venus Rd, SE18 .... 132 A4
Vera Rd, SW6....... 159 F4
Verbena Cl, E16...... 72 A1
Verdi Cres, W10...... 29 F3
Vereker Rd, W14 .... 135 F3
Vere St, W1.......... 85 E1
Verity Cl, W11 .... 79 E1
Verney Rd, SE16 .... 149 D4
Verney Way, SE16... 149 E3
Vernon Ms, W14 .... 135 F1
Vernon Pl, WC1 ...... 59 F4
Vernon Ri, WC1 ...... 38 B4
Vernon Rd, E3 .... 46 B2
  E15 .... 27 F3
Vernon Sq, WC1...... 38 B4
Vernon St, W14..... 135 E1
Vernon Yd, W11...... 80 A2
Verulam Bldgs, WC1 . 60 B3
Verulam St, WC1..... 60 C3
Vesey Path, E14..... 97 F1
Vestry Ms, SE5..... 171 E4
Vestry Rd, SE5..... 171 E4
Vestry St, N1 .... 40 C4
Viaduct Pl, E2....... 43 E5
Viaduct St, E2 .... 43 E5
Vibart Wk, N1....... 15 F5
Vicarage Av, SE3 ... 181 D2
Vicarage Ct, W8.... 109 E1

Vicarage Cres,
  SW11 .... 162 C4
Vicarage Gdns, W8 ... 81 D5
Vicarage Gate, W8 .. 109 E1
Vicarage Gro, SE5 ... 171 D3
Vicarage La, E15 ..... 27 F5
Vicarage Wk,
  SW11 .... 162 C4
Vicars Cl, E9 .... 44 A1
Viceroy Ct, NW8 .... 33 F2
Viceroy Rd, SW8 .... 167 E3
⇌ Victoria 113 F5
⊖ Victoria 113 F5
★ Victoria & Albert Mus,
  SW7 .... 111 D4
★ Victoria Coach Sta,
  SW1 .... 141 E1
Victoria Dock Rd,
  E16.............. 101 F2
Victoria Embk, EC4 ... 88 A3
  SW1 .... 115 F1
  WC2 .... 88 A3
★ Victoria Embankment
  Gdns, WC2....... 87 F3
Victoria Gdns, W11... 80 C4
Victoria Gro, W8 .... 110 A3
Victoria Gro Ms, W2 .. 81 D3
Victoria Ms, E8 ...... 20 C1
  NW6 .... 8 C5
★ Victoria Park, E9... 23 E5
Victoria Pk Rd, E9 ... 43 F1
Victoria Pk Sq, E2 .... 44 A4
Victoria Pas, NW8 .... 54 C1
Victoria Pl, SW1..... 113 F5
Victoria Rd, NW6..... 30 B1
  W8 .... 110 A4
Victoria Sq, SW1 .... 113 F3
Victoria St, E15 ...... 27 E3
  SW1 .... 114 A4
★ Victoria Twr,
  SW1 .... 115 E3
Victoria Way, SE7 ... 157 E2
Victoria Wf, E14 ..... 95 F3
Victoria Yd, E1 ...... 93 D1
Victory Pl, E14....... 95 F2
  SE17 .... 118 B5
Sch Victory Prim Sch,
  SE17 .... 118 B5
Victory Wk, SE8.... 176 C4
Victory Way, SE16... 123 F2
Vigo St, W1......... 86 A3
Viking Cl, E3......... 45 F3
Viking Ct, SW6...... 137 D4
Viking Gdns, E6 ..... 75 E2
Villa St, SE17 ...... 147 D3
Villiers St, WC2 ..... 87 E3
Vincent Cl, SE16 .... 123 E2
Vincent Rd, SE18.... 133 E5
Vincent Sq, SW1 .... 114 B5
Vincent St, E16 ...... 72 B4
  SW1 .... 114 C5
Vincent Ter, N1 ...... 39 E2
Vince St, EC1 .... 41 D5

Vine Ct, E1 .... 65 D4
Vinegar St, E1 .... 93 E4
Vinegar Yd, SE1 ..... 119 E1
Vine Hill, EC1 .... 60 C2
Vine La, SE1 .... 91 F5
Vine Sq, W14 .... 136 B3
Vine St, EC3 .... 92 A2
  W1 .... 86 B3
Vine St Br, EC1 .... 61 D2
Vine Yd, SE1 .... 118 B1
Vineyard Wk, EC1 .... 60 C1
★ Vinopolis, SE1 ..... 90 B4
Vintners Ct, EC4 ..... 90 B2
Violet Cl, E16 .... 71 F2
  SE8 .... 152 A4
Violet Hill, NW8 ...... 32 A3
Violet Rd, E3 .... 69 E2
Violet St, E2 .... 65 F1
Virgil Pl, W1 .... 56 A4
Virgil St, SE1 .... 116 B3
Sch Virginia Prim Sch,
  E2 .... 42 A5
Virginia Rd, E2 .... 42 A5
Virginia St, E1 .... 93 D3
Viscount Dr, E6 ...... 76 A3
Viscount St, EC1 ..... 62 A2
Vista Bldg, The,
  SE18 .... 133 D5
Sch Vittoria Prim Sch,
  N1 .... 38 C2
Vivian Ct, W9 .... 31 E2
Vivian Rd, E3 .... 45 E2
Voss St, E2 .... 43 D5
Vulcan Cl, E6 .... 105 D1
Vulcan Rd, SE4 ..... 176 A5
Vulcan Sq, E14 ..... 153 D1
Vulcan Ter, SE4 ..... 176 A5
Vulcan Way, N7 ...... 16 B1
Vyner St, E2 .... 43 F2

W

Wadding St, SE17 ... 146 C1
Waddington St, E15 .. 27 D1
Wadeson St, E2 ...... 43 F2
Wades Pl, E14 .... 97 E2
Wadham Gdns,
  NW3 .... 11 E5
Wadhurst Rd, SW8 .. 166 A3
Wager St, E3 .... 68 A3
Wagner St, SE15 .... 174 A1
Waite St, SE15 ...... 148 A4
Waithman St, EC4 ... 89 E1
Wakefield Ms, WC1 .. 37 F5
Wakefield St, WC1 ... 59 F1
Wakeham St, N1 ..... 18 C2
Wakeling St, E14 ..... 95 E1
Wakelin Rd, E15 ..... 49 E2
Wakeman Rd,
  NW10 .... 28 C4
Wakerley Cl, E6 ..... 104 A1
Wakley St, EC1 .... 39 E4

Walberswick St,
  SW8 .... 167 F2
Walbrook, EC4 .... 90 C2
Walburgh St, E1 ..... 93 E1
Walcorde Av, SE17 .. 146 B1
Walcot Sq, SE11 .... 117 D5
Walcott St, SW1 .... 114 B5
Waldair Ct, E16 ..... 133 E1
Waldair Wf, E16 .... 133 E1
Waldemar Av, SW6 .. 159 F4
Walden St, E1 .... 65 E5
Waldron Ms, SW3 ... 139 D4
Wales Cl, SE15 ...... 173 E1
Waley St, E1 .... 67 D3
WALHAM GREEN,
  SW6 .... 161 E2
Walham Grn Ct,
  SW6 .... 161 E2
Walham Gro, SW6 .. 160 C1
Walham Yd, SW6 ... 160 C1
Walkers Ct, E8 .... 20 C1
  W1 .... 86 C2
Walkynscroft,
  SE15 .... 173 F5
★ Wallace Collection,
  W1 .... 56 C5
Wallace Rd, N1 ...... 18 B1
Waller Rd, SE14 .... 174 C4
Waller Way, SE10 ... 177 F1
Wallgrave Rd, SW5 .. 109 E5
Wallingford Av, W10 .. 50 C4
Wallis All, SE1 ...... 118 B1
Wallis Rd, E9 .... 24 B2
Wallside, EC2 .... 62 B4
Wall St, N1 .... 19 D2
Wallwood St, E14 .... 68 B4
Walmer Pl, W1 .... 56 A3
Walmer Rd, W10 .... 78 B1
  W11 .... 79 E2
Walmer St, W1 ...... 56 A3
Walm La, NW2 .... 6 B2
Walney Wk, N1 ...... 18 B1
Walnut Cl, SE8 ..... 152 B5
Walnut Tree Rd,
  SE10 .... 155 F3
Walnut Tree Wk,
  SE11 .... 116 C5
Sch Walnut Tree Wk
  Prim Sch, SE11 ... 116 C5
Walpole Ms, NW8 ... 32 C1
Walpole St, SW3 .... 140 A2
Walsham Rd, SE14 .. 174 C5
Walters Cl, SE17 .... 146 B1
Walters Ho, SE17 ... 145 E5
Walter St, E2 .... 44 C5
Walter Ter, E1 .... 67 D5
Walterton Rd, W9 ... 52 B2
Walton Cl, SW8 .... 167 F1
Walton Pl, SW3 .... 112 A3
Walton St, SW3 .... 111 F5
WALWORTH, SE17 .. 146 A2
★ Walworth Garden Fm -
  Horticultural Training Cen,
  SE17 .... 145 F3

Walworth Pl, SE17 .. 146 B3
Walworth Rd, SE1 .. 118 A5
  SE17 .... 118 A5
Sch Walworth Sch,
  SE1 .... 147 F3
  Lwr Sch, SE17 .... 147 D2
Wandon Rd, SW6 ... 161 F2
Wandsworth Br Rd,
  SW6 .... 161 E3
Wandsworth Rd,
  SW8 .... 143 E4
Wanlip Rd, E13 ...... 73 E1
Wansbeck Rd, E3 .... 24 B3
  E9 .... 24 B3
Wansdown Pl,
  SW6 .... 161 E1
Wansey St, SE17 ... 146 B1
WAPPING, E1 .... 93 D4
⊖ Wapping 94 A5
Wapping Dock St,
  E1 .... 93 F5
Wapping High St,
  E1 .... 92 C5
Wapping La, E1 ...... 93 F3
Wapping Wall, E1 .... 94 A4
Warburton Cl, N1 .... 19 E1
Warburton Rd, E8 ... 21 F5
Warburton St, E8 .... 21 E5
Wardalls Gro, SE14 .. 174 B1
Warden Rd, NW5 .... 13 D1
Wardens Gro, SE1 ... 90 A5
Wardo Av, SW6 .... 159 E4
Wardour Ms, W1 .... 86 B3
Wardour St, W1 ..... 86 C2
Ward Pt, SE11 ...... 144 C1
Ward Rd, E15 .... 26 C5
Wardrobe Ter, EC4 ... 89 F1
Wards Wf App, E16 .. 130 C1
Warfield Rd, NW10 .. 28 C5
Warfield Yd, NW10 .. 28 C5
Warham St, SE5 .... 169 F1
Warley St, E2 .... 44 C4
Warlock Rd, W9 .... 52 C1
Warmington St,
  E13 .... 73 D1
Warndon St, SE16 .. 150 B1
Warneford St, E9 .... 21 F5
Warner Ho, SE13 ... 177 E5
Warner Pl, E2 .... 43 D3
Warner Rd, SE5 .... 170 A4
Warner St, EC1 ...... 60 C2
Warner Ter, E14 ..... 69 D4
Warner Yd, EC1 ..... 60 C2
Warren Ho, E3 ...... 47 E4
Warren La, SE18 ... 133 E4
Warren La Gate,
  SE18 .... 133 E4
Warren Ms, W1 ...... 58 A2
⊖ Warren Street 58 B1
Warren St, W1 .... 57 F2

Warriner Gdns,
SW11 . . . . 164 B4
Warrington Cres,
W9 . . . . 54 A2
Warrington Gdns,
W9 . . . . 54 A2
Warspite Rd, SE18 . . 131 E3
Warton Rd, E15 . . . . . . 26 A4
Warwall, E6 . . . . 77 E5
◉ Warwick Avenue . . 54 A2
Warwick Av, W2 . . . . . . 54 A2
W9 . . . . 54 A2
Warwick Bldg, SW8 . . 165 E1
Warwick Ct, WC1 . . . . . 60 B4
Warwick Cres, W2 . . . . 54 A3
Warwick Est, W2 . . . . . 53 F4
Warwick Gdns,
W14 . . . . 108 B4
Warwick Ho St,
SW1 . . . . 87 D4
Warwick La, EC4 . . . . . 89 F1
Warwick Pas, EC4 . . . . 61 F5
Warwick Pl, W9 . . . . . . 54 A3
Warwick Pl N, SW1 . . 142 A1
Warwick Rd, SW5 . . . 108 A5
W14 . . . . 108 A5
Warwick Row, SW1 . 113 F3
Warwickshire Path,
SE8 . . . . 176 B1
Warwick Sq, EC4 . . . . . 61 F5
SW1 . . . . 142 A2
Warwick Sq Ms,
SW1 . . . . 142 A1
Warwick St, W1 . . . . . . 86 B2
Warwick Way, SW1 . . 142 A1
Warwick Yd, EC1 . . . . . 62 B2
Washington Cl, E3 . . . . 47 F4
Watercress Pl, N1 . . . . 19 F4
Waterford Rd, SW6 . . 161 F3
Waterfront Studios
Business Cen,
E16 . . . . 100 C4
Water Gdns, The,
W2 . . . . 55 F5
Watergate, EC4 . . . . . . 89 E2
Watergate St, SE8 . . . 152 C5
Watergate Wk, WC2 . . 87 F4
Waterhouse Cl, E16 . . 74 C3
W6 . . . . 135 D2
Waterhouse Sq, EC1 . . 60 C4
Wateridge Cl, E14 . . . 124 C4
Water La, E15 . . . . 27 F1
EC3 . . . . 91 E3
NW1 . . . . 13 F4
SE14 . . . . 174 B1
⇌ Waterloo 116 C1
◉ Waterloo 116 C1
Waterloo Br, SE1 . . . . 88 A3
WC2 . . . . 88 A3
⇌ Waterloo East 88 C5

Waterloo Est, E2 . . . . . 44 A2
Waterloo Gdns, E2 . . . . 44 A2
N1 . . . . 17 E4
⇌ Waterloo
International 116 B1
Riv Waterloo Millennium
Pier 116 A1
Waterloo Pas, NW6 . . . . 8 B4
Waterloo Pl, SW1 . . . . . 86 C4
Waterloo Rd, SE1 . . . . 116 C1
Waterloo Ter, N1 . . . . . 17 E4
Watermans Wk,
SE16 . . . . 123 E3
Waterman Way, E1 . . . 93 E4
Waterside Cl, E3 . . . . . 24 A5
SE16 . . . . 121 D2
Waterside Pl, NW1 . . . 13 D5
Waterside Pt,
SW11 . . . . 163 F1
Waterside Twr,
SW6 . . . . 162 B5
Waterson St, E2 . . . . . 41 F4
Water St, WC2 . . . . . . 88 B2
Water Twr Pl, N1 . . . . . 39 E1
Waterview Ho, E14 . . . 67 F4
Watford Cl, SW11 . . . 163 F3
Watford Rd, E16 . . . . . 73 D4
Watkinson Rd, N7 . . . . 16 A1
Watling Ct, EC4 . . . . . . 90 B1
Watling Gdns, NW2 . . . 7 F2
Watling St, EC4 . . . . . . 90 A1
SE15 . . . . 147 F5
Watney Mkt, E1 . . . . . 93 F1
Watney St, E1 . . . . . . 93 F1
Watson's Ms, W1 . . . . 55 F4
Watson's St, SE8 . . . . 176 C2
Watts Gro, E3 . . . . 69 E3
Watts St, E1 . . . . 93 F4
SE15 . . . . 172 B3
Watts Way, SW7 . . . . 111 D3
Wat Tyler Rd, SE3 . . . 178 B5
SE10 . . . . 178 B5
Wavel Ms, NW6 . . . . . . 9 E4
Waveney Cl, E1 . . . . . . 93 D4
Waverley Gdns, E6 . . . 75 F4
Waverley Pl, NW8 . . . . 32 C2
Waverley Wk, W2 . . . . 53 D3
Waverton Ho, E3 . . . . . 24 B5
Waverton St, W1 . . . . . 85 D4
Waylett Ho, SE11 . . . 144 C3
Wayman Ct, E8 . . . . . . 21 E2
Waynflete Sq, W10 . . . 78 C2
Weald Cl, SE16 . . . . . 149 E2
Wear Pl, E2 . . . . 43 E5
Weatherley Cl, E3 . . . . 68 B3
Weaver Cl, E6 . . . . . . 105 E2
Weavers Ter, SW6 . . . 137 D5
Weaver St, E1 . . . . 64 C2
Weavers Way, NW1 . . . 14 C5
Webb Cl, W10 . . . . 50 A2
Webber Row, SE1 . . . 117 D3
Webber St, SE1 . . . . . 117 D1
Webb Gdns, E13 . . . . . 73 D1
Webb Rd, SE3 . . . . . . 156 B4

Webb St, SE1 . . . . 119 E4
Webheath Est, NW6 . . . 8 B3
Webster Rd, SE16 . . . 121 D4
Wedgwood Ms, W1 . . . 87 D1
Wedlake St, W10 . . . . 51 F1
Weighhouse St, W1 . . . 85 D1
Weir's Pas, NW1 . . . . . 37 D4
Welbeck St, W1 . . . . . . 57 E5
Welbeck Way, W1 . . . . 57 E5
Welby St, SE5 . . . . . . 169 F4
Welfare Rd, E15 . . . . . 27 F3
Welland Ms, E1 . . . . . . 93 D4
Welland St, SE10 . . . . 154 A4
Wellclose Sq, E1 . . . . . 93 D2
Wellclose St, E1 . . . . . 93 D3
Call Wellcome Trust,
NW1 . . . . 58 C1
Well Ct, EC4 . . . . 90 B1
Weller St, SE1 . . . . . . 118 A1
Wellesley Ct, W9 . . . . . 32 A4
Wellesley Pl, NW1 . . . . 36 C5
Wellesley St, E1 . . . . . 66 C4
Wellesley Ter, N1 . . . . . 40 B4
★ Wellington Arch,
W1 . . . . 113 D1
Wellington Bldgs,
SW1 . . . . 141 D3
Wellington Cl,
SE14 . . . . 174 C4
W11 . . . . 80 C1
Wellington Ct, NW8 . . 32 C3
Wellington Gro,
SE10 . . . . 178 C2
H Wellington Hosp,
NW8 . . . . 33 D3
Wellington Pl, NW8 . . . 33 D4
Sch Wellington
Prim Sch, E3 . . . . . . 46 C5
Wellington Rd,
NW8 . . . . 32 C2
NW10 . . . . 29 D5
Wellington Row, E2 . . 42 B4
Wellington Sq, SW3 . 140 A2
Wellington St, WC2 . . 87 F2
Wellington Ter, E1 . . . . 93 E4
Wellington Way, E3 . . 46 C5
Wells Ms, W1 . . . . 58 A4
Wells Ri, NW8 . . . . 34 A1
Wells Rd, W12 . . . . . . 106 A2
Wells Sq, WC1 . . . . 38 A5
Wells St, W1 . . . . 58 A4
Well St, E9 . . . . 21 F4
E15 . . . . 27 E1
Wells Way, SE5 . . . . . 147 D4
SW7 . . . . 110 C3
Welsford St, SE1 . . . . 148 C2
Welshpool Ho, E8 . . . . 21 D5
Welshpool St, E8 . . . . 21 D5
Welwyn St, E2 . . . . . . 44 B4
Wendle Ct, SW8 . . . . 143 E5
Wendon St, E3 . . . . . . 24 B5
Wendover, SE17 . . . . 147 E3
Wenlock Ct, N1 . . . . . . 41 D3
Wenlock Rd, N1 . . . . . . 40 A2

Wenlock St, N1 . . . . . . 40 B3
Wennington Rd, E3 . . . 45 D3
Wentworth Cres,
   SE15 . . . . 173 D2
Wentworth Ms, E3 . . . 67 F1
Wentworth St, E1 . . . 64 A5
Werrington St,
   NW1 . . . . 36 B3
Wesley Av, E16 . . . . . 101 E4
Wesley Cl, SE17 . . . 145 F1
★ Wesley's Ho, EC1 . . 63 D1
Wesley Sq, W11 . . . . . . 79 E1
Wesley St, W1 . . . . . . 57 D4
Wessex St, E2 . . . . . . 44 B5
West 12 Shop Cen,
   W12 . . . . 106 C1
West Arbour St, E1 . . 66 C5
Westbourne Br, W2 . . 54 A4
Westbourne Cres,
   W2 . . . . 82 C2
Westbourne Cres Ms,
   W2 . . . . 82 C2
Westbourne Gdns,
   W2 . . . . 53 E5
WESTBOURNE GREEN,
   W2 . . . . 52 C4
Westbourne Gro,
   W2 . . . . 81 D1
   W11 . . . . 80 B2
Westbourne Gro Ms,
   W11 . . . . 80 C1
Westbourne Gro Ter,
   W2 . . . . 53 E5
◉ Westbourne Park . . 52 B3
Westbourne Pk Ms,
   W2 . . . . 53 E5
Westbourne Pk Pas,
   W2 . . . . 53 D4
Westbourne Pk Rd,
   W2 . . . . 53 D4
   W11 . . . . 79 F1
Westbourne Pk Vil,
   W2 . . . . 53 D4
Westbourne Rd, N7 . . 16 C2
Westbourne St, W2 . . 82 C2
Westbourne Ter, W2 . . 54 B5
Westbourne Ter Ms,
   W2 . . . . 54 A5
Westbourne Ter Rd,
   W2 . . . . 54 A4
Sch Westbridge Prim Sch,
   SW11 . . . . 163 E3
Westbridge Rd,
   SW11 . . . . 163 D4
WEST BROMPTON,
   SW10 . . . . 137 E4
⇌ West Brompton . . 137 D3
◉ West Brompton . . 137 D3
Westbrook Rd, SE3 . . 181 E4
West Carriage Dr,
   W2 . . . . 83 D5
West Cen St, WC1 . . . 59 E5
Westcombe Ct,
   SE3 . . . . 180 A1

Westcombe Hill,
   SE3 . . . . 157 D4
   SE10 . . . . 156 C3
⇌ Westcombe Park . 157 D3
Westcombe Pk Rd,
   SE3 . . . . 155 F5
Westcott Rd, SE17 . . 145 E4
West Cromwell Rd,
   SW5 . . . . 136 C1
   W14 . . . . 136 A2
West Cross Route,
   W10 . . . . 78 C2
   W11 . . . . 78 C2
West Eaton Pl, SW1 . 112 C5
West Eaton Pl Ms,
   SW1 . . . . 112 C5
West End La, NW6 . . . 31 D1
Westerdale Rd,
   SE10 . . . . 156 C3
Western Beach Apartments,
   E16 . . . . 100 C4
H Western Eye Hosp,
   NW1 . . . . 56 A3
Western Gateway,
   E16 . . . . 100 C3
Western Ms, W9 . . . . . 52 B2
Western Pl, SE16 . . . . 122 B1
DLR Westferry 96 C2
Westferry Circ, E14 . . 96 C4
Westferry Rd, E14 . . . 96 B4
Westfield Cl, SW10 . . 162 A2
Westfield St, SE18 . . 130 C4
Westfield Way, E1 . . . 45 E5
West Gdn Pl, W2 . . . . . 83 F1
West Gdns, E1 . . . . 93 F3
Westgate St, E8 . . . . . 21 E5
Westgate Ter,
   SW10 . . . . 137 F3
West Gro, SE10 . . . . . 178 B3
Westgrove La,
   SE10 . . . . 178 B3
West Halkin St,
   SW1 . . . . 112 C3
⇌ West Ham 49 E4
◉ West Ham 49 F4
West Ham La, E15 . . . . 27 E4
⇌ West Hampstead . . . 9 D2
◉ West Hampstead . . . 9 D2
West Hampstead Ms,
   NW6 . . . . 9 E2
⇌ West Hampstead
   (Thameslink) 9 D1
West Harding St,
   EC4 . . . . 61 D5
West India Av, E14 . . . 96 C4
West India Dock Rd,
   E14 . . . . 96 B1
DLR West India Quay . . 97 E3
◉ West Kensington . 136 A2
West Kensington Ct,
   W14 . . . . 136 A2
WEST KILBURN, W9 . . 30 A4
Westland Pl, N1 . . . . . . 40 C4
West La, SE16 . . . . . . 121 E2

Coll West London Coll,
   W1 . . . . 85 D1
West Mall, W8 . . . . 81 D4
West Mersea Cl,
   E16 . . . . 101 E5
West Ms, SW1 . . . . . . 141 F1
WESTMINSTER,
   SW1 . . . . 114 A3
◉ Westminster 115 F2
★ Westminster Abbey,
   SW1 . . . . 115 E3
Sch Westminster Abbey
   Choir Sch, SW1 . . . 115 D3
★ Westminster Abbey Mus,
   SW1 . . . . 115 E3
Coll Westminster
   Adult Ed Service,
   Amberley Rd Cen,
   W9 . . . . 53 E2
   Ebury Br Cen,
   SW1 . . . . 141 E2
   Frith St Cen, W1 . . . 87 D1
Westminster Br,
   SE1 . . . . 115 F2
   SW1 . . . . 115 F2
Westminster Br Rd,
   SE1 . . . . 116 B2
★ Westminster Cath,
   SW1 . . . . 114 A4
Sch Westminster Cath
   Choir Sch, SW1 . . . 114 B4
Sch Westminster Cath RC
   Prim Sch, SW1 . . . 143 D2
Sch Westminster City
   C of E Sch, SW1 . . . 114 B3
★ Westminster City Hall,
   SW1 . . . . 114 B3
Westminster Gdns,
   SW1 . . . . 115 E5
Coll Westminster
   Kingsway Coll,
   Battersea Pk Cen,
   SW11 . . . . 165 D3
   Castle La Cen,
   SW1 . . . . 114 B3
   Gray's Inn Cen,
   WC1 . . . . 38 A5
   Kentish Town Cen,
   NW5 . . . . 13 E1
   Lucas-Tooth Gymnasium,
   WC1 . . . . 38 A5
   Peter St Cen, W1 . . . 86 C2
   Regent's Pk Cen,
   NW1 . . . . 58 A1
   Vincent Sq Cen,
   SW1 . . . . 114 C5
Riv Westminster Millennium
   Pier 115 F1
Sch Westminster Sch,
   SW1 . . . . 115 E3

🅢 Westminster Under Sch,
SW1 . . . . 142 C1
Westmoor St, SE7 . . 130 B4
Westmoreland Pl,
SW1 . . . . 141 F3
Westmoreland Rd,
SE17 . . . . 146 B4
Westmoreland St,
W1 . . . . 57 D4
Westmoreland Ter,
SW1 . . . . 141 F3
Westmoreland Wk,
SE17 . . . . 147 D4
West One Shop Cen,
W1 . . . . 85 D1
Weston Ri, WC1 . . . . . . 38 B3
Weston St, SE1 . . . . . 119 D3
Weston Wk, E8 . . . . 21 F4
West Parkside,
SE10 . . . . 128 B4
West Pier, E1 . . . . 93 E5
West Pt, SE1 . . . . 148 C2
Westport Rd, E13 . . . . 73 E2
Westport St, E1 . . . . . . 67 D5
West Poultry Av,
EC1 . . . . 61 E4
West Rd, SW3 . . . . . . 140 B3
West Row, W10 . . . . . . 51 E1
🅓 West Silvertown . . 101 D5
West Smithfield,
EC1 . . . . 61 E4
West Sq, SE11 . . . . . . 117 E4
West St, E2 . . . . 43 F3
WC2 . . . . 87 D1
West Tenter St, E1 . . . . 92 B1
Westview Cl, W10 . . . . 50 B5
West Warwick Pl,
SW1 . . . . 142 A1
Westway, W2 . . . . 52 C3
W9 . . . . 52 C3
W10 . . . . 51 F5
Westwick Gdns,
W14 . . . . 106 C2
Westwood Rd, E16 . . 101 E5
Wetherby Gdns,
SW5 . . . . 138 A1
Wetherby Ms, SW5 . . 137 E2
Wetherby Pl, SW7 . . 138 A1
🅢 Wetherby Sch,
W2 . . . . 81 D1
Wetherell Rd, E9 . . . . . 23 D5
Weybridge Ct,
SE16 . . . . 149 D3
Weybridge Pt,
SW11 . . . . 164 B5
Weyhill Rd, E1 . . . . 65 D5
Weymouth Cl, E6 . . . 105 E1
Weymouth Ms, W1 . . 57 E3
Weymouth St, W1 . . . 57 D4
Weymouth Ter, E2 . . . 42 B2

Whalebone Ct, EC2 . . 63 D5
Whalebone La, E15 . . 27 E4
Whales Yd, E15 . . . . . . 27 E4
Wharfdale Rd, N1 . . . . 37 F2
Wharfedale St,
SW10 . . . . 137 E3
Wharf Pl, E2 . . . . 43 D1
Wharf Rd, N1 . . . . 40 A2
N1 (King's Cross) 37 E2
Wharfside Rd, E16 . . . 71 E4
Wharf St, E16 . . . . 71 E4
Wharton St, WC1 . . . . 38 B5
Wheatfields, E6 . . . . . . 77 E5
Wheatley St, W1 . . . . . 57 D4
Wheat Sheaf Cl,
E14 . . . . 125 E5
Wheatsheaf La,
SW6 . . . . 158 B1
SW8 . . . . 167 F1
Wheatsheaf Ter,
SW6 . . . . 160 B2
Wheatstone Rd,
W10 . . . . 51 F3
Wheeler Gdns, N1 . . . . 15 F5
Wheelwright St, N7 . . 16 A3
Wheler St, E1 . . . . 64 A2
Whetstone Pk, WC2 . . 60 A5
Whichcote St, SE1 . . . . 88 C5
Whidborne St, WC1 . . 37 F5
Whiskin St, EC1 . . . . . . 39 E5
Whistler Ms, SE15 . . . 172 B2
Whistlers Av, SW11 . . 163 D2
Whistler Twr, SW10 . 162 B1
Whiston Rd, E2 . . . . . . 42 A2
Whitacre Ms, SE11 . . 145 D3
Whitby Rd, SE18 . . . . . 132 A5
Whitby St, E1 . . . . 64 A1
Whitcher Cl, SE14 . . . 151 E5
Whitcher Pl, NW1 . . . . 14 A2
Whitchurch Rd, W11 . 79 D2
Whitcomb St, WC2 . . . 87 D3
Whiteadder Way,
E14 . . . . 125 F5
Whitear Wk, E15 . . . . . 27 D1
Whitebeam Cl,
SW9 . . . . 168 B2
WHITECHAPEL, E1 . . . . 92 C1
⊖ Whitechapel 65 E3
★ Whitechapel Art Gall,
E1 . . . . 64 B5
Whitechapel High St,
E1 . . . . 64 B5
Whitechapel Rd, E1 . . 64 C5
White Ch La, E1 . . . . . . 64 C5
White Ch Pas, E1 . . . . . 64 C5
⊖ White City 78 B3
White City Cl, W12 . . . 78 A3
White City Rd, W12 . . 78 A2
White Conduit St, N1 . 39 D2
Whitecross Pl, EC2 . . . 63 D3
Whitecross St, EC1 . . . 62 B1
Whitefriars St, EC4 . . . 89 D1
Whitehall, SW1 . . . . . . 87 E4
Whitehall Ct, SW1 . . . 87 E5

Whitehall Gdns, SW1 . 87 E5
Whitehall Pl, SW1 . . . 87 E5
White Hart St, EC4 . . . 61 F5
SE11 . . . . 145 D2
White Hart Yd, SE1 . . . 90 C5
Whitehaven St, NW8 . 55 E2
Whitehead's Gro,
SW3 . . . . 139 F2
White Horse All, EC1 . . 61 E3
White Horse La, E1 . . . 66 C2
White Horse Ms,
SE1 . . . . 117 D3
White Horse Rd, E1 . . . 95 E1
White Horse St, W1 . . 85 E5
White Horse Yd, EC2 . . 62 C5
White Kennett St, E1 . 63 F5
Whiteleys Shop Cen,
W2 . . . . 81 E1
White Lion Ct, EC3 . . . 91 E1
White Lion Hill, EC4 . . 89 F2
White Lion St, N1 . . . . 38 C3
White Post La, E9 . . . . 24 B3
White Post St,
SE15 . . . . 174 B1
White Rd, E15 . . . . 27 F3
Whites Grds, SE1 . . . . 119 F2
White's Row, E1 . . . . . 64 A4
Whitethorn St, E3 . . . . 69 D2
Whitfield Pl, W1 . . . . . 58 A2
Whitfield Rd, SE3 . . . 179 D4
Whitfield St, W1 . . . . . 58 C4
Whitgift St, SE11 . . . . 116 A5
Whitings Way, E6 . . . . 76 C3
Whitman Rd, E3 . . . . . 67 F1
Whitmore Est, N1 . . . . 41 F1
Whitmore Gdns,
NW10 . . . . 28 A2
🅢 Whitmore JMI Sch,
N1 . . . . 41 D1
Whitmore Rd, N1 . . . . 41 E1
Whitstable Ho, W10 . . 79 D1
Whittaker St, SW1 . . 140 C1
Whittaker Way, SE1 . 149 D1
Whittingstall Rd,
SW6 . . . . 160 B4
Whittington Av, EC3 . . 91 E1
Whittlesey St, SE1 . . . 88 C5
Whitton Wk, E3 . . . . . . 46 C4
Whitworth St,
SE10 . . . . 155 F2
Wicker St, E1 . . . . 93 E1
Wickford St, E1 . . . . . . 66 A1
Wickham Cl, E1 . . . . . . 66 B4
Wickham St, SE11 . . 144 A2
Wick La, E3 . . . . 46 C2
Wicklow St, WC1 . . . . . 38 A4
Wick Rd, E9 . . . . 22 C2
Widdin St, E15 . . . . . . 27 D4
Widegate St, E1 . . . . . 63 F4
Widgeon Cl, E16 . . . . . 73 E5
Widley Rd, W9 . . . . 31 D5
Wigmore Pl, W1 . . . . . 57 E5
Wigmore St, W1 . . . . . 84 C1
Wigston Rd, E13 . . . . . 73 E1

Wigton Pl, SE11.....145 D3
🕬 Wilberforce
  Prim Sch, W10 ....29 F4
Wilbraham Pl, SW1..112 B5
Wilby Ms, W11........80 B4
Wilcox Cl, SW8.....167 F1
Wilcox Pl, SW1......114 B4
Wilcox Rd, SW8.....167 E1
Wild Ct, WC2 ....60 A5
Wilde Cl, E8 ....20 C5
Wild Goose Dr, SE14.174 B4
Wild's Rents, SE1 ..119 E3
Wild St, WC2 ....87 F1
Wilfred St, SW1 ....114 A3
Wilkes St, E1 ....64 B3
Wilkinson Rd, E16....74 B5
Wilkinson St, SW8..168 A2
Wilkin St, NW5 ......13 E1
Wilkin St Ms, NW5 ...13 E1
Wilks Pl, N1 ....41 F3
Willan Wall, E16 ...100 A2
⊖ Willesden Green 6 B1
Willesden La, NW2 ....6 B2
  NW6 ....7 F4
Willes Rd, NW5 ......13 F1
🕬 William Davis
  Prim Sch, E2 ......64 C1
William Dunbar Ho,
  NW6 ....30 A3
William Ellis Way,
  SE16............121 D4
William IV St, WC2 ..87 E3
William Guy Gdns,
  E3 ....47 F5
William Henry Wk,
  SW8 ....142 C5
William Margrie Cl,
  SE15.............173 D5
William Ms, SW1....112 B2
🕬 William Morris Acad,
  W6 ....134 C3
William Pl, E3........46 A2
William Rd, NW1......36 A5
William Saville Ho,
  NW6 ....30 B3
Williams Bldgs, E2....66 A1
Williams Cl, SW6....159 F1
Williamson Cl, SE10 .156 A2
William Sq, SE16 .....95 F3
William St, SW1.....112 B2
🕬 William Tyndale
  Prim Sch, N1 ......17 F3
Willis St, E14 ....97 F1
Willoughby Pas, E14..96 C4
Willoughby St, WC1 ..59 E4
Willoughby Way,
  SE7 ....129 E5
Willow Br Rd, N1......18 A2
Willowbrook Rd,
  SE15.............148 B5
Willow Ct, EC2.......63 E1
Willow La, SE18....132 B5
Willow Pl, SW1 .....114 B5
Willow St, EC2 ....63 E1

Willow Tree Cl, E3 ....45 F1
Willow Wk, SE1 .....119 F5
Willow Way, W11 ....79 D3
Wilman Gro, E8 ......21 D3
Wilmcote Ho, W2 .....53 E3
Wilmer Gdns, N1.....41 E1
Wilmer Lea Cl, E15 ...26 C4
Wilmington Sq, WC1..38 C5
Wilmington St, WC1 ..38 C5
Wilmot Cl, SE15 ....172 C2
Wilmot Pl, NW1......14 A3
Wilmot St, E2........65 E1
Wilsham St, W11.....79 D4
Wilshaw St, SE14 ...176 C3
Wilson Gro, SE16....121 E2
Wilson Rd, SE5 .....171 E4
Wilsons Pl, E14 ......96 A1
Wilsons Rd, W6.....135 D2
Wilson St, EC2 ....63 D3
Wilton Cres, SW1 ...112 C2
Wilton Ms, SW1.....113 D3
Wilton Pl, SW1......112 C2
Wilton Rd, SW1.....113 F4
Wilton Row, SW1 ...112 C2
Wilton Sq, N1........18 C5
Wilton St, SW1 .....113 E3
Wilton Ter, SW1 ....112 C3
Wilton Vil, N1 ....40 C1
Wilton Way, E8 ......20 C2
Wiltshire Cl, SW3 ...112 A5
Wiltshire Row, N1....40 C1
Wimbolt St, E2.......42 C4
Wimbourne Ct, N1 ...40 C2
Wimbourne St, N1 ...40 C2
Wimpole Ms, W1.....57 E3
Wimpole St, W1.....57 E5
Winchendon Rd,
  SW6 ....160 A2
Winchester Av, NW6...7 F1
Winchester Cl, E6 ...104 A1
  SE17.............145 F1
Winchester Ms, NW3 .11 D3
Winchester Rd, NW3 .11 D3
Winchester Sq, SE1 ...90 C4
Winchester St, SW1 .141 F2
Winchester Wk, SE1 ..90 C4
Wincott St, SE11....117 D5
Windermere Av,
  NW6 ....29 F1
Windermere Pt,
  SE15.............174 A1
Winders Rd, SW11 ..163 E5
Windlass Pl, SE8 ....151 F1
Windmill Cl, SE1 ....121 D5
  SE13.............178 B5
Windmill Ct, NW2 .....7 F1
Windmill Ho, E14 ...124 C5
Windmill La, E15.....27 D1
Windmill Row, SE11.144 C3
Windmill St, W1 .....58 C4
Windmill Wk, SE1 ....89 D5
Windrose Cl, SE16...122 C1
Windsock Cl, SE16 ..124 A5
Windsor Gdns, W9 ...52 C3

Windsor Pl, SW1 ....114 B4
Windsor St, N1.......17 F5
Windsor Ter, N1......40 B4
Windsor Way, W14...107 D5
Windspoint Dr,
  SE15.............149 E5
Wine Cl, E1 ....94 A3
Wine Office Ct, EC4...61 D5
Winford Ho, E3 ......24 B4
Winforton St, SE10..178 A3
Wingrave Rd, W6 ...134 B5
Winifred St, E16 ....104 B5
Winkley St, E2 ....43 E3
Winnett St, W1 ......86 C2
Winsland Ms, W2 ....54 C5
Winsland St, W2 .....54 C5
Winsley St, W1 ......58 A5
Winslow, SE17......147 E3
Winslow Rd, W6 ....134 B4
🕬 Winsor Prim Sch,
  E6 ....104 C1
Winsor Ter, E6 ....76 C4
Wintergreen Cl, E6 ...75 E4
Winterton Ho, E1 .....93 F1
Winterton Pl, SW10 .138 B4
Winthrop St, E1......65 E3
🕬 Winton Prim Sch,
  N1 ....38 A3
Wise Rd, E15 ....48 B1
Witan St, E2.........43 F5
Woburn Pl, WC1.....59 D1
Woburn Sq, WC1 ....59 D2
Woburn Wk, WC1 ....37 D5
Wodeham Gdns, E1...65 D3
Wodehouse Av, SE5 .172 A3
Wolfe Cres, SE16 ...122 C3
Wollaston Cl, SE1 ...118 A5
Wolseley St, SE1 ....120 B2
Wolsey Ms, NW5 .....14 A1
Wolsey St, E1 ....66 A4
Wolverley St, E2......43 E5
Wolverton, SE17 ....147 D2
Wolverton Gdns,
  W6 ....106 C5
Wontner Cl, N1 ......18 A4
Woodall Cl, E14 ......97 F2
Woodbine Ter, E9 ....22 B1
Woodbridge St, EC1 ..61 E1
Woodchester Sq, W2..53 E3
Woodchurch Rd, NW6 .9 D4
Wood Cl, E2 ....64 C1
Woodcocks, E16 .....74 B4
Woodcroft Ms, SE8 ..151 E1
Woodfall St, SW3 ...140 A3
Woodfield Gdns, W9 ..52 B3
Woodfield Pl, W9.....52 B2
Woodfield Rd, W9 ....52 B3
Woodford Ct, W12 ..106 C1
Woodger Rd, W12...106 B2
Woodget Cl, E6 ......75 E5

Woodhatch Cl, E6 . . . . 75 E4
Woodhill, SE18 . . . . . 131 F5
Woodland Cres,
 SE10. . . . . 155 E4
 SE16. . . . . 122 C2
Woodland Gro,
 SE10. . . . . 155 E3
Woodland Hts, SE3 . . 155 F4
Woodlands Pk Rd,
 SE10. . . . . 155 E4
Woodland St, E8 . . . . . 20 B1
Woodland Wk,
 SE10. . . . . 155 F3
Wood La, W12 . . . . 78 B2
Woodlawn Rd,
 SW6 . . . . 158 C1
Woodman St, E16 . . . . 105 D5
Woodpecker Rd,
 SE14. . . . . 151 E5
Wood Pt, E16 . . . . 73 D4
Woodrush Cl, SE14 . . 175 E1
Wood's Bldgs, E1 . . . . . 65 E3
Woodseer St, E1. . . . . . 64 B3
Woodsford, SE17. . . . . 146 C3
Woodsford Sq, W14 . 107 F2
Woodside Rd, E13 . . . . 74 A1
Woods Ms, W1 . . . . 84 B2
Woods Pl, SE1 . . . . . . 119 F4
Woods Rd, SE15 . . . . 173 E4
Woodstock Gro,
 W12 . . . . 107 D1
Woodstock Ms, W1 . . . 57 D4
Woodstock St, W1 . . . . 85 E1
Woodstock Ter, E14 . . 97 F2
Wood St, EC2 . . . . 90 B3
Woodville, SE3 . . . . . . 181 F3
Woodville Rd, NW6 . . . 30 B2
Wood Wf, SE10 . . . . . 153 F4
Wooler St, SE17 . . . . . 146 C3
Woolf Ms, WC1 . . . . . . 59 D1
⌂Sch Woolmore Prim Sch,
 E14 . . . . 98 B2
Woolmore St, E14 . . . . 98 A2
Woolstaplers Way,
 SE16. . . . . 120 C4
WOOLWICH,
 SE18. . . . . 133 D3
⇌ Woolwich
 Arsenal 133 F5
Woolwich Ch St,
 SE18. . . . . 131 E4
⇌ Woolwich
 Dockyard. 132 A5
Woolwich Ferry Pier,
 E16. . . . . 132 C2
Woolwich Foot Tunnel,
 E16. . . . . 132 C2
 SE18. . . . . 132 C2
Woolwich High St,
 SE18. . . . . 132 C4

Woolwich Manor Way,
 E6. . . . . 76 B2
 E16. . . . . 105 E5
Woolwich Mkt,
 SE18. . . . . 133 E5
Woolwich Rd, SE10. . 156 A2
Wooster Gdns, E14 . . . 70 C5
Wooster Pl, SE1 . . . . . 119 D5
Wootton St, SE1 . . . . . 117 D1
Worcester Ms, NW6 . . . 9 F1
Wordsworth Rd,
 SE1 . . . . 148 A1
Worfield St, SW11. . . 163 F2
Worgan St, SE11 . . . . 144 A2
 SE16. . . . . 123 D4
⌂Coll Working Men's Coll, The,
 NW1 . . . . 36 B2
Worland Rd, E15 . . . . . 27 F3
World's End Est,
 SW10 . . . . 162 B1
World's End Pas,
 SW10 . . . . 162 C1
Worlidge St, W6 . . . . 134 A2
Wormwood St, EC2. . . 63 A5
Wornington Rd, W10 . 51 E2
Woronzow Rd, NW8 . . 33 D1
Worship St, EC2 . . . . . . 63 D2
Worth Gro, SE17 . . . . 146 C3
Worthing Cl, E15. . . . . 49 E1
Wotton Rd, SE8 . . . . . 152 B5
Wouldham Rd, E16 . . . 72 A5
Wren Cl, E16. . . . . 72 B5
Wren Landing, E14 . . . 97 D4
Wren Rd, SE5 . . . . 170 C4
Wren St, WC1. . . . . 60 B1
Wrentham Av, NW10 . 28 C2
Wrexham Rd, E3 . . . . . 47 D3
Wricklemarsh Rd,
 SE3 . . . . 181 E4
Wrigglesworth St,
 SE14. . . . . 174 C1
Wright Rd, N1 . . . . 19 F1
Wrights La, W8 . . . . . 109 E3
Wrights Rd, E3 . . . . . . 46 A2
Wrotham Rd, NW1 . . . 14 B4
Wyatt Cl, SE16. . . . . . 124 A2
Wybert St, NW1. . . . . . 57 F1
Wycherley Cl, SE3 . . . 180 A1
Wyclif St, EC1 . . . . 39 E5
Wycombe Sq, W8 . . . . 80 C5
Wyfold Rd, SW6 . . . . 159 E3
Wyke Rd, E3 . . . . 24 C4
Wyllen Cl, E1 . . . . 66 A2
Wymering Rd, W9 . . . . 31 D5
Wynan Rd, E14 . . . . . 153 E2
Wyndcliff Rd, SE7 . . . 157 E3
Wyndham Est, SE5 . . 170 B1
Wyndham Ms, W1 . . . . 56 A4
Wyndham Pl, W1. . . . . 56 A4
Wyndham Rd, SE5 . . 169 F2
Wyndham St, W1 . . . . 56 A3
Wyndham Yd, W1 . . . . 56 A4
Wynford Rd, N1 . . . . . . 38 A2
Wynnstay Gdns, W8 . 109 D3

Wynyard Ter, SE11 . . 144 B2
Wynyatt St, EC1 . . . . . 39 E5
Wythburn Pl, W1. . . . . 84 A1
Wythes Rd, E16. . . . . 103 E5
Wyvil Est, SW8 . . . . . 167 E1
⌂Sch Wyvil Prim Sch,
 SW8 . . . . 167 F1
Wyvil Rd, SW8. . . . . . 143 E5
Wyvis St, E14 . . . . . ,. . 69 F3

Y

Yabsley St, E14 . . . . . . 98 B4
Yalding Rd, SE16 . . . . 120 C4
Yardley St, WC1 . . . . . . 38 C5
Yarmouth Pl, W1 . . . . . 85 E5
Yarnfield Sq, SE15 . . . 173 D4
Yarrow Cres, E6 . . . . . . 75 E3
Yateley St, SE18 . . . . 131 D4
Yates Ct, NW2 . . . . 7 D2
Yeate St, N1 . . . . 18 C4
Yeldham Rd, W6 . . . . 134 C3
Yeoman Cl, E6 . . . . . . 105 E2
Yeoman's Row, SW3 . 111 F4
Yeoman St, SE8 . . . . . 123 E5
Yeomans Yd, E1 . . . . . . 92 B2
Yeo St, E3 . . . . 69 E3
Yoke Cl, N7 . . . . 15 F1
York Br, NW1 . . . . 56 C1
York Bldgs, WC2 . . . . . . 87 F3
York Cl, E6 . . . . 104 A1
York Gate, NW1 . . . . . . 56 C2
York Gro, SE15 . . . . . 174 A4
York Ho Pl, W8 . . . . . 109 E1
York Pl, WC2 . . . . 87 F3
York Rd, SE1 . . . . 116 B1
Yorkshire Grey Yd,
 WC1 . . . . 60 A4
Yorkshire Rd, E14 . . . . 95 E1
York Sq, E14 . . . . 95 E1
York St, W1 . . . . 56 B3
York Ter E, NW1 . . . . . 57 D2
York Ter W, NW1 . . . . 56 C2
Yorkton St, E2 . . . . 42 C3
York Way, N1 . . . . 15 D1
 N7 . . . . 37 F1
York Way Ct, N1 . . . . . 37 F1
York Way Est, N7 . . . . 15 E2
Young Rd, E16 . . . . 74 A4
Young's Bldgs, EC1 . . . 62 B1
Young St, W8 . . . . 109 E2

Z

Zampa Rd, SE16 . . . . 150 A3
Zander Ct, E2 . . . . 43 D3
Zealand Rd, E3. . . . . . . 45 E2
Zetland St, E14 . . . . . . 69 F4
Zoar St, SE1 . . . . 90 A4

★ Place of interest ⇌ Railway station H Hospital ⊖ London Underground station